NEW ENGLAND'S CRISES AND CULTURAL MEMORY

In this magisterial study, John McWilliams traces the development of New England's influential cultural identity. Through written responses to historical crises from early New England through the pre-Civil War period, McWilliams argues that the meaning of "New England," despite claims for its consistency, was continuously reformulated. The significance of past crises was forever being reinterpreted for the purpose of meeting succeeding crises. The crises he examines include starvation, the Indian wars, the Salem witch trials, the revolution of 1775–76, and slavery. Integrating history, literature, politics, and religion, this is one of the most comprehensive studies of the meaning of "New England" to appear in print. McWilliams considers a range of writing including George Bancroft's *History of the United States*, the political essays of Samuel Adams, the fiction of Nathaniel Hawthorne and the poetry of Robert Lowell. This compelling book is essential reading for historians and literary critics of New England.

JOHN MCWILLIAMS is Abernethy Professor of American Literature at Middlebury College in Vermont. He is the author of *Political Justice in a Republic: James Fenimore Cooper's America* (1972), *Hawthorne, Melville and the American Character* (Cambridge, 1984), and *The American Epic* (Cambridge, 1989).

NEW ENGLAND'S CRISES AND CULTURAL MEMORY

Literature, Politics, History, Religion, 1620–1860

JOHN McWILLIAMS

Middlebury College

CAMBRIDGE
UNIVERSITY PRESS

PUBLISHED BY THE PRESS SYNDICATE OF THE UNIVERSITY OF CAMBRIDGE
The Pitt Building, Trumpington Street, Cambridge, United Kingdom

CAMBRIDGE UNIVERSITY PRESS
The Edinburgh Building, Cambridge, CB2 2RU, UK
40 West 20th Street, New York, NY 10011-4211, USA
477 Williamstown Road, Port Melbourne, VIC 3207, Australia
Ruiz de Alarcón 13, 28014 Madrid, Spain
Dock House, The Waterfront, Cape Town 8001, South Africa

http://www.cambridge.org

First published 2004

Printed in the United Kingdom at the University Press, Cambridge

Typeface Adobe Garamond 11/12.5 pt.   *System* LATEX 2ε   [TB]

A catalogue record for this book is available from the British Library

Library of Congress Cataloguing in Publication data

McWilliams, John P.
New England's crises and cultural memory: literature, politics, history, religion,
1620–1860 / by John McWilliams.
p.   cm.   (Cambridge studies in American literature and culture, 142)
Includes bibliographical references and index.
ISBN 0 521 82683 7
1. American literature – New England – History and criticism.   2. Politics and literature – New
England – History.   3. Religion and literature – New England – History.   4. Literature and
history – New England – History.   5. New England – Intellectual life.   6. New England –
Historiography.   7. New England – In literature.   8. New England – History.   I. Title.   II. Series.
PS243.M38   2004
810.9′358 – dc22   2003069584

ISBN 0 521 82683 7 hardback

For Mireille, Christopher, and Isabel

Calamities are the caustics and cathartics of the body politic. They arouse the soul. They restore original virtues.

John Adams, writing as John Winthrop,
"Governor Winthrop to Governor Bradford,"
Boston Gazette, January 1767

The generations of men are not like the leaves on the trees, which fall and renew themselves without melioration or change; individuals disappear like the foliage and the flowers; the existence of our kind is continuous, and its ages are reciprocally dependent. Were it not so, there would be no great truths inspiring action, no laws regulating human achievements; the movement of the living world would be as the ebb and flow of the ocean; and the mind would no more be touched by the visible agency of Providence in human affairs.

George Bancroft, *History of the United States*, IV (1852)

Contents

Acknowledgments

The press readers for this book, the late Sargent Bush and Paul Downes, provided informed and insightful criticism of a long manuscript. The range of their knowledge and their acute questioning of my argument have been invaluable. Colleagues and friends have given the great gift of their reading time in assessing one or more chapters: Joyce Appleby, Lawrence Buell, James Calvin Davis, Murray Dry, Robert Ferguson, Robert Ferm, William Hart, and Will Nash. I am grateful to the National Endowment of the Humanities for a Research Fellowship and to the staff of the Boston Public Library, the Houghton Library, the Middlebury College Library (especially Robert Buckeye and Joanne Schneider), the New York Public Library, and the Widener Library. During research trips, lifelong friends Gordon and Susan Weir, David Breakstone, and Sharon Bauer have provided a home away from home, lightening the skies of even a Cambridge March. Reneé Brown and Cynthia Slater provided competence and comfort during my crises of computer anxiety. For help in securing funding and time, as well as for good counsel, I am grateful to George Dekker, Stephen Donadio, Robert Gross, Brett Millier, Robert Schine, and Thomas Wortham. The opportunity to serve on the editorial board of *Early American Literature* under the editorships of Philip Gura and David Shields proved to be a tonic as well as a learning experience. A project of this extent has special need of longtime encouragement. I have been blessed to have received sustained support for many years from the late Alan Heimert and, more recently, from Albert Gelpi.

As published, this book is a much shortened version of a manuscript entitled "New England's Crises," which can be consulted in the Abernethy Collection of the Middlebury College Library. Three of the nine chapters contain revisions of parts of previous essays. Chapter 2, "Thomas Morton: Phoenix of New England Memory," is a reworking of "Fictions of Merry Mount," published in *American Quarterly*, 29 (1977), 3–30. The first half of chapter 6, "Race, War, and White Magic: The Neglected Legacy of Salem," includes a revised version of "Indian John and the Northern Tawnies," first published in *New England Quarterly*, 69 (1996), 580–604, and since republished in Alden Vaughan's *New England Encounters* (Northeastern University Press, 1999). Chapter 8 includes revised portions of "Lexington, Concord and the 'Hinge of the Future'" (*American Literary History*, 6 [1993], 1–29) and "The Faces of Ethan Allen" (*New England Quarterly*, 49 [1976], 257–282).

The incorporating of parts of these essays into a much larger argument has demanded a broadening of historical and literary contexts in order to reflect new critical approaches and recent scholarship. But it would be disingenuous not to say that, in revising my earlier forays into the Matter of New England, I have discovered a need to write with greater tolerance and less smarty definitiveness. This tradition is complex, interwoven, self-reflexive, and deserving of more than one lifetime of study. Despite many an exclusionary sin and consequent affliction, New England historical writing has given us a profound and enduring cultural legacy. It would be folly not to respect it, especially because it stands so self-accused.

Introduction
Crisis rhetoric: exclusion in New England history

First, the inevitable question about a well-traveled road. Why, in a time of cultural studies that assimilate race and gender criticism, should anyone write yet another book centering on the Anglo-protestant northeastern writers, mostly male, who seem to comprise that regrettably inescapable term "Puritanism"? The field would seem to be as overworked, as exhausted, as a New England upland farm during the 1890s. One undeniable rejoinder would be that, since Vernon Parrington launched this academic complaint in the 1920s, hundreds of scholarly books on New England Puritanism and its authorial galaxy have testified to the lasting importance of the tradition.[1] Nor has Puritanism remained a dead letter, recalled only in scarlet, in twentieth-century literature. The famed title of Santayana's novel notwithstanding, we are perennially ready to entertain yet another rediscovery of "the last Puritan," whether in the guise of T. S. Eliot's assimilation of his New England roots to his Anglican present (*Four Quartets*), Robert Lowell's decidedly protestant Catholicism (*Lord Weary's Castle*), John Updike's witty broodings on sin and sexuality in New England suburbia (*Couples*), or Donald Hall's up-country generational pastoralism (*String too Short to be Saved*). The overhasty foreclosure of George Bancroft's insistence that Samuel Adams had been "the last Puritan" in America has been demonstrated again and again.[2]

The lasting power and sheer volume of New England literary tradition, from William Bradford's *History* and John Winthrop's *Journal* onward, surely originate in the Puritan faith in the power and authenticity of the written word. God's Word, rather than the liturgy of any Anglo-Catholic priest, was to be the absolute standard for human conduct. *Sola scriptura.* But just as man's words, spoken or written, could draw near to God's Word, so later New England generations could draw near to the spirit of the forefathers by reading – and revising – the words of their community and regional histories. The opening of the good news from St. John, "In the beginning was the Word," would continue to be applicable to immediate secular history as long as the New England past remained demonstrably imbued with divine purpose and the prospect of spiritual fulfillment. To antebellum New Englanders, the postmodernist distinction between signifier and signified was literally inconceivable. Until the time of Henry Adams, word was assumed to correspond to thing; truth was ultimately one. Properly understood, the deeds and discoveries of "the Puritan forefathers" held forth standards of spiritual value and communal conduct upon which contemporaries could, should, and ultimately must build.

The resulting search was to continue much longer, however, than we usually believe. Robert Lowell's splendid posthumous essay on the region he loved and hated, "New England and Further," attacks New England's pretension by symbolizing its empty contemporary end ("And inland, still shunning the light of day though now elmless, stand the white rectilinear houses, marked 1810 – nothing changed without, nothing regained within"), but simultaneously insists that there remains something "spiritual, or rather invisible . . . a longing in New England so strong for what is not that what is not perhaps exists."[3] The betrayal and the longing, Lowell knew, had been complementary, even symbiotic responses for three centuries. When intense longing for a perhaps unrealizable spirit becomes the defining trait of a regional culture, that unrealizable spirit paradoxically exists in the very words used to try to describe it. Not for nothing did Robert Lowell once plan a book – and write three vivid poems – on Jonathan Edwards, whose search for God's grace had left him continually conscious of his inability to describe the fleeting moment of union with the divine through the flawed medium of human words.

The fact that the Puritan and neo-Puritan tradition has yielded durable harvest is, however, no excuse for a scholarly book that would merely pick the same fruits and align them into slightly different patterns. The contribution I hope to make to the study of American Puritanism rests on three conceptual differences. Perry Miller established a tradition of studying Puritanism from within, citing as American Puritanism's defining texts the sermons, theological works, diaries, and histories of New England Protestant leaders, mostly clergymen. From Perry Miller to Sacvan Bercovitch and beyond, although differences among Puritans have often been emphasized, the predominant assumption has been that collective abstractions like "the New England Way," "the New England Mind," "the American Jeremiad," and especially "the Puritans" not only existed but continuously outlasted any theological/political impasses proclaimed during particular controversies. Within this scholarly tradition, evolving traditions of Puritan rhetoric have thus often been emphasized at the expense of their origins in historical events.[4] In fact, however, the verifiable stuff of harsh and hard-won conflict – starvation, covenants, extradition, wars, revolution, mob violence, battle bravery, self-sacrificial protest – had given rise to the tropes and evolving symbology through which New England historical writers reinterpreted past crises. By summarizing what historians now believe "actually happened" during perceived crises, I hope to put the floor of recoverable historical fact back beneath and beside the grand designs of New England mission, and to see what emerges. I aspire to the quality Clifford Geertz once called "thick description"; I assume that cultural history has a "shifting collection of meanings" from which one must draw "explanatory conclusions from the better guesses."[5]

Secondly, recent scholarship has made it indefensible to maintain that the selection of primary texts, and their alignment to genres, should follow the unbranching path of regional male leadership. For Perry Miller, belief in the existence of the New England Mind meant that Puritan beliefs and Puritanism's major doctrinal controversies had to be clarified through study of the works of expository prose written by those Puritans most directly involved in them. Novelists, poets, and dramatists, especially those from without New England's borders, were excluded from scholarly view as if their contributions had been merely imaginative, often Menckenite, and therefore uninformed. In recent years, American exceptionalism has been rather roundly attacked, and the canon of literary works pertinent to Puritanism has been considerably broadened, but American exceptionalism has been criticized chiefly by noting similarities and unanimities within the experiences, and within the expository prose, of British and American Puritans.[6]

I seek multiple kinds of widening. I propose to select crises based on events within New England history, and then to study recreations of those crises in writings of many genres, by women and men from diverse traditions, with a time of publication ranging from Bradford's and Winslow's *Mourt's Relation* (1622) through Lydia Maria Child's *The First Settlers of New England* (1829), through the histories of the fourth generation Adamses (1880–1920), to the poetry of Robert Lowell and to Maryse Condé's *I, Tituba, Black Witch of Salem* (1986). To me, it is the cumulative discourse among these voices that has always, at any historical juncture, made up "American Puritanism" as it should be understood, then and now. Nor is this cumulative discourse obtainable by simply adding in writings by women, Native Americans and blacks. Are Samuel Adams's rebellious editorials and Theodore Parker's jeremiads still to be excluded from the American Puritan tradition because their authors (certainly of old New England lineage) were not neo-Calvinist preachers? Are Edith Wharton's *Ethan Frome* and Arthur Miller's *The Crucible* to be excluded from the "matter" of Puritanism because their authors were not New Englanders? Or, to turn the tables against more recent assumptions, are we now to slight the importance of Mather's *Magnalia* or Bancroft's *History* because neither the works nor their authors represent diversity and diverging traditions as we now understand those terms? Ours is a postcanonical, and therefore revisionist, time, but surely, if we are to understand the past on its own terms, the very real benefits of searching for diversity within New England's first two hundred years must be supplemental and corrective rather than substitutional.

The third difference: in spite of this book's broad time range, my focus in examining the reconstruction of "American Puritanism" will be upon the historical memory of early nineteenth-century New England.[7] It was at this time that the crosscurrents in attitudes toward the Puritan heritage became most acute and arguably most important. Tenth generation descendants of the founding families of 1620 and 1630 needed to make sense of their heritage. In particular, they needed to find the providential connections between the three eras of greatest significance to the presumed advance of protestant virtue: the plantations of 1620 and 1630, New England's Time of Troubles from 1675 to 1700, and New England's early leadership of the revolution that would form the American Republic. (Hence the tripartite division of this book's chapters.) Nineteenth-century immigrants needed to be encouraged to understand that heritage and those connections. Whether "the Puritans" had ever been synonymous with "New England," and whether America was in any sense New England writ large, posed complementary definitional problems that elicited both pride and anxiety, creating multiple possibilities for the use of synecdoche and metonymy in writing about the regional past.[8] The many New England commemorative addresses, which began in Plymouth in 1776 and climaxed in the bicentennial addresses of Massachusetts settlements' foundings between 1820 and 1840, effectively replaced Election Day sermons as occasions for lending remembrance of forefathers. While serving contemporary political purpose, these bicentennial orations added a national dimension to local history in ways that show the difficulties of assimilating Calvinism into Republicanism.[9] The complexity and significance of Hawthorne's historical short stories derive from his artful ways of negotiating these same crosscurrents.

We need to recognize that by the mid-1830s an acute and ominous tension existed between New England's pride in its past and the growing signs that New England, despite its recurrent claim to represent the entire

Republic, might soon become a geographically enclosed backwater, isolated from an America growing ever westward and gravitating ever southward. Such a shift in the Republic's geopolitical center diminished the prospects for the growth of both New England's economic prosperity and its protestant mission. More importantly, it threatened to transfer power from the very intellectual tradition through which Republican liberty had evolved, toward the misconceived claim that the Great American Republic would, like Greece and Rome, support as well as condone slavery. Hence my final chapter will explore the neglected connection between the Garrisonian abolitionists of Massachusetts and their need to reassert New England's national leadership through remembrance of the forefathers.

Insofar as this book has a single major figure, it can only be the now neglected literary historian who endeavored, as Bercovitch noted, to make a grand synthesis out of New England and the South, Calvinism and Republicanism, American nationalism and the growing worldwide power of Liberty as exercised through the popular will – namely, George Bancroft. Although Bancroft may have grown up on a Worcester farm, attended Unitarian Harvard, and served as a collector for the Port of Boston, he was neither the parochial New Englander nor the spread-eagle nationalist zealot he is popularly assumed to be. When Bancroft returned to Cambridge after four years of *wanderjahren* earning a Gottingen Ph.D., Andrews Norton judged him a Europeanized fop and promptly cut his acquaintance. Recurrent mention of Bancroft's founding of the Naval Academy at Annapolis has obscured his stints as ambassador to the court of St. James and to Berlin. Most important for our purposes, however, is Bancroft's decision, after his term in Polk's cabinet in Washington, to move to New York, rather than return to Boston, in order to complete the remaining seven volumes of his *History*.[10] Here is the equivalent of William Dean Howells's move from Boston to New York a generation later – both a cause and a sign that the center of the American intellectual/publishing world was shifting away from Boston.

Revering both the Puritans and Thomas Jefferson, writing about providential causation like a Unitarian while insisting he was a Congregationalist, hating slavery but unwilling to sever liberty from constitutional union, Bancroft remains, in his determination to make one whole out of all sequential controversies, the New Englander who best serves as the template for his age's view of the American past. So many editions and reprintings of Bancroft's *History* were published in the half-century after 1834 that sales figures have not been hazarded. Compared to the stylistic power and daring breadth of Bancroft's immensely popular *History*, John Gorham Palfrey's still useful *History of New England* (1858–1890) seems dutiful and pedantic, ultimately parochial in spite of its undeniable corrective contributions.

Setting out in the early 1830s to write national history after a New England upbringing and years of European travel, Bancroft faced formidable problems of mediation. At the exact moment when the new demand for the immediate abolition of slavery broke apart the era of good feelings, Bancroft faced the challenge of balancing, for a national if not international readership, the competing claims to be advanced for Columbus or Cabot, Jamestown or Plymouth, John Smith or John Winthrop, Patrick Henry or Sam Adams, Thomas Jefferson or John Adams. The contributions of all needed to be seen as one even at a time of increasingly recognized sectional hostility between Virginia and Massachusetts, North and South. There was the need to show how American protestantism was an outgrowth of old world reformation, while still somehow preserving what we now call American "exceptionalism." Even more pressingly, there was the need to praise the wisdom of the popular will, emerging as the undirected consensus of a free Republican people, while still acknowledging that national leadership must be exercised by those individuals most qualified, and often best educated, to do so.

Training and circumstance left Bancroft with fruitfully conflicted attitudes. In Germany he had absorbed the international positivism of Comte, the nationalism of Herder, and the beginnings of Von Ranke's empiricism ("how things really were").[11] The resulting tension between Bancroft's desire to record fact and his desire to pen narratives of democratic progress would never be resolved. While recognizing the origins of regional distinctions that were increasingly apparent after 1830, Bancroft also yearned to write of one undifferentiated American people, *e pluribus unum*. On the one hand, he isolated and insulated the United States of America as the special preserve of Republican virtue; on the other, he celebrated America as an open nation, today's exemplar of the worldwide force of individual liberty and democratic voluntarism. Like Tocqueville, he negotiates the most powerful contrarieties of his day (perhaps also of ours?) even when he does not directly confront them.

Historical mediation had been needed even among Bancroft's immediate predecessors. Harlow Sheidley has shown that, between 1800 and 1830, the Federalist élite of Massachusetts had sought to "exorcise the American past of its potentially radical thrust, so that it would reinforce deference, hierarchy and due subordination and serve as a weapon in the battle with the South for historical preeminence and present predominance."[12] Such purposes would lead Webster, Story, and Everett to aggrandize Puritans as ur-Republican gentlemen devoted to retaining civil liberty. Bancroft knew full well, however, that the "élite" Federalist view did not accord very well with the *History* of Mercy Otis Warren, for whom the Puritans had been of little interest in contrast to the Provincial Massachusetts citizen's courageous revolt against the luxuries and centralized power of British empire. American exceptionalism and old world origins might be assimilated to each other by insisting that, under God's Providence, America was leading the world toward democratic progress, but how exactly were Anglican and Congregationalist, Separatist and non-Separatist, the country party and the town party, Federalist and Republican, section and nation, all to be plausibly seen as working together to comprise the American Republic as the vanguard of Liberty and Democracy? The challenge to the historian was immense, but as a devotee (like Webster) of Liberty and Union, while also being a devotee (unlike Webster) of iconoclasts who had spoken the popular will against privilege, Bancroft knew how high the stakes were in trying to hold the Republic's historical origins together.

New Englanders of Bancroft's generation had an uncomfortable sense of being stalled, caught, or even mired, in historical time between the great achievements of Puritan forefathers and Revolutionary fathers, the limitless future promised by their regional and national heritage, and an uncertain, deeply compromising present. Their own era, the mostly prosperous, expansive, and peaceful decades from 1830 to 1860, did not seem to portend any crisis comparable to 1630, 1688, or 1775, except possibly the darkening cloud of slavery, yet New Englanders often spoke and wrote as if theirs was a time of special urgency, perhaps because they longed for crisis in order to show they were worthy of their heritage. Theirs was a situation to which Frank Kermode's model of personal and cultural "crisis" seems particularly applicable. Rephrasing Aristotle in an attempt to uncover human assumptions about time, Kermode argues that "Men die because they cannot join the beginning and the end."[13] If we were present at the beginning or the end, we would be not only be immortal; we could *know* absolutely. In fact, however, every human being has been born in the middle of linear time, unable to see the beginning or the end, longing to find coherence in time's passing and meaning in life's happenings, yet sensing that, unless beginnings and ends could be truly seen, coherence and meaning remain doubtful at best. We therefore need to live through identifiable crises, because crises are spots in time that enable us to define our beginnings and, more importantly, our ends.

Antebellum New Englanders never voiced their unease in precisely this way, of course, but they approached their history in similar spirit. To know how the fathers and forefathers had met their crises could never be exactly applicable today, but the cultural past provides a guideline for worthy conduct that could transcend the confusing present. The many familiar words written and rewritten within New England's ever-accumulating historical tradition were certainly not to be regarded as the Word, but their moments of illumination should be recalled for purposes of collective self-understanding, and then adapted to today's actions on behalf of Liberty and/or Democracy. New Englanders' investment in their past was thus clearly shifting toward presentist concerns. While holding forth eighteenth- or even seventeenth-century standards, the import of Calvinism and Congregationalism upon models of communal mission turned outward in ever-growing anxiety about the relation of region to nation.

How, then, are we to best define the terms "New England" and "New England Literature" from the perspectives both of our time and of the antebellum decades? As early as the 1830s, New Englanders recognized that their literature was becoming increasingly subdivided into two overlapping halves. At first there had been the founding literature of Puritan Mission, emanating from Boston and Plymouth, with its offshoots in Hartford, New Haven, and Providence plantations, and its continuing self-revisions from Nathaniel Morton onward. But later, first emerging to prominence in the *Narrative of Colonel Ethan Allen's Captivity* (1779), came the literature of up-country or rural New England, a literature that existed in uneasy resentment of Boston's claims, and of which the later prominence of "New England Local Color" would be only a part, not a separate nor exclusively women's tradition.[14] This division admittedly required modification as early as the writing of the post-constitutional state histories (Benjamin Trumbull in Connecticut, Jeremy Belknap in New Hampshire, James Sullivan in Maine, Samuel Williams in Vermont). This dichotomy should no longer lead us to overlook important texts written outside its parameters from a woman's, an Indian's, a slave's, a non-New Englander's, or an ex-New Englander's perspective. Although the urban–rural, country party–town party, Boston–up-country distinction remains essential, I hope to bring selected important up-country and minority texts into comparison with the 'mainstream' literature of Boston and eastern Massachusetts, which was of the origin and was still dominant in Bancroft's era.[15]

The name and identity of the region itself poses even greater problems. The term "New England," which all of us use with confidence in its shared meaning, has in fact always been remarkably elusive. Consider just a few of the more common, still current visual images: has "New England" ever really been definable as staid town communities of white clapboard houses built around a village green, dominated by a Congregational Church steeple, and surrounded by farms on which the constant labor has more often been admired than experienced? Is "New England" more accurately imaged as the once struggling mill town or decaying seaport that has turned its brick mills and warehouses into condos for retirees and shopping malls for chain stores? Is New England best conceived, in John Elder's title phrase, as *The Mountains of Home*, a human-size, low-mountain landscape backed by the expansive forests that have now reoccupied the largest tracts of New England acreage? Or does the name "New England" continue to signify, as it did for Cotton Mather, an expanding community centered on Boston, now a leveled trimont with back bays filled, but still and recently a "city on a hill" to those with Fidelity Investments or Fleet Bank in mind? Of course, a formidable case can be made that whatever was once culturally distinct about New England disappeared at an accelerating rate after the cataclysm of the Civil War and the subsequent incorporation of America. Is "New England" now merely an accident of political geography, six states circumscribed by New York, Canada, and the Atlantic, an anachronism collectively promotable for the tourist dollar in either its quaint or gleaming guises?[16]

Although the mind protests against images at once so hackneyed, so superficial and so enduringly profitable, agreement upon a deeper historical definition is not easy to achieve. Is a credible New England heritage still recognizable in the many late nineteenth-century claims for a stubborn strength of inner character (mal)nourished by daunting climactic extremes and by New England's geographic isolation, leading to the culture that Henry James, somewhat wistfully but mostly satirically, referred to as "plain living and high thinking"?[17] If James's words evoke the Protestant work ethic (now entirely outmoded?), we might remember that performing hard labor for earthly or heavenly reward was admired in Philadelphia and Charleston, New York and London, as well as Plymouth and Boston. And then there is the most intellectually demanding and perhaps most reverential definition of them all. To Perry Miller, the lasting essence of the New England way was the spiritual and political complex he called the "New England Mind" – a federal theology, accepting good works as partial evidence of grace, struggling to maintain a godly community gathered through Congregational covenant – a mindset long maintained by the determination of a New England educated élite. Entirely an anachronism?

Behind all these formulations, however, lies the question raised implicitly by John Smith's *A Description of New England* (1616) and its famous map, the promotional work that for the seventeenth century, and ever thereafter, would give New England its name and its first geopolitical definition. What did the two words "New England," mapped as the shoreline from Cape James (Cape Cod) to Pembrock's Bay (Penobscot Bay), actually signify in addition to an imperial land claim? To Smith, the two words probably meant little more than England renewed, transported across the sea with lowered barriers of class privilege, a fertile land but not a cornucopia, a place where economically struggling English families and artisans could find a fresh start through good farming, better fishing, and mercantile trade.[18] But by the time Smith wrote his *Advertisements for the Unexperienced Planters of New England* (1631), he was well aware that, to many an embarking Pilgrim or Puritan making use of his map, New England was now being reenvisioned as Old England in a new form, transformable in ways somehow paralleling the biblical transformation of the old man into the new, holy Jew into saved Christian, the Covenant of Works into a Covenant of Grace still requiring Works – a remaking that might well entail an explicit or virtual separation from the Anglican Church, though not, surely, from England.[19]

Nobody could know, of course, which of the multiple meanings of "New England" – "new" as "the old renewed," "new" as "the old transformed" or the many shades between them – was to prove the more accurate. Successful plantation was to require settlers of both persuasions, and fortunately both sorts of settlers came. For decades, the planters were too busy constructing their communities and institutions to worry overmuch about a definitional problem that was potentially inflammatory and probably irresolvable. From the time of William Bradford and John Winthrop through Edward Johnson and William Hubbard and up to the time of Cotton Mather, early historians of the migration would write their own New Englands into God's providential scheme without becoming overly self-conscious about alternative models.[20]

What therefore emerged in New England historical writing was a markedly oppositional way of defining their distinctive culture. Protest against Anglican abuses and Laudian persecution, together with a desire to escape straightened economic circumstance, had been recognized causes of migration from the outset. Proclaiming a separate identity was, however, another matter. Although Robert Cushman and William Bradford, John Winthrop and Edward Johnson had praised both religious and economic motives for removing from England, no official document defining collective intent had emerged. Hoping that the eyes of the world would indeed remain upon them, New Englanders looked backward in anger and regret, as well as forward with promise and anxiety.[21] By the 1770s, leaders of Massachusetts and Connecticut had begun to look sideways as well, at

New York with envy, at the South with moral and economic concern, and at their own northern frontier with class condescension. The continuing lack of any publicly acknowledged consensus about the essential purposes and outcome of the New England venture created special opportunities, and a special need, for separating self from other, our new community from their old one, and then, after the Revolution, our old community from their new one. If there was no consensus about New England's identity, New England could best be defined by contrast to those whom New Englanders had sequentially opposed.[22] We might discover who we are by demonstrating, in deed or word, who we are not.

To know oneself by one's opponent led memorializers to an intense, sometimes overheated preoccupation with crises both real and imagined. The true mettle/metal of New Englanders could be discovered in the ways they had overcome the trials sent upon them in a sequence of interrelated communal crises. The applicability of the term "Affliction" thus needed to be broadened from those trials through which God tested the individual soul's preparation for salvation, to those trials through which God tested New England's possibly premillennial virtues as a collective people. When John Adams, in the immediate aftermath of the Stamp Act crisis, rebuked Governor Bernard for wielding an "iron sceptre of tyranny," Adams chose to write, pseudonymously, as Governor Winthrop to Governor Bradford in order to demonstrate that, although "calamities are the caustics and cathartics of the body politic," calamities also "restore original virtues."[23] The organizing structure of Cotton Mather's *Magnalia* provides the chief example of writing cathartic history based upon communal affliction. Beneath the obtrusive numerology of seven parts, seven days of creation, twice-seven times seven "Golden Candlestick" New England churches, and the seven vials of apocalyptic revelation, Mather defines the "Great Things of Christ in America" as a series of embattled crises with those forces that would undo New England. Mather's New England is not a culture of conflicting interest groups, but rather of one undifferentiated people threatened by deviants without and within. Metaphors of warfare, self-sacrifice, and conquest are everywhere as Mather recounts New England's struggle against Anglican persecutors, Antinomians, inner heretics, Separatists, vagrants, Quakers, Indians, royally appointed governors, witches, wizards, and the French.[24]

Oppositional self-definition, combined with the Protestant faith in the power of both Word and word, thus lent lasting power to New England historiography. To meet the next crisis required New Englanders to summon from their heritage the spiritual and physical strength necessary to prevail – a form of civic preparationism. As the decades wore on, measuring New

England's present spiritual worth increasingly required comparisons between the ways past and present crises were met. The assumptions behind the post-Revolutionary motto on the seal of Boston, "*Sicut Patribus, Sit Deus Nobis*" (As with our fathers, so may God be with us) had implications beyond the obviously patriarchal insistence that today's males must continue to earn God's favor by being worthy of their distinguished heritage. It would require of today's New England historian a special concern for the words of regional tradition. By reading of the ways God had "been with" the fathers, the sons might discern their duties and, hopefully, their expectations.

The line of distinguished New England historians who built upon the work of their predecessors, from Bradford and Winthrop, through Cotton Mather, Hannah Adams, and Mercy Otis Warren, to Bancroft and Palfrey, thus faced an exhilarating conundrum. The generations and ages of mankind, as my epigraph from Bancroft's *History* insists, were assumed to be "reciprocally dependent"; in no other way could the "great truths inspiring action" ever be measured and known. If the regional past demonstrated God's progress either toward the Millennium or the Divine Republic, then the way in which today's New Englanders meet current crises should prove to be even more glorious than those of their predecessors. But if New England's prospect seemed to prolong a bewildering stasis or, worse, to show communal decline, then the remembrance of historical crises through the historical word would become more threatening, but no less precious. Preceding historians, it would be assumed, had recorded those afflictive failures that contained God's contingent offer of recoverable spiritual worth.

This book will therefore be not so much a study of familiar claims for New England integrity as of the process of their constant reformation. Behind the peaceful images of self-contained villages, family farms, and Cotton Mather's Boston as "Theopolis Americana" lay a culture driven to define itself through successive crises of spiritual embattlement. Seventeenth-century plantation began in theocratic conflict and economic need; the limited but real challenge New Englanders faced was to somehow remain a non-Separatist *new* England within the bounds of the outsetting British empire. During the American Revolution, however, New England needed to be reimagined as the Separatist leader of the new world's republic; the Revolution had to demonstrate that the defiant virtues of Puritan forbears could be adapted to the new values of a more enlightened age, but that it had not been fundamentally changed. After 1820, when New England's primacy was increasingly threatened by the expansion of slavery

into the old southwest, the Garrisonian abolitionists began to see themselves as defenders of New England's besieged citadel of virtue. Whether
New Englanders conceived of themselves (in good times) as the vanguard of
the Republic or (in not so good times) as its fighting remnant, the constant
in the process of historical self-definition was to be a region forever in conflict, forever reestablishing its own cultural integrity through opposition to
some inner or outer "other."

My selections among New England's perceived crises are admittedly
subjective and necessarily incomplete. Nothing will be written here about
Roger Williams, about the Gortonists and the Remonstrants, nor about
the Quaker persecutions, nor about the Half Way Covenant, nor about
the first or second Great Awakenings, nor about the French and Indian
War, nor about Shays Rebellion, nor about the Hartford Convention. All
could have served and all are important. With the exceptions of the first
and last chapters, the crises I have selected follow three criteria: the crisis
occurred as a dateable historical event; it was perceived as a crisis, and
constantly rewritten within the historiographical tradition as an important
testimony to New England's self-definition; the crisis would prove to be
readily shapeable into a quasifictional narrative, with dramatic moments of
confrontation, a narrative that would lend itself to recasting in important
historical literature.

These criteria will sometimes privilege the perception of historical importance, rather than the reality of it. It is arguable that the Merry Mount
controversy, the Salem witch trials and even Concord Fight, which figure
prominently in this book, had no influence on the development of New
England life or institutions at all. Given the quality and prominence of the
literature concerned with these two events, however, Merry Mount, Salem,
and Concord are indispensable to the development of New England historical identity. Conversely, institutional agreements as clearly formative as
the Cambridge Platform, the New England Confederation of 1643, and the
Massachusetts Constitution of 1780 – as well as the changes wrought by
turnpike and railroad, clipper ship and schooner – shall not be considered
here. All were to prove notably static and barren for purposes of historical
reconstruction; they readily lent themselves to panegyric or denunciation,
but not to the kind of narrative that embodies regional character.

Hidden beneath my predilection for historical events whose historical
importance has been perceived rather than proven lies a personal quandary
the reader deserves to know. Educated during the 1950s and early 1960s to
accept the usually unadmitted assumptions of logical positivism, I began
writing and teaching with the belief that truths about literature, history,

and historical literature could be ascertained and proven. Knowledge was its own justification, learning was cumulative, and the academy was not subject to careerist ideological fashions. Since that time, I have been increasingly convinced by (or should it be "afflicted with"?) the relativistic assumption, prevalent in nonscientific disciplines, that we can know only a sequence of perceptions, themselves historically conditioned. Having added the second set of assumptions without discarding the first, I nonetheless hope that, in writing a book on this particular topic, such an inner conflict in fundamental assumptions is transformable into a merit.

The sequence of perceived crises promoted an increasingly exclusionary mentality. To be a New Englander, as these crises were historically understood, was to be in continuing, embattled protest against enemies both without and within. Whoever the New Englander might be, he (or occasionally she) was clearly not a Merry Mounter, not an Antinomian, not an Indian, not a French Canadian, not a royalist place man, not a loyalist, not a New Yorker, and, finally, not a slaveholder. As New England merit was redefined through these successive eliminations, the accumulating of excluded groups and communities narrowed and circumscribed the region, not only in race, religion, and gender, but also in origin, politics, and geography. Questions of exclusion/inclusion in New England's evolving identity surface in the debates over the Half Way Covenant, over Stoddardism, over the right of taxation in the Province, over who is or is not wearing homespun and drinking tea. But exclusionary issues also, in the early nineteenth century, underlie such diverse developments as the Federalist claims to justify the Hartford Convention, the protest against Irish immigration, and the worried praise for the many native-born emigrants who were suddenly carrying another version of the New England way (town meeting, open church, and public school) out of New England, across upper New York State, into the Western Reserve, and thence into the undefined America that lay beyond.

As republicans of the newly United States began to recognize that the best America was yet to be, their limited awareness of the actualities of the extraregional world allowed them to project their New England identities upon the Great Republic as if it were a *tabula rasa*. We understand the geopolitical parochialism prompting William Hubbard in 1680 to declare that New England was bordered on the west by "the Pasificke or South Sea, the distance how farre being as yet unknowne"[25] and why Cotton Mather in 1702 assumed that the "*Magnalia Christi Americana*" was synonymous with "the Ecclesiastical History of New-England." We do not, however, as readily recognize the energizing innocence of similarly projective leaps in post-Enlightenment New England. A few examples. The New Englander who in 1804 surely knew more about American geography than anyone else, Jedidiah Morse of Charlestown, could surmise in print, with utter disregard for North Carolina's Mount Mitchell (6,684 ft.) and for the possibilities of the recent Louisiana Purchase, that New Hampshire's Mount Washington (5,249 ft.) is "probably between ten and eleven thousand feet above the surface of the ocean; and much the highest land in the United States."[26] The title of New England's quickly and deservedly venerated journal, the *North American Review*, was from the outset misleadingly presumptive; until the Civil War, it was to remain, for the most part, Whig Unitarian Boston and Whig Unitarian Cambridge reviewing the world. New Englanders, and perhaps others as well, managed to convince Tocqueville that the "whole destiny of America is contained in the first Puritan who landed on these shores as that of the whole human race in the first man."[27]

Decade after decade, such claims of regional self-aggrandizement, whether in the form of a speech, an institutional title, or the written word, were to be offered with serious intent.[28] Not until a national civil war loomed could an insider like Oliver Wendell Holmes gain affection as well as notoriety by mocking the Bostonian's imagined, centrifugal expansion of his local virtue: "Boston State-House is the hub of the Universe; you couldn't pry that out of a Boston man if you had the tire of all creation straightened out for a crowbar."[29] It is telling that the metaphor of "the hub," which Holmes offered in a spirit of bemused though complacent satire, was later to become an unofficial motto at the very moment Boston was overtaken by New York City.

Boston speaking for New England speaking for America speaking for humanity. Before Holmes's time, that series of projections can be found in speeches by Webster and Everett, in the plays of Mercy Otis Warren and the prose of Lydia Maria Child, in the histories of Hildreth and the earliest volumes of Bancroft, but it can also be found where one might least expect it.[30] Emerson's neglected essay "Boston" was first delivered as a speech in Boston in the spring of 1861, when President Lincoln was calling for 75,000 volunteers to put down the rapidly growing secession of southern states. Without ever mentioning the immediate context of southern rebellion, Emerson issued a communal call based upon the continuance of local, not national tradition:

This town of Boston has a history. It is not an accident, not a windmill, or a railroad station, or cross-roads tavern, or an army-barracks grown up by time and luck to a place of wealth; but a seat of humanity, of men of principle, obeying a sentiment and marching loyally whither that should lead them; so that its annals are great historical lines, inextricably national; part of the history of political liberty. I do not speak with any fondness, but the language of coldest history, when I say that Boston commands attention as the town which was appointed in the destiny of nations to lead the civilization of North America.[31]

To envision Boston leading the loyal march of Unionist sentiment is here justified, not on the basis of present urban fact, but rather on the evidence of "coldest history" expressed in references that reach out beyond the city to its immediate environs. For Emerson to so heatedly deny economic causation (Boston is "not a windmill or a railroad station") in order to emphasize that Boston's annals are both "inextricably national" and "part of the history of political liberty" is in exact accord with Bancroft's reading of the way post-Puritan history had developed through the Revolution. By 1861, however, Bancroft was less prepared than Emerson to insist that only Boston could be regarded as "the town which was appointed in the destiny of nations to lead the civilization of North America." It was Emerson, not Bancroft, who at this moment made an exclusionary claim for Boston's leadership in the progress of collective liberty.

Toward the end of the essay, after issuing his call for Bostonians to loyally march for liberty, Emerson makes a virtue out of that then most troubling of words, "rebellion":

Boston never wanted a good principle of rebellion in it, from the planting until now; there is always a minority unconvinced, always a heresiarch, whom the governor and deputies labor with but cannot silence; Some new light, some new doctrinaire who makes an unnecessary ado to establish his dogma; . . . some noble protestant, who will not stoop to infamy when all are gone mad, but will stand for liberty and justice, if alone, until all come back to him. (203)

Suddenly Boston's "noble protestant" is recast as the defiant individual-ist who defines liberty by revolting against Boston Puritanism, specifically against the governor and his deputies. Lest the historical force of this redef-inition be slighted, Emerson provides in midparagraph a chronological list of those Bostonians, or Boston sojourners, who have nobly protested: John Wheelwright, Thomas Maule and Richard Sewel, George Whitefield, John Adams and Josiah Quincy, Governor Andrew and "some defender of the slave against the politician and the merchant" (surely Theodore Parker). There need to be surprising bedfellows in Emerson's list (long-vilified John Wheelwright linked with sainted John Adams, for instance) because to qualify as a "noble protestant" is to be neither Antinomian nor Deist, but to assume the mantle of principled solitary rebel against the compromised

Massachusetts establishment. Praise of the collective Bostonian march to liberty has vanished; instead, the defiant pilgrim for liberty has been so long prominent that his role in "coldest" Boston history can be expanded from "heretic" into "heresiarch."

Emerson's "Boston" illustrates a pattern of recreating the New England past built upon a double rhetoric of liberty that succeeds in having it both ways. Depending on the context, Emerson can urge his audience toward good work in the present by tracing Boston's tradition of Puritan and neo-Puritan Liberty back either to early governors *or* to Roger Williams, to John Winthrop *or* John Wheelwright, to George Whitefield *or* to Charles Chauncy. However handy such dualism may be in realigning the New England past, an acute problem of antebellum political thought surfaces here. If the popular will to liberty is embodied in the collective authority of the Bostonian community, who are nonetheless opposed by rebels much as Wheelright or Adams, then New England's crises reveal the recurring threat of the tyranny of the majority. Lest belief in the providential justice of New England history disappear, *vox populi* must still contain *vox dei*, but whenever the voice of the people threatens to outshout the voice of God, Boston's history shows that a libertarian heresiarch, not unlike Hawthorne's Gray Champion, will arise, and will somehow not only be heard but also followed.

ASSURANCE, ANXIETY, AND REGIONAL SALVATION

A last introductory issue emerging from the contrast of two famous passages from New England's long canonical texts. The most confident statements about New England's intergenerational resilience cloak doubt bordering on fear or satire. Before immersing his reader in 850 pages of fact, legend, and hagiography that recount the Lord's battles for New England, Cotton Mather exclaimed: "But whether New England may Live any where else or no, it must Live in our History!"[32] This remark, so characteristic of Mather's will to triumph, shows how deeply his certitude depends on overcoming acknowledged anxiety. Mather's opening phrase raises the astonishing possibility of the present death, the literal erasing, of the very entity he will write about. Perceiving the achievements of New England's past thus becomes inseparable from forewarning that all the golden candlesticks might be extinguished. In one way, Mather's sentence justifies the labors involved in making his massive book (New England "must live in *our History*" – italics mine), but in another way Mather's sentence advertises his book as already an anachronism, a memorial to all he fears is dead. No wonder that the

Magnalia repeatedly searches out those providential forces that might turn the newly created Province of Massachusetts into a New England/American polity still more glorious than the former Commonwealth.

The second to last paragraph of *Walden* uses regional legend for a seemingly opposite rhetorical end:

Every one has heard the story which has gone the rounds of New England, of a strong and beautiful bug which came out of the dry leaf of an old table of apple-tree wood, which had stood in a farmer's kitchen for sixty years, first in Connecticut, and afterward in Massachusetts, – from an egg deposited in the living tree many years earlier still, as appeared by counting the annual layers beyond it; which was heard gnawing out for several weeks, hatched perchance by the heat of an urn. Who does not feel his faith in a resurrection and immortality strengthened by hearing of this?[33]

Unlike Mather, who imagined New England's imminent death in order to bring its past alive, Thoreau offers us a dead New England apple tree in order to bring present life out of it. The four consecutive "which" clauses narrow the reader's vision to the embryo of the "strong and beautiful bug" from which will come renewal. Mather's concern had been communal salvation perceivable through providential signs; Thoreau's concern is individual "resurrection and immortality" signified through the working of nature's organic law.

When we consider the contexts of the two statements, the change from a communal biblicist perspective to an individual and naturalist one proves to be anything but simple. Mather applies to all New England the vocabulary of assurance, certitude, and security which had for decades been used to assess the inner spirit of the visible saint.[34] Conversely, Thoreau's parable about a "resurrection and immortality" originating in ordinary New England farm life comes at the very end of a text in which he has alternately satirized and attacked the New England farmer's thoughtless pursuit of superfluous luxury – a way of life that has clearly earned, for most New Englanders, no inner peace, no natural understanding, no spiritual grace. His readers ("you who read these pages, who are said to live in New England," p. 1) may have heard the story of the apple-tree table but are presumed to be no more alive than the dead tree itself; Thoreau's very last paragraph, indeed, informs us that the Yankee Johns and Jonathans are not likely ever to "realize all this" until they awake to dawn and see beyond today's morning star (227). But there is, in fact, no more assurance of renewal, communal or individual, at the end of *Walden* any more than at the beginning of the *Magnalia*. For Thoreau, there is only the "faith in resurrection and immortality" that depends upon the utterly inexplicable miracle that one New England bug has somehow emerged after a century of encasement in dead, dead wood. The consciousness of communal mission that sustained Cotton Mather despite all his doubts is, in Thoreau's concluding "story," no longer available.

Thoreau's regional iconoclasm was not, however, a perspective shared by many contemporary New England leaders. Thoreau was not arguing for New England "resurrection and immortality" on historical grounds; for him, both of these words had accrued non-Christian and extracommunal meanings that John Winthrop or Thomas Shepard would have decried. Thoreau's rhetoric does not proceed from the same patterns of analogy we find in Bancroft's *History*, Hawthorne's historical tales, many a commemorative oration, and even in Emerson's "Boston." For them, self and local community, local community and New England, New England and America were three pairs defined symbiotically either as mirror reflections or mirror opposites of each other. Moreover, the pairings continued on through historical time. Because there could be no absolute assurance from without, no verifiable saint except an invisible one, one could only look back upon and try to connect meaning-laden crises in the lives of self, community, and region.

PART ONE

Plantation and settlement

CHAPTER I

Of corn, no corn, and Christian courage

For understandable reasons, New England's first crisis – its Starving Time – has remained its least considered and least remembered communal trial. From the 1820s until at least midway through this century, young America was to be invoked by prominent New England historians both as a land of limitless natural bounty and as a state whose true spiritual glory was yet to be. Because land and republicanism were forces forever beckoning progressive Euro-Americans, the Anglo-American had to be freed from late medievalism, the Indian had to be (unjustly) dispossessed, then removed, and the Negro had to be (justly) freed into a position of political equality quite consonant with social inferiority. Under such circumstances, the past crises through which America had emerged were likely to seem political, economic, racial, and religious in kind. When Merry Mounters, Antinomians, Indians, and royalist placemen were looming immediately over the New England historical horizon, why linger over the hunger trials of first settlement? The new land's natural bounty had not been initially abundant, to be sure, but the widespread feeling that it should have been served to divert historical attention elsewhere.

In the eyes of such influential national historians as George Bancroft, Henry Adams, and Samuel Eliot Morison the great republic had emerged from a two-hundred-year mingling, a long unplanned working together, of the best traditions of Virginia and New England, but with New England subtly granted primacy. Opechancanough's rebellion and the Pequot War were to be regarded as premonitions both of King Philip's War and of the Indian's losing alliance with the British during the Revolution. The signing of the Mayflower Compact, the powers claimed by the House of Burgesses, the changing definition of "Freeman," and Roger Williams's presumed belief in "Liberty of Conscience" led directly to Jefferson's Declaration and to systems of republican representation based upon individual natural rights. For scholars of New England culture, community values had evolved in a broadly similar spiritual way. To Cotton

Mather, John Gorham Palfrey, Perry Miller, and Sacvan Bercovitch, the *Magnalia* among regional crises remained those of independence politics and the New England religious mind: the Antinomian Crisis, the Half Way Covenant, the loss of the charter, the revolution of 1689, Stoddardism and then (after Mather's time) secularization and the Great Awakening, with their divided influences upon the American Enlightenment and the American Revolution. Here is a tradition which, however valid it may be in its revealing of colonial or postcolonial spiritual and political purposes, gives short shrift to the physical. Little space for scurvy, even less for corn.[1]

In Jamestown, in New Plymouth, and in Massachusetts Bay the first crisis of new world settlement had been survival: to live until tomorrow. The settler's body had to remain sufficiently healthy to digest food; somewhere, enough unspoiled food had to be found to sustain the body. Severe famine did not end after one year, but continued for at least three. During those first years many a planter's innermost plea, John White's promotional title notwithstanding, must have been "Give us this day our daily bread." To those settlers believing themselves sent on the mission of a just God, anxiety over daily bread must have raised Job-like questions that would have been both personal ("What sin have I committed?") and collective ("What might God's purpose be if He has sent us plague and famine even before we have set up our godly commonwealth?"). These questions, one suspects, were too agonizing, too unanswerable (and the few healthy planters were probably too busy) to be written down.

Many of the often ignored statistics of disease and famine had been there in the historical record from the beginning.[2] Of the spiritual responses of famished men and women who faced immediate death, there are only remembered traces, usually penned by someone else. There are enough such traces, however, to make their recovery more than an historical curiosity, perhaps even a corrective. At least since President Lincoln's 1863 proclamation of Thanksgiving as a national holiday, we have lived in a culture that pauses, once a year, to associate the settlement of the new world, especially in Massachusetts, with the quick harvesting of an overflowing plenty. If the settlement of New England is remembered at all on the last Thursday in November, it is associated with the groaning bounties of an American festive board that seems, like Thanksgiving itself, forever self-replenishing. The reality of what happened in New Plymouth and Charlestown (let alone Jamestown) is what we do not even know we have forgotten. Both Pilgrims and Puritans gave thanks to God by fasting; do we honor what they endured and achieved by eating to surfeit?

My purposes in these pages are 1. to convey the continuing gravity of those first bodily crises, 2. to discriminate between Virginian and New England responses to similar deprivations, and 3. through study of later historical remembrances to suggest the cultural needs that made silence or selective recall of those physical sufferings so advantageous. Contrasting the hunger of first settlement with the plenty of the antebellum Republic might provide a clear instance of New England material prosperity, or of the good life in protestant America, but it would also have undermined the assumption that America had somehow always been (with apologies to Scott Fitzgerald) the green breast of the new world. During the 1830s, to dwell upon the first trials of the Pilgrims and Puritans risked offending Virginians for whom any similar claim advanced for Jamestown was hard to justify. North or South, doubts of a beneficent Providence would surely have arisen if the macabre details of the first years were to be examined too closely. Although this concern gradually receded after the Civil War, a reluctance to disfigure the first fathers by dwelling upon unseemly physical realities grew in its stead. By 1886, the "Puritan" of memory had become the massive, striding, purposeful, and fully clothed figure of Saint-Gaudens's statue.

The overall pattern of first sufferings had been remarkably the same in all three plantations. Shortly before the publication of promotional tracts in England, all three settlements had been chartered as joint stock trading companies, headed by protestant planters of Puritan persuasion, who were expected speedily to ship raw materials, especially fish, lumber, or perhaps even gold, back to English adventurers from a port city in the new world. As Edward Winslow noted, these were to be commonwealths "where religion and profit jump together," but the returnable "profit" (in the increasingly economic sense of that term) did not "jump" nearly as quickly as adventurers or planters anticipated.[3] There was precious little corn or fresh water. Whatever the recurrent terms "bloody fluxes" and "burning fevers" may have signified medically (at the very least scurvy, dysentery, pneumonia, tuberculosis, malnutrition, and exposure), their collective toll was prompt and terrible. Within nine months after arrival, 72 of 105 colonists in Jamestown, 47 out of 102 in New Plymouth, and about 200 out of 1,000 in Massachusetts Bay were dead. Destructive, costly fires aggravated the anxiety of remaining. Prisoners and/or apprentices were released to avoid the expense of feeding them. At the end of the first winter, 80–100 people returned to England from Massachusetts Bay, none chose to return from Plymouth, and almost everyone reputedly wished to return from Jamestown.

To use the biblical terms, famine followed hard upon plague. Not a famine that disappeared with the first harvest (as our Thanksgiving mythology would have it), but a famine that weakened bodies and spirits until at least the gathering in of the third harvest. In all three colonies, these conditions provoked disputes about increased community control over housing conditions, water supplies, and the procuring of foodstuffs. Without the aid of Native Americans in providing the English with Indian corn, whether through advice, trade, gift, or settlers' theft, none of the three colonies could have survived the first full winter, and only Massachusetts Bay might have survived the second.

Before the starving times ended, shallops and pinnaces were to range far and wide in search of Indian corn, often procured at exorbitant prices in trade. At various times during the first three years, all three colonies were reduced to living, probably exclusively, on whatever shellfish could be gathered and eaten before spoilage. Dispersal of the population from the port community was primarily due to the need for fresh water and unharvested shorefront. The clearing of new acres by the kind of hardy frontiersmen evoked by the Turner thesis did not occur.[4]

Corn – not squash and certainly not wild turkey – was the cause of both starvation and thanksgiving. As the generic term for grain, corn was the commodity that could last through winter months and be replanted on fallow Indian fields near the seashore without risking inland forays. Corn, therefore, would quickly become a recurring concern in law and letters home, as well as in promotional tracts. But the generic term soon acquired two tellingly different meanings. Boat-imported wheat and barley came to be called "English Corn" because it was conceived as a relief supply, secondary in importance and time of arrival to the "Indian corn" that could be procured through trade with the Indians, and then used as seed corn for planting. Corn as grain, ground and baked into the staff of life, also had welcome Eucharistic associations that would become explicit in later historical remembrance. But during the starvation times, the desperately short supply of corn provoked telling demands for supplements and alternatives. Immigrants were told to bring a three-month corn supply with them, but they were also told to bring over cattle, cows for milk, sheep for wool and mutton, and then, somewhat later, oxen for clearing new fields. Only in hindsight can these experiences be collectively seen in William Cronon's manner as ecological change; during the first five years of plantation, they must have been felt as new ways of life or death.

What might have been called "arrival narratives" seeking to account for the sufferings of famine (sufferings as acute as any "captivity narrative") were not to be forthcoming at a time when promotional literature was clearly needed. Mention of a few fleeting notations suffice, however, to convey the extremity of the planters' affliction. George Percy in Jamestown, 1607: "Our men were destroyed with cruel diseases as swellings, fluxes, burning fevers, and by wars, and some departed suddenly, but for the most part they died of mere famine."[5] John Smith in Jamestown, 1610: "Of 500, within 6 months after there remained not many more than 60 most miserable and poore creatures. It were to vild [*sic*] to say what we endured."[6] William Bradford, on the Pilgrims' appropriation of sixteen bushels of the Nauset Indians' corn in 1620: "a special providence of God and a great mercy to this people, that here they got seed to plant them corn the next year, or else they might have starved."[7] Thomas Dudley discovering the condition of the settlers at Naumkeag (Salem) in 1629: "All the corn and bread amongste them all [were] hardly sufficient to feed upon a fortnight."[8] Roger Clap recalling the settling of Dorchester and Charlestown: "Provision was not to be had for Money . . . Meal & Water & Salt boil'd together. . . . Oh, the Hunger that many suffered, and saw no hope in an Eye of Reason to be supplied."[9]

Only the governors of the plantations, who were most immediately responsible for the welfare of their people, seem to have attempted even a tentative explanation. (The leading ministers had not come with the first boats.) All three governors respond only to particular moments of extreme suffering, as if the very considering of the problem of providential justification had to be coerced from them by dire circumstance. However, the differences between the Virginian and the two New Englanders are startling because they do not depend on social class (Winthrop and Percy both came from the lesser nobility), nor upon education or position, but upon the consequences of observed Christian faith.

George Percy's manuscript narrative entitled "A Trewe Relacyion" ends its account of the Starving Time by recounting a startling incident that has received only the scarcest mention in Virginian or American historiography, even after its eventual publication in 1922.

And amongst the rest, one thing happened which was very remarkable wherein God showed his just judgment. For one Hugh Pryse, being pinched with extreme famine in a furious distracted mood did come openly into the market place blaspheming, exclaiming and crying out there was no God. Alleging that if there were a God, He would not suffer his creatures whom He had made and framed to endure those miseries and to perish for want of foods and sustenance. But it appeared the same day that the Almighty was displeased with him, for going that afternoon with a butcher, a corpulent fat man, into the woods to seek for some relief, both of them were slain by the Salvages. And after being found, God's indignation was showed upon Pryse's corpse, which was rent in pieces with wolves or other wild beasts, and his bowels torn out of his body, being a lean spare man. And the fat butcher not lying above six yards from him was found altogether untouched, only by the Salvages' arrows whereby he received his death.[10]

To Percy, the ultimate misery of the Starving Time was not the shriveling of a body into a skeletal "anatomy," not disease, not cannibalism, not infanticide, not even eating one's wife (all of which had already occurred in Jamestown) but rather the growing conviction that there is no God. Because written admissions of atheism were rare among early seventeenth-century Englishmen, and public pronouncements of atheism even more rare, George Percy presents Hugh Pryse's spiritual distress, not as representative of all of Jamestown's survivors, but as an indication of the depths to which the human spirit can be reduced. Pryse had pursued blasphemy beyond tacit atheism into public proclamation. He "came openly into the market place" and there stated "that there was no God" rather than "I believe there is no God." Under the circumstances, Pryse's reasoning seems a troublingly logical conclusion. For him to allege "that if there were a God, He would not suffer his creatures whom He had made and framed to endure those miseries" is a plausible outcry that, on the one hand, takes us back to the Book of Job, but on the other constitutes clearly unacceptable behavior within a Christian community struggling for a foothold in a new world.

It may be that George Percy was driven to write about Hugh Pryse because Percy was inwardly drawn to accept the logic of Pryse's blasphemy. What is sure is that Percy found relief for his own spirit by adducing that God promptly intervened through a double Secondary Cause (the bloodthirstiness of both the savage and the wolf) to demonstrate not only His "just judgment" but His continuing presence in Virginia. Pryse's merely human logic can therefore be discredited as "a furious distracted mood" and Percy can end his passage by contrasting the deserved bestial desecration of Pryse's body to the bodily remains of the "fat butcher," who had evidently found more than sufficient corn, and probably not a little meat, amidst Jamestown's famine. Percy is unwittingly describing a Jamestown that is no longer a community in any quality save proximity. His memory of Hugh Pryse is, understandably, not one which Virginians proud of their heritage have wanted to exhume.

Nowhere in the extant records of the dire first years of Plymouth or Massachusetts Bay is there any passage comparable to Percy's reflections on Hugh Pryse. If atheism was ever entertained in New Plymouth or Massachusetts Bay, it seems never to have been acknowledged in writing. Perhaps the force of protestant errand or respect for clerical leadership, even in the absence of John Robinson and John Cotton, made any avowal of atheism impossible. Perhaps the strength of the family unit, so absent among Jamestown's males, lessened the likelihood of individual heresy.[11] Or perhaps St. Paul's words about the "mystery of iniquity" provided a genuine inner check on the very temptation to blaspheme. We do not know.[12]

In recounting Plymouth's time of comparable distress (March of 1621), Bradford offered no explanation beyond commenting that the settlers' conduct toward each other had been truly admirable, even wondrous. Bradford's words would become, for nineteenth-century Americans, among the most cherished passages in *Of Plymouth Plantation*:

So as there died some times two or three of a day in the foresaid time, that of 100 and odd persons, scarce fifty remained. And of these, in the time of most distress, there was but six or seven sound persons who to their great commendations, be it spoken, spared no pains night or day, but with abundance of toil and hazard of their own health, fetched them wood, made them fires, dressed them meat, made their beds, washed their loathsome clothes, clothed and unclothed them. In a word, did all the homely and necessary offices for them which dainty and queasy stomachs cannot endure to hear named; and all this willingly and cheerfully, without grudging in the least, showing herein their true love unto their friends and brethren; a rare example and worthy to be remembered. (85)

The conduct remembered here, Christian charity at its finest, is the opposite of the divisive, self-seeking, and finally blasphemous acts George Percy and John Smith, in their several ways, recalled in Jamestown. Although Bradford does not say so, his account implies that, by not raising metaphysical questions about God's equity, the Pilgrims not only maintained their faith, but saved their energies to succour their fellows. Bradford's only mention of the Deity in the passage occurs in its closing hope that such charities shall eventually receive their due: "And I doubt not but their recompense is with the Lord."

The crisis that most settlers of the Great Migration endured on the Mishawum peninsula during the late summer of 1630 was to be preserved in the Charlestown town records, but not known in detail until Thomas Prince's *Chronological History of New England* (1736). The settlers, "Sick of the Scurvy," were living in "cottages, booths and Tents about the Town-Hill" with "no fresh Food to cherish them." The dead had to be buried about the town hill, aggravating the dire sanitary conditions caused by summer heat. By mid-August, despite two separate days of Thanksgiving, Humiliation and Fasting, the planters and their families were in "great and threatening straits for want of Food"; by December, at least 200 were dead and 100 had returned to England. The remarkable letters John Winthrop wrote during the crisis to his wife Margaret and son John back in Groton had to somehow strike the proper balance between providing information and reassurance, between recounting disaster and searching for remedies, between discerning natural causes and special providences. On July 16, he had to write Margaret of the death of their son Henry and of other "sad and discomfortable things"; he nonetheless observed "yet for all these things, I praise my God I am not discouraged, nor do I see cause to repent or despair of those good days here which will make amends for all."

In Winthrop's letter of July 23, specifics about the scarcity and "coarse" quality of the settlers' fare precede the claim that "if we have corn enough we may live plentifully." Although a crisis was clearly pending, the very fact that "He begins with us in affliction" is advanced as "the greater argument to us of His love and of the goodness of the work which we are about" (46). By August 14, Winthrop acknowledged to his son John that "the Lord's hand had been very heavy upon our people" while refraining from telling John "that which I conceived to be the reason." On September 9, confessedly in the midst of "much mortality, sickness and trouble," Winthrop first admits to Margaret that, though the remaining members of the Winthrop family were alive, it was difficult to find "the comfort of it" in the midst of so many deaths and other "afflictions of our bretheren." Instead of the City on a Hill, Winthrop bluntly warns, "We may not look at great things here," even suggesting that "It is enough that we shall have Heaven, even though we should pass through hell to it." Unable to see God's will amid the bewildering mix of so many "corrections" and so many "mercies," Winthrop remains persuaded on faith that "He will not cast us off, but in His due time will do us good, according to the measure of our afflictions." God's grace, be it noted, is here assumed to grow in proportion to the severity of the afflictions properly born. No assumption could be more foreign to George Percy, and no "greater argument" more characteristic of Puritan inner resources. Amid corpses, heat, drought, and famine, but after the forming of the Church Covenant, Winthrop could summon the confidence to write his wife: "We here enjoy God and Jesus Christ; is not this enough? What would we have more?"[13]

Winthrop's reflections on famine and providential justice end with his letter to Margaret of November 29. After naming the twelve members of the Winthrop household who have died, along with many "principal persons" of the company, Winthrop warns Margaret of disease and poor diet in order *not* to discourage her:

I trust that, that God, who hath so graciously preserved and blessed us hitherto, will bring us to see the faces of each other with abundance of joy. My dear wife, we are here in a Paradise. Though we have not beef and mutton, etc., yet (God be praised) we want them not; our Indian corn answers for all.[14]

Winthrop sees no inconsistency between his persistent ascribing of all causation to God, and his unremitting personal activity on behalf of the company's survival. Here is John Cotton's well-known paradox, "diligence in worldly business and yet deadness to the world," a paradox similar to Jonathan Edwards's ability to acknowledge achievements of the human will while denying the freedom of the will.

In written memory, the harvesting of amber waves of grain as the source for settlers' love of land was to surface long before Jefferson and Crevecœur. Perry Miller called Samuel Sewall's 1697 "prose poem" on Plum Island the "point at which the English Puritan had, hardly with conscious knowledge, become an American, rooted in the American soil."[15] Whether Miller's claim for Puritan primacy is justified or no, Sewall's affirmations rise through a baroque rhetoric of parallel clauses quite unlike Bradford's or Winthrop's concision. Sewall's love of river and pasture is firmly based upon the continuing plenty of that very same Indian corn which the first planters had sought with such difficulty:

And as long as *Plum Island* shall faithfully keep the commanded Post, Notwithstanding all the hectoring Words and hard Blows of the proud and boisterous Ocean; as long as any Salmon or Sturgeon shall swim in the streams of *Merrimack*, or any Perch or Pickeril in *Crane Pond*; as long as the Sea-Fowl shall know the Time of their coming, and not neglect seasonably to visit the Places of their Acquaintance; as long as any Cattel shall be fed with the Grass growing in the Medows which do humbly bow down themselves before Turkie-Hill; as long as any Sheep shall walk upon Old Town Hills, and shall from thence pleasantly look down upon the river Parker and the fruitful Marshes lying beneath; as long as any free and harmless Doves shall find a White Oak or other Tree within the Township to perch, or feed, or build a careless Nest upon, and shall voluntarily present themselves to perform the office of Gleaners after Barley-Harvest; as long as Nature shall not grow old and Dote, but shall constantly remember to give the rows of Indian Corn their education by Pairs; So long shall Christians be born there, and being first made meet, shall from thence be Translated, to be made partakers of the Inheritance of the Saints in Light.[16]

To Sewall, the climactic event in nature's restorative annual cycle is the "leading out" ("*education*") of the Indian Corn to feed still another generation of settlers. As a visible Providence, the growing of the corn demonstrates that "nature shall not grow old and dote." But in the closing rhetorical shift of the passage (from "as long as" to "so long shall"), the growing corn becomes a metaphor for the invisible process by which those Christians fortunate enough to be "born there" shall become Invisible Saints.

In Sewall's prose poem, nature provides as much assurance of sainthood as man can have. No first generation New Englander could have written such a passage, not only because of the corn shortage, but because Sewall's love for his father's land depends on recalling the stability afforded by generations of farming in one fruitful place. Although Sewall would have heatedly denied it, the opportunity to grow to maturity on such a land seems more important than the Bible in leading men to grace. The paired rows of corn lead up toward the light, year after year. Would not Cotton, Shepard, and Hooker have suspected heresy in such language?

And yet, when we put Sewall's hymn to Plum Island back into the context of *Phaenomena* as a whole, something other than the consoling cycles of bountiful natural law emerges. Sewall's passage occurs at the very end of a tract searching out the Book of Revelation and early Massachusetts history for reassurances that America will still be the site of the New Jerusalem.[17] The corn provided by Squanto and the providential rain that fell upon Plymouth's withered corn in 1623 are, to Sewall, crucial signs of New England's hope. The rarely read last words of *Phaenomena* warn that the "invaluable privileges" God granted to New England may not continue. "For our God is a consuming Fire," Sewall notes, and then closes with a prayer that "this very year, notwithstanding the Blast, the Worm, the Frost, the Drought, the War . . . the end of the Lord with New England will be that, though He Slay us, yet will we trust in him. October 7, 1697" (60).

The power of Sewall's prose poem to Plum Island's fertility, we should acknowledge, depends on its having been written during a year of drought and worm-eaten harvest, amidst the many other horrors (French and Indian attacks, loss of the Old Charter, the guilty aftermath of the Salem witch trials) that beset northern Massachusetts during the 1690s. Sewall's love for the stable pastoral life of Plum Island depends on the presumed absence, in that particular place, of the cultural crises that were engulfing New England as a whole. By isolating Plum Island and the Newbury/Newburyport area, Sewall sought to make it the New England of his historical imagination. Corn, given its familial and Eucharistic implications, provided Sewall with the ultimate sign of a regional and personal regeneration arising from memory of place.

Among Edward Taylor's more than two hundred "Preparatory Meditations," none has proven more enduringly satisfying than "I Kenning
Through Astronomy Divine" written in 1684. Linking man's fallen condition to his need for the bread of the Eucharist, without accepting tran-
substantiation, Taylor recounts the "Celestial Famine sore" into which all
men have fallen by eating "the Fruite forbad." Angels now show "an Empty
Barrell," in a world where there is no longer "the smallest Crumb" for
sustenance. When God then grinds His Son's body into the bread of life,
thereby giving grace, "knead in this Loafe," to all true believers, man gains
eternal salvation through a crumb altogether different in kind.[18]

However considerable the harvest privations in Taylor's Westfield may
have been during the 1670s, the glory of church communion, and the poem's
text from St. John ("I am the Living Bread"), are not the only reasons for
this meditation's striking force. Behind its metaphors lay founding communal experiences widely though selectively remembered. In 1669 Nathaniel
Morton had contended that the starvation of Charlestown, the Days of
Humiliation and Fasting, and the "great work of Erecting a Way of Wor-
shiping Christ in Church Fellowship" had been directly connected in spirit
as in time. Thomas Prince would follow suit, declaring that the July 30,
1630 formation of Boston's first Church Covenant at Charlestown was an
outgrowth of the "Christian Courage" the settlers had exhibited "amidst
these calamities." No one in this act of dual remembrance would outdo
Roger Clap, who in the 1670s recalled his hunger, in July of 1630, for "the
very Crusts of my Father's Table" while also remembering how "God's holy
Spirit in those Days" led many to "Pray for Grace, beg for Christ; and it
was not in vain."[19] Extreme famine, which had led Hugh Pryse and George
Percy from God, had brought Roger Clap and John Winthrop to God.

VOICING THE SILENCE

No seventeenth-century Puritan attempted a sustained examination of exactly why God had allowed corpses to accumulate and crops to wither
during the first three to five years of settlement. By century's end, however,
New England historians had clearly discovered the uses of ancestral reti-
cence for the present purpose of praising New England's beginnings. To
be sure, the historians' silence could on occasion be of their own making,
as for instance when Cotton Mather, Thomas Hutchinson, and George
Bancroft, all of whom were writing with Bradford's and Winslow's accounts of Plymouth Plantation before them, simply omitted all mention of

the Pilgrims' "taking" of the Nausets's corn.[20] More often, however, New England historians turned the settlers' silence into a virtue, by rendering restraint as faith, voicelessness as endurance, and death as prospective salvation. To discern the sustaining of faith through severe early trials was logically demanded by the beginning and end of their historical errand. Plymouth and Massachusetts Bay were reenacting the founding struggles of the primitive Christian churches, but they were also exemplifying the virtues of a new world commonwealth (later a republic) which the historians could not quite foresee.[21]

It is not just to claim, however, that by interpreting the planters' voiceless survival as Christian courage, New England's historians were distorting provable facts. Given the scarcity of primary evidence, historians beginning with Nathaniel Morton, and continuing for generation after generation, were to quote, reword, or otherwise reaffirm two retrospective eyewitness summaries they read in their histories: William Bradford's account of the "rare example" of "true love" Plymouth's dying settlers had shown during the Starving Time and Edward Johnson's tribute to the sufferers at Charlestown: "most admirable it was to see with what Christian courage many of these Souldiers of Christ carried it amidst all these calamities."[22]

Timely variations on these passages would become standard practice. Softening Edward Johnson's model of the New England church militant, Cotton Mather would ascribe the survival at Charlestown to the combined affective powers of fasting and faith: "it was their manner with *heart-melting*, and I may say, *Heaven-melting* devotions, to fast and pray before God."[23] To Hannah Adams, the Pilgrims had survived because they were unwittingly planting the seeds of the first amendment: the "heroic fortitude" and "religious fervor" of the Plymouth settlers, inspired by their need "to enjoy full liberty to worship God, according to the dictates of their Consciences," Adams declares, "enabled them to surmount every difficulty."[24] George Bancroft, whose standards for understanding historical sources were half providential but half empiricist, was the first to admit the value of absent evidence in penning consolations of the sufferings of New England settlers: "Not a hurried line, not a trace of repining, appears in their records," Bancroft correctly observed, thereby allowing his reader to assume that records existed elsewhere demonstrating the less worthy motivations of other new world colonies.[25]

Beginning with Nathaniel Morton, regional historians paraphrasing Bradford had noted that, unlike the 100 Puritans who had returned from Charlestown to England in 1630, none of the Pilgrims had chosen to return on the *Mayflower* in 1621, even though the Pilgrims' condition was more desperate. The pride in humility so evident in Bradford's *History* thus proved the most engaging source for commemorative oratory on behalf of New England/America's progressive future. Daniel Webster's reputation for eloquence originated in the rhythmic balance of his famed 1820 Discourse at Plymouth:

> We have come to this Rock, to record here our homage for our Pilgrim Fathers; our sympathy in their sufferings; our gratitude for their labors; our admiration of their virtues; our veneration for their piety; and our attachment to those principles of civil and religious liberty, which they encountered the dangers of the ocean, the storms of heaven, the violence of savages, disease, exile, and famine, to enjoy and to establish.[26]

Although "sympathy for sufferings" is here listed first, and "famine" last, Webster's speech never visualizes these particulars. Instead, he creates a hypothetical forefather who predicts that descendants of the Pilgrims, following their guiding star of civil liberty, shall so subdue the continent that "the waving and golden harvest of autumn, shall extend over a thousand hills" (29).

Webster's refashioning of Puritan separatism, first into national independence and then into New England's westward destiny, allows for only one further reminder of initial trial. Glossing over details of the Pilgrims' first winter, Webster acknowledges: "Hardly had they provided shelter for the living, ere they were summoned to erect sepulchres for the dead." His very next sentence, however, wholly transforms the pilgrims' suffering into a sacramental memorial of regional pride. "The ground had become sacred by inclosing the remains of some of their companions and connections. A parent, a child, a husband, or a wife, had gone the way of all flesh, and mingled with the dust of New England" (23). Unlike Sewall's prose poem, Webster's speech asks its audience to believe that the Pilgrims had as early as 1621 become "at home in their country" because the body of a family member was already dissolving into New England soil (22).

Grief and suffering thus pass away as the loved one's body is absorbed into the new land. "That which we sow in weakness shall be raised in strength" (29), intones Webster's hypothetical Pilgrim forefather, whose nameless voice transforms today's orator back into William Bradford, the pilgrim into the contemporary, and all New England's generations ultimately into one. The voice Webster here creates is both libertarian and commanding, regional and national, a kind of collective Protestant muse from the past that is perfectly calculated to speak to a citizenry for whom beloved national hymns about the "land of the Pilgrims' pride," "The memory of that holy hour" when "our exiled fathers crossed the sea," and "amber waves of grain" were all soon to be written.

By the time Rufus Choate delivered "The Age of the Pilgrims the Heroic Period of our History" before the New England Association of New York in 1843, he had heard the rhetoric of Pilgrim futurism often enough, but he was also well aware that his speech would be compared to Webster's. Like Webster, Choate traces American constitutional democracy back to the Mayflower Compact, American freedom of religion to John Robinson and William Brewster, and the virtues of the New England way to "'plain living and high thinking.'" Both "the securities of conservatism" and "the germs of progress" were already there "in the Mayflower cabin," Choate claims, even before the Pilgrims first stepped ashore.[27]

In all these respects Choate spoke as Webster's fellow Whig conservative, concerned to advance a version of the New England/American way in which reasoned popular liberty as defined by patriarchal leadership had always prevailed. And yet, Daniel Webster, who was in Choate's audience on that occasion, must have been taken back by Choate's implicit challenge to Webster's emphasis on today's harvests as visible proof of the forefathers' virtues. "We can think of nothing and of nobody, here and now, but the Pilgrims themselves," Choate insists. "I cannot and do not wish for a moment to forget that it is their festival we have come to keep" (77). Although the word "heroism" or "heroic" must appear on Choate's every page, his controlling point is that "The Age of the Pilgrims" *was* "the Heroic Period of our History." The truly heroic quality of the Pilgrim martyrs were that they died alone, without the eyes of a nation upon them, died for principles infinitely higher than a full granary or military glory in defense of a political state.

Choate recounts how "in a late visit to Plymouth, I sought the spot where these earlier dead were buried" (96). His visit to a Plymouth graveyard allegedly enabled him to see, in Edward Winslow's words, "strong men staggering through faintness for want of food" (97). As Choate stands in the graveyard, a pilgrim to the Pilgrims, the entire desolate winter of 1620/1621 reemerges from history's oblivion as in a panorama before him until the climactic moment when a collective ancestral voice, most unlike Webster's expansionist prophet, finally speaks (102). It is the voice of venerated elder William Brewster who informs Choate that Plymouth Rock is henceforth to be hallowed primarily by "the precious dust which we have committed to its bosom . . . I would be near them in the last day, and have a part in their resurrection" (103).

Whereas Webster had merely touched upon the putative consolation of a burial in New England soil, the very purpose of Choate/Brewster's reflections is morbidly regressive: "gazing on these long and intently and often, we may pass into the likeness of the departed, – may emulate their labors, and partake of their immortality" (105). Combining the conventions of the British graveyard poets with those of New England filiopietistic historians, the voice of Choate/Brewster serves as the most lugubrious kind of corrective to Webster's progressivism. Only in context does its macabre excess become understandable. The New York audience who heard Choate's speech consisted mostly of New England émigrés for whom regional nostalgia was surely an essential motive for attending. In the 1840s, as New England's national power was ebbing away, Choate began by reminding his audience that the eyes of the world could no longer be on Boston; he and his audience were now well met in Gotham, "in the heart of this chief city of the nation into which this feeble land has grown" (74). By 1843 both Webster and Choate were trying to negotiate conflicting commitments both to sectional nationalism and unionism, but the contrast between their two speeches shows the price exacted upon New England in the intervening quarter-century.

To show the beneficent hand of Providence at work during the Puritans' Starving Time at Charlestown posed a greater challenge than for the Pilgrims at Plymouth, where all reported conduct during the first winter had been exemplary in both senses of the word. Not only had 100 planters returned from Charlestown to England; memories surely lingered of the specific incidents behind John Winthrop's vague reference, in his July 23, 1630 letter to Margaret, to "some persons who never showed so much wickedness in England as they have done here" (*Letters*, 46). The potential for embarrassing contrast between the two foundings only grew as it became ever more evident that Boston had far surpassed Plymouth as New England's leading community.

No room for doubt about the Great Migration had been allowed, however, by Edward Johnson, who wrote the first published account of the sufferings at Charlestown. Andrew Delbanco and Stephen Carl Arch have argued persuasively that Johnson wrote his history amid worries that Massachusetts Bay might be emptied by emigration to join Cromwell's Commonwealth and/or its army; in Delbanco's words, Johnson was writing "to stem the tide of defections."[28] Because many planters had returned after the summer of 1630 in Charlestown, no moment in Massachusetts's brief history needed more careful explanation. Omitting any incident of the wickedness to which Winthrop had referred, Johnson summarized the "piteous case" of the needy settlers at Charlestown, then penned his tribute to the "Christian courage" with which "many of these Souldiers of Christ carried it amidst all these calamities" (66). Describing the settlers' preparations to move to Boston, Johnson made no mention of the many who returned, but focused instead on the growth and prosperity of present-day Charlestown, giving particular thanks that a plantation of only 150 dwellings should now have "Corne Land in Tillage in this towne about 1200 Acres" (69).

After picturing the prosperity of present-day Charlestown, Johnson penned quasifictive anecdotes to bolster his readers' historical memory:

> The Women once a day, as the tide gave way, resorted to the Mussells, and Clambankes, which are a Fish as big as Horsemussells, where they daily gathered their Families food with much heavenly discourse of the provisions Christ had formerly made for many thousands of his followers in the wildernesse. Quoth one, "My Husband hath travailed as far as Plimoth" (which is neere 40 miles,) "and hath with great toile brought a little Corne home with him, and before that is spent the Lord will assuredly provide". (77)

Two other wives, whose husbands' efforts had also procured their families less than a loaf, then voice similar concerns, but the worry of all three is momentarily lessened by observing that their children remain "cheerefull, fat and lusty" on a shellfish diet. Ultimately the Lord provides all three women their due reward for faith in the shoreline's bounty: "And as they were incouraging one another in Christs carefull providing for them, they lift up their eyes and saw two Ships comming in" (78). By elaborating so miraculous a providence, Johnson's history reinforces the collective power of a new world army that suddenly seems composed less of "souldiers of Christ" than of sturdy women who trust the plenitude of the new land. In Johnson's handy mixing of genres, the arrival of English corn confirms the women's trust, while Britain's ships seem to sail only and forever westward.

After the publication of Thomas Prince's *Chronological History*, the troubling evidence of the Charlestown records became impossible to ignore. Prince quoted Edward Johnson's tribute to "Christian Courage," but he also revealed the gruesome details of the summer's suffering, acknowledged that some settlers had been "imprudently selling" scant boat provisions to the Indians, and quoted Thomas Dudley's statement that the settlers who chose to remain were glad to be rid of the 100 returnees.[29] When, therefore, on June 28, 1830 Edward Everett delivered in Charlestown the open-air bicentennial address for Governor Winthrop's arrival, he faced a problem of commemoration exceeding his need to rival Daniel Webster's oratory at Plymouth. Everett's solution was to palliate past Puritan failings by evidence of recent restitution. Everett repeated most of Prince's gruesome account of the summer of 1630 in Charlestown, including the heat, famine, fouled water, daily deaths, and the returnees.

At speech's end, however, Everett pointed portentously downward to the soil of Charlestown's Town Hill, observing that "We are gathered over the ashes of our forefathers. We live on holy ground . . . Beneath our feet repose the meek and sainted martyrs whose flesh sank beneath the lofty temper of their noble spirits" (230). "And there," Everett continued, pointing upward to Bunker Hill, "rest the heroes who presented their dauntless foreheads to the God of Battles, when he came to his awful baptism of blood and of fire." Hearers were clearly meant to have their viewpoint literally uplifted by Everett's concluding, sensory contrast between the body of the 1630 Puritan, silently "sinking beneath the burning sun into the parched clay," with the body of the Bunker Hill Minuteman, fallen amid "wheels of maddening artillery, ringing with all the dreadful voices of war, wrapped in smoke, and streaming with blood" (230). To Everett, the bodies of the Puritan and the Bunker Hill martyr laid near each other in Charlestown soil have physically and spiritually become one; both Puritan and Minuteman died for civil liberty, "the early and the later champions of the one great cause" (231). Could there be a better example of the power of Archibald Alison's theory of place "Association" in enabling a commemorative orator both to bind and to transform history?

Because George Bancroft shifted allegiance to the Democratic Party in the very year the first volume of his *History* was published, he was still, in 1834, very much a Massachusetts clergyman's son with a Harvard education, regional loyalties, and associations with former leaders of the National Republican Party. The first two volumes of Bancroft's national history unfold the causes of New England's primacy in a manner that would only rarely have offended such recently prominent Massachusetts Whigs as Daniel Webster or Edward Everett. Because Bancroft's faith in the continuing power of New England was not yet dimmed, he could close his first volume by remarking: "I have dwelt the longer on the character of the early Puritans of New England, for they are the parents of one-third the whole white population of the United States."[30] In context, the statement is hardly an apology, but it nonetheless begs the question of the historical balance to be struck between Virginia's and Massachusetts's claims to national and republican origins.[31] Knowing that his readers were increasingly aware of divisive issues posed by slave versus free labor, low versus high tariffs, Cavalier versus Yankee, Bancroft had to find the most effective ways of validating

New England's cultural leadership without offending Virginian sensibilities past and present.

Toward this perhaps unachievable end, Bancroft allocated three chapters of his first volume to Spanish, French, and English explorations, three chapters to Virginia, one to Maryland, and three concluding chapters to the Pilgrims and the Puritans, together with a vigorous attack on slavery. Careful to give every group its due save Native Americans (an early nineteenth-century form of political correctness?), Bancroft rightly emphasized that the charters of both the Virginian and Massachusetts Bay colonies had granted no democratic principles of self-government. Instead, proto-American liberties were later to be grafted upon monarchical charters by a combination of new world conditions and the courage of protestant planters.

This careful balancing of regional influence goes tellingly and perhaps deliberately awry when Bancroft considers the first settlements' responses to plague and famine. Summarizing conditions during the nine months of George Percy's governorship, Bancroft passes the following judgment on the character of Virginia's planters during the Starving Time:

The emigrants of the last arrival were dissolute gallants packed off to escape worse destinies at home, broken tradesmen, gentlemen impoverished in spirit and fortune; rakes and libertines, men more fitted to corrupt than to found a government. It was not the will of God that the new state should be formed of these materials; that such men should be the fathers of a progeny, born on the American soil, who were one day to assert American liberty by their eloquence, and defend it by their valor. (138)

Here is providential history with a misleading vengeance. Because the survivors of the winter of 1609/1610 did not in historical fact abandon Jamestown, despite their decision to do so, at least some of those survivors had to have become the biological "fathers" of Virginia's progeny. Conversely, Bancroft's claim that Captain John Smith was "the Father of Virginia" deprives paternity of all physical definition, obviating the genetic evidence of blood in the name of Smith's metaphorical paternity as "the true leader" (138). Readers who claimed descent from those Virginia families Mark Twain was to mock as the FFV ("First Families of Virginia") would hardly have been pleased to be informed that the "will of God" could never have made "American liberty" from their "dissolute" ancestral "materials."

Although Virginians and Puritans had both, by 1700, managed to transform chartered privileges into settlers' rights, Bancroft circumscribed the origin of "the enfranchisement of the mind from religious despotism" (267) by placing it within his tribute to John Calvin, which begins the chapter entitled "The Pilgrims." Daniel Webster or Rufus Choate, but surely not Nathaniel Beverley Tucker or Hugh Swinton Legaré, would have warmed to Bancroft's summary of the virtues arriving in the *Mayflower*: "As the Pilgrims landed, their institutions were already perfected. Democratic liberty and independent Christian worship at once existed in America."[32] So suspect a regional claim created an additional problem within the requisite sequence of narratives of the plantings. Having ascribed priority to New England, how was Bancroft then to explain the compromised, divisive summer of the Great Migration's arrival? Like Edward Everett, Bancroft did not shirk facts that Thomas Prince had made known. Although the 100 who returned to England were not written off as contemptible malcontents, as Dudley had done, they were said to have been so "disheartened by the scenes of woe" that "dreading family and death, they deserted Massachusetts" (357).

Accompanying these admissions, however, was an overlay of compensatory metaphor whose authority depended on contemporary assumptions about natural law. Johnson's anecdotes of the faithful women on the beach were transformed, in Bancroft's version, into spiritual support provided to sensitive, stoic Puritan husbands by their physically vulnerable but spiritually resilient wives: "Woman was there," Bancroft wrote, "to struggle against unforeseen hardships, unwonted sorrows; the men, who defied trials for themselves, were miserable at beholding those whom they cherished dismayed by the horrors which encompassed them" (357). Conjugal misery, however, was not to last for long, because the children who died at Charlestown, anticipating Mrs. Stowe's Little Eva, "in their last hours, awoke to the awful mystery of the impending change, awaited its approach in the tranquil confidence of faith, and went to the grave full of immortality" (358).

For Bancroft, the enduring consolation for both the survivors and the dead of Charlestown had been revealed, not through any scriptural passage, nor any specific Providence of 1630, but through the timeless moral law of nature:

In the midst of want, they abounded in hope; in the solitudes of the wilderness, they believed themselves in company with the Greatest, the most Benevolent of Beings. Honor is due not less to those who perished than to those who survived; to the martyrs, the hour of death was an hour of triumph; such as is never witnessed in more tranquil seasons; just as there can be no gorgeous sunset, but when the vapors of evening gather in heavy masses round the west, to reflect the glories of declining day. (358)

Bancroft has here created a verbal landscape akin to many a Hudson River School painting, particularly Thomas Cole's *Landscape with Dead Trees*, Sanford Gifford's *Passing Storm in the Adirondacks*, and, most especially, Frederick Church's *Twilight in the Wilderness*. The promise of the westward-setting sun, emerging in all its glory through the clouds, contains the promise both of individual salvation/resurrection and of the Republic's future – without the need to specify either of them. There is nothing biblical in Bancroft's passage except its essence: Nature has shown us that the Puritans at Charlestown were right to have "believed themselves in company with the Greatest, the most Benevolent of Beings." In Bancroft's first volume, Virginia is granted no such sunsets.

A final thought on a brilliant (mis)use of silence in "Children of Light" (1946), Robert Lowell's terse, angry onslaught against two centuries of Pilgrim hagiography:

> OUR FATHERS wrung their bread from stocks and stones
> And fenced their gardens with the Redman's bones;
> Embarking from the Nether Land of Holland,
> Pilgrims unhouseled by Geneva's night,
> They planted here the Serpent's seeds of light;
> And here the pivoting searchlights probe to shock
> The riotous glass houses built on rock,
> And candles gutter by an empty altar,
> And light is where the landless blood of Cain
> Is burning, burning the unburied grain.[33]

The validity of Lowell's attack depends on the dubious assumption that Puritanism, now transformed into a wasteful secular drive for technological conquest, has remained the dominant force in American cultural life. The poem's rhetorical power depends on the implosion of ironies held within tightly compressed language (the double meanings of "stocks," "riotous" and (Plymouth) "rock"; the associations of "Nether Land" with "Nederland," "unhouseled" with "unhoused"; the contemptuous capitalization of OUR FATHERS; the irony of planters becoming "landless," and of a proudly able people whose true identity is Cain).

Lowell's controlling metaphor for assessing the Pilgrim legacy is, appropriately, one of spiritual planting; from the outset, the New England people have tried to fashion the bread of life from stocks and stones, to feed themselves by planting Serpent's seeds of light. Some of the consequences are expressed in rather expectable images (glass houses and empty altars) but Lowell's ending is a startling fusion of past and present. Today's spiritual light derives only from the governmental disposal by fire of the stockpiled grains of Depression farmers, including, as the second line implies, Indian corn. Instead of feeding or enlightening the people, the "unburied grain" is visualized as "burning, burning" – two words surely meant to recall the "burning, burning" of St. Augustine with which T. S. Eliot had closed "The Fire Sermon" in *The Waste Land*.[34]

The brilliance and intensity of Lowell's apocalyptic denunciations render it all the more necessary to protest that Lowell's account of their presumed origin is as historically false as it is prejudicial. There were, at the outset, precious few planted gardens and no wringing of bread from stocks. A far more plausible argument is that the immediate effect of the Starving Times of 1610, 1620, and 1630 was to harden settlers' resolves never again to be without corn or the wherewithall to get it. Such determination probably did not mean rapid dispossession of the Indian (fencing gardens with the Redman's bones), but rather trading with the Indian to one's own advantage, while bringing ever more land under cultivation. Such a resolve would also have required a rapid consolidation of ship trade through which British-manufactured goods could be sent to the new world whenever possible, including "English corn" as needed. The deepest and most lasting effect, however, was to be upon the suppressions of the historical mind. By remaining the horror memory that parents and children would prefer not to recall, the first three years of disease, death, and starvation provoked the most strenuous of efforts toward a different and better future, both individual and collective.

CHAPTER 2

Thomas Morton: phoenix of New England memory

To turn from the Starving Times of first arrival to the razing of Merry Mount is to shift perspective from *opera seria* to *opera buffa*, from unspeakable crisis to overwritten scuffle, from inner trial of the communal spirit to public trial of the outsider. Famine had been a crisis within the body and the soul; Merry Mount was a passing controversy later elevated for purposes of group self-definition into a crisis. Bradford, Endicott, and Winthrop strove to eliminate from New England all that Merry Mount might represent, first by alleging a wide spectrum of Thomas Morton's villainies, then by extraditing him. Morton's revenge was to try to deprive the "precise Separatists" of all significance by using Cavalier literary satire to serve the legal end of revoking the Massachusetts Bay Company's charter.[1] This was a war of unforgettable words that was to reduce the sporadic quasimilitary actions, but not the underlying theological politics, to burlesque.[2]

The great irony of Morton's prominence in New England legend is that the purposes of both historical antagonists would utterly fail. Just as Morton was extradited from Massachusetts three times, yet died in New England after his third return, so the shrill clarity of Bradford's and Winthrop's denunciations would highlight Morton's memory, not obscure it. Similarly, even though Morton may insist upon the beauty, fertility, and erotic power of the New English Canaan, both his satire and his outrage depend on his assuming, from the outset, that "Nature's Masterpeece" has been handed over to the defacing hand of the Puritan. His climactic proof of Puritan sadism can only be the moment in which he witnesses, for himself and his reader, the root and branch eradication of Merry Mount:

All was burnt downe to the ground, and nothing did remaine but the bare ashes as an embleme of their cruelty; and unles it could (like to the Phenix,) rise out of these ashes and be new againe (to the immortall glory and renowne of this fertile Canaan the new,) the stumpes and postes in their black liveries will mourne; and

44

piety it selfe will add a voyce to the bare remnant of that Monument, and make it cry for recompence (or else revenge,) against the Sect of cruell Schismaticks.[3]

Merry Mount was erased within three months of the Great Migration's arrival, the charter revocation scheme came to naught, and Morton himself was to die "old and crazy" in Maine.[4] In the realm of written remembrance, however, Morton's hope for continuing resurrection would prove to be remarkably prophetic. At the time Miles Standish apprehended him, Merry Mount probably consisted of no more than seven male planter/traders, but in historical memory Merry Mount would, phoenix-like, rise from its own ashes again and again to symbolize cultural values that New England had rightly eliminated or self-righteously lost.

The bedrock dispute of legal land title was promptly obscured. The proceedings against Merry Mount by William Bradford in 1628, by John Endicott in 1629, and by John Winthrop in 1630 were all part of a larger process of establishing regional jurisdiction by clearing New England of resident dissidents – Thomas Morton being the most vocal and alien. Never sizeable by comparison even with Plymouth, Merry Mount became, upon the arrival of the Winthrop fleet, quite negligible as a rival for the fur trade, as a source of guns for Indians, or as a nest of godless revelers led by the Lord of Misrule. It is doubtful whether the Merry Mount community ever posed a threat commensurate with the crisis rhetoric with which it was to be denounced. But the 'pagan' amorality of the Merry Mount settlement, Hawthorne's canonical tale notwithstanding, had not been the paramount issue at the time it was destroyed. In his time, Thomas Morton, as I hope to show, had been a greater threat in England than in Massachusetts, a more dangerous adversary with his lawyerly and literary pen than with his gun, his maypole, or his fur profits. Would Bradford, Endicott, and Winthrop have been half as incensed at the paganism of Morton's May Day had not Morton been engaged, perhaps as early as the late fall of 1628, in Sir Ferdinando Gorges's continuing attempt to subvert the Puritan occupation of New England?

As a writer, Morton possessed the wit and the learning to characterize himself as the opposite of the stock Puritan in every conceivable way; he then displayed the courage (or the folly) to return to New England, where he would be imprisoned in part for having written, in Bradford's words, "an infamous and scurrilous book against many godly and chief men of the country, full of lies and slanders against their names and persons and the ways of God."[5] Bradford's description only insured that Morton's *New English Canaan* would be remembered and reread. The sweeping nature of Bradford's accusations, written at least nine years after Morton's book was published, and sixteen years after the events it records, allowed later historians and writers plenty of opportunity for doubt, revisionism, and reinvention.

The "crisis" posed by Morton and Merry Mount was, therefore, an entirely reimagined one, even as Bradford and Morton penned their first accounts of it. From the outset, it was a crisis of opposed symbology, readily adaptable to shifting cultural and personal needs. Wherever Morton was thought to reside on the spectrum from conspiratorial villain to innocent victim, the only constant in the literature of Merry Mount would be that the actions subjugating Morton, taken by those three worthies, Bradford, Endicott, and Winthrop, were to associate New England's strength with patriarchal Puritan authority for the historically foreseeable future. Conversely, whatever qualities Thomas Morton and his community were thought to embody had been in 1630 defined out of New England's moment of historical origin.

The isolating of Morton and Merry Mount is therefore a thoroughly understandable, perhaps inevitable scholarly exercise. Again and again we are told that Morton was the only seventeenth-century writer who wrote of New England with a sense of humor, that only he integrated his community with the land and the Indian, and even that Morton was the only (English)man ever to fly falcons in Massachusetts. The oddity of the *New English Canaan*'s publication in Amsterdam has served to reinforce the colorful and comic singularity associated with Morton's name. In fact, however, much of the imaginative literature about Merry Mount proceeds in a more integrative fashion by following Morton's own practice of defining identity by symbolic character contrasts. Morton is seen and judged by comparison with his presumed opposite. The obvious oppositions (Morton as the foil to Standish, Bradford, Endicott, or Winthrop) become more complex once when we recognize that the four Puritan patriarchs were themselves perceived as different models of Puritan character. Whether a writer juxtaposes Morton to Standish rather than Bradford, Endicott rather than Winthrop, thus has consequences for how Morton is perceived and what values were presumably eliminated from New England. As a further consequence, the characters of Morton's symbolic opposites evolve through the process of literary "imitation" (Robert Lowell's John Endicott, for example, is conspicuously unlike Hawthorne's). The most important, and certainly the most neglected, of these couplings is the doubling of Morton with an alternative model of ostracized villainy. For nineteenth-century writers of romance, Thomas Morton almost immediately summoned up the figure of Morton's coconspirator Christopher Gardiner in ways that suggest acutely divided, even inconsistent, judgments of New England's origin.

REDIRECTING THE ACCUSATIONS

If we reconstruct the history of Merry Mount by following the chronology and honoring the context of the written accounts, the importance of Bradford's famous accusation against Morton as the Lord of Misrule diminishes sharply. John Winthrop's journal entries and Thomas Dudley's letter to the Countess of Lincoln then emerge as the only extant primary and contemporary sources, Morton's *New English Canaan* is shown to have been a literary weapon written to further a political overturn, and Bradford's denunciations can be seen as a retrospective judgment written at least nineteen years after the maypole celebration, but only two years after the aging Morton's final extradition by Governor Winthrop. There is no evidence whatever that Morton's May Day rites were central to Plymouth's decision to extradite him in 1628, nor was Morton's May Day of any concern to John Winthrop in 1630 when he ordered Merry Mount to be burned and Morton stocked and extradited. Instead, the issues that emerge in the records written before 1631 center on the fur trade, selling guns to the Indians, the alleged mistreatment of the natives and, above all, jurisdiction. There may be good reason to conclude that Thomas Morton was persecuted by Pilgrims and Puritans, but there is no reason to believe that he was prosecuted for worship of Flora and Bacchus, for use of the Book of Common Prayer, or for sleeping with lasses in beaver coats. It would be Morton himself, writing in England in the mid-1630s, who was to raise these allegations, knowing as he did exactly how to mock the "precise Separatists" as envious, bigoted killjoys. A few years later, it would be the existence of Morton's "scurrilous" book that would lead Bradford, sometime after 1646, to write his counter-account of May Day and of Morton, an account designed to situate Morton among the many models of godless roguery that Plymouth's sons were henceforth to avoid.

Winthrop's journal for September 1630 notes simply: "Thomas Morton adjudged to be imprisoned till he were sent into England; and his house burnt down, for his many injuries offered to the Indians, and other misdemeanors" (31). Thomas Dudley's letter of March 12, 1631, which provides a much fuller account of Winthrop's sentencing, characterizes Morton as "a proud, insolent man" about whom a "multitude of complaints were received" regarding the many injuries he had done "both to the English and

Indians" – all of them involving the use of guns.[6] Dudley's letter makes not one mention of Merry Mount, May Day, pagan ceremonies, or Morton's religion, even though John Endicott, who had cut down Merry Mount's maypole two years before, had been present in court when Winthrop had sentenced Morton.

Among the leaders of Massachusetts Bay, Morton did not begin to acquire the significance of a genuine threat until June 1631, when Winthrop opened a packet of letters sent from Sir Ferdinando Gorges to Sir Christopher Gardiner in Weymouth and found among them a letter that had been sent from Gorges to Morton in England. Winthrop then became rightly convinced that Morton had become an integral part of Gorges's "secret design to recover his pretended right" to govern all New England.[7] By May 1633, Winthrop learned that Gardiner, Morton, and Ratcliffe had petitioned the King and the Council for New England, "accusing us to intend rebellion, to have cast off our allegiance, and to be wholly separate from the church and laws of England" (54). Soon thereafter the Massachusetts General Court issued orders to fortify Castle Island, Dorchester, and Charlestown, to gather guns and ammunitions, to drill the trainbands in all covenanted towns, and to impress all the labor that would be needed to complete these defensive preparations. If Winthrop had known that, in late May 1634, Morton had been appointed the Council for New England's prosecutor for repeal of the Massachusetts Patent, he would surely have had the foresight to take even more extreme measures.

The similarity of this moment to the writ of Quo Warranto against the Massachusetts Charter fifty years later, with the subsequent sending of Sir Edmund Andros as appointed Governor-General of New England, is striking and would be noted, most especially by Sam Adams at the time of the "Intolerable Acts" of 1774. Although the takeover crisis of 1634–1637, unlike those of 1685 and 1774, would eventually dissipate, preparatory responses against it would continue. When the trainband of Salem was mustered in November, Endicott cut the red cross out of the British flag, thereby gaining local military support at the expense of lending credence to Morton's charge that the Puritans were political as well as religious separatists. In May a warning beacon was ordered to be built upon Sentry (now Beacon) Hill, a military commission was appointed, and the Freeman's Oath was exacted of all the commission's members, whether they were saints or not. The expectation was for a military conflict that many a New England settler must have feared to lose. Although no gun was fired, Massachusetts would lose the paper war when the King's Bench, after receiving Morton's writ of *quo warranto* arguing that all Massachusetts land titles were invalid, declared in 1637 that the charter had always been void and was about to be vacated.

It is in the midst of this crisis mentality that Thomas Morton wrote and published the *New English Canaan* (1637).[8] Its rhetoric and structure cannot be fully understood by those who persist in viewing Morton as a harmless cavalier or as a pioneer settler at one with the Edenic land and its inhabitants – although Morton took passing delight in striking both poses. Morton writes as a trader, adventurer, ur-planter, lover, Royalist, friend to Indians, courtier, lawyer, bon vivant, pious Anglican, sportsman, cataloguer of flora and fauna, jokester or classicist, adopting whatever guise might be most handy in the immediate context. Never one to hide his skills at shape-shifting, Morton ends his account of his supposedly unparseable May Day poem by celebrating his own powers of deception: "Hee that playd Proteus, (with the helpe of Priapus,) put their noses out of joynt" (281).[9] Through laughter and through law, Morton's aim was to write the Separatists out of New England at the very moment they seemed to have eliminated all dissidents within. If Morton was to gain support for Gorges's overturn of the charter and reallocation of New England lands, incidents of Puritan illegality needed to be convincingly presented and the Separatists' charter rights to occupy the land of the Massachusetts needed to be implicitly challenged.

The *New English Canaan* never directly confronts the overriding issue of the right of native versus European possession of new world lands. As a lawyer charged with preparing new deeds for Gorges's associates, Morton was far too clever to directly question either the validity of a paper patent or the argument of the *vacuum domicilium*. He conveniently fails to mention whether he or Wollaston ever had a patent for the land on which Merry Mount had stood.[10] Instead, he preceded his account of the Puritans by descriptions of New England and its natives, descriptions drawn from a blissful summer of coastal exploration when there were apparently no Pilgrims or Puritans in sight. The impression created by reading Morton's entire book consecutively is that ownership of land is an implied right of the first occupant – in this case, Merry Mount would "belong" to the Merry Mounters (Wollaston remaining conveniently unmentioned). Surely the purpose of Morton's continual, half-facetious references to himself as "mine host" is to reaffirm his priority of right, as an established landholder, to dispense the generosity of his board to all newcomers who, unlike the Puritans, show Merry Mount due respect and grace of manner.

Because land ownership implies rights of jurisdiction, Morton knew by 1636 that his conflict with the Massachusetts Bay Company, rather than

Plymouth, would be determinative in law. He began his account of the Great Migration with satire. The fiddling Cowkeeper and "great swelling fellow of Littleworth" (John Endicott), with the help of "Master Charter party" had "crept over to Salem" and then displayed "the Patent of the Massachusetts" in order to awe already established planters with his "pretended" authority as "chiefe Justice of the Massachusetts Bay" (304, 305). When, however, John Endicott summoned all settlers to Salem and insisted that every planter sign articles subscribing to the principle "That in all causes, as well Ecclesiastical as Politicall, wee should follow the rule of Gods word," the humor of the narrative suddenly drops away. Morton had agreed to attend the public meeting but had refused to sign. "Onely Mine Host," Morton writes, had had the courage to publicly object, insisting that he would be willing to grant the Massachusetts Bay Company jurisdiction over him only "*So as nothing be done contrary or repugnant to the Lawes of the Kingdome of England*" (307). In the political context of the mid-1630s, this alleged amendment was a master stroke, allowing Morton to imply that the Puritans were irresponsible Separatists bent on independence, while singling himself out as the only planter who had had the courage to remember and to observe the actual wording of the Massachusetts Bay Company charter.

The argument Morton then offers on behalf of his supposed amendment shows him at his brilliant best:

> *So as nothing be done contrary or repugnant to the Lawes of the Kingdome of England.* These words hee knew, by former experience, were necessary, and without these the same would prove a very mousetrapp to catch some body by his owne consent, (which the rest nothing suspected,) for the construction of the worde would be made by them of the Separation to serve their own turnes; and if any man should, in such a case, be accused of a crime, (though in it selfe it were petty,) they might set it on the tenter hookes of their imaginary gifts, and stretch it to make it seeme cappitall; which was the reason why mine Host refused to subscribe. (307)

Once theocracy has become the governing principle of New England, Morton argues, the Word of God will be twisted into whatever "construction" the Separatists choose to place upon it. Small sins will readily become capital crimes in the hands both of powerful local ministers who determine the Word, and of powerful local governors who determine the word.

Morton's refusal to subscribe should be seen as New England's first instance of public civil disobedience, but his disobedience was undertaken, not on behalf of the higher law, but because the higher law usually turns out to be nothing more than what fallible men say it is. Although it may be a stretch thus to trace Thoreau's and Parker's ideas of civil disobedience back to Mine Host, there surely is a connection between Morton's legal challenge to Endicott's jurisdiction and the compromised position of loyal diplomats such as Increase Mather and Thomas Hutchinson, who would love both New England and the supremacy of English law, and who would, in their later years, pay a dear price for retaining both allegiances.

At the time Bradford began writing about Morton, sometime between late 1646 and 1648, he knew Winthrop had forced Morton out of Massachusetts and may already have learned of Morton's death in Agamenticus (York), Maine in 1647.[11] Despite Edward Winslow's apprehensions, once the Puritans had assumed power in England, neither Morton nor Gorges was any longer a jurisdictional threat to New England's plantations.[12] The annals in the final chapters of *Of Plymouth Plantation* show that, at the time of Morton's rearrival in Plymouth, Bradford was preoccupied with other worries: an outbreak of "wickedness" signaled by Thomas Granger's execution for buggery, the death of William Brewster, the arrival of "many untoward servants" and "many unworthy persons" in the Massachusetts Bay area, dispersal of Plymouth settlers to Eastham and Nauset, possible war with the Narragansetts, the departure of Edward Winslow to England, and the collective sense of "this poor church left, like an ancient mother grown old and forsaken of her children" (370).

These immediate circumstances shaped the very substance of Bradford's historical recreation. Four long paragraphs are written about the threat posed by Morton's arming of local Indians. Morton's subversive skills at undoing terms of indenture and attracting "unclean birds" to a roost that was near to, but outside of, Plymouth Plantation are remembered as having been a paramount concern. Bradford reinvents Morton's destroyed community as the sum of those remembered evils that continue as a present threat. May Day 1627 serves as a prototype for the "many wicked persons and profane people" whom Bradford says have "so quickly come over into this land" in 1642 and 1643 (356).

After this they fell to great licentiousness and led a dissolute life, pouring out themselves into all profaneness. And Morton became Lord of Misrule, and maintained (as it were) a School of Atheism. And after they had got some goods into their hands, and got much by trading with the Indians, they spent it as vainly in quaffing and drinking, both wine and strong waters in great excess (and, as some reported) 10 pounds worth in a morning. They also set up a maypole, drinking and dancing about it many days together, inviting the Indian women for their consorts, dancing and frisking together like so many fairies, or furies, rather; and worse practices. As if they had anew revived and celebrated the feasts of the Roman goddess Flora, or the beastly practices of the mad Bacchanalians. (227)

Groping to define the precise category of immorality to which Morton belonged, Bradford here adds one old world term to another (pagan, Lord of Misrule, fairie, fury), until he arrives at the beastly, mad Bacchanalian, which subsumes the other four. Surely the repetition of the unnamable "worse practices" as "beastly practices" reflects Bradford's worry over the recent outbreak of wickedness signaled by Granger's buggery. Neither in this remarkably focused presentation of Morton as the essence of immoral and irreligious man, nor in Bradford's equally focused attack on Morton's supplying of guns to the Indians, are the original historical issues of juris-diction, colonial law, and land use any longer of lasting consequence.

Any attempt to factually resolve any issue of the controversy leads one back to the shifting sands of the two major texts. For both Bradford and Morton, creation of character was more important than recall of fact. Neither Bradford nor Morton made efforts to record controversial episodes precisely as they remembered them, or even in chronological order. Neither determined which of the other's objectionable traits had aggravated dislike into action. The power of their recreations derives from their allowing present circumstance and a priori notions of character to shape their recall of long-past events. To Bradford, Thomas Morton represents ancient but re-curring godlessness; civilized in externals but pagan in allegiance, cunning in strategy but carnal in desire, equally heedless of racial distinctions, society's needs, and biblical morality. To Morton, William Bradford represents the absurd but cruel Separatist: lower class, clumsy, antiintellectual, and busily self-righteous, anxious to display his bogus purity by bursts of oppression.

Morton's caricatures of Bradford, Endicott, Winthrop, and Standish seem to merge into one figure because they serve to introduce generaliza-tions about the Puritan character. All Puritans are "elephants of wit"; all have "special gifts for envy and mallice" (339); all "wink when they pray, be-cause they thinke themselves so perfect in the highe way to heaven that they can find it blindfould" (334). Morton has relied upon a preformed character type, traits of which can readily be invoked to appeal to Anglicans or lawyers. Bradford's moments of hesitant lenience can be interpreted as bungling, Bradford's fear of armed Indians as financial envy, and Bradford's distaste for Indian "consorts" as a sign of prurience. Beginning in Washington Irving's time, the Separatists' destruction of Merry Mount would therefore become the perfect primary resource for all those who, for various motives, wished to attack "the Puritan" as a racist, nature-hating killjoy.

The gradual emergence of Morton's viewpoint, first into consideration and eventually into favor, depended on a timely coincidence of publishing conditions and change in cultural attitudes. Because the *New English Canaan* was not republished until 1838, and *Of Plymouth Plantation* not until 1856, New England's early historians long retained literal physical control over both texts. Edward Johnson, who had been in England at the time of Morton's greatest political influence, appears to have read the *New English Canaan* after his return to Massachusetts, because he refers to Morton as "the Host of Merrimount" who had also been one of the Saints' "Malignant adversaries," "a wretched fellow" who had effectively supported the "lording Bishops" until the Lord providentially delivered him up into Governor Winthrop's restraining hand.[13] Johnson's contemptuous dismissal would prove to be the mildest of beginnings. For at least the next 150 years, Morton's memory would be at the mercy of regional historians who consulted only Bradford's manuscript and/or their own predecessors. Nathaniel Morton, Cotton Mather, William Hubbard, Thomas Prince, Thomas Hutchinson, Hannah Adams, and Joseph Felt were all content to quote Bradford's account as the historical truth – and then add their own terms of invective – without considering either the date Bradford had written the passage or Bradford's view of Plymouth's already declining place in history. Their unwillingness even to entertain Morton's viewpoint shows how much New Englanders felt they had to lose.[14]

Despite the impressive information assembled in his long standard Prince edition of the *New English Canaan* (1883), Charles Francis Adams Jr. has continued to be associated with the virulent detractors of Morton and Merry Mount. His lengthy prefatory essay "Thomas Morton of Merry Mount" contains more than a few judgments, such as the claim that Morton had "absolutely nothing to be said in his favor. He was a lawless, reckless, immoral adventurer."[15] Such evidence for Adams's narrow-mindedness has seemed the stronger because of the particular kinds of privilege evident in his life and lineage. Charles Francis Adams Jr. served as president of the Massachusetts Historical Society in decidedly chauvinist times. The site of Merry Mount, which had been deeded to Edmund Quincy in 1635, had long since been absorbed within Adams family lands, on which Charles Adams was then living in an imposing, newly built house atop "Presidents Hill."[16] However, between 1883, when Adams published the Prince edition of Morton's book, and 1893, when he published his now less read *Three Episodes in Massachusetts History*, Adams had undergone experiences likely to make him more tolerant and more understanding of Thomas Morton. Adams had spent much time in the far West, becoming president of the Union Pacific Railroad in 1884, but driving it into bankruptcy by 1890, when Jay Gould forced him to resign. Failed speculations in western lands, together with showy expenditures on his homes in Quincy and Boston, depleted family resources and provoked sibling rivalries with Henry Adams and Brooks Adams. As Charles's house on President's Hill began more and more to resemble a woeful mount, he retreated into early Massachusetts history, writing of his three chosen "episodes" (Thomas Morton and the earliest settlers, Anne Hutchinson and the Antinomians, and the growth of Quincy), while acknowledging in his diary: "I go out of the present world which I can't manage into the past where I am master."[17] Adams was now writing, incisively but with divided attitudes, about dissident individuals and their minority adherents, dissidents who had been forced out by a people stronger, and perhaps more able, than they.

If one wishes to present Charles Adams as the condemnatory voice of New England's neo-Puritan heritage, it is easy to do. Adams's opening judgment was that "Morton was a born Bohemian and reckless libertine, without either morals or religion, and he probably cared no more for the Church of England than he did for that of Rome."[18] However, throughout Adams's history, here is another, engaging Thomas Morton whom Adams is often at pains to quell. Morton was, Adams notes, "a man of convivial temper and a humorist" (172). In a passage resembling the "Quincy" chapter of his brother Henry's *Education*, Charles Adams credits Morton with "an innate love of nature" that made him an "exhilarated" and appreciative survivor of "the harsh, variable New England climate" (173). Charles cannot resist penning a Hawthorne-like "picturesque effect" of Merry Mount's May Day, in which the pageantry "breaks in upon the leaden gloom of the early New England annals like a single fitful gleam of sickly sunlight, giving the chill surroundings a transient glow of warmth, of cheerfulness, of human sympathy" (179). At some perhaps subconscious level, Charles Adams sensed his affinity with Morton, "this man – born a sportsman, bred a lawyer, ingrained a humorist and an adventurer," who, like himself, had lost so much through his own recklessness and bravado.

The more Adams contemplated the pleasures of May Day, the more he was attracted to them. Morton's revelry and the "rolicking choruses" of his poems emerge as "a protest of human nature at the attempted suppression of its joyous and more attractive half" (181). But in summarizing the significance of Merry Mount, Charles Adams, still the New Englander, needed to elevate past eastern pleasures over recent western ones that he may, or may not, have observed:

Incongruous and laughable, the situation had its dramatic features also. It was not a vulgar modern instance of the frontier dance-hall under the eaves of a conventicle.

There was a certain distance and grandeur and dignity about it, – a majesty of solitude, a futurity of empire. On the one hand, the sombre religious settlement; on the other the noisy trading-post, – two germs of civilized life in that immeasurable wilderness, unbroken, save at Merry-Mount and Plymouth, from the Penobscot to the Hudson. Yet that wilderness, though immeasurable to them, was not large enough for both. (182)

Even when today's west is thus transferred back into New England's past ("noisy trading-post"), the two "germs of civilization" had to remain utterly incompatible, not at all one Commonwealth, any more than east and west now formed one national culture. Merry Mount and Plymouth were to remain, in historical imagination, two conflicting ur-republics, placed in fatal proximity in the midst of limitless wilderness.

Adams thus emerges as the first New Englander willing to defend Morton on historical terms. He charges that in 1630 John Winthrop had imposed a "root and branch sentence" without a hearing – a travesty of legal process likenable only to "the Star Chamber or the Court of High Commission" (242, 241). Adams's conclusion about the razing of Merry Mount, so long vengefully celebrated by New England historians, is that "the confiscation and the burning were unmistakable acts of high-handed oppression" (247). Broadening his attack, Adams then writes that "The School of New England historians" has customarily defended "the whole long record of not dissimilar acts which disfigure the early annals of Massachusetts" (247). Naming only Palfrey and Robert Winthrop, Adams exposes the illogic in the familiar argument that, because "freedom of opinion" could not be tolerated in establishing the Commonwealth, repressive measures of such "extreme severity" were therefore justified. New England's filiopietism has been based on shifting sand. Justifying means by ends, New England's historians have created a tradition in which tyrannical measures are first cloaked and then "venerated" because something like "democracy" would eventuate from them.

Among the many attacks on Puritanism as the source of all the nation's present ills, no text of the 1920s has more fully retained its impact than *In the American Grain* (1925).[19] William Carlos Williams struck directly at the metaphor so precious to Bancroft and his contemporaries. As "the seed of Tudor England's lusty blossoming," as well as the "seed" of the American Republic, the Pilgrims had in fact not expanded as Nature's nation, but had shriveled in fear and hate as soon as they were forced to confront the wilderness. "The jargon of God, which they used, was their dialect by which they kept themselves surrounded as with a palisade."[20] The inevitable result was that Pilgrims and Puritans declined to a "nadir" of "little pips," a people so afraid of flesh and forest that they "praised a zero in themselves" and "produced a race incapable of flower" (66). No liberty, progress, or democracy here.

William Carlos Williams was, however, anything but a close reader. In order to portray Thomas Morton as the first of the anti-Puritan pioneer iconoclasts who would ultimately flower into Daniel Boone (that "great voluptuary born to the American settlements against the niggardliness of the damming [*sic*] Puritanical tradition," p. 130), Williams selected Charles Adams as his scapegoat, stalking horse, and straw man. Misspelling the author's name as "A. C. Adams," Williams wrongly charged Adams with "parochialism," neo-Puritan bigotry, squeamishness, and lack of proportion in failing to realize that Morton was not a "vulgar Royalist libertine" but a "New World Pioneer taking his chances in the wilderness" (75). Like H. L. Mencken and Randolph Bourne, Williams was so intent upon debunking the Puritan as part of the modernist effort to "make it new" that he could not see, or would not admit, that a revisionist of a different sort might have been there before him.

In a manner suggestive of Joseph Conrad before him, and D. H. Lawrence after him, Williams searches out forgotten figures who brooded over the mysterious darkness of a savage continent and found regeneration by dying back into the wilderness. In this regard, Morton served as the symbolic victim upon whom Puritans laid their hands "with malice, with envy, insanely," simply because Morton had laid his hands upon the red flesh which the Puritans desired yet feared to touch. The possibilities of bringing Morton to literary life, under such a burden of psycho-historical import, are virtually nil. In Charles Adams's edition of the *New English Canaan*, Williams had read just enough evidence of Morton's love of profit, survival, and witticism to know he should not allot Morton more than five pages.[21]

Scholarly study of the romance versus novel approach to antebellum American fiction has virtually disappeared, in part because its implications for literary genre have been exhausted, in part because it promises a small yield for more recent interests in gender, ethnicity, and cultural studies. For literary characterizations of Morton and Merry Mount, however, a regard for romance remains indispensable. Hawthorne referred to "The May-pole of Merry Mount" as the foundation for a "philosophic romance" as well as "a sort of allegory"; Motley subtitled *Merry Mount* "A Romance of the Massachusetts Colony"; Scott's historical romances were as much a model for Sedgwick's *Hope Leslie* as Scott's romantic poems were for Longfellow. One convention of historical romance was to prove especially suited to recreating the historical significance of Merry Mount's demise. The pairing of opposites, so habitual in the fictions of Scott and Cooper, freed New England writers of romance to escape the straightjacket imposed by gener- ations of New England historians who, devising small variations upon their predecessors, had continued to publish one-sided redactions of Bradford's and Winthrop's histories. What is most remarkable about the post-1820 romantic literature of Merry Mount is the near total absence from it of characterizations and references to William Bradford and John Winthrop. Winthrop's and Bradford's histories had been read carefully, of course, and events described in them were then fictionalized, but in the visualizing of Morton's life and community, Bradford and Winthrop were moved off stage and replaced by either Sir Christopher Gardiner or John Endicott. Although Sir Christopher Gardiner – knight, Catholic, royalist, and bigamist – was at the farthest imaginable end of the Anglo-American character spectrum from John Endicott – "the Puritan of Puritans" – the two paired figures would share important thematic and literary functions. They represent unacknowledged, repugnant qualities that the New England tradition has tried, not entirely successfully, to exclude. The characterizing of Gardiner and Endicott would grow on their creators until the paired opposite dom- inates the reader's attention, threatening to reduce the historical Thomas Morton, but not the symbolic import of Merry Mount, to near irrelevancy.

Although scholarly study of *Hope Leslie* has focused on the interra- cial complexities of Magawisca's suffering, on the two heroines, and on Sedgwick's revisionist account of the Pequot War, the novel's narrative has received very little attention.[22] Twenty of *Hope Leslie*'s twenty-seven chap- ters take place in 1644–1645, beginning with Sir Philip Gardiner's return to New England to rejoin "my old friend and patron Thomas Morton" at Merry Mount.[23] Sedgwick can disregard all charges pertaining to Merry Mount's paganism, because the immorality of Morton's behavior is not, for her, at issue. Sedgwick perceives that, Bradford's account notwithstanding, Morton's historical importance was due to his having been "the old polit- ical enemy of the colony" (338) – an associate of Gorges and therefore by extension an agent of Laud.

As Sedgwick characterizes Sir Philip Gardiner, he and not Thomas Morton is the opposite of everything the admirable American Puritan is expected to be. Entering Boston as the mysterious stranger, the Byronic Gardiner proves to be, not only a knight, Catholic, royalist, urbanite, lecher, and bigamist, but also a remarkably skillful dissembler. By his smooth tongue, sham piety, and sham adherence to British liberties he has quickly earned the trust of the remarkably naïve fathers of the Plymouth Church. His engagingly villainous qualities are, however, cloaked within Puritan garb so that he will not appear to be "a man of the world" (124). Gardiner represents, in sum, the infective power of all worldly old world values that would challenge a New England protestant commonwealth still in the process of formation.[24]

Only three New Englanders have the capability to penetrate Gardiner's dissembling, and none of them is a Puritan patriarch. The two contrasting heroines, Magawisca and Hope Leslie, have so strong an intuitive sense of Gardiner's untrustworthiness that, by novel's end, the reader must infer that woman's power to discriminate true virtue – and not male authority – has been New England's saving grace. After Gardiner's plan to abduct Hope Leslie is first exposed, then literally blown up in a boat explosion, Sedgwick observes of her conspicuously male devil: "All the bodies of the sufferers were finally recovered, except that of Sir Philip Gardiner; and the inference of our pious forefathers, that Satan had seized upon that as his lawful spoil, may not be deemed, by their skeptical descendants, very unnatural" (348). Gardiner can be killed, but the composite evil he represents seems to have remained in New England, never to be fully expunged, nor perhaps did Sedgwick wish it to be.

The third person instrumental in Gardiner's undoing is, ironically, Thomas Morton himself. At the height of his influence in Boston, Gardiner determines to visit Morton, now a reputed maniac, in his jail cell. Without uttering a word, Morton pulls Gardiner inside the prison cell, snatches the key, locks the door on the inside, and then throws the key through the window bars. On a symbolic level, the "maniac" Morton then acts out the reader's desire by pinning Gardiner to the floor and "stuffing his cloak into his mouth" (259). At some level, the wordless and crazed Morton seems to sense that Gardiner's mouth, not Morton's merrymaking, is the true threat to a better New England. Sedgwick closes the scene by observing "perhaps no culprit ever turned his back on a jail with a more thorough conviction that he deserved there to be incarcerated, than did Sir Philip" (261).

John Lothrop Motley began *Merry Mount* (1849) with a prefatory note insisting that only one work of fiction had yet been written about his subject (Hawthorne's "The May-Pole of Merry Mount") and that he, Motley, had not read it. The claim is somewhat disingenuous. Although Morton's willfully historical narrative is quite different from Hawthorne's fanciful allegory, Motley seems to have forgotten that, as George Bancroft's student at Round Hill School in 1829, he had read Sedgwick's novel and had written, with evident excitement: "I think 'Hope Leslie' is a great deal better than 'The Prairie.' It is the best new novel that I have read for two or three years, excepting Scott's."[25] Motley's disclaimer is especially suspect when we consider that, in his recreation of Massachusetts from Morton's May Day celebration through his first trial before Winthrop (1628–1630), Motley allots as many pages to Gardiner as to Morton, and characterizes Sir Christopher Gardiner in a manner that is virtually identical to Sedgwick. Like Sedgwick's Hope Leslie, Motley's fair heroine Esther Ludlow resists the seductive appeal of the Byronic Gardiner, thereby thwarting the subversive old world forces that Gardiner represents and making possible the marriage of the loving Puritan maiden and her all-capable suitor, a marriage that represents a more tolerant and hopeful future.[26]

Motley's Morton, unlike Sedgwick's, is "eloquent, adroit, bold, good-humored" and fully self-possessed.[27] In order to reenact "the stirring memories of brighter ages" (165), he organizes the May Day revels as a pageant of medieval English culture, replete with morris and milkmaid dances. His greatest joy is badinage, quoting Horace and Ovid, not primarily to provoke the Puritans, but to expose the cultural emptiness of the new world, even if it means embracing illusion. His downfall is his failure to plan and to act. Knowing that Winthrop's agents will soon arrest him, Morton spends his time enjoying the aesthetics of falconry, "totally lost to everything in the world below" (II, 168). Motley's Morton would never expend the effort, or devise the strategy, needed to draw up a *quo warranto* for prosecution at the King's Bench.

The common feature in Sedgwick's and Motley's characterizations of Morton is that, in both novels, Morton becomes increasingly subsidiary to the threat of Sir Christopher Gardiner. Indistinguishable in appearance, manner, and motive from Sedgwick's villain, Motley's Gardiner is determined to "build a colony such as the world has never seen": "a strong proprietary government, a new order of nobility" and "a peasantry working the bountiful soil," with himself as "The Lord Palatine of Massachusetts" (28). Gardiner has, Motley claims, all the depraved qualities necessary to realize his "visions of a new empire in a virgin world" (73). On one occasion, Gardiner even mocks justification by faith as a cliché, then uses it as a tool of seduction. For the early nineteenth-century reader, Christopher Gardiner and not Thomas Morton embodied the bad dream of Puritan settlement. As Gardiner suddenly looms up from nowhere, be it in Salem, Plymouth, Boston, or the forest, wronging women, falsifying language, and subverting nascent democracy, he is granted the power of a nightmare sufficiently attractive that we do not quite want to escape from it. He represents the might-have-been of New England aristocracy, aesthetics, elegance, and seductive power.

On the one hand, the historical romancers wish to dismiss Gardiner. Motley concludes, for example, that Gardiner's endless masking, his ability to reappear anywhere while residing nowhere, ultimately made him "but an unreal shadow, a phantom, appearing, vanishing and reappearing in different places and seasons without a definite purpose, and almost without a real existence" (ii, 91). On the other hand, Gardiner's lingering shadow presence is clearly the sign of his appeal. Because overweening lust finally undid his aristocratic and Catholic machinations, Gardiner could readily seem, especially to protestant women readers of historical romance, attractively satanic. Because Satan had appeared in an old world embodiment that had been officially cast out of New England, all that might have been lost could be extensively reimagined.

Longfellow's "The Rhyme of Sir Christopher" (1873) draws upon this hidden appeal by, once again, doubling Gardiner with his associate Thomas Morton. Gardiner endures a disfiguring public humiliation before the General Court, not primarily for the adulteries at the center of the poem's narrative, but for "evil deeds in church and state" with which the reader is presumed to be familiar (257). "Deformed, . . . disheveled and unshorn," Gardiner wishes he could resume a more innocent way of spending "idle hours":

> With roystering Morton of Merry Mount,
> That petitifogger from Furnival's Inn,
> Lord of misrule and riot and sin,
> Who looked on the wine when it was red. (254)

Known for serving fine wine as the host of Craigie House, Longfellow grants Morton's way of life a freshness of sensual response that belies Bradford's now clichéd branding of Morton as "Lord of misrule and riot and sin." Because the clarity of Morton's red wine seems to partake of New England's time of origin, Longfellow ends his poem by ascribing complementary identities to the two reprobates. The last two lines of the poem castigate Gardiner as "The first who furnished this barren land / With apples of Sodom and ropes of sand" (258). Whereas Gardiner's words proved to be but ropes of sand, apples cindered by God's avenging justice, Morton's roistering appeals to an innocence lost. His love of the wine when it was red, even though it had no Eucharistic associations, was as pure as it was harmless. The pairing of the confederates thus allows the reader to enjoy what he or she condemns.

Motley's *Merry Mount* has fictional failings that need no belaboring. Immediately after its publication, however, Motley's years of research into Morton's life and times led him to write "The Polity of the Puritans," a review essay that remains a major nineteenth-century statement about the goals and cost of New England's first settlement, as well as a searching criticism of George Bancroft. Comprehensive, forceful, and concise, it is the transitional essay that turned Motley from a failed novelist into a prominent historian.

Motley begins with a forcing question about the nation's mid-century expansionism. Who or what is responsible for the emergence of America into a "great empire, so much superior in extent and importance to any ever acquired and governed by the Demos before, without limit or hindrance from any other political power?"[28] On the evidence of present-day success, the likely candidates would seem to be the ancestors of slaveholding southern planters, or of Massachusetts mill owners (Cotton Whigs), or of treasure seekers (Virginia's foolish 1609 gold seekers now reborn in California):

This vast democracy was rather the work, the unconscious work, of a different set of adventurers. From 1620 to 1630, the region of ice and granite, now called New England, was taken into the grasp of those men of ice and granite called the Puritans. That grasp never slackened nor flinched, although it clutched no gold. A single idea led those rigid colonists hither. Supported by that single idea, they maintained their position in spite of obstacles enough to freeze the souls of common men, – in spite of starvation, consumption, pestilence, scurvy, arctic winters, tropical summers, tomahawks, wolves, and wild-cats – all the dangers of the wilderness, all the loss of civilization and its advantages; and the result, the unintentional result, as we believe, has been the establishment of the great American democracy. The idea of a pure church, which was the single idea of New England colonization, has after two centuries produced a pure democracy. (472)

To this point, Motley has affirmed Bancroft's widely accepted argument tracing the power of American democracy back to Puritanism, adding to it a determinism of climate that would become common in the next half-century.

Motley's challenge to the claim upon the Puritan origins of national virtue proves to be already implied, however, in his triple repetition of the word "single." He is willing to grant that "the seeds of political liberty were unconsciously contained and concealed in the great principle of resistance to, or rather of flight from, religious oppression, which was the

mainspring of the [Puritan] movement" (477). But Motley will not allow
the current, handy confusions of purpose with result, and of liberty with
democracy, to continue. Although Massachusetts's defense of its "Liberty"
in the 1770s may be derivable from its Puritan origins, the punishments
meted out to Samuel Maverick and Richard Brown, Roger Williams and
Anne Hutchinson, the Gortonists and the Quakers prove that, at the moment of origin, "it was not liberty of conscience which the Puritans came
to establish, but the kingdom of the saints" (486).

Because the "single idea" of New England's colonization was to establish the "kingdom" of the saved minority, Motley's contemporaries must
disabuse themselves of Bancroft's comforting notion that the power of today's Demos arrived with Winthrop on the *Arbella*. Motley interrogates the
supposedly democratic Mayflower Compact, discovering within its stated
loyalty to King James no challenge to indenture and no notion of equality
of individual right or popular rule. He applies clear logic to the General
Court's determination in May 1632 that all Saints must be Freemen, contending "thus the aristocracy became a theocracy, and the colony was less
democratic than ever" (484). Although the political power thus indirectly
granted to the Saints may well have established a commonwealth of piety
and virtue, "there was no democracy, but on the contrary, great danger
to the sacred principle of liberty, in such a polity" (585). Quoting John
Cotton's insistence that "God never intended the democracy as a proper
government for church or commonwealth" (483), Motley argues for the
importance of clear thinking about the nation's origins. Until and unless
Americans can realize that there is an immense difference between claiming
Democracy and Liberty to have been the aims, rather than the results, of
the Puritan settlement, the Demos is likely to remain as muddle-headed
and overconfident about its future, as it has proven to be about its past.

Motley makes no attempt to uncover the origin of these confusions, but
he knows the identity of their most celebrated proponent:

> Present history belongs to the Bancroft school, and it is not therefore surprising
> that the colonization of New England is treated as a democratic movement . . . To
> say that the forefathers of New England came here to establish a democracy seems
> to us as erroneous as it would be to say that the fugitives from the great Gothic
> invasion, who took refuge, like beavers, in the lagunes of the Adriatic, meant to
> establish a commercial aristocracy. (477)

Motley chose to overlook the fact that Bancroft had been sharply critical
of Puritan intolerance, and that Bancroft had periodically expressed his
own reservations about regarding Puritans as America's ur-democrats or

ur-libertarians. But Motley was right to perceive that Bancroft had wanted to ascribe to Puritan settlement those presentist virtues which, as an historian, he could not always validate in the historical evidence. Surely aware of Bancroft's self-contradiction on this point, Motley nonetheless cites only Bancroft's logically fuzzy claims that the broad-based rule of the Saints established the principle of democracy – and then sharply criticizes Bancroft for his simplistic thinking!

In the main, Motley understood, even revered, Bancroft's accomplishment: "The secret of Bancroft's success is, that by aid of a vigorous imagination, and a crisp, nervous style, he has been enabled, by a few sudden strokes, to reveal startling and brilliant pictures, over which the dust had collected and hardened, as it seemed, forever" (473). The proximity of tribute to criticism is the sign of a younger revisionist emerging from an admired mentor's influence, but it also shows Motley's real concern for the integrity and importance of Bancroft's subject. Motley's angry but defensive response to the distortion of the filiopietists should be seen as a prototype for the position assumed by Charles Francis Adams Jr. "To praise the mildness of a system under which men were sold as slaves for immoralities, mutilated for censuring the magistrates, and put to death for professing a different religious belief from Calvinism," Motley observes, "is not, we think, the best way to serve the cause of the Puritans" (476).

Ultimately, Motley remains understandably unsure of exactly how the Puritans should be perceived. When "weighed in the scales of justice," the Puritans deserve the following summary judgment:

Their virtues were many, and among the noblest which can adorn humanity; indomitable courage, patience, fortitude, self-denial, generosity, extreme purity of morals, piety, energy and singleness of purpose almost superhuman – all these elements of the heroic, and even the saintly, they possessed in an eminent degree, and no man can gainsay it. Their virtues were many and colossal; their vices were few but formidable, for they were intolerance, cruelty, tyranny and bigotry. (476)

Does the concluding listing of four vices subvert the nine virtues or only qualify them? Is the phrase "extreme purity of morals" a compliment or an implied criticism? Does a "colossal virtue" compensate for a "formidable vice"? Motley does not say. These are still questions asked of the Puritan heritage, and Motley was, to his credit, no more capable of easily resolving them than are we.

And what part did Thomas Morton and Merry Mount play in Motley's searching critique? Reminding the reader of Nathaniel Ward's straightforward defense of religious intolerance, Motley offers up Thomas Morton as the culminating example of the "fact" that "religious toleration, so far from being considered a virtue at that day, was rather accounted a crime" (487). In the context of "The Polity of the Puritans," the rantipole illusionist of Motley's novel *Merry Mount* is transformed into the representative victim of Puritan "intolerance, cruelty, tyranny and bigotry" (487).

If the Plymouth people were incensed beyond endurance at Morton's pranks, and, squatters as they were themselves, could not refrain from inflicting lynch law upon a man whose only offence was dancing round a Maypole upon his own ground, how much more unlikely were the dignified and wealthy magistrates of Massachusetts, strong in their charter and their patent, to permit the least deviation from the true path on the part of any indweller of their territory. To tolerate heresy in religion was in their eyes a heinous offence. (487)

If even the harmless Morton was not to be endured, what chance would a forthright advocate for separation of church and state, a man like Roger Williams, ever have had?

The limit of Motley's challenge to New England filiopietism surfaces clearly in his essay's conclusion. Motley is proud to remind readers that Massachusetts has remained "one of the main portals of a great Republic," and that, in the westward emigration of its citizenry, "New England has reached the Pacific" (491). The metaphor of the "portal" of the Republic ultimately serves the interests of regional primacy and sectional nationalism. "New England is not America, to be sure," Motley concedes, "but she has been so long the great portal through which the tide of population and civilization has flowed" that New England's democratic influence has necessarily proven dominant (497). More important, New England's recent leadership in reform movements shows that Yankee pragmatism and Puritan piety have never been separable.

Motley's view of New England present eventually blunts his criticisms of New England past. From the perspective of 1849, a scant year before the Compromise of 1850, pragmatism seems to have been at least as important as piety, and the survival of the impulse toward virtue in government at least as important as the compromises it had, to date, entailed. Near his essay's end, Motley arrives at what should have been a new rationale:

With all the faults of the system devised by the Puritans, it was a practical system. With all their foibles, with all their tyrannical and arbitrary notions, the Pilgrims were lovers of liberty as well as sticklers for authority. The seeds of liberty contained in Puritanism expanded in the soil of England till they overthrew a throne which had stood six centuries. The same seeds in New England ripened after two centuries to an absolute democracy. (490)

Nowhere in Bancroft's *History* would Motley's passage seem out of place; its last sentence is arguably a more absolute and regionalist variant of Bancroft's thesis about American democracy than Bancroft himself ever penned. The reluctance of educated mid-nineteenth-century Americans to truly disbelieve Bancroft's progressivism could hardly be better illustrated.

Contrasting Thomas Morton to Sir Christopher Gardiner had made Mine Host of Merry Mount seem an engaging bon vivant, free of evil intent. Juxtaposing Morton to John Endicott had far different implications. Gardiner's shadowy unreality had been traceable to aristocratic and Catholic qualities ruled out of Protestant New England; John Endicott's blunt durability enabled him to serve as the most solid embodiment of New England Puritan reality. Not Bradford or Winthrop, whose marmoreal virtues had long since been constricted by the filiopietists, but John Endicott, who had conveniently written almost nothing, but whose settling of Salem had preceded the founding of Boston. Unlike John Winthrop, a lawyer/governor renowned for caution and wisdom, John Endicott offered the promising figure of the bluff Puritan soldier, the commoner who spoke and acted with terrifying honesty, thereby revealing the Puritan character at its least self-conscious but deepest level. Although Endicott's impulsive brutalities made Morton's pleasure-seeking seem almost regenerative, Endicott's uplifted sword also made Morton's badinage and his maypole seem weak, evanescent, impotent.

At stake here was the reconstructed meaning of the act of separation. Bradford and Winthrop had defined Merry Mount as the godless community separate from Puritan New England, but Endicott's outspoken claims for self-government, together with his forthright anti-Anglo-Catholicism, had positioned him as the Separatist among avowed non-Separatists. After the American Revolution, Endicott had to be seen, on one level, as the Puritan precursor for the declaring of independence. In this regard, his impulsive violence and self-reliant courage posed a troubling inconsistency, both about Puritanism and about the Revolution. But Endicott's leveling of the maypole would also serve as the occasion for making him over into the *ne plus ultra* of New England's anti-libertarian orthodoxy, "the Puritan of Puritans." This last phrase, however, carried its own ambivalence. Was John Endicott truly the essence of American Puritanism or was he, rather, like Anne Hutchinson but in a very different way, more Puritan than the Puritans themselves?

Hawthorne's preoccupation with Endicott as the truly representative Puritan led him to introduce Endicott into no less than six of his tales and sketches. Morton, however, receded into insignificance. Although Merry

Mount as a community was obviously of importance to Hawthorne's symbolizing of New England history, Morton himself is described only in "Main Street" where he is rather airily dismissed as the cliché of the gaily ineffectual Cavalier.[29] Surprisingly, there is no reference to Thomas Morton either in "The May-Pole of Merry Mount" (1836) or in "Endicott and the Red Cross" (1838). Readers of "Endicott and the Red Cross" are never told that Endicott's verbal and visual claim for New England's separation from Old England derives, in historical fact, from Thomas Morton's activities in support of charter revocation. These omissions do not mean that Hawthorne had little interest in the worth or fate of Morton's allegiances as they had affected New England history. Morton's absence rather suggests Hawthorne's desire to separate the controversial but often stereotyped qualities of the historical man from the issues his presence had raised.

No reader of "The May-Pole of Merry Mount" can forget the dramatic entrance of John Endicott "from the black surrounding woods" after some twenty paragraphs of Hawthorne's metaphorically complex but utterly static descriptions: "So stern was the energy of his aspect, that the whole man, visage, frame and soul, seemed wrought of iron, gifted with life and thought, yet all of one substance with his head-piece and breastplate. It was the Puritan of Puritans; it was Endicott himself."[30] Here is the energy and strength of the New England future deeply tainted by an impervious bigotry and intolerance. After Endicott has forthrightly "assaulted" the "flower-decked abomination" of the maypole, Hawthorne arranges for him to command a sequence of sadistic brutalities for which there is no historical evidence. Nor is there any evidence for the equally unforgettable softening of John Endicott's heart as he places the garland of the Lord and the Lady of the May around Edith and Edgar's heads, thereby uniting the pagan marital ceremony of their Merry Mount past with the Christian marital ceremony of their Salem future. There is a mingling by literary addition here, a mingling which will not allow single judgments of any kind, and which was in 1836 quite new to the historiography of Merry Mount. After an opening paragraph luring his reader into the simplistic belief that "jollity and gloom were contending for an empire," Hawthorne convinces us that there can be no satisfactory choice between "grisly saints" and "gay sinners," even if "the future complexion of New England was involved in this important quarrel" (54, 62).

As the tale develops, happiness is increasingly dissociated from mirth, while love is associated with "earth's doom of care and sorrow" (58). The ending of the narrative, in which Edith and Edgar are ushered from Merry

Mount as if it were a false paradise lost through the cruel judgment of an all too human God, invites us to imagine for New England's Adam and Eve a better but more sorrowful future. If Hawthorne's intent in penning "a sort of allegory" (54) was to devise one of his Allegories of the Heart, his ending plausibly renders the growth of human love through the experience of grief. But if an historical allegory is also intended, as it seems to be, Hawthorne's ending is curiously unresolved. The Salem of John Endicott, to which Edith and Edgar return, is not a community in which their newly gained sensitivity is likely to flourish, and Merry Mount itself, Hawthorne reminds us, has ceased to be. Edith and Edgar might therefore embody a *via media* for the human heart, but not for "the future complexion of New England."

"Endicott and the Red Cross" builds to a similarly irresolvable paradox by introducing Endicott as a sadistic autocrat, and then persuading the reader to admire him, while keeping Thomas Morton unmentioned and off stage. In John Endicott's breastplate we first see reflected all the warped agencies and tangible evidence of Puritan intolerance, cruel abridgments of human liberty that Hawthorne makes no attempt to justify because of the exigencies of the frontier. Endicott remains a harshly repellent figure until Roger Williams delivers Winthrop's letter warning Endicott of Gorges's imminent arrival as governor-general (information based upon Thomas Morton's 1634 letter to Jeffrey). At this juncture, Hawthorne's temporal perspective shifts: Endicott the sadistic intolerant of the Puritan era acquires the mantle of the ur-Revolutionary patriot. Because Endicott is, as early as 1634, made to advocate home rule of "our own soil" and even to conclude his speech with the fervent rhetorical question "What have we to do with England?," it is clear that Hawthorne regards the anti-Catholic sacrilege of excising the cross from the flag as but a secondary consideration. We are rather witnessing, as Hawthorne's last words tell us, "the first omen of that deliverance which our fathers consummated, after the bones of the stern Puritan had lain more than a century in the dust."[31] The declaring of independence in 1634, and presumably in 1776, is explicitly identified as a moment of "deliverance" and certainly not as the beginning of a polity based upon individual "liberty." Nonetheless, Endicott's deed of courage and strength prompts the narrator to exclaim, without any sign of irony, "for ever honored be the name of Endicott" (441). Endicott thus rises to honored status through the quelling of Gorges's charter threat and the complete submergence of Thomas Morton's part in it. But Hawthorne simultaneously forces the recognition that John Endicott's fierce assertion of independence derives from the narrow exclusions of his religion. From John Endicott's inner rage, and not from John Winthrop's stately piety, has the strength of New England/America's origins been formed.

"Endicott and the Red Cross," the first play in Robert Lowell's trilogy entitled The *Old Glory* (1964), combines Morton's May Day celebration of 1627, Endicott's expedition to cut down the maypole in 1629, Winthrop's burning of Merry Mount in 1630, Gorges's scheme to take over New England, and Endicott's cutting the red cross from the British flag, all into the events of one day at Merry Mount in the 1630s. Hawthorne's Edith, Edgar, and Peter Palfrey reappear, and phrases from the Puritan historiographical record are worked unobtrusively into the dialogue. Lowell's play shows a scrupulous regard, not for historical dates but for the words of the written tradition which Hawthorne and the historians had created. Morton and Endicott now confront one another directly, speaking familiar words of the literary tradition that acquire altered meanings because of changes in character and circumstance. Lowell is here employing the technique he would call "Imitation," a way of recasting notable literature that is immediately derivative from Eliot's "Tradition and the Individual Talent" and ultimately derivative from Renaissance poetic practice.

Lowell is not concerned to demonstrate that the demise of Merry Mount represents historical progress or decline, nor to create exemplars of persecuted sensualists and worthy founders. Freedom of will and action, which his literary and historical predecessors had sought to preserve for both parties, no longer exists. Whatever Puritans or Merry Mounters may profess, they are compelled by circumstance toward pragmatic decisions which work destruction for others as well as themselves. Among the many accounts of Merry Mount, Lowell's alone assumes as an axiom that history is an incomprehensible muddle, impelling leaders of all kinds to snatch at simplistic absolutes and then to act on them to everyone's detriment. Such is the murderous sham, not only of old glory but of the flags that all nations raise in order to excite patriotic enthusiasm.[32]

Lowell has freed Thomas Morton from judgmental identities as a devil, Cavalier, blithe pagan, or aficionado of the senses. The gaily dressed gentleman of Hawthorne and Motley appear on stage "overweight," "complacent," and "oily," dressed in a "shabby coffee-colored suit, part cloth and part deerskin," that suggests frontier negligence, not British social class.[33] Morton feels no yearning for "noblemen, cathedrals, or plays" because he has established Merry Mount for three new world purposes: "love" of the "rough land," "money," and a "renewal" which his appearance constantly belies (11). Beneath the stereotypical literary guises in which Morton had been dressed, Lowell detects a cynical self-interest that is as vulgar as it is instinctive. For Lowell, Thomas Morton should be regarded as the universal *l'homme moyen sensuel* especially prevalent in materialistic America and during times of new settlement. Morton's Massachusetts is "a waste of animals, Indians and the nine-month winter" (25) that in no way recalls the New English Canaan. Although his small community is constantly threatened by clever royal agents and Puritan killers, Morton shows no regard for potential Indian allies beyond the minimal protection he might obtain from them. As the play develops, Morton's love of land is replaced by disgust for Puritans, politicians, and Indians; whatever love he might once have felt, whatever money he might have made, both disappear in the chaos of contending forces around him.

The grimness of Morton's situation accounts for the transformation of his character. His powers of ridicule and irony are exercised not for the joy of language but for the need of self-protection. The falconer who had quoted Ovid, the sensualist who had sought the natural life, now reduces the options and meanings of his world to joyless practicalities expressed in flat diction and curt phrases. Of his society at Mount Wollaston, Morton says, "it's very lonely here" (17); of his trade, "We have to give them liquor and guns to get their furs" (24); of kings and churches, "Our supply of both is endless" (21); of his life in the new world, "I have a plantation. I have to make it pay, I have to live" (17). Because his hope for survival in the new world demands his playing off Indians, Puritans, Anglicans, and the home government against each other, he habitually dehumanizes his world by metaphor. He calls his Merry Mount followers "animals," the Indians "beasts," the Puritans "May flies," and plans to divert Laud's soldiers with red concubines because "you've got to throw these dogs a little flesh / if you want them to fight the Puritans" (16). Morton then justifies his duplicity by observing, quite correctly, "The world is changeable. It's like a playing card" (16). Because, however, Morton holds only losing cards, his cynicisms can end only in displays of futility. When he returns on stage to witness the razing of Merry Mount at play's end, we see him, for the first time in the written tradition, as a human being stripped of all defenses, "partly drunk, but more in a state of despairing recklessness" (55).

Like the Pilgrims in "Children of Light," the Puritans of Lowell's "Endicott and the Red Cross" are collectively judged to be benighted and violent. But Morton's thoroughly venal character suggests that, in spite of Lowell's rage at the sins of the forefathers, he will not allow "the Puritan" to remain the scapegoat for all national ills, as "the Puritan" surely had been in the 1920s. The most perceptive, complex character in the play is the destroyer of Merry Mount, John Endicott. No longer Hawthorne's "Puritan of Puritans" (64), sure of his rectitude and proud of his severity, Endicott is the only figure in Lowell's play to recognize that "Each city is a Jerusalem" (45), "Nothing is clear" (44), "No one is too clean or free" (60). After shooting all of Morton's Indians and burning Merry Mount to the ground, Endicott pointedly subverts his own triumph by proclaiming "a day of mourning" both for himself and "for the other Indians, all those who are fighting / with unequalled ferocity, and probably hopeless courage / because they prefer annihilation to the despair of our conquest" (77). By insisting that every flag arouses simplistic violence, Endicott introduces the motif that will bind all three of Lowell's plays into an indictment of an American mentality that had persisted from the 1620s through the Cold War. At the same time, however, Endicott's nihilistic impulses, born of despair over universal relativism, cast a shade of inscrutability over all things, including the very motive for reenvisioning Merry Mount. No longer can we assume that the author strives for a clear resolution of values, whatever those values might be.

Endicott knows that his "Puritan" absolutism is a momentary compensation for growing inner emptiness. His inner void derives partly from his worrying of ultimate questions, but also partly from the humanizing grief of destroyed and worn-out allegiances. Endicott tells Palfrey: "When my wife died, I served in the army, / Somehow I found I couldn't stomach killing / without an iron faith. I found that iron faith" (42). At one moment, Endicott even sees himself as Christ militant crucified for his old world loyalties. Pointing to the red cross flag flying above Morton's doorway, he remarks: "You see our flag, the Red Cross; it still flies high; my arms are nailed to this cross" (71). When Palfrey expresses anxiety that the glory of the New Israel might fall to the combined influence of King Charles, Merry Mounters, and savages, Endicott grimly admits that he can sustain no trust in Christianity, the King or the future of Massachusetts Bay: "I have little faith. The faith of the armies. / I am only alive when I am fighting for my life. / I detest this, but it is so" (49).

Endicott's doubts lead him into ever-swifter brutalities, followed by deepening depression. He enters acknowledging, "I am the hollowness inside my armor" (41). He believes that his true historical identity has been revealed to him in a recurrent nightmare in which he is a "Jesuit general . . . reading black sentences on the black page of a ribboned book," forever condemning a world of nameless men to death with the approval of his self-made God (45–47). Before cutting the red cross from the flag, Endicott declares, as in Hawthorne's tale, "What have we to do with England?," but the lengthy speech that follows, one which Hawthorne had rendered as a glorious premonition of national independence, is to Lowell's Endicott merely instrumental rhetoric, "a hollow dishonest harangue, / half truth, half bombast" (50). The play's last stage direction shows John Endicott kicking the mutilated red cross flag off Morton's steps while Merry Mount burns to ashes in the background. Endicott's final words, "it's a childish thing," the words which end the play, clearly refer both to the flag and to his own gesture of kicking it.

The intent of Lowell's characterization of Endicott is elusive, but the analogies which suggest themselves all speak of a postmodernist mentality of the darkest kind. When asked why he had "changed Endicott from Hawthorne's ironclad Puritan – a man who tramples on the English flag – into a far more ambiguous character," Lowell replied: "it was an instinct to make him a sort of crumbling figure, like Hamlet, though rather brusque and attractive when he's being a brutal ruler."[34] Insofar as Endicott's outlook is answerless, nihilistic, and drawn to historical irony as well as to Old England, he resembles Robert Lowell – to say nothing of Hamlet. To many a member of the 1965 audience at the American Place Theatre, the seeming assurance and brutal outcome of Endicott's military decisions must have been seen as a topical allusion to Robert McNamara or Lyndon Johnson. Those who find comfort in ideological labels, then or now, could plausibly perceive Endicott as an existentialist turned fascist. There is, as Lowell himself said, something disturbingly "attractive" in the brutality arising from Endicott's despair.

Lowell has turned Thomas Morton from anachronistic Cavalier into the prototype of American materialism and sensual indulgence, then shown Morton to be no match for the repulsive but acute power of John Endicott's judgments, ideological and political. While Morton shrivels into insignificance, the presumably timeless nihilism symbolized in Endicott becomes the true destroyer of the joys Merry Mount was supposed to represent, but probably never did. To Robert Lowell, William Bradford and John Winthrop are, therefore, quite literally nowhere.

It seems hard to believe that, after Lowell's play, there can be another truly new and plausible "imitation" of the Merry Mount materials. As its title indicates, Peter Ackroyd's *Milton in America* (1996) turns an historical novel into willful fantasy, but then fills its fictive world with names, events, and especially phrases from the written record. Fleeing the Restoration late in 1660, John Milton founds the community of New Milton near

Tiverton, Rhode Island. New Milton is his New England "mansion house of liberty," a four-street "commonwealth" made up of meetinghouse, prison, and farm fields, in which only Freemen have the vote, a just price is fixed for all goods, and neither witches nor adulterers shall, in law, be suffered to live. These historical accuracies notwithstanding, Ackroyd's John Milton is also, however, a neo-Cromwellian, idol-smashing megalomaniac, who announces, consecutively, "I leave England in order to save England," "I leave England in order to be England," and "I shall be Milton among the Americans."[35]

Milton's antagonist, in a startling anachronism, proves to be Thomas Morton, renamed Ralph Kempis, a red-bearded, blue-coated, white-hatted refugee from Jamestown who establishes the colony of "Mary Mount" across the river from New Milton, sets up both a maypole and a statue of the Virgin Mary, and proceeds to live with Wampanoag women. Whereas the Puritans of New Milton are given such names as Preserved Cotton, Hallelujah Deakin, and Sanctified Coffin, Ralph Kempis sings Morton's maypole song ("Drink and be merry, merry, merry boys / Let all your Delight be in the Hymen's joys," p. 194), then prays to the Virgin Mary, and ultimately defends religious tolerance, without there being, apparently, any contradiction among the three.

At novel's end, John Milton outdoes even John Endicott in rousing New England to battle, arguing that Mary Mount combines three satanic forces into one. "The Indian savages may soon be converted by the Papists into a warlike and subtle nation, and become like so many Irishmen loosed upon us." "God's people will clean out that hole of Satan in our midst," Milton exclaims: "the chosen race will be saved!" (268). The cannon of New Milton, reinforced by the trainbands of the United Colonies of New England, eventually lay waste to Mary Mount and Kempis/Morton is stabbed to death. John Milton is last seen wandering blind in the forest, crazy with guilty lust for a deer-skinned maiden with "bare breasts. Lustrous and sweet" (304). Readers who believe there were any admirable qualities in Puritanism, in the wilderness, or in John Milton had best be wary! In Ackroyd's novel, the fearful emptiness of the New England forest has so aggravated Puritan religious intolerance that a writer of great power has been reduced into a hateful bigot. As John Milton's page discovers about his former master, "He has turned himself into a devil" (297).

At this moment of writing, Ackroyd's *Milton in America* would seem to be the finale of the Merry Mount *opera buffa*, a coda written in a dark minor key. But it would be foolish to assume that the Merry Mount of literature has, like the Merry Mount of Wollaston, been razed forever. The matter of Merry Mount has proven to be the most durable Rorschach test of New England identity. Despite all mishaps, Thomas Morton correctly prophesied his own kind of immortality. The historical memory of Merry Mount is sure to be reborn in yet another guise, just as the phoenix forever arises from its own ashes.

CHAPTER 3

Trying Anne

The first word of this chapter title is intended to be both an adjective and a verb. Without the protection of any codified judicial procedures, Anne Hutchinson was twice tried, first banished and later excommunicated, at the end of lengthy "examinations" conducted first by civil magistrates and then by the clergy, both functioning as de facto courts. No one has denied that the so-called "Antinomian Controversy" nearly wrecked the Boston church, if not New England's Commonwealth, at the very outset.[1] The crisis divided the ministers, the churches, the deputies and the Freemen among themselves and against each other, and ended in the exile, forced and unforced, of a goodly number of Boston's most wealthy, zealous, and influential church members. Nor has anyone denied that, once John Winthrop regained the governorship, most ministers and deputies supported him in using every legal and newly legal measure at the Commonwealth's disposal – including private conferences, a fast day, a synod, a listing of no less than eighty-two heresies, paper reconciliations, an alien law, disarming, elections, disenfranchisement, banishment, and excommunication (in that order) – in order either to bring the Antinomians to bay or to root them out of the Bay forever.

Even Anne Hutchinson's most committed defender should acknowledge, however, that she had proven to be constantly and implacably trying. "Trying" because she possessed, as John Cotton said when admonishing her, "a sharpe apprehension, a ready utterance, and abilitie to represe yourselfe in the Cause of God."[2] Trying because, unlike John Wheelwright, she would make no accommodations with authority, but would, at both trials, defend herself by the challenging command "prove it," thereby voicing in 1637 the post-Enlightenment notion that an accused criminal is innocent until proven guilty. And, most importantly, Hutchinson proved to be "trying" because her idea of salvation, individual and communal, comprised an unliveably logical development of the Pauline and Reformation emphasis on Justification by Faith. However elusive the various Antinomian or

74

Cottonian positions on Sanctification and Justification may be, they illustrate Kenneth Burke's insight that a heresy is best understood as a logical extension of a previous orthodoxy over the bounds of its present acceptability.

The Merry Mount conflict has proven adaptable to lasting purposes of cultural symbolism because in origin it had all the advantages of visual, often physical confrontation between clearly contrasted individuals and groups. Its issues were of known worldly allegiances and its antagonists so sharply differentiated that it could readily serve as the ur-conflict portending New England's cultural future. Even though many a later writer, beginning with Edward Johnson, would not hesitate to sanctify or villainize Winthrop, to revere or revile Anne Hutchinson, the Antinomian Crisis was never to enjoy, for literary purposes, the same miniaturist clarity. Unlike confrontations over Merry Mount, which involved physical acts set down in a few concise sentences, the Antinomian Crisis remained, until its very end, persistently and exclusively verbal. The conventicles that Anne Hutchinson conducted in her home after John Cotton's sermons provoked spoken accusations, sermons, queries, remembrances, a synod, and what can only be called theological position papers, many of them bafflingly abstract and inconsecutive. Ever-multiplying queries to which clear resolution could not be found. In lasting historical effect, however, the wranglings in the theological murk would have far more consequence than the razing of Merry Mount. The gathering flood of words promoted as well as reflected conflicts that affected every aspect of the Commonwealth's newly evolving culture: the inner spirit and public conduct of a New England Christian, how to determine qualifications for church membership, the need for unanimity among churches called in the Congregational way, adjusting the powers of church versus state, the place of new merchants among an empowered landed class, setting the limits of woman's sphere. Changing the totality of New England life, the reach of the Antinomian Crisis shows that the concerns we now distance and categorize as "theology" were, to all Puritan parties in 1637, the very essence of human life, spiritual and societal.

Any definitive pronouncement upon the Antinomian Controversy had best be advanced with wary humility.[3] David Hall's indispensable compilation of primary sources, *The Antinomian Controversy 1636–1638: A Documentary History* (1968), reveals that crucial gaps of factual information remain: 1. we do not know whether Anne Hutchinson ever denied that Sanctification evidenced in good works was *an* evidence of salvation; 2. we do not know whether she believed that "free" grace meant only that grace was freely given by an unencumbered God, or given "free" of any responsibilities for preparation or visible sainthood; 3. we do not know what John Wilson said in his inflammatory speech on the "very sad" condition of the Boston Church; 4. we do not know what John Wheelwright said about "the seal of the spirit" during the October 1636 meeting of leading ministers in John Cotton's house; 5. we do not know whether, during the crucial private conference of December 1636, Anne Hutchinson explicitly accused the ministry (except John Wheelwright and John Cotton) of preaching a covenant of works. Even the reason(s) for Anne Hutchinson's sentencings cannot be finally determined because, first, John Winthrop refused to specify exactly why she was being banished and, second, John Wilson did not specify exactly which heresy or heresies warranted her excommunication. What civil law had Mrs. Hutchinson broken that made her so criminal as to deserve banishment from the Commonwealth? Which of the eighty-two recently determined heresies justified her excommunication from the Church? On the basis of the extant evidence, no one can ever know.

The primary documents show us an Anne Hutchinson who, strikingly unlike Thomas Morton, is virtually mute. Except for the records of her testimony at the two hearings, no words that are verifiably hers have survived. Consequently, nothing she is alleged to have said or believed before November of 1636 can be substantiated. John Winthrop and John Wilson pronounced final sentences of banishment and excommunication, not for specific, named charges, but for all the confusing, varied, and contradictory evidence brought forth at the hearings. Above all, we need to remember that the very term "Antinomian" is itself an act of historical reconstruction advanced in 1644 by Thomas Weld and John Winthrop for the purposes of discrediting Anne Hutchinson after her death. Neither Anne Hutchinson, John Wheelwright, nor John Cotton, none of whom put any such label on themselves, seems ever to have advocated free grace *against* the Law. Nor is there evidence of their advocating the familist heresy, associated with John Eaton, that "God sees no sin in his elect." For New England "Antinomians" – and here I admittedly hazard my own formulation – the religious issue was more subtle but no less controversial: in a newly founded Christian commonwealth, how important is Christian conduct in gaining spiritual regeneration through "union" with the Holy Spirit?

When making first mention of Anne Hutchinson in his *Journal,* John Winthrop formulated the terms of conflict in so clear and forceful a way that they long seemed determinative, especially to later New England historians impatient with theological dispute but eager to exonerate the forefathers:

One Mrs. Hutchinson, a member of the church of Boston, a woman of a ready wit and bold spirit, brought over with her two dangerous errors: 1. That the person of the Holy Ghost dwells in a justified person. 2. That no sanctification can help to evidence to us our justification – From these two grew many branches.[4]

Although the trope of Hydra-like multiplication is already clearly in Winthrop's mind, his fastening upon these particular seeds of error cannot be proven to be misleading, nor does his wording of the terms of disagreement seem unfair. As early as spring 1636, related controversies had arisen (public criticism of the ministry, a woman conducting a conventicle that included men), but the two "errors" Winthrop emphasized pervade the lengthy doctrinal exchanges then being written down between Thomas Shepard, John Cotton, the elders of the Boston Church, and the ministers of other Bay congregations – exchanges in which John Wheelwright's beliefs are cited, but not Anne Hutchinson's.

Winthrop's phrase "brought over with her" suggests that the two errors were ultimately those of John Cotton, who had been Mrs. Hutchinson's revered minister in old Boston as well as new. What can be gained from a close reading of John Cotton's testimony on these two points? Cotton's most direct replies to these two charged "errors" (in "Sixteene Questions of Serious and Necessary Consequence") are guardedly inconclusive. On both points at dispute, Cotton's thinking takes tentative logical steps toward later forms of protestant protest but then withdraws them.

Consider the crucial two-letter preposition at issue in Winthrop's phrasing of the first "error." If the Holy Ghost dwells "in" a justified person, could not the justified person therefore have a "sealed assurance" that would turn God's gift of inner grace into a continuing, self-defined union with the Deity – a condition of holiness almost as asocial and even more permanent than Emerson's "part or parcel of God"? In response to the elders' phrasing of this problem in their fifth question ("Whether the testimony or Seal of the Spirit be so clear, as to witnesse immediately by it self, without respect of any work of Christ in a Man?"), Cotton wrote: "The Testimony of the Spirit (it self) is so cleare, as that it may witnesse immediately, though not without some worke of Christ in a man, yet without respect unto (that) Worke" (49). The logic of this rejoinder is, to say the least, perplexing. If God's grace can be witnessed in a man "immediately" and "without respect of any work," then why would any accompanying "worke of Christ in a man" still be as necessary, as Cotton claims it to be?

Trying to unravel the wording of Cotton's response, the elders expressed understandable bafflement at his qualifications ("immediately," "not without," and "without") and then stated: "we humbly entreat to see your grounds for it." But in the anxiety of impending crisis, the elders immediately leaped to predicting that Cotton's wording would lead to disrespect for the Christian life, wondering whether, if they were understanding Cotton aright, "such an opinion may be a seed of much hypocrisie and delusion in the Churches, and that it may train up people to a plain forsaking of the Scriptures in deed, while they cleave to them in shew" (65).[5]

The tenth question the elders posed for Cotton ("Whether this Sanctification being discerned by us, be not a true Evidence of Justification?") is worded in almost exactly the same pointed terms as Winthrop's formulation of Mrs. Hutchinson's second error. This time Cotton's response seems clear in syntax and orthodox in meaning: "If this [true Christian] Sanctification be evidently discerned, it is a true evidence of Justification, *a Posteriori*; as Justification is likewise a true Evidence of Sanctification, *a Priori*" (51). However, there are problems even here. Cotton's first phrase allows that doing good works is one kind of after-the-fact evidence of true faith, but his conditional wording also raises a question of the validity of the evidence for Sanctification. His second phrase then uses the word "evidence" in a troubling way, implying that having true faith not only gives promise of doing good works, but is somehow a "true evidence" of it before the fact.

The point here is not to rehearse the familiar charge that, during the Antinomian Controversy, John Cotton acted the part of a dodgy, self-protective casuist who was, in George Bancroft's phrase, "pliant in dialectics."[6] Our main concern should be the larger process in which Cotton was engaged, an elaborate two-year winnowing out of New England's theocratic identity through a controversy that Cotton and John Winthrop were futilely trying to mediate. If there were at first only two Antinomian errors, there were soon sixteen, then eighty-two, then an unsuccessful attempt to reduce to three, and then confusion. Questions, replies, counterreplies, and counterquestions. Brilliance as well as pliancy in dialectics lost in the collective swirl of words, meetings, and hearings. No one engaged in the controversy seems to have considered the possibility that the debated issues were of God's determination and therefore might be irresolvable to the human mind. No one could see that a heresy might be the logical extension of an orthodoxy. From time to time, the controversialists would cite Romans 3, the ultimate scriptural authority on faith versus works in the Christian life, but not even John Cotton seems to have noticed that, twenty verses before insisting "For we hold that a man is justified by faith apart from works of law," Paul had written "For He will render to every man according to his works." Even John Calvin, despite his emphasis on Justification by Faith alone, had admitted both "we confess with Paul that the doers of the Law are justified before God" and that the Saints recognize good works "as signs of the calling by which they realize their election."[7] Like nearly all seventeenth-century contemporaries, the Bay Colony protestants made the energizing assumption that all truth must ultimately be one, and that it was New England's special glory and special burden to find it. The year 1637 was, moreover, one in which New Englanders were especially unwilling to admit to ambivalence.

Common to both sides was the ever unprovable charge of "hypocrisie" in assessing the inner state of supposed regenerates born in sin. From the "Antinomian" perspective, if there are no visible saints, then the ministry's claim to select the probable elect by Sanctification according to the Law might be based upon faulty evidence that cloaks a desire to maintain power. From the "Legalist" perspective, if doing good works is no sign of true faith, then the claim upon free grace may be based on imagined evidence that cloaks selfish conduct weakening the bonds of community. By January 1637, charge and countercharge had led to simplistic falsification of both positions in the public streets. John Winthrop was keenly aware that the labeling and dividing of people into opposed sides aggravated conceptual hostilities he was helpless to prevent: "it began to be as common here to distinguish between men, by being under a covenant of grace or a covenant of works, as in other countries between Protestants and papists."[8] Just as Merry Mount and Plymouth, twenty-five miles apart, somehow could not coexist on a continent, so the elders and Antinomians, both of them followers of Paul, Calvin, and Covenant theology, began to conceive their differences in utterly oppositional terms.

In this overcharged atmosphere, the court conducted its two-day "Examination" of Anne Hutchinson, trying to separate the civil from ecclesiastical charges of a controversy in which the two had clearly become inextricable. The widely read record of the trial, printed by Anne's great-great-grandson, Thomas Hutchinson, is more intensely dramatic than any playscript based upon it could ever be. The sharply intelligent opening exchanges between John Winthrop and Anne Hutchinson, the slow gathering of suspiciously uniform charges by the country ministers, Hutchinson's insistence that the ministers give testimony under oath, the climactic and clearly reluctant testimony of Cotton on the second day, Hutchinson's avowal of her immediate revelations, Dudley's and Endicott's immediate grasping of that easy opportunity, their aggressive questioning of Cotton, William Coddington's courageous protest to Winthrop when all was clearly lost ("you know it is a rule of the court that no man may be a judge and an accuser too," p. 344), and Hutchinson's last forcing question ("I desire to know wherefore I am banished?" p. 348) – who could imagine a scenario of such gathering intensity? Or, perhaps it would be more pertinent to ask: who was able to write down the essence of two days of testimony in so terse and shapely a form?

If one wishes to place gender issues at the center of the Antinomian Crisis, one need only ignore John Wheelwright and fasten upon selective details of Anne Hutchinson's civil trial. Governor Winthrop charged Anne Hutchinson with conducting a conventicle in a manner "not tolerable nor comely in the sight of God nor fitting for your sex" (312). A few minutes later, clearly angered by Hutchinson's insistence that those she taught were "children of God" who "do honour the Lord," Winthrop snapped back: "We do not mean to discourse with those of your sex" (314). The court was concerned to discover whether Anne Hutchinson taught men as well as women at her conventicles. When Winthrop sentenced Hutchinson, he banished her as "a woman not fit for our society" (348). These details, considered collectively, abundantly demonstrate that women were thought to be intellectually inferior and therefore expected to acquiesce, but they are too scattered and too few to substantiate the charge that the trial was *about* patriarchy's need to suppress nascent feminism. Anne Hutchinson defended herself, not as a woman, but as a regenerate Christian falsely charged by ministers whose ability in spiritual matters she questioned. She herself dismissed the court's concern with her teaching of men as something of a red herring. Theological and churchly issues dominated the court's questioning. In Winthrop's words, Mrs. Hutchinson had "troubled the peace of the commonwealth and the churches here" (312), first by breaking the Fifth Commandment and second by claiming the authority of immediate personal revelation.

The connection of these quasicivil charges to the two theological errors that Winthrop ascribed to her should remain at the heart of any effort of historical reconstruction. If the Holy Ghost dwells "in" a justified person, then, as John Cotton argued on the trial's second day, God's Providence *might* well speak to and through a fully justified saint apart from the biblical word, though not in substance inconsistent with the Word. Wary of the possibility of illusory revelation, Cotton phrased his admission of that providential power in the negative: "that she may have some special providence of God to help her is a thing that I cannot bear witness against" (341). This particular issue, although unquestionably relevant, finally immersed everyone in fruitless conjecture about the elusive authority of inner belief.

Had Mrs. Hutchinson dishonored the ministers by her contemptuous disagreements with them? No one, in November 1637, could possibly prove what Mrs. Hutchinson had or had not said in her conference with the clergy in December 1636, nor could anyone prove what she had said in conventicles more than a year past. What everyone did know was that the court testimony of John Cotton on this matter would be crucial. His testimony ends with a sentence defending Mrs. Hutchinson ("I must say that I did not find her saying they were under a covenant of works, nor that she said they did preach a covenant of works," p. 334), but his recall of the December meeting is far more evasive: "The elders spake that they had heard that she had spoken some condemning words of their ministry . . . she told them to this purpose that they did not hold forth a covenant of grace as I did, but wherein did we differ? why she said they did not hold forth the seal of the spirit as he doth" (334). Even after many rereadings, John Cotton's word "as," used twice in consecutive sentences, remains as tellingly ambiguous as John Winthrop's preposition "in." Did Cotton intend the word "as" to establish an implied comparison meaning "as effectively as" or "in the same manner as"? If so, Cotton was testifying to nothing more than that Mrs. Hutchinson had said there was an understandable difference of degree and kind among ministers, all of whom preached the Covenant of Grace. But if Cotton used the word "as" as a coordinating conjunction, the equivalent in meaning to the word "which," then Mrs. Hutchinson had claimed that, although Cotton himself preached the Covenant of Grace, other Bay ministers did not. Although these differences of meaning, too subtle for any court to explore in the heat of the moment, were never clarified at Mrs. Hutchinson's hearing, the differences among them remain all-important.

When Deputy Governor Dudley, always anxious to arrive at simple certainty, told Mrs. Hutchinson, "I will make it plain that you did say that the ministers did preach a covenant of works," she countered with the simple certainty "I deny that" (318). Although repeated accusations of this frontal kind brought the court no satisfaction, they brought Mrs. Hutchinson to such a point of exhaustion (or was it pride in first principles?) that she claimed to know Cotton and Wheelwright comprised "the clear ministry" "by an immediate revelation" (336, 337). To a majority of the deputies, she had finally expressed the error of believing that the Holy Ghost dwells "in" a justified person in clearly heretical form. We should not presume, however, that if we possessed an exact transcript of Mrs. Hutchinson's words, we could resolve the problematic multiple meanings of "as" and "in." We can conclude only that the written record brings us up against the limitations of human language, against the ways in which our words, in T. S. Eliot's memorable phrasing, "slip, slide, perish, / Decay with imprecision, will not stay in place."[9]

The civil banishment of Mrs. Hutchinson in November did not make the outcome of her ecclesiastical trial the following March either secondary or inevitable. Among a people who had hazarded so much for faith, civil banishment may well have seemed secondary to heresy and excommunication. The primacy of the civil trial in time did, however, enable the civil government to lead in arriving at a communal decision. In Alan Heimert's phrase, the ministry was "reduced in effect into the handmaids of the Massachusetts magistrates."[10] The ministers' inquiry into Mrs. Hutchinson's spiritual beliefs pursued tangential or sensational accusations that now seem motivated by an intent to convict. The matter of Sanctification and Justification was supposed to be addressed in a sequence of seven allegations prepared by John Eliot and Thomas Weld, but these charges were only passingly explored. Instead, Thomas Shepard questioned Anne Hutchinson at length about her belief in the mortality of the soul and the nonresurrection of the body, issues important to the recently completed synod's worry over "Familism," but not central to Mrs. Hutchinson's view of Good Works as evidence of Justification. Cotton stooped to luridly denouncing her future, predicting that anyone who denies the resurrection of the body must soon engage in sexual transgressions associated with old world familism:

that filthie Sinne of the Comunitie of Woemen and all promiscuus and filthie cominge togeather of men and Woemen without Distinction or Relation of Marriage, will necessarily follow. And though I have not herd, nayther do I thinke, you have bine unfaythfull to your husband in his Marriage Covenant, *yet that will follow upon it.* (372)

Charles Adams Jr., sensitive to the immediate courtroom context of inflammatory words, judged Cotton's testimony at Hutchinson's church trial to have been "the ignominious page in an otherwise worthy life." Oversimplifying Cotton's theology, but capturing the effect of his strategy, Adams concluded that Cotton had "made haste to walk in a Covenant of Works — and the walk was a very dirty one."[11] As Charles Adams had done for the forefathers' judgment against Thomas Morton, so he did for their judgment against Anne Hutchinson: he was the first to frontally accuse the accusers.

Throughout the two proceedings, John Winthrop and John Wilson showed as little regard for the inner spirit of the sanctified person as Anne Hutchinson showed for the Commonwealth's need for ministerial authority. Hutchinson would not consider whether her position on Sanctification denied the community any basis for determining what is Christian conduct according to the Law. Conversely, although church and civil authorities admitted in theory that granting assurance of sainthood on the basis of good works might be an error of "Legalism," they showed no living suspicion of it. Without such mutual consideration of opposed positions, resolution was impossible.

However, the charge of religious "Intolerance," later leveled at both sides, is an anachronism appropriate to neither. Religious tolerance in Thomas Jefferson's (not Roger Williams's) sense is only possible in already established communities in which individual spiritual belief has become a matter of secondary concern. As a considerable number of lay and clerical seventeenth-century New Englanders were to proclaim, a people determined to construct a godly community under divine law cannot tolerate the kinds of perceived error that allow evil free reign. The more appropriate charge against both parties (excepting, until the end, John Cotton) is excessive confidence and overhasty suspicion in identifying error.[12] Before condemning the ministry as legalists, why not consider the communal demands of their office, and why not provide evidence that saints who were doing good works had fallen away from grace? Before proceeding against the Antinomians, why not wait until their prospective heresies had produced a few visibly poisoned fruits?

There were, however, in the particular circumstances, compelling reasons why allowing Mrs. Hutchinson's conventicles and John Wheelwright's preaching to continue did not seem feasible. Consultation and theological querying had led to more acrimony, but not retraction. The success and even the survival of the Commonwealth had, for the past three years, been threatened by other major difficulties: the continuing dispersion of congregations around the Bay; the threat of an appointed governor from England, who would remove the charter; the protracted banishing of Roger Williams; the bloody Pequot War; the removal of a large body of settlers with Thomas Hooker to found Hartford. These are the kinds of collective circumstances that lead people in power to determine upon actions that will demonstrate and reclaim the basic values of the founding community.[13]

What exactly, however, had those values been? For many decades, students of "American Puritanism" assumed that orthodoxy in Massachusetts was a known commodity as soon as the *Arbella* touched anchor.[14] In fact, however, after five years of settlement there was still no communal definition of New England theology, no body of legal statutes, and no educational institution to prepare able young men to assume positions of authority. The major early statements of founding purpose by John Winthrop and John Cotton, however broad their claim to speak for a new order, were all general in prophecy, vague in their details, and written by single individuals. For five years, only the sketchily detailed charter of the Massachusetts Bay

Company provided any institutional definition for the Commonwealth, whose singleness of body John Winthrop had invoked. But just as the individuality latent in old world protestantism had encouraged the proliferation of individual sects, so New England congregationalism as a method of church polity encouraged the growth of communities that were physically and politically separate from each other. The forced codification of communal values was ironically to be the Antinomian Crisis's immediate and lasting consequence. "Antinomian" criticism of the Massachusetts ministry, not the a priori principles of the first migrants, led to the synod that defined New England heresy (1637), to the creation of Harvard College (1638), and to the compiling and approving of the Massachusetts Body of Liberties (1641). These fundamental institutions of New England's future were thus created more in a spirit of retrospective defense than they were in accord with any prospective model of Christian charity.

The first synod grasped after theological certainty and churchly self-definition by special defense of the authority of Scripture against any claim to new light. The synod defined error 40 as the belief that "There is a testimony of the Spirit and voyce unto the Soule, merely immediate, without any respect unto, or concurrence with the word"; to claim any "merely immediate" testimony, the ministers commented, would be an "Enthusiasme justly refused by all the Churches" (230). The synod logically pursued Antinomian heresy to its horrific future. Two "errors," neither of which Anne Hutchinson nor John Wheelwright seem to have voiced, cast a particularly long shadow: error 51, "The soule need not to goe out to Christ for fresh supply, but is acted by the Spirit inhabiting" (233); and error 79, "If a member of a Church be unsatisfied with any thing in the Church, if he express his offence, whether he hath used all meanes to convince the Church or no, he may depart" (241). Both of these errors, soon to be enforced against the Quakers, can be seen as negative definitions of the spiritual individualism F. O. Matthiessen would identify as the essence of the American Renaissance. In departing from the Unitarian and Congregational churches, many a New England transcendentalist and abolitionist come-outer was to be transformed by the "Spirit Inhabiting."

Although the General Court began consideration of funding a college in 1635, it set aside no funds for doing so until its October 1636 meeting, at which there was extensive discussion of the Hutchinsonians. During the November 2 meeting in Newtowne (Cambridge), John Harvard was sworn in as a Freeman and John Wheelwright was disenfranchised and banished. The first Harvard Board of Overseers, appointed in 1638, included none of the Antinomians, but it did include Thomas Dudley, Hugh Peter, Thomas

Shepard, John Wilson, John Winthrop, and John Cotton, who had recently admonished Anne Hutchinson at her ecclesiastical hearing. Two later recollections make the exclusionary origin of Harvard College unmistakable. Edward Johnson, after affirming the death of Anne Hutchinson and the founding of Harvard in unconnected but successive sentences, envisions a student body filled, not with the knowledge of Harvard's classical curriculum, but with the grace of Christ: "The breath of life is added, they no Antinomians are, / But loving Him who gives them life, more zealous are by far."[15] Thomas Shepard, who had kept Antinomianism out of his Newtowne congregation, linked the recent expulsions of the Pequot savage and Hutchinsonian "familist" to the Lord's will for the "erecting a school or college, and that speedily, to be a nursery of knowledge in these deserts, and supply for posterity."[16] From the statements of Johnson and Shepard, it is only a metaphoric leap to Samuel Eliot Morison's approving conclusion: "The suppression of Hutchinsonianism was the price that New England had to pay for a college."[17]

There is substantial evidence that rancor against the Antinomians was essential to the first written statutes designed for New England's self-governance. Completed by Nathaniel Ward in 1641, the codification of Massachusetts Laws had first been proposed at the time of Anne Hutchinson's civil trial. Ward, one of many country ministers opposed to the Antinomianism of the Boston Church, had not been present at Hutchinson's civil trial, but he had given Deputy Governor Dudley a letter testifying he had heard Anne Hutchinson say that New England's ministry was "in a state of damnation, being under a covenant of Works, or to that effect."[18] Six years after the Massachusetts *Body of Liberties* had become law, Ward opened *The Simple Cobler of Aggawam in America* with a trenchant attack on "Toleration of divers Religions, or of one Religion in segregant shapes." Donning the mantle of the plain dealer, Ward announced: "I dare take upon me, to be the herauld of *New-England* so farre, as to proclaim to the world, in the name of our Colony, that all Familists, Antinomians, Anabaptists, and other Enthusiasts shall have free Liberty to keepe away from us, and such as will come to be gone as fast as they can, the sooner the better."[19] In the figure of the simple cobbler, common country wisdom is thus associated with the newly established, exclusionary orthodoxies of magistracy and ministry.[20] As the comic voice of rural New England, Ward's simple cobbler is the literary point of origin for Lowell's Hosea Biglow, even though Hosea's attack on the Massachusetts Cotton Whigs shows how the Puritan/Yankee voice could be used, equally effectively, for oppositional purpose.

The 1641 *Body of Liberties* allows precious little room for disagreement with civil or ecclesiastical authority. Of its ninety-eight sections, all of them conferring a "liberty" upon an individual or a group, only the seventy-fifth contains any reference to a right of dissent. In the seventy-fifth section, a "Libertie" of religious dissent was granted, not to all Freemen, but only to those Freemen who were both members of governing bodies and engaged in making or executing laws concerning religion.[21] Any protest must be conducted "respectively for the manner"; dissent, if written, was to be briefly noted in court records without the "tediousness" of adducing any reasons for it. Sam Adams, who would cite Puritan forefathers as heroic resistors of civil tyranny, would not have recognized this "Libertie" as worth the protest, had he read it closely.

Other provisions of the *Body of Liberties* show the mark of a new need for unanimity and social control. While granting extensive liberties to all citizens in some spheres (freedom from taxation on foreign property, freedom from all kinds of impressment and feudal tenure, equality before the law and under trial), the provisions close down on the threat of inner religious division. Permission to hold lay conventicles ("private meetings for edification in religion amongst Christians") is granted "so it be without just offence for number time, place, *and other circumstances*" (201, italics mine). The state is granted power over the churches in all matters save ecclesiology and theology: "Civill Authoritie hath power and libertie to see the peace, ordinances and Rules of Christ observed in every church according to his word, so it be done in a Civill and not in an Ecclesiasticall way" (190). Throughout the document, the word "liberty" refers not to an individual right but to a limited power, exercised by an individual, that serves the common good. The liberties of all men and the powers of the Freemen are to work apart but together, very much as Winthrop had implied in his phrase defining the Commonwealth: "a due form of government, both civil and ecclesiastical."[22] Historical circumstances were, however, making the paradoxical basis of Winthrop's ideal ever more clear. By 1645, in a forceful speech to the General Court at Hingham, Winthrop would need to be even more explicit, insisting that, just as faithful submission to Christ makes a believer free, so a consideration of true "civil or federal" liberty can only lead to the conclusion that "this liberty is maintained and exercised in a way of subjection to authority."[23] There was in fact nothing new or unexpected in these words; they were a reminder with a hint of warning. In 1641 John Winthrop's idea of liberty became the stipulated principle and statutory fact of legal living in New England, a restatement of what he had long believed, and Nathaniel Ward had recently helped to codify.

RISE, REIGN, AND RUIN: SHORT STORIES

For a century after Anne Hutchinson's banishment, the primary source consulted by regional and national historians would not be Winthrop's *Journal*, which was long available only at second hand, but *A Short Story of the Rise, Reign and Ruine of the Antinomians* (1644), a selection of documents initially made by Winthrop, but published in England with a preface by Thomas Weld. Their compilation, which enjoyed four printings in the seventeenth century, was to be cited as authoritative by historians as late as Palfrey.[24] Its structure reveals how the magistracy and clergy had become codeterminants of the New England will. In order to demonstrate communal authority over individual heresy, Governor Winthrop chose to reprint, first and foremost, the list of eighty-two spiritual errors determined by the 1637 synod in its imposing entirety. The petition of protest on behalf of John Wheelwright is quoted in full, but is surrounded by a triumphantly partisan narrative of the civil and ecclesiastical trials of Wheelwright and Hutchinson. The cumulative effect of the volume is to identify those theological heresies which most undermine the combined authority of a reformed ministry and a civil commonwealth. The individual most thoroughly silenced by the *Short Story* is not the recently deceased Anne Hutchinson, whose words are quoted, whose positions are summarized, and with whose expulsion the volume ends, but the Reverend John Cotton, whose name rarely appears, and whose tracts and testimony are never quoted.

After the English revolution of 1640, at a time when Protestantism was in power but the congregational way was under attack, Winthrop and Weld clearly desired that the complicating voice of past mediation be no longer heard. Pages of the transcript of Hutchinson's trial are glossed over, or shifted into indirect discourse, in order to arrive at this misleading summation: "And thereupon she told them, that there was a wide difference betweene Master *Cottons* Ministery and theirs, and that they could not hold forth a Covenant of free Grace, because they had not the Seale of the Spirit, and that they were not able Ministers of the New Testament" (270). Here is exactly the kind of clear, straightforward acknowledgment Winthrop had tried but failed to elicit from Mrs. Hutchinson in court. Although Winthrop's summary cannot be dismissed as a falsity or a lie, it is a simplifying, court-serving distortion in which all of Mrs. Hutchinson's denials, wit, and equivocation have disappeared, as has John Cotton's testimony in qualified defense of Anne Hutchinson's beliefs, with its ambiguous uses of the word "as."

In the early historiography of the controversy, no passage would prove more influential than the opening paragraphs of Thomas Weld's preface. "Antinomians" are visualized as spiritual confidence peddlers, migrants who, immediately on their arrival from England, "began to open their packs, and freely vent their wares to any that would be their customers." These peddlers offered only poisoned goods, however, so that "some being tainted conveyed the infection to others: and thus that Plague first began amongst us." The power of Weld's interconnected metaphors depends on a fact of life any seventeenth-century reader, but especially the first planters of Massachusetts, would have known: despite the triumphant cleansing of the land, infections will replant themselves and plagues forever recur. Introduced from Old England hard upon the founding, the Antinomian poison is to be seen as "this great and sore affliction" (218) periodically sent by God from outside the community whenever the Saints grow too secure in life's weary pilgrimage. In this way, the alliterative words of the volume's title, "rise, reign and ruin," both proclaim an end to one crisis and provide a pattern readily applicable to new ones.

Weld and Winthrop are particularly concerned to explain why, amid their godly commonwealth, such a plague of heresies could ever have multiplied so quickly. The appeal of Antinomian doctrine, Weld's preface concludes, was not so much its novelty but the fact that it offered "a fair and easie way to heaven" by which a sinner need not try to prepare for grace through walking legally and doing good deeds, but could instead "stand still and waite for Christ to doe all for him" (204).[25] If Christ does all, Winthrop and Weld recognize, the church becomes unnecessary; its spiritual and civil authority may be attacked simply because it is authority. Those drawn to Antinomian conventicles are likely soon to believe, even if they do not admit to it, that "the darker our sanctification is, the cleerer is our justification" (264). If self-assurance of free grace in spiritual matters leads the unwary to assurance of right-doing in matters of state, then the restriction of the Freeman's suffrage to the saints would soon become indefensible. For New England, this disbonding process could end only in the almost unspeakable word, "anarchy."

For a theocratic commonwealth in the wilderness, John Winthrop's warning was every bit as logical and as plausible as Anne Hutchinson's insistence that election is election, Christ's grace is freely given, and visible sainthood is a contradiction in terms. Unfortunately, the integrity of both viewpoints would be promptly lost – first in sexist villification of Anne Hutchinson as a seductive and/or murderous woman (Eve, Sisera, Jezebel, etc.) and later in smug dismissal of theological subtleties which later historians disdained to try to comprehend.[26] Nonetheless, the frequency with which later writers of all kinds would return to the controversy suggests that they had uses (or misuses) for it that were far more important than condemning Mrs. Hutchinson or reattacking a dead heresy.

To Edward Johnson, who foresaw the New England Millennium arriving sooner rather than later, the synod's finding of eighty-two errors did more than establish a needed orthodoxy:

And verily Satans policy here (as in all places where the Lord Christ is acknowledged) was to keepe men from that one right way, by the which hee applies himselfe to the soule, no marvell then if so many Errours arise, like those fained heads of Hidra, as fast one is cut off two stand up in the roome, and chiefly about the uniting of a soule to Christ by Faith.[27]

The constant multiplication of Antinomian "Erronists" only raises the stakes of New England's affliction and calls forth the army of saviour saints into combat. God's wonder-working Providence, speaking through the synod, uses true words as Heracles used his sword and brand, cutting and searing all monsters' heads that emerge. The more heresies the synod uncovers, the more soldiers will be found to combat them. Eighty-two for eighty-two.

Contemplating the Antinomian Hydra leads Johnson to heightened appreciation of all that might be lost. In a passage characteristic in stylistic vigor but rare in its coherence, Johnson reverses the promotional tropes of New England as desert or wilderness:

These Erronious, and Hereticall persons batter off the fruit from the goodly branches of Christs vines and make bare the flourishing trees planted in the house of the Lord, and yet professe themselves to be Scholars of the upper forme, that have learned as far as their Masters can teach them, but let me tell you friends you'l prove but trewants if you fall thus to Robbing of Orchards, and its an offence far beyond petty Larceny to rob Christs Garden, let your pretences be what they will: can it possibl[y] be for the magnifying of Christs Grace that the branches growing upon his root should remain fruitless? No assuredly, herein God is glorified that his people bring forth much fruit. (126)

To Johnson, the inner garden remains, the spiritual fruit can still be eaten. Although the orchard may be fallen, it is still God's will that New England bear the fruit that will glorify Him. To what extent this garden is a geographical place as well as an inner state, Johnson does not declare. His metaphors are designed to promote commitment. Just as a vision of desert wilderness had been necessary to release the energy needed for settlement, so the prospect of an Edenic orchard is now needed to release the energy needed for the Saints to protect themselves.

At a time when New England's churches were no longer clearly expanding, Cotton Mather assumed the sensible and diplomatic position that, for a life of Christian piety, both inner faith and good works are obviously needed. "The truth," he writes about the Antinomian Controversy, "might easily have united *both* of these persuasions."[28] For Mather, it is as futile to argue about priorities between faith and works as it is destructive to attack the spiritual authority and civic leadership of the protestant ministry, especially in a commonwealth newly become a province. He therefore dismisses Johnson's metaphor of the Hydra's heads: "What these errors were, 'tis needless now to repeat; they are dead and gone; and for me, beyond hope of resurrection; 'tis pity to rake them out of their graves; 'tis enough to say they were of an Antinomian and Familistical tendency" (II, 443). By declaring that the substance of Antinomian beliefs is "for me, beyond hope of resurrection," Mather momentarily quells apprehension of their recurrence by writing as if Antinomian beliefs are a now forgotten anachronism, a past heresy that has no future.

It was not to be so. Once the controversy over the Great Awakening became public, the assumption that "Antinomianism" was an expired threat suddenly seemed a comforting illusion. The title page of Charles Chauncy's *Seasonable Thoughts on the State of Religion in New England* (1743) introduces its attack on back-country revivalism by noting that the book will contain "a Preface Giving an Account of the Antinomians, Familists, and Libertines, who infected these Churches, above an hundred Years ago: Very needful *for these days*; the LIKE SPIRIT and ERRORS, prevailing *now* as did *then*."[29] Citing Weld and Winthrop, Edward Johnson, and John Norton's life of John Cotton, but not Wheelwright or Hutchinson, Chauncy characterizes Antinomianism as "an erroneous, enthusiastic Spirit" driven by "an excess of Heat in their imaginations" (iii, iv). Passing silently over differences between yesterday's Antinomians and today's New Lights, between itinerant preachers and visiting preachers, between conventicle teaching and revival sermon, Chauncy's rhetoric blurs Wheelwright and Whitefield, Hutchinson and Edwards, into one dangerously enthusiastic mentality that gains power wherever preparationism is neglected.[30]

TOLERATING ANNE

For nineteenth-century New England historians, the import of the Antinomian Crisis was no longer an issue of heresy or orthodoxy, but its place in the history of religious intolerance. Honoring the right of individual conscience is elevated into the definitive virtue of spiritual politics, then seen within later contexts of England's Act of Toleration or the First Amendment to the US Constitution. Suspecting that man's theology will never yield God's Truth, the historians assume that the importance of the Antinomian Controversy must lie in its societal consequences. The issue of Justification by Faith versus Works is approached with resigned ambiguity, melancholic pity, or amused contempt. The historians' true concern is to ferret out the way New England (dis)honored individual rights at its moment of origin, yet subsequently maintained a cultural mission that kept Puritan culture at the vanguard of enlightened liberty and progress. New England's vindication might now best be seen as coming about through the eventual triumph of "Antinomian" ideas, rather than their suppression, but triumph there must be. This was not a perspective that, under the pen of male historians, was likely to perceive gender issues as central, or even germane. But it was certainly a perspective fully able to give the sanctity of individual belief its political due.

Bancroft's pages on the Antinomian Crisis are among his *History*'s most far-reaching revisionist achievements. Bancroft's search for the power of Liberty's divine spirit leads him toward uncovering its true protestant origins, not in John Winthrop's Commonwealth, but in Anne Hutchinson's rebellion against it. Because the South has no religious dispute of remotely comparable importance, New England assumes spiritual center stage. Bancroft sees two "parties" in the Massachusetts of 1636: the recent magisterial/clerical establishment worried about separation, and a party of newly arrived idealists, the Hutchinsonians who "came fresh from the study of the tenets of Geneva."[31] Refusing to smear Antinomians as libertines, familists or illusion-prone egoists, Bancroft asserts in their defense that they were driven to follow "the principles of the reformation with logical precision to all their consequences" (387). Instead of enthusiasts, the Antinomians are the puritans among the Puritans, rationally seeking the logic of their orthodoxy. While Antinomian ideas of absolute, invisible election looked back to Calvin, the underlying rational and individualistic spirit of the Hutchinsonians looks historically forward.

Instead of immersing readers in the regional past, as so many New England historians had done, Bancroft places Anne Hutchinson's revolt in a prophetic context of the philosophy of mind:

In the very year in which she was arraigned at Boston, Descartes, like herself a refugee from his country, like herself a prophetic harbinger of the spirit of the coming age, established philosophic liberty on the method of free reflection. Both asserted that the conscious judgment of the mind is the highest authority to itself. Descartes did but promulgate, under the philosophic form of free reflection, the same truth which Anne Hutchinson, with the fanaticism of impassioned conviction, avowed under the form of inward revelations. (391)

Knowing Descartes claimed that the individual mathematical mind could provide the fullest insight into God, even through a vision, Bancroft begins by noting that Descartes had therefore "established philosophic liberty on the method of free reflection." His subsequent reference to Anne Hutchinson then allows the reader to discover a prior avowal of the transcendent authority of the individual mind within a much disparaged New England source.

In structuring his narrative, Bancroft's decision to precede the suppression of the Antinomians with an account of the suppression of Roger Williams is no accident of historical chronology. In Bancroft's view, Hutchinson developed for the group what Roger Williams developed for the individual: "he was the first person in modern Christendom to assert in its plenitude the doctrine of the liberty of conscience, the equality of opinions before the law" (376). Although the historical Roger Williams had certainly not believed that "all" opinions are equal, even before the law, Williams's defense of "the liberty of conscience" was, as Bancroft sees it, promptly taken up by Anne Hutchinson. She was the rational Calvinist who "had come to the wilderness for freedom of religious opinion," then sought to gather around her a group who "avowed their determination to follow the impulses of conscience" (387, 390).

Hutchinson's victimization at the hands of Winthrop's intolerance is, however, not at all Bancroft's point. "The true tendency of the principles of Anne Hutchinson is best established by examining the institutions which were founded by her followers" (390). Returning the reader to Roger Williams's Rhode Island, Bancroft demonstrates that elected Judge William Coddington, together with three elders, fought for a constitution in which "liberty of conscience was perpetuated" (393). Bancroft's climactic quotation from the preamble of the 1641 Rhode Island Constitution then introduces a wholly new dimension to the historiography of the Antinomian Controversy:

It is unanimously agreed upon, that the government which this body politic doth attend unto in this island, and the jurisdiction thereof, in favor of our Prince, is a DEMOCRACIE, or popular government; That is to say, it is in the power of the body of freemen orderly assembled, or major part of them to make or constitute just Lawes, by which they will be regulated. (393)

Massachusetts may have long regarded Rhode Island as a sinkhole for heretics and libertines, but the seeds of America's democratic republic and the first amendment of the Constitution, are nonetheless to be traced back to Rhode Island's founding. Democracy and religious liberty are thus retained for New England and simultaneously identified as the logical end of Puritan independence. In a footnote as defiant as it is triumphant, Bancroft suggests that his printing of the preamble to Rhode Island's 1641 Constitution may be the first time the Republic's citizens could ever have known about it: "I copied this, word for word, from the Records, now in Providence" (393).

Because Bancroft assumes that "every political opinion, every philosophical tenet, assumed in those days a theological form" (388), Anne Hutchinson can therefore, without apology, emerge as a fanatic for Truth rather than Error. Bancroft is so little afraid of the word "fanatic" that he uses it twice, concluding that the Hutchinsonians "sustained with intense fanaticism the paramount authority of private judgment" (388). What Bancroft conveniently ignores here, while clothing Hutchinson in Jeffersonian or perhaps Emersonian robes, is that the Hutchinsonian revolt against the ministry was prompted by the stated conviction that "paramount authority" must ultimately reside in God's Free Grace, and only secondarily in "private judgment." Contemporaries alert to the compliment of literary imitation might well have heard, in Bancroft's claim that the Antinomians "resisted every form of despotism over the mind," a deliberate echo of Jefferson's famous vow, "I have sworn upon the altar of God, eternal hostility against every form of tyranny over the mind of man."[32]

Bancroft's faith in the popular will could easily accommodate the reluctant tyranny of Winthrop or the pliability of John Cotton, but how was Bancroft to explain the reelection of Winthrop and Dudley in May 1637? How could the Freemen, whom Bancroft calls "the people," and who are presumed to have an innate Teutonic love of Liberty, ever have voted the anti-Hutchinsonians back into political power? The answer, Bancroft says, lies in the fact that John Wheelwright was threatening to make an appeal to the King against the government of the Bay: "The contest appeared, therefore, to the people, not as the struggle for intellectual freedom against the authority of the clergy, but as a contest for the liberties of Massachusetts against the power of the English government" (389). Through this understandable misapprehension, the people's turning against Antinomians who trust in the paramount authority of the private mind can be explained as the people's courageous independence in asserting a right of self-government against England. One good is sacrificed to another in a way predictive of New England's pre-revolutionary protest against British governance.

By the late 1850s John Gorham Palfrey, who was increasingly worried about the prospect of separatism within the American Republic, no longer had patience with Bancroft's revisionism. "Received accounts" of the Antinomian Controversy have led, Palfrey says, to "unjust impressions."[33] Forty pages of carefully selected facts are assembled "to prove the substantial rectitude of the course taken for their [the Antinomians] overthrow" (508). Palfrey's Winthrop is a reluctant judge who, after allowing the Antinomian revolt to develop unchecked, exhibited "moderation and good temper"; "there was no confiscation, no imprisonment, except for safe-keeping, and no danger to life or limb" (507, 506). As for the worth of the exiles, "She [Massachusetts] scarcely lost a citizen whom it was desirable to retain" (509). Those prone to sneer at the incidentals of scriptural politics, Palfrey says, are likely to overlook the "real justification" of the leaders of the Bay, a justification "resting on the grounds of political duty and common sense" as understood in 1637 and not two centuries thereafter (508).

Like Bancroft, Palfrey assesses the Antinomian Controversy by its Revolutionary fruit. Whereas Bancroft sees Rhode Island exiles establishing the all-powerful Ideas of constitutional democracy and liberty of conscience, Palfrey surveys events from the Stamp Act to the Battle of Lexington and then asks who precisely were to serve as America's Revolutionary leaders? Descendants of Massachusetts Puritans, men like Mayhew, Otis, and the Adamses, and *not* the descendants of Rhode Island Antinomians, like, say, Thomas Hutchinson! Before consigning the Antinomians to their deserved exile, Palfrey confronts his reader with a rhetorical question: "If by unchecked internal dissension, or by foreign force, the little colony of Massachusetts had been broken up two centuries and a quarter ago, where would have been the American Revolution of the last century, with its influence on the authority of free principles of government in the Christian world?" (510). To Bancroft, DEMOCRACIE was a Kantian Idea which, in a new world context, has an irrepressible, independent force. To Palfrey in the late 1850s, however, the value of lasting union through consensual rule of law must not be compromised: "When two scores of years passed before the recurrence of any serious internal dissension in Massachusetts, the substantial wisdom of the course now pursued may be deemed to be vindicated by the event" (1, 509). Both Bancroft and Palfrey justify the Revolutionary end by the Puritan means, but they imagine the process differently. To adapt Lincoln's phrases: Bancroft, who was no Abolitionist, nonetheless emphasizes that, though the Puritan Commonwealth could not have existed permanently half-slave and half-free, constitutional freedom as enshrined in the first amendment must continue to prevail. To Palfrey, writing a crucial twenty years later, loyalty within New England, both at the time of its colonial origins, and perhaps soon again for the sake of a greater union, must and shall be preserved.

For half a century after *Three Episodes in Massachusetts History* was published (1892), Charles Adams's lively account of the Antinomian Controversy would remain the standard narrative. As president of the Massachusetts Historical Society, Adams was the first writer in a position to order and compile all essential documents, and he remains the only writer to insist on a satiric aspect to its unfolding. His wit proceeds from patrician, genteel, secular, and sometimes sexist assumptions. Because seventeenth-century Massachusetts was without "dances, parties, concerts, theatres or libraries," "there must be religious sensation, seeing there could be no other."[34] In so impoverished a culture, Anne Hutchinson's conventicles were "a school of criticism – a *viva voce* weekly religious review" (401). Theology itself, not just Antinomianism, became the plague infecting the Commonwealth: "A community living in a state of religious exaltation," Adams remarks, "is, of course, predisposed to mental epidemics" (398). Adams summarizes the particulars of sanctification and free grace plausibly and clearly, but he also dismisses discussion of them as "hot wrangling over the unknowable" (493). The calling of any synod, Adams declares, is "the last recourse of perplexed theologians" (468). Throughout the synod of 1637, "no one in the assembly had any distinct conception of what they were talking about" (473). "As for real danger to the existence of the colony, there was none" (ii, 570). The whole affair, as Adams sees it, was driven by "the implacable spirit of theological hate" behind which lay, on both sides, only "the hard substratum of injured pride" (ii, 570).

Adams's desire to thus reduce the stakes was only partly due to his writing a local history of Quincy and Hingham, albeit with synecdochal intent.[35] The Civil War, in which Adams had fought, had provided the nation with a second point of origin and had led many a soldier, including Adams, to be wary of sacred causes and easy abstractions. Industrialization had led to a new economy of incorporation, making older notions of the primacy of religion and politics seem obsolete. Not until Perry Miller began writing *The New England Mind* would Adams's condescension to Puritan theology become, in its own turn, academically unacceptable, even quaint.

There is nothing quaint or dated, however, in Charles Adams's account of the injustice of pre-Republican court procedures. Expanding on William Coddington's silenced objection that John Winthrop was acting both as judge and accuser, Adams quotes the summary of Hutchinson's civil trial in order to argue that civil "examination" was "a mockery of justice, rather – a barefaced inquisitorial proceeding" in which Anne Hutchinson was "badgered, insulted, and sneered at, and made to give evidence against herself" (488). Adams's forthright attack, far beyond anything previously written, has as its contemporary target the historical whitewash recently granted Winthrop and the clergy by John Gorham Palfrey. Palfrey's rewriting of New England history, Adams protests, has glossed over persecution and intolerance in order to praise a debatable unanimity of little worth. Mired in the *post hoc ergo propter hoc* fallacy, Palfrey is reduced to arguing that the refractory child deserved all his "stripes and starvation" because such "bad instruction and worse discipline" led to presumably "better things in manhood" (578).

Instead of crediting Palfrey with understandable worry over separatism within the Union, Adams lambastes him for fantasizing that revolutionary European mobsters of 1848 had been conspiring in Puritan Boston:

In their anxiety to justify the subsequent proceedings of the magistrates and the clergy, the New England historians have imagined a condition of affairs existing in Massachusetts in 1635–1637 which the evidence does not warrant. They have transformed the self-contained little New England community into something like a French or German mob. (441)

Adams will allow no room for Cotton Mather's and Palfrey's belief that post-Antinomian orthodoxy had led to a healthy cultural stability. Referring to "the sterile conformity which for more than a century after the suppressions of 1637–1638 prevailed in the Puritan Commonwealth," Adams contends that, decade after decade, Massachusetts could produce only "a literature of forgotten theology and unreadable homilies" (577).

Adams's characterization of Anne Hutchinson is revealingly conflicted. On the one hand she voices "New England's earliest protest against formulas," thereby vitalizing a deadening culture like "the movement of sap in a young tree" (367). Against the "privileged class" of the New England clergy who were "living in the full odor [*sic*] of sanctity among God's people," Anne Hutchinson "persistently intimated that, as a class, God's prophets in New England were not what they seemed" (392). Her able self-defense at her civil trial is the one bright spot in a prosecution that is "dreary and repellent, – in a word, New England wintry" (483). Hutchinson's courage in court is contrasted, unfairly, to the cowardice of John Cotton's hasty and "dirty" retreat back to a Covenant of Works. Because Adams views theology as the rationale rather than the cause for prosecution, the significance of

Hutchinson's trial can only be that "a woman's preference among preachers was somehow to be transmuted into a crime against the state" (493).

Although Adams believes Hutchinson to have been the target of a judicial inquisition, he declines to ennoble her as a victim. Stereotypical qualities of the forward woman recur in her characterization. Although Hutchinson was unjustly arraigned merely because "she had criticized the clergy" (483), she criticized the clergy because she had "an unruly tongue as well as an insatiable ambition" (398). While she was devising her theology, "visions of political greatness also began to float before her" (399). Without evidence, Adams remarks that Mrs. Hutchinson was "devoid of attractiveness of person" (393). Although a long-standing ploy for maligning Margaret Fuller surely lies behind this particular slur, (Hutchinsonians are derisively labeled "the Transcendentalists of that earlier day," p. 435), Adams is primarily concerned with a civic threat in a more present form, namely "the emancipation of women" which, "unfortunately for Mistress Hutchinson... had not been formulated among political issues."[36] Anne Hutchinson's friendship with Mary Dyer is evidence that a shared "doctrine of an inward light" links Antinomian to Quaker to Transcendentalist, but Adams acknowledges no spiritual empowering of women through this rebellious tradition (394).

Although Adams risks no overview at the end of his narrative, his reader would be hard pressed not to see the Antinomian Controversy as the beginning of New England's decline. An overprivileged clergy, ambitious women, and worried autocrats mouth theological absurdities in a political power struggle that seems to have yielded nothing but "sterile conformity." Dismissing the Antinomian Controversy by wishing a plague on both houses, Adams concludes: "it illustrated with singular force the malign influence apt to be exercised by the priest and the woman as active elements in political life" (II, 568–569). Like brothers Brooks and Henry, Charles evidently enjoyed writing New England history into a *cul-de-sac*, if not a dead end, all the while demonstrating, through his knowledge and the power of his sardonic prose, the superiority of the tradition he so freely criticizes.

DUX FOEMINA FACTI

In the gender-conscious climate of the late 1970s, Charles Adams's sneer at the political threat of emancipated women was but a small part of the accumulated misogyny Anne Hutchinson had been made to bear. To Winthrop's retrospective labeling of her as "this *American Jesabel*," Edward Johnson and Cotton Mather had added the image of Eve whispering un-Christian Error in the ears of other women. In the eighteenth century Charles Chauncy had used Anne Hutchinson as a way of discrediting the presumably feminine Enthusiasm associated with the Great Awakening. To these kinds of charges, Hawthorne added a fear not only for the sanctity of the hearth, but also for the supremacy of male authorship, worrying – now famously – that the aggressive public spirit of Anne Hutchinson would soon be reincarnated in a host of "ink-stained Amazons" likely to "expel their rivals by actual pressure, and petticoats wave triumphant over all the field."[37] Even Edmund Morgan's admirable and widely read *The Puritan Dilemma* (1958) was written from a viewpoint sufficiently sympathetic to Winthrop that gender considerations were left out, and the chapter on the Antinomian Controversy was misleadingly entitled "Seventeenth-Century Nihilism."

Given this continuing bias, women writing at any time about Anne Hutchinson were likely to find themselves caught in a bind: to castigate Hutchinson was to follow the male lead, but to vindicate Hutchinson was to risk the charge of condoning a social rebel, a dangerous enthusiast, a false prophetess. Hannah Adams declined to judge Hutchinson on the grounds of gender; Harriet Cheney referred to her as "the golden apple of discord"; Eliza Lee concluded, somewhat reluctantly, that Hutchinson was a woman of "intellectual superiority" and "inordinate self-esteem" who "must have feared that the slimy trail of spiritual pride had sullied the white robes of her martyrdom."[38]

Aggressive assertion of Hutchinson's worth as a woman was not to emerge until the second wave of late 1970s feminism prompted a need for women to avenge a wronged foremother against gendered slurs of the kind advanced by Emory Battis.[39] Marcy Moran Heidish's vivid novel *Witnesses* (1980) portrays Hutchinson as a woman who believes from the outset that God's grace comes only through faith, but that works are one sign of election. In Heidish's recreation of Anne Hutchinson's December 1636 meeting with the clergy, Anne admits only to having pointed out differences of degree among ministers' opinions on Grace and Works, leaving the reader to conclude that the ministers were jealous of, and threatened by, her popularity. Heidish brings forth long-ignored evidence in the historical documents to show Hutchinson as a skilled herbalist and midwife whose care for family earned her the love of women. By novel's end, however, she has become a woman with some confusions but no failings, a dignified victim stripped of liberty, power, and health, who will stoop neither to personal meanness nor to forgiving her oppressors. This model of womanly heroism and courage is achieved only at the price of a seventeenth-century outlook. To Heidish's

Hutchinson, family is a greater priority than God; her weekly discussions of sermons are not concerned with free grace or sanctification, but resemble a stereotypical Quaker meeting where one speaks only when moved to do so, thereby conveying "the sweetest sense of peace, deep and blue as a mountain lake" (82).[40]

In *The Puritan Ordeal,* Andrew Delbanco observes of the Antinomian Crisis that "its historical meaning has eluded our full understanding."[41] This observation is surely true, if for no other reason than that the issues the crisis aroused (Sanctification versus Justification, the authority of the ministry, the meaning of "free grace," and of "union" with the Holy Spirit) arise from within Puritanism itself, rather than being external to it. If the meaning of the Antinomian Crisis has remained elusive, however, its effect has not. Although few have gone quite so far as Charles Francis Adams Jr. in arguing that a "sterile conformity" descended on New England after 1637, the sense of something narrowed and something lost has been, since Adams's time, nearly unanimous. The institutions set up in the wake of the Antinomian expulsion gave to New England, or at least to Massachusetts claiming to be New England, a culture coherent in education, law, and church doctrine – but at a very great price. The quality which the Hutchinsonians called "Legalism" is apparent in the intended workings of those institutions. This legalistic spirit would long exercise a force for restraint that would promote all those qualities Thoreau was to attack, 150 years later, as New England conformity. When we speak so readily of the transformation of Puritan into Yankee at some point during the eighteenth century, we are acknowledging that, in a New England culture now perceived as regional, there was a waning of inner religious enthusiasm and its replacement by calculated codes of external behavior and tangible success. From the times of Royall Tyler, John Trumbull, and Seba Smith onward, the comic qualities that were so promptly ascribed to "the Yankee" could never fully hide the diminishment.

PART TWO

Time of troubles

Headnote

As New England's first century drew to a close, its troubles and crises, both real and imagined, accumulated with the force of a prolonged nightmare. The Stuart Restoration, Indian wars, crop failures, Boston fire, smallpox plague, charter revocation, witchery, promiscuous dancing, admired emigrants, undesirable immigrants, alcoholism, luxury, poverty, empty treasuries, religious nonconformity – these signs of a presumably failing mission became confusingly intermingled as New Englanders struggled to discern the operative secondary cause(s) of God's evident disapproval. Seen as a biblical genre, these exhortations were to be grouped as the literature of the jeremiad, a form whose conventions, even as explored by Perry Miller and Sacvan Bercovitch, rapidly acquire the deadening sense of a collective clerical competition to devise tropes to quicken spiritual anxiety and promote covenant renewal. Along this particular academic path, what was once a living fear of communal decline is likely to devolve into the study of hermeneutic rhetoric.

To try to recover something of the experience of self-recrimination amidst a sea of troubles, let us glance, not at Samuel Danforth's "Brief Recognition of New England's Errand into the Wilderness" (1670), which has by now surely served its exegetical purpose, but rather at two contrasting sermons by Urian Oakes. "New England Pleaded With," an Election Day sermon of 1673, denounces only the inward causes of corruption: swearing, drunkenness, filthiness, Sabbath-breaking, greed, "garish attire," and "Grinding the Faces of the Poor" – all of them tolerated by New England's many "dreaming Professors" who have become "sermon proof."[1] Oakes also, however, exhorts his audience to maintain New England's founding purpose as a citadel for the righteous remnant. In New England, God still offers his people "Sanctuary Mercies"; He has built "a Wall of Fire about us"; He has made us "as a City upon a Hill, though in a remote and obscure wilderness."[2] Persistent metaphors of a walled civilization evoke unnamed, terrifying enemies without, while aggravating an irresolvable tension within. What protection can God's surrounding "wall of fire" possibly provide if the truly corrosive corruption is inside us? What good can it do to denounce "unbounded Toleration as the first-born of all Abominations," while also acknowledging that the piety of New England's "giddy Professors" has become "customary, formal, superficiary, lukewarm, neither hot nor cold" (54, 15). Why praise the calling of the New England farmer if one also admits, in accusatory words that anticipate Thoreau, that "There is so much rooting in the Earth, that there is little growing upward" (33)? From time to time, to be sure, Oakes resorts to the comfort of oppositional self-definition, praising the suppression of Antinomian, Pequot, and Quaker, but in the main New England's walls seem to him to be clearly down, and he nowhere suggests where or how they might be rebuilt. Convinced only that "God is certainly angry with New England" (61), Oakes offers no consolation until his last page, and then only in an abrupt and explicitly official manner: "Though there be a Day of Gloominess and thick Darkness coming upon the Reformed Churches, and there should be a Day of Trouble, and Treading down, and perplexity in this Valley of Vision; yet I have Commission from the Lord to say, 'It shall be well with the Righteous'" (63).

If Oakes delivered all sixty-four pages of his printed text, his election sermon must have lasted four hours. The remarkable success of his subsequent career as minister of the Cambridge Church and acting president of Harvard suggests that his hours of public prominence had been well received. In turn, the public's appetite for such a relentlessly accusatory performance suggests that "gloom," "thick darkness," and "perplexity in the valley of Vision" were more than a metaphoric prediction; they spoke to a directionless obscurity of *communal* purpose within the minds of the Election Day audience. By 1693 the confusions of 1673 would in retrospect seem as nothing, but they had evidently been, in Oakes's time, immobilizing enough.

Shortly after Urian Oakes's death, Increase Mather published Oakes's Fast Day sermon entitled "A Seasonable Discourse" with a preface lamenting "How doth New England shake since this Oak whom Christ hath made a Pillar in the temple of his God, is removed."[3] Despite its conventional subdivisions into numbered points of text, explication, and application, Oakes's appropriately brief sermon is an elaboration of one word. Our New England "Professors" of religion are weary of God, weary of the service of God, weary of Divine Truth, weary of Commonwealth Government, weary of church government, weary of family government, weary of our spiritual privileges, weary of our own murmurings, and, finally, weary of ourselves for being weary of God. And what is the sermonic "use" to which this obsessive explication is to be put? "To realize that a people weary of God are not God's People" and thus to force the audience to confront the rhetorical question: "Are we not a sick people?"[4] If weariness is a condition produced by long labor or long contemplation without release or resolution, then Oakes may be said to have selected a word remarkably "seasonable" in its descriptive accuracy. In this sense, the word applies to his own effort; absent any proposal for cure, weary contemplation of the end of New England's mission can only reproduce itself. Hence Oakes ends his sermon by reminding his congregation that God will neither endure nor pity the weariness his listeners now feel.

What issues from such a cloud of perplexity? A myriad possible outcomes over an extended time, to be sure, but in the short run, swift and probably excessive responses to the most immediately visible among the cloud of enemies. Walls breached and crises rising everywhere. Not knowing any longer who they were, New Englanders had to define themselves anew by expelling visible enemies beyond new geographical borders and reconstructed spiritual boundaries. To shift the metaphor and postdate the analogy, many a late seventeenth-century New Englander must have felt like the title character in Hawthorne's "The Ambitious Guest." Marginalized in the White Mountains during the boundless ambition of late adolescence, Hawthorne's nameless New Englander flees from an overheard avalanche only to run directly into its obliterating path.

CHAPTER 4

A cloud of blood: King Philip's War

The apocalyptic literary legacy of King Philip's War extends farther forward than currently recognized, to writers as different as Robert Lowell and Bharati Mukherjee. "The Park Street Cemetery," the lead poem of Lowell's first book of poetry, immerses the reader in the "dusty leaves" and near forgotten spiritual/political pretensions of Boston's long-buried dead, culminating in the avenging depersonalizing question "What are Sam Adams or Cotton Mather?"[1] When Lowell expanded this "graveyard" poem for inclusion in *Lord Weary's Castle*, he retitled it "At the Indian Killer's Grave," thereby suggesting that the prevailing motivation of the Puritans had been, not salvation but domination, not king-killing but Indian-killing. The poem's narrator, clearly Lowell himself, discovers upon a visit to King's Chapel Burial Ground that the cracked gravestones of Boston's sanctified progenitors cannot hide a half-covered well in a ruined garden. Through the well, the narrator catches glimpses of the underworld fashioned by the Puritans' descendants, a mechanic hell where the screechings of the Green Line subway literally undermine the virtues that the blackened gravestones strove to commemorate.[2]

The "Indian Killer" of the poem's title turns out to be an unnamed composite figure made up of Lowell's first American ancestors (John and Mary Winslow, whose cenotaph is in the cemetery), John's nephew Josiah Winslow (governor of Plymouth and commander of New England's army during King Philip's War) and Benjamin Church, the war hero who captured King Philip. Like the mythical Cadmus, Lowell's composite Indian Killer, "that fabulous or fancied patriarch," may have slain the dragon, but he then "sowed the dragon's teeth," thereby planting the seeds of today's corruption. Faced with this kind of multiplying cultural dead end, Lowell concludes his poem by pleading to be gospelled to a truer garden, "Where Mary twists the warlock with her flowers."

While pondering over last things at the cemetery's gray railing (newly repainted red), the narrator has a vision of the ghostly presence of King Philip:

> Philip's head
> Grins on the platter, fouls in pantomime
> The fingers of kept time:
> "Surely, this people is but grass,"
> He whispers, "this will pass;
> But Sirs, the trollop dances on your skulls
> And breaks the hollow noddle like an egg
> That thought the world an eggshell. Sirs, the gulls
> Scream from the squelching wharf piles, beg a leg
> To crack their crops. The Judgment is at hand;
> Only the dead are poorer in this world
> Where State and elders thundered *raca*, hurled
> Anathemas at nature and the land
> That fed the hunter's gashed and green perfection
> Its settled mass concedes no outlets for your puns
> And verbal Paradises. Your election,
> Hawking above this slime
> For souls as single as their skeletons,
> Flutters and claws in the dead hand of time.

The irony of Lowell's devising so vindictive a speech depends on the reader's knowing that the body of the historical King Philip (Metacom) had *not* been buried in King's Chapel, but had been quartered, beheaded, and cut up for saleable souvenirs. The voice of Philip, as a prophetic, beheaded John the Baptist, emerges from the buried history within his enemy's sanctuary, proclaiming both the shell-like fragility of the Puritan's verbal world and the predatory nature of Puritan "election," whether spiritual or political. Philip's is the submerged voice of historical truth, hurling anathema at Puritan Indian Killers who had themselves "hurled Anathemas at nature and the land / That fed the hunter's gashed and green perfection."

"At the Indian Killer's Grave" illustrates Jill Lepore's insight that the wordlessness of the historical Philip would compel later writers of many persuasions to devise a prophetic speech for him.[3] But why does Robert Lowell, the most inside of self-declared outsiders, need to cloak himself in Philip's voice as if his were a voice altogether outside New England? The answer is surely not to be found in another neo-Freudian recounting of Robert Lowell's rebellion against father, fathers and Father, nor in Lowell's passing Mariolatry, but in the literary and historiographical tradition out of which "At the Indian Killer's Grave" was written. The Indians had, in theory, been a part of "New England" and its errand from the first statement of missionary purpose, through the adoption of the Massachusetts Commonwealth Seal with its Indian pleading "Come Over and Help Us," to the building of Harvard's Indian College, and to the gathering of the Indian "Praying Towns." Whether valid or not, Edward and Josiah Winslow's insistence on English contractual purchase of Indian lands, rather than the English seizing of them, shows that the Indian had long been conceived as integral to New England, somehow belonging to the land even if it were a *vacuum domicilum*.

The thesis of this chapter is that King Philip's War was the crisis that would end this conceptual inclusion for the next two centuries of New England life. Just as the literature of King Philip's War fixed New England's western and southern boundaries, it simultaneously wrote the Indian, including surviving Wampanoags, Narragansetts and Nipmucs, out of New England. This conceptual change allowed the Indian as tractable heathen to be rather rapidly replaced by the Indian as uncivilizable savage. When, therefore, nineteenth-century white historical writers wished to elegize or savagize the Indian, it was comparatively easy for them and their audience to assume that Mohicans, Pequots, and even Wampanoags no longer existed. By Robert Lowell's time, however, adopting the voice of King Philip had become the perfect vehicle for a son of New England to avenge his own willed exclusion by denouncing New England's historical sins. To enter into the voice of Philip was to imagine oneself as the extinct inside/outsider of another race.

WALLING IN AND WRITING OUT

Of the severity of King Philip's War, its measurably cataclysmic quality, there can be no doubt; at least nine frontier towns totally destroyed, eleven others badly burned (including Providence and Springfield), almost every noncoastal community in Massachusetts and Rhode Island attacked. By April 1676, the de facto western border of Massachusetts had receded to the Concord River. Statistical estimates of the carnage vary, but the war seems to have killed somewhere near 10 percent of the adult male English population of Massachusetts, making fugitives of hundreds of families, setting back white settlement for half a century, and leaving the United Colonies 80,000 pounds in debt by 1678, and Massachusetts still 40,000 pounds in debt in 1690.[4] The costs to the Wampanoags, Narragansetts, Nipmucs, and Pocumtucks were far worse; except for the Christian Wampanoags on Cape Cod, Nantucket, and Martha's Vineyard, southern New England's

Indian peoples lost nearly all their hunting lands, their cleared fields, their warriors and their cultural independence. Accordingly, King Philip's War has in the mind of regional history remained "New England's Crisis" from the time of the mid-war publication of Benjamin Tompson's poem of that title, through Richard Slotkin's insistence, almost exactly two centuries later, that King Philip's War was "the great crisis of the early period of New England history."[5]

Jill Lepore has argued persuasively that an underlying cause of the war was fear of acculturation on both sides. Through trade and missionary activities, white adaptation of Indian practices, and Indian adaptation of white technologies, interracial contact had been prolonged until British protestants feared they were losing their English culture, and Indians feared they were losing their native cultures.[6] If this is true, we should expect the English to fight the war with rhetoric of even more than the customary degree of totalizing the oppositional qualities of the enemy. And so it was.

Although there has been mixed advantage in the conventional naming of the conflict as "King Philip's War," the historical reason for the name is clear.[7] In the fearful or contemptuous eyes of Massachusetts citizens and historians the dreaded enemy could readily be symbolized in one barbaric Indian "King" named after Philip of Macedonia, whose people had beseeched the Apostle Paul to "Come over to Macedonia and help us" (Acts 16:9). Once the killing began, however, the name "Philip" externalized New England's proven enemy as a warlike autocrat who had resisted conversion. Not until the twentieth century would New England writers insist upon referring to King Philip as Metacom, sachem of the Pokanokets, leader of an important Wampanoag tribe, but not a man possessed of absolute authority, even among his own people.[8]

Through the end of the nineteenth century New England pursued a bait and switch strategy to the Indians' disadvantage. Increase and Cotton Mather saw King Philip's War as a confrontation between the powers of Christ and Satan; Bancroft and Palfrey saw it as a regional death struggle between the civilized man and the savage; William Hubbard's *Narrative* (1677) – long thought to be the authoritative "history" – saw it as a combination of the two. As personal memory of the conflict receded and the era of trans-Allegheny expansion approached, King Philip's War was increasingly viewed as a race war between red and white, a confrontation in which the white protestant way emerged deservedly victorious and the fertile lands of the Narragansetts and Nipmucs were opened for "settlement." By the 1820s and 1830s, dwelling on the atrocities of King Philip's War became a useful way of demonstrating that Andrew Jackson's policy of forced Indian removal offered a comparatively bloodless and progressive solution to the presumably unchangeable problem of two separate races, one advancing toward world domination, the other declining inevitably toward extinction. By this time the Puritan commitment to Indian conversion, "Come over and help us," had become an errand relegated to missionaries who no longer voiced the nation's imperial theme.

Care must be taken, however, that the New Englanders not be seen as monolithic apologists for conquest. If it is true, as Francis Jennings claimed, that "Puritans had long known the power of propaganda presented as history," why then should it be that the very first historian of the war, that self-proclaimed Puritan of Puritans named Increase Mather, insisted upon tracing the causes of the war to "the Heathenisme of the English People," among whose sins is the worship of a new god called land.[9] "Land! Land!," Mather insisted late in 1675, "hath been the idol of many in New England."[10] And if, as Jennings claimed, "During the nineteenth-century, and much of the twentieth, the whole historical profession was dominated by historians who not only were trained in New England but at the same time were steeped in the accepted traditions of that region,"[11] why is it that condemnatory questioning of Puritan conduct during King Philip's War should have begun with the late eighteenth-century New England histories of Thomas Hutchinson and Hannah Adams? It was George Bancroft, and not Francis Jennings, who first forcibly argued that the underlying cause of King Philip's war had been the economic pressures caused by land dispossession. Are we to dismiss charges of racial bigotry leveled against the Puritan conduct of the war in writings by Washington Irving, Fenimore Cooper, and Lydia Maria Child simply because those writings have been traditionally classified as "literature" and not "history"? The first unapologetic Native American claim for the heroic justice of the New England Indian rebellion did not need to await the aftermath of the late 1960s Red Power movement; it may be found in Pequot William Apess's bitterly revisionist eulogy of King Philip, delivered twice in Boston in 1836.

The long-standard twentieth-century historical and military narrative of the war, Douglas Edward Leach's carefully researched *Flintlock and Tomahawk* (1958), ends with the familiar but false conclusion that "the two races had fought a war of extermination," even though much of the historical evidence Leach cited points to a different conclusion.[12] In fact, the Mohegans, Pequots, Niantics, and Sakonnets fought with the English, not against them; Joshua Tift was beheaded for fighting with the Narragansetts. The four most notorious Indian chiefs were all put to death by hostile Indians: Pequot chief Sassacus by the Mohawks, Narragansett chief Miantonimi by the brother of Mohegan chief Uncas, Miantonimi's son Conanchet through combined execution by Pequots, Mohegans, and Niantics, and finally King Philip himself by a Sakonnet called Alderman. Even if one contends that, in all four instances, Indian executioners were acting at the virtual command of white authorities, the deaths are dramatic proof of how divided among themselves New England tribes had been since the time, long before 1620, when the invading Pequots had conquered lands held by Mohegans and Narragansetts.[13]

These were the kinds of divisions that contemporaries were likely to remember, but later generations were apt to overlook or slight. Even though Increase Mather supported the Puritan mission to convert the Indians, he also openly approved the New Englanders' policy of divide and conquer: in allowing Conanchet to be executed by three tribes, Mather wrote "the English dealt wisely, for by this means, those three Indian Nations are become abominable to the other Indians."[14] Reaffirming his father's idea of expedient policy, Cotton Mather raised its stakes, rejoicing that the hostility between Mohegans and Narragansetts "produced such a division in the kingdom of Satan against itself, as was very serviceable to that of the Lord."[15]

Unlike later New England historians, however, seventeenth-century Puritans were prone to discerning God's incidental providences without claiming to know their cumulative meaning, even after the presumably deserved, climactic killing of Philip. Near the end of his "Brief History of the Warr," Increase Mather warns of another "dark cloud rising, in respect of Indians in these parts."[16] No clarity here. Thirteen years later, Cotton Mather's *Decennium Luctuosum* contends that the continuing hostility of the hydra-headed Eastern Indians after 1676 is but another sign of the degeneracy of New England's godly Commonwealth. In the final book of the *Magnalia*, Mather is still searching for convincing evidence of New England's leadership in the spiritual redemption of the world. To have to conclude New England history during the dreary aftermath of King Philip's War prompts Mather to end the *Magnalia*, not with pride in "great things" accomplished, but with a paragraph bemoaning "our own backsliding heart." Because "The Wars of The Lord" seem to have brought forth "so wonderful a degeneracy," Mather must lay down his pen by exclaiming, in a one-sentence paragraph, "God knows what will be the End."[17]

At the time John Smith's map had been published, "New England" had meant, for all practical purposes, the coastline. From 1635 to the 1650s, "New England" remained ill defined, but in common usage it meant the Massachusetts lands east of the Connecticut River plus their most immediate offshoots, including Hartford, New Haven, and Maine coastal ports. But by the 1670s the Massachusetts and Connecticut tribes to the west, the congregated eastern towns, and the communities of Praying Indians between them were perceived as inhabiting one land, one geographical entity called New England. Since 1643 the United Colonies of New England had claimed jurisdiction over this entire land mass without reaching any determination about the land rights of Indians residing within it. Awareness that New England would be bounded to the west by the Hudson River suddenly emerged when Governor Andros of New York and the Mohawks showed their hostility toward encroachments from the east.[18] It is not accidental, therefore, that in so many of the jeremiads at century's end the formulaic phrase for lamenting God's deserved displeasure becomes "O New England" (an imitation of Jeremiah's "O Israel") and not "O Massachusetts" or even "O New Israel." "O New England" is a claim upon a newly circumscribed geographical region as well as upon English cultural identity.

In 1670, however, this sense of New England's enlarged geographical bounds still somehow needed to include Indians residing within, while also indicating that unconverted heathen, but not necessarily all red men, must be expunged. Here was an untenable compromise to which the resolution, precisely because of King Philip's War, would be the externalizing of the Indian. At the conclusion of the war, Samuel Nowell found the exactly appropriate and therefore perverse metaphor for conveying this sense of the enemy within who must nonetheless be expelled. No friend of the Indian, Nowell shaped his Artillery Company sermon of 1678 as a warning on the need for continuing military preparedness, but he summarized his sense of the recently concluded war by stating: "Two nations are in the womb and will be striving."[19] To see Christian whites and heathen Indians as nations striving against each other within one womb gave large-scale geographical reinforcement to the Puritan belief that attacking Indians were God's agents embodying New England's inner sins. The unconverted Indian thus becomes the saint's sinful inner twin who must first be conquered, then expelled, if a godly commonwealth is to be restored.

The conceptual walling-out of the Indian was forged in sermons and addresses delivered during and immediately after the war. While western Massachusetts settlements were still burning, Increase Mather warned that a pacifist countryman fleeing to the city for protection might find himself like the man who "went into the house and leaned his hand on the wall and a serpent bit him."[20] Samuel Willard's "The Heart Garrisoned," an Artillery Company sermon delivered June 5, 1676, urges the fortification of New

England's soul by metaphors of military aggression and enclosure: "Get a Shield of Faith, a Helmet of Salvation, a Girdle of Truth, a Breastplate of Righteousness," Willard insists, because those who would rob you of your soul are "sculking in every bush to surprise."[21] William Hubbard's Election Day sermon of the same year walls the Indians out of New England because of their own inexplicable violations. "Why" Hubbard exclaimed, "are our hedges broken down, and the wild boar out of the wood doth waste it [God's vineyard], and the wild beast of the field doth devour it?"[22] Urian Oakes, applying the inscrutabilities of Ecclesiastes to the present conflict, felt compelled to conclude "The Battle is not to the Strong... There is, as it were, a kind of Lottery, a great Uncertainty in Warre... a breaching of fences."[23] And finally, Samuel Willard's 1679 funeral sermon for Governor John Leverett elaborated a similar metaphor into God's commandment for war's end. New England is now "to repair and make up the wall that is broken down. That our fence is tottering & in many places open, is a thing obvious." "Pray for the peace of Jerusalem," Willard urged: "Thus shall the breeches in New England's hedge be made up." To repair New England's hedge (a very British kind of boundary) now clearly entails shutting the Indian entirely out.[24]

During the war, its underlying cause was not thought to be Indian malignancy; even if the Indian were the devil, he had to be the agent of God's scourge upon New England's degeneracy. Such self-accusation was not, as is often assumed, a view held only by Increase Mather and a few backward-looking ministers. It surfaces everywhere, even among laymen opposed to Boston's ministerial establishment. As early as December 1675, Deputy Governor John Easton of Rhode Island blamed the onset of the war squarely on the "spiret of persecution" of the New England clergy.[25] Immediately after the Great Swamp Fight, Captain Wait Winthrop published a broadside concluding:

> O New-England, I understand,
> With thee God is offended:
> And therefore He doth humble thee,
> Till thou thy ways hath mended.[26]

Nathaniel Saltonstall, a magistrate from Haverhill, wrote that God's sword was now drawn against New England's many sins and apostasies because of "our abiding very much unreformed."[27] Schoolmaster Benjamin Tompson's prologue to "New England's Crisis" (1676) lists the number and severity of the sins of coastal communities, from merchant gold and rental housing down to hot chocolate and imported aristocratic fashions. Tompson's satiric spirit did not prevent him from concluding that New Englanders sorely needed "To fear and fare upon their fruits of sinnings."[28]

If Indian and Englishman were warring twins within New England's womb, self-purging and not interracial understanding was the needed supplement to military action. Accordingly, Hartford, Boston, and Plymouth observed thirteen separate days of fasting or public humiliation before the end of the war. The Massachusetts General Court passed statutes restricting tavern licenses and controlling prices as well as forbidding scanty dress, long hair, and public idling. The episodic, often structureless qualities of the accounts written during wartime reflect a people that had become frighteningly perplexed, not only about where the next attack might erupt, but also about which combination of their own backslidings, or which kind of inner division, had provoked it.

This viewpoint, most memorably developed in the sermons and histories of Increase and Cotton Mather, could produce no insight into Indian motives, Indian strategy, or Indian cultures. By objectifying the Indian as the evil twin within, it could only end in an exorcism destructive to both peoples. But the notion of the Indian as God's afflictive agent was a brilliant vehicle for searching out divisions within New England's Commonwealth. "The Cloud of Blood" Increase Mather predicted eighteen months before Philip attacked Swansea led Mather to fasten upon corruptions hidden within New England's expansion as the true cause of the war's onset.[29] In his "Earnest Exhortation to the Inhabitants of New-England" some fifteen separable aspects of "The Heathenisme of the English People" are condemned as God-provoking sins. The economic and social strains caused by more luxury, more poverty, and more transience, a shift "from a religious to a worldly interest," excessive regard and excessive disregard for the founding fathers, a need for external force to spur covenant renewal, the increasing separation of a rhetorically ambitious ministry from their pastoral duties, tardy and inadequate missionary efforts to convert the Indian – all these developments, still reaffirmed in twentieth-century historians' accounts of seventeenth-century change, pass under Increase Mather's worried and sometimes self-condemnatory review.[30]

Increase Mather's audiences, already suspicious of the treachery of nearby Praying Indians, must have deeply resented his rhetorical question "Are not some Praying English as perfidious, as hypocritical in heart, as profane as some Praying Indians?"[31] Readers of his "Brief History of the Warr" must have inwardly protested at his linking the bow that had recently appeared in the Massachusetts sky to the Antinomian Crisis. By observing "As in the days of our Fathers, it was apprehended that God did testifie from heaven against the monstrous Familitical opinions that were then stirring," Mather connected two crises in order to suggest that the cancer of Familist/Antinomian heresies was still alive within.[32] At war's end, Richard Hutchinson, Anne's nephew, was to assign blame to the opposite quarter by alleging that attacking Indians had conveyed God's punishment on Massachusetts's unjust extradition of "Dissenters."[33] However opposed Hutchinson and Mather were in identifying New England's sinners, they divined causation by the same mode of reasoning.

Such powerful condemnations were not likely to be long tolerable among the increasingly secular and varied population that resided around Massachusetts Bay. A comfortingly moderate tone was clearly needed, a voice that would not insist on tracing all secondary causes to one primary cause, a comprehensive view of the recent war that would, in the main, shift the blame from oneself to the Indian. One year after the war's end, William Hubbard provided the needed adjustment to Mather's judgmental absolutes. Hubbard skirted the issue of agency by titling his account *A Narrative of the Troubles with the Indians in New England*, a subject presumably synonymous with the title of the London edition, *The Present State of New England*. Hubbard's Indians, unlike Mather's, attack with "no cause of provocation being given by the English."[34] Although Hubbard acknowledges that Indian attacks must be God's scourge upon English failings, he engages in no communal soul searching. Instead he gives us narrative after narrative of Indian atrocity followed by providential deliverance. The assumption behind such narratives is that heathenism and race combine to identify all Indians as one people separate from New England's continuing identity.

Hubbard's rarely considered conclusion redefined New England political geography from this secular, exclusionist perspective. Throughout his narratives Hubbard assumed, unlike Increase Mather or Urian Oakes, that war can have wholly naturalistic causes; burned fields, starvation, and "fevers and fluxes," none of them traceable to the finger of God, contributed greatly to the sudden weakening of Indian military forces in May 1676 (81–83). At war's end, any regard for restoring the Christian mission to the heathen can thus disappear in a celebration of the war's geopolitical outcome for all New England, now including Rhode Island dissenters. "To be short," Hubbard concludes in a very long final paragraph, "we are all but one Political body, which ought to be sensible of the Sorrows that befell any particular members thereof" (84). Although New England's settlements became "farther disposed upon the Sea Coasts and Rivers, than was at first intended," the war has shown us the need for regional political unity. We now realize we have been "in our Government and Jurisdiction, and being likewise where we live, encompassed with people of several Nations, which may prove injurious, as they have formerly committed Insolencies, and Outrages upon several of our Plantations." In Hubbard's view, a grand necessity of union emerged, first through the 1643 Articles of Confederation and then through the armies of the United Colonies of New England, which have defeated the external enemy and secured our borders. Although Hubbard knows that in 1677 many an Indian still resides within the region's geographical borders, he insists on seeing the "Savages," retrospectively, as one enemy "people" who have "encompassed" us. The six editions of Hubbard's *Narrative* to be published before 1865, together with John Foster's map, would help to define New England for generations of regional, overwhelmingly protestant readers.

BEHEADING: THE USES OF ATROCITY

The narrating of King Philip's War established a set of conventions about Indian warfare that would recur in captivity narratives, the historical literature of the French and Indian War, the frontier novels of Cooper and Simms, the histories of Francis Parkman, and persist, in slightly altered form, in film westerns. In many self-justifying accounts of Massachusetts Christians, from the time of Nathaniel Saltonstall through John Gorham Palfrey, bands of nameless New England Indians, identifiable only by tribe, attack suddenly and without explanation from marshy southern swampland and dense western forests. Whatever the writer may claim about Philip's intertribal conspiracy to rid New England of the white man, the purposes of warfare as rendered for the reader remain terrifyingly local: scalps, arson, crop destruction, captives, the erasing of a particular settlement. The more racist the author's attitudes, the more likely that specific atrocities will be used to deflect attention from the territorial causes of genocidal war.

Under such circumstances, the handiest means for a Christian to demonstrate heathen immorality, or for a post-Revolutionary romancer to demonstrate red barbarity, was to dwell upon scenes of torture that would condone dispossession. How many of the torture scenes in *The Last of the Mohicans* and *The Conspiracy of Pontiac*, in *Nick of the Woods* and *The Yemassee*, have their origin in one remarkable sentence from Cotton Mather's *Magnalia*:

The Indians took five or six of the English prisoners; and, that the reader may understand *crimine ab uno*, what it is to be taken by such devils incarnate, I shall inform him: they stripp'd these unhappy prisoners, and caused them to run the gantlet, and whipped them after a cruel and bloody manner; they then threw hot ashes upon them, and cutting off collops of their flesh, they put fire into their wounds; and so, with exquisite, leisurely, horrible torments, roasted them out of the world.[35]

Although the way these five prisoners died was historically inconsequential, Mather chose this sentence to end an entire section of the *Magnalia*. With what exquisite leisure and evident relish his sentence lingers over the details of torture, building on the power of this representative example (*"crimine ab uno"*) until its final ten words, all in dactylic rhythm, slowly and satisfyingly end in "roasted them out of this world." The Christian's fascination for the abomination of the "devil incarnate" could not be better rendered.

Narratives of the war gave disproportionate attention to the assault upon Quabag (Brookfield) in early August 1675. At every point, the siege of Brookfield satisfied an archetypal sense of the war around which colonists could rally: an unexpected attack from Indians hiding in swamps and hillsides upon English troops who were on a peace mission; a Puritan's son who proves himself worthy of his heritage by rescuing his wounded father (Thomas Wheeler); twenty-five Christian men and fifty women and children in one garrison house "encompassed" by 300 faceless Indians; the heathen shooting "like Haile through the walls" and "continually yelling like wolves gaping for their prey"; Indian mockery of the Christian's Bible and his God; the burning of all other buildings in the town; dwindling ammunition and food; a desperate three-day repulse of continuing strategies of arson (fire arrows, burning hay, burning horse carts); a shower of rain, perhaps providential; the unexpected and surely providential arrival "in the very nick of opportunity" of Major Simon Willard and his "flying army of sixty horse" (together with five often unmentioned Indian guides); and, finally, the sullen withdrawal of the heathen attackers after the Christian families are reunited by military deliverance.[36]

The siege of Brookfield is surely the prototype for the many sieges of the blockhouse which, beginning with *The Wept of Wish-ton-Wish*, recur in Fenimore Cooper's frontier novels. It is also the ultimate origin of that moment, eventually *de rigeur* in B westerns, when the pioneers and their cowboy allies circle the Conestoga wagons to prepare against Indian attack, while their helpless but protected wives clutch sleeping babes to their breasts. Everything heathen, savage, and inscrutable is outside, threatening the elevated inner center that contains the reader's known world of moral order. As William Hubbard, imagining the Brookfield garrison house surrounded by "barbarous Miscreants," reminded his readers: *In the Mount of the Lord it shall be seen.*[37]

In accord with the revisionist historical purposes advanced by late twentieth-century women novelists of color, Bharati Mukherjee's novel *The Holder of the World* (1993) turns the conventional retelling of the assault on Brookfield inside out. Instead of attack and abduction, we see a Nipmuc lover leading a Puritan widow and her daughter from the dangers of British settlement back to a mutually fulfilling tribal life. The Puritan father, a man of comically painful paradoxes, is put permanently aside as the daughter and the Indian depart to a better life. By novel's end, the daughter metaphorically becomes the Holder of the World in colonial India. Mukerjee's reader is thus compelled to join Brookfield to wider worlds rather than to celebrate the New England town's isolated integrity.[38]

Mukherjee notes that in 1661 Oliver Cromwell's exhumed head had been "stuck on a pole in Westminster Hall" and that, fifteen years later in Brookfield, Hannah Easton heard terrifying rumors of King Philip "impaling scalped heads" (22, 28). There is nothing unhistorical in such seeming fictionalization. The long-standing practice most compellingly abhorrent to seventeenth-century chroniclers of the war had been the postmortem beheading of an enemy's corpse for purposes of public display.[39] In accord with the medieval, church-approved policy of *Ad terrorem malefacorum*, the heads of evildoers, whether heretics or the king's enemies, had been placed on pikes on London Bridge. Why, however, was military beheading still practiced during King Philip's War with such (disgusted?) relish both by Indians and by God's reformed people? Why do Christians who believe themselves regenerate and born in God's image fix an enemy's bloody, rotting head on a fencepost or on a town palisade? Why send a chief's (Canonchet's) head in a bag to the Governor's Council? To be sure, such trophyism can terrorize, proclaim victory, deliver a warning, or satisfy vengeance through a form of testimony neither God nor Nature seems to have honored. But to any protestant Christian trying to follow New Testament law in the new world, staring at a decapitated Indian head must have aroused a perhaps inadmissible sense of guilt over setting aside such basic ethical principles as "Blessed are the merciful" and "Thou shalt not kill."

William Hubbard presents Indian beheading of Englishmen and Indian contempt for the Bible as the twin horrors that provoked New England's retaliation. When Plymouth's troops first march into Philip's stronghold at Mount Hope, they see "a Bible newly torn, and the leaves scattered about by the enemy in hatred of our Religion therein revealed; two or three miles further they came up with some Heads, Scalps, and Hands cut off from the bodies of some of the English, and stuck upon Poles near the Highway."[40] The climactic atrocity of the assault on Groton was that the Nipmucs, "with their wonted subtlety and barbarous cruelty . . . stripped the body of him whom they had slain in the first onset, and then cutting off his head, fixed it upon a pole looking towards his own Land. The corpse of the man slain the week before, they dug up out of his Grave, they cut off his head and one leg, and set them upon poles" (75). Hubbard evidently would have his reader believe that decapitation is a pagan cruelty Christians do not share. Yet Hubbard surely knew that in 1623 Miles Standish's pilgrims had impaled Chief Witawamet's head on a pole at Wessagusett, that Mohegans had sent in Narragansett heads to Boston in the 1640s, and that, in 1671, the head of the son of Nipmuc sachem Matoonas had been impaled on a pole on Boston Common. The effect is a reverse silencing. By refusing to consider that Indians might, like the English, convey the very same message through the same gruesome sign, Hubbard denies the Indian even the power of symbolic language.

A turning point for New England's wartime spirit was the capture of the defiant Narragansett chief Canonchet. Canonchet's reward for reputedly saying "he liked it well, that he should dye before his heart was soft, or had spoken anything unworthy of himself"[41] was to be described most fully by Nathaniel Saltonstall:

And that all might share in the Glory of destroying so great a Prince, and come under the Obligation of Fidelity each to other, the Pequods shot him, the Mohegins cut off his Head and quartered his Body, and the Ninnicrofts Men made the Fire and burned his Quarters; and as a Token of their Love and Fidelity to the English, presented his Head to the Council at Hartford.[42]

Saltonstall's account renders the Indian complicit in his own obliteration. Allied Indians serve as wordless factotums subservient to English power – shooting, beheading, quartering, burning. The end of their service is to present the trophy of Conanchet's forever silenced head to New England's recently federated civil authority, the Council at Hartford.

The execution of Canonchet prompted Benjamin Tompson to pen lines particularly revealing of wartime psychology:

> Some captiv'd, others wounded, many slain,
> Like Hydra's Heads, yet ne'r the less remain,
> And here that Lucifer receives defeat,

Who scorns with any less then Princes treat,
What necklace could New England better please
Then Heads strung thick upon a thred of these,
Him they dispatch, and hundreds more are hurl'd.
Him to attend upon in th'other world:
Whose hunting bouts will heavily go on,
His Legs must stay until the Head come on.[43]

Even though Conanchet has been decapitated, the heads of Indian Lucifers multiply in the forest of the mind without end. Tompson satirizes the Indian "phansie" of the hunting afterlife by taking perverse delight in imagining headless warriors hunting in their forest heaven. Unlike poets, Indians can never speak, even in the afterlife. When Tompson exclaims that the most pleasing outcome would be for (feminine) New England to display a necklace whose jewels would be a string of Indian heads, one wonders whether Tompson could conceive of any vengeance against the heathen Hydra that might be excessive.

The climax and resolution of the Indian wars was the sight of Philip's silenced head on a pike in Plymouth. Increase Mather first fashioned this outcome as a metaphor for triumphant walling out, then made the triumph conditional: "And *Philip*, who was the *Sheba*, that began & headed the Rebellion, his head is thrown over the wall, therefore have we good reason to hope that this *Day of Trouble* is near to an end, if our sins doe not undoe all that hath been wrought for us."[44] Philip's head may have been "thrown over the wall," but it would long rest on Plymouth's palisade. Although Cotton Mather, writing two decades later, knew the Indian wars were still continuing to the north, he elaborated his father's reference into an even headier triumph: "His [Philip's] *head* was carried in triumph to Plymouth, where it arrived on the very day that the church there was keeping a solemn thanksgiving to God. God sent 'em in the head of a leviathan for a thanksgiving-feast. *Sic pereat quisquis caeperit talia posthac.*"[45] A generational comparison here serves as the measure of Massachusetts's triumph. After nearly sixty years, the first Thanksgiving feast with Massassoit has evolved into the metaphoric devouring of Massassoit's son's head at yet another Plymouth Thanksgiving feast. To so cannibalize leviathan is, in Cotton Mather's view, not an act of savagery but one of triumph over it. No passage in New England historiography is more darkly perverse or oddly comparable to George Percy's account of the cannibalizing of Indian corpses in Jamestown. Mather's words show how fully New England had become immersed in its own time of trouble, its dark night of the soul.

In the folklore of New England Indians that William Simmons has preserved, there remains only one surviving native memory of King Philip's War. It was set down in 1936 and concerns a head.

Stories from the Leonard's and King Philip's families passed down from generation to generation say, that when Philip was killed his faithful warriors, not being able to steal the whole body, for fear of detection, stole the head of their chief, and hid it under the door step of the old Leonard homestead, in Taunton, until they could safely bury it, with all the sacred rituals due the mighty chief, who died for home and people. Indian tradition disputes history, and there are those who believe it, that the great sachem's head is buried between Taunton and Mt. Hope, and no one knows its resting place.[46]

History written in English leaves Philip's head on a pole in Plymouth for some twenty-five years, long enough for the curious or perhaps possessive fingers of Cotton Mather to detach Philip's jaw from his skull.[47] If the merciful God worshipped by New England's Christians exists, we should hope that the Wampanoags' restitutional legend about Philip's burial and the Leonard homestead records the truer version of the relic of Metacom's body.

Historians debate whether the war gained land wealth and promoted intercolonial cooperation – or bankrupted the treasury, aroused hostility in England and New York, and aggravated intercolonial rivalry. Francis Jennings argued plausibly that, although the English gained Indian land, New England became at war's end a "closed pocket," its growth halted by the aroused, hostile presence of Governor Andros and the newly formed Covenant Chain of Iroquois and Delaware tribes.[48] Stephen Saunders Webb has provided evidence of closure in the opposite direction. Because of contemptuous wartime articles published in the *London Gazette*, the Restoration government in England began regarding Boston magistrates as incompetent, backward-looking Puritans who could not protect their own settlers.[49] The depletion of New England's men and resources thus provided the first practicable opportunity as well as the rationale for turning the virtually independent trading company of Massachusetts Bay into a royal province. In Webb's view, "King Philip did more than any Englishman to end the independence of New England" (411).

King Philip's War had, however, an even more lasting geographical outcome. It consolidated and confined New England's regional identity in the very act of defining its expanded borders. The opening sentence of Cotton Mather's *Decennium Luctuosum* (1699) speaks of boundaries in a way not possible before 1675: "Twenty three years have Rolled Away since the

Nations of Indians within the Confines of New England, generally began a fierce War upon the English Inhabitants of that country."[50] The restricting word "confines" is here countered by the self-defining word "country," a term suggesting the known borders of an independent culture threatened from without yet defended by inner power. Its identity confirmed by unity within mapped limits, the New England *patria* could transform the defeats of the war into a sign that God's newly saved people could still achieve great things – if they could summon the faith needed for Justification and the energy needed for Sanctification.

Spiritual insight and literary skill are not the only reasons for the immediate and sustained popularity of Mary Rowlandson's *Narrative* (1682). The captivity narrative, as Rowlandson first established it, was conveniently ahistorical, written as if personal affliction should dominate communal or territorial concerns. From her opening sentence describing the moment of onslaught ("On the tenth of February 1675, Came the Indians with great numbers upon Lancaster"[51]) through the account of her ransom/redemption, Rowlandson shows little interest in discovering the group motives, past actions, future purposes, or even the tribal name of her captors. The brutalities committed against her family and community are an atrocity so collectively terrible that any consideration of historical circumstance is made to seem inhumanly dispassionate. The reader is given personal glimpses of Philip and Weetamo with no indication of their historical importance. The twenty "Removes" that organize the narrative create an almost placeless wilderness, in which the Indians are outside Christian time, *beyond* New England. Rowlandson's forced interest in Indian customs never enables her to see her captors as starving fugitives from at least three different tribes, who are being driven north away from supply lines and who need a seamstress to prepare winter coats as much as a monetary reward for ransom.[52]

The three powerful paragraphs with which Rowlandson's *Narrative* closes liken her personal sufferings, not to the possibly prideful model of Christ's suffering, but to the pre-Christian spirit of Ecclesiastes:

I have seen the extrem vanity of this World: One hour I have been in health, and wealth, wanting nothing: But the next hour in sickness and wounds, and death, having nothing but sorrow and affliction . . . The Lord hath shewed me the vanity of these outward things. That they are the Vanity of vanities, and vexation of spirit; that they are but a shadow, a blast, a bubble, and things of no continuance. (166)

To live among Indians is evidently to have nothing, even to be nothing except the memory of one's Christian identity. Unlike Increase Mather, who had listed all the likely reasons why God is afflicting New England, Mary Rowlandson can find no cause. At various moments, she suggests that God is deservedly chastising her people for their sins, or her community for its sins, or herself for her sins. But what those sins might be, she does not speculate. Consequently, her final words more closely resemble the Book of Job than the Congregational Way of Lancaster. Needing to believe that her afflictions must have been sent for just cause and good purpose, she can only have faith and wait: "Stand Still and see the salvation of the Lord" (167).

TRANSFORMING METACOM

Because the English colonists knew even less about "King Philip" than they would later know about Pontiac, Metacom readily served as a conveniently protean symbol, first of the worst, and later of the best, qualities that were not of New England/America. In 1675 and 1676 nearly all English colonists knew only that he was out there, just beyond the limits of Christian frontier communities, and that he was called "King Philip." As the war continued it became clear that the English had given him a name prophetic of far more than heathen conversion. Many a New Englander read Plutarch, who informed them that Philip of Macedon had unified barbarous northern tribes under his kingship and then made war against Athens for nearly twenty years, twice conquering the Athenian armies at Thermopylae. The Macedonian Philip had finally been brought down, not by a Greek army but like Metacom by an assassin from among his own people. In a kind of classical typology, Plutarch's remarks about the uncivilized loutishness of Macedonians living beyond the polis were being reenacted in the new world. As New England's Philip, Metacom readily assumed the face both of a wily diplomat and of an implacable militarist anxious to seize lands that, according to the true God(s), were not his.[53]

John Easton's "Relacion" brings us as close to the motives of the historical Metacom as we are ever likely to get. In early June 1675, just one week before the war began in Swansea, Deputy Governor Easton convinced "king Philop" and forty armed Wampanoags to join five Rhode Island officials in exploring prospects for securing a peace. Philip and his men limited their stated grievances almost entirely to long-standing practices of land dispossession: "They said all English agred against them, and so by arbetration thay had had much rong, mani miles square of land so taken from them ... now thay had no hopes left to kepe ani land"[54] Neither a forest Satan nor Nature's melancholy nobleman, Easton's Metacom is a clear-sighted pragmatist who leads his people into hard fighting only when he has to. Not until George Bancroft wrote his *History* was Easton's viewpoint to reemerge.

Benjamin Tompson's contradictory characterization of Philip, like his fragmented narrative, reflects his inability to resolve conflicting attitudes toward the event he called "New England's Crisis." Pity, curses, ridicule, and affectionate satire are meted out to both the English and the Indians. Even though Tompson laments New England's fall from the founders' "golden times" of love and faith, he himself clearly prefers rum to water, chocolate to Indian maize, fine houses to smoky huts, and gold to wampum.[55] Philip is introduced by speculations about his being the dupe of "some Romish Agent" (the French), or the victim of his own envy, or a deluded patriot who "to our lands pretended right" (86). But the question of Philip's motive is then dismissed as of no importance because "Indian spirits need / No grounds but lust to make a Christian bleed" (86).

After preparing to damn Philip for his heathen lust, Tompson's next lines reduce him to comic vulgarity as a "greazy *Lout*" (80). The twenty-line speech by which Philip then rouses tribal chieftains for war careens wildly in attitude and tone. Although Philip begins by denouncing both English greed and the naïveté of his own ancestors, the threat of credible protest against an English land grab is suddenly dissipated by his speaking gibberish and bad grammar. Phrases such as "Me meddle Squaw me hang'd" (87) and "This no wunnegin, so big matchit law" (86), show that Benjamin Tomson already well understood the rhetorical benefits of what was to be called "Hollywood Injin." The speech by which Philip then rouses his warriors makes no appeal to tribal pride, deserved vengeance, or even land repossession:

> Now if you'le fight Ile get you english coats,
> And wine to drink out of their Captains throats.
> The richest merchants houses shall be ours,
> Wee'l ly no more on matts or dwell in bowers
> Wee'l have their silken wives take they our Squaws. (87)

What is the reader to conclude when Tompson ascribes to the Indian the same greed for sensual pleasure he has smilingly condemned in his own generation of Englishmen and in himself?

Philip's role as Satan, much restrained in Tompson's poem, was to receive the fullest imaginable support from William Hubbard, who needed to depict Philip as the swampy source of external evil, not the agent of divine justice. Hubbard described Philip, severally, as "this treacherous and perfidious Caitiff" (13), "this bloody wretch" (102), "a spectacle of divine vengeance" (102), and "a Salvage and Wild Beast" to whom "The Devil appeared in a dream."[56] Like Cooper's Magua, Hubbard's Philip may be understood as a projection of the Englishman's worst qualities onto an external enemy, but Hubbard's evil Indian has not, like Cooper's, been brutalized by the military whip, nor does Hubbard allow Philip to question European principles of land title.

It was, surprisingly, the winning of the American Revolution that made a new perspective possible. The fact that in 1776 the still powerful Mohawks had sided with the British in New York City, rather than the patriots in Boston, showed that, at least since 1675, the Mohawks had had good reason to resent the incursions of westward-moving New England farmers. Even more important was the new, general association of true heroism with native-born resistance of imperial armies that included European mercenaries. Suddenly gone was the power of the Reverend Nathan Fiske's linking hypothetical redcoats threatening Brookfield in 1775 to the very real redskins who had decimated Brookfield in 1675.[57] Instead, a retrospective identification between the Minuteman and the Indian could be advanced on the grounds that both of them fought defensive wars for their natural right to determine their own lives on their own land. Hannah Adams provided, on behalf of King Philip, the same kind of revisionist challenge that Bancroft was to provide for Anne Hutchinson. Challenging the authority of William Hubbard and Daniel Neal, Adams praised Philip for his "undaunted courage" and "energy of mind," virtues that are inseparable from a "love of country" that is defined geographically.[58]

For the restitution of the Indian cause through literature, the importance of Washington Irving's inclusion of "Traits of Indian Character" and "Philip of Pokanoket" in his long popular *The Sketch Book* (1820) is hard to overestimate. Generations of readers were to discover, amidst ingratiating sketches of comic Dutchmen, genteel idlers and John Bull Englishmen, two abrasive essays in which Irving's cultivated bonhomie gives way to memorable denunciation of white racism. Provoked by anger at Andrew Jackson's 1814 campaign against the Creeks, Irving frontally attacked the genocidal implications of Indian dispossession, even though his test case lay in the New England past:

It is painful to perceive even from these partial narratives how the footsteps of civilization may be traced in the blood of the aborigines; how easily the colonists were moved to hostility by the lust of conquest; how merciless and exterminating was their warfare.[59]

To allege genocide by subverting the rhetoric of Hubbard and Mather was, however, a strategy made easier by existing tensions of regional identity. As a New Yorker speaking for expiring Dutch lassitude against selfish Yankee expansionism, Irving assesses New England historiography from without. He attends to the avalanche of Puritan defamation of King Philip and selects appropriate quotations to expose its prejudices. Would Irving's attack had been equally aggressive had the Iroquois rather than the Algonquin been the Indian people at issue?

Irving's Philip is fighting for even more than Hannah Adams's "love of country." "A patriot attached to his native soil," Philip fought "with an untamable love of natural liberty" (246–247). In the context of Philip's pre-Enlightenment era, when "aborigines" were all presumably savage and New Englanders acted with "disregard of the natural rights of their antagonists" (242), Philip is to be seen as a Byronic hero comparable to a "lonely bark foundering amidst darkness and tempest" (247). The sachem who seems never to have led Indians in an attack has become a "soldier daring in battle, firm in adversity, patient of fatigue, of hunger, of every variety of bodily suffering, and ready to perish in the cause he had espoused" (246). Such constancy of purpose, at odds with Irving's sense of the passing impetuousness of Indian attack, elevates Philip to possession of those "heroic qualities and bold achievements that would have graced a *civilized* warrior and have rendered him the theme of the poet and the historian" (247, emphasis mine). By such tacit exceptionalism, Irving's Philip is, like Cooper's Uncas, elevated beyond the race whose best qualities he exemplifies.

By 1829, when Lydia Maria Child published *The First Settlers of New England*, the refusal of many Cherokees to cede their land to Georgia had made Andrew Jackson's pending Indian Removal Bill a national controversy. Like Irving, Child recreates past Indian wars in order to suggest that the hypocrisies of today's land grab have a long history, but her indignation at racial and religious injustice is even more pointed and vehement. The book opens and closes with an attack on "the insatiable cupidity of the Georgians" and an explicit call to oppose Indian Removal, whether contractual or forced.[60] Granddaughter of a Medford Minuteman who had fought at Lexington, but daughter of an authoritarian Calvinist, Mrs. Child turns New England's Revolutionary love of liberty against New England's Puritan past, just as she turns her admiration for Milton's poetry against Milton's approval of male dominance.[61] Her purpose is "to prove, from the most authentic records, that the treatment they [American as well as New England Indians] have met with from the usurpers of their soil has been, and continues to be, in direct violation of the religious and civil institutions which we have heretofore so nobly defended, and by which we profess to be governed" (iv).

Purchasers encouraged by Mrs. Child's title to expect another exercise in regional filiopietism must have found that *The First Settlers of New England* unsettled all complacencies. Philip is presented as a proto-Revolutionary libertarian patriot, an "heroic chief" who "had displayed the most un-daunted determination to preserve his independence and guard the rights of his country against a foreign power" (145). Conversely, the Puritans who dispossessed New England Indians were guilty of far more than the "bigotry and cruel zeal" (90) charged against them by Hannah Adams and Washington Irving. To Mrs. Child, King Philip's War shows that the Puritan forefathers were not Christians: "It is highly derogatory to the character of our divine Master to call by his name those who have acted in direct op-position to his precepts and example" (42). Even worse, the anti-Christian conduct of New England soldiers is clearly accountable to "the odious doctrines set forth by Calvinistic preachers" (115). In 1675, New England's protestant spirit was revealed to have been corrupted in its Reformation origin.

To defend her generation's belief in God's libertarian Republic, Child at-tacks the determinism underlying the biblical notion of the chosen. To her, "the elect" refers not to the minority of saints within a given community, but to Puritan New England's way of seeing itself entire as a militantly holy region. She thus insists on separating the true Christianity of the loving Jesus from Deistic rationalism, from New England Calvinism, and from the spirit of the Old Testament. Instead of drawing lines of continuity in New England intellectual history across the Revolution, Child severs them, denying that the male Calvinistic past lives on in New England's present generation. Evangelical piety is thereby joined to post-Revolutionary lib-ertarian politics and to notions of enlightened New England womanhood in a way that prefigures the fictions of Harriet Beecher Stowe.

William Apess delivered his "Eulogy on King Philip" (1836) after Jackson's Removal Bill had been passed in Congress, shortly after Georgia began selling Cherokee lands in a lottery, and at the time when a majority of the Cherokee, supported by some Christian churches and many a Whig politician and newspaper, were protesting vehemently against the forced removal that would soon result in the Trail of Tears. It was the exact his-torical moment for the gathering spirit of protest to be expressed in its most outspoken form by someone living between red and white traditions. William Apess was a Pequot of half- and mixed blood whose white grandfather had married the granddaughter of Metacom. By 1835 he had spent some ten years as a Methodist preacher riding circuit among white, red, and black congregations.[62]

Apess's multicultural heritage enabled him to devise a new conception of Philip as defender of the Indian peoples. Because Irving and Child had objectified Philip as a noble victim belonging to a wronged and separate race, neither writer had been able to conceive of the Indian, past or present, as a participant citizen of New England or America. Apess is the writer who, after 150 years of literary and historiographical exclusion, writes the Indian back in to New England/America. By his bodily presence before the audience in Boston's Odeon, delivering the Lord's Prayer in Pequot and claiming descent from Philip, Apess refuted the popular fictional ideal of "the last of" a native people. When Apess claimed, in his second paragraph, that Philip died for a cause "as glorious as the *American* Revolution," he removed Philip from the contemporary bipolar rhetoric of civilization versus savagery, transforming him into an able leader whose defense of his people would "appeal to the lovers of liberty" wherever in the new world they might arise.[63] Apess's comparisons of Philip to George Washington acknowledged the cultural differences between the two heroic leaders while insisting that both acted upon revolutionary American notions of Liberty.[64]

Whether Apess was more strongly influenced by the Jeffersonian principle that all men are created equal or by the biblical claim that all men are descended from Adam is not easy to discern. Whichever it may be, the chief casualty of Apess's reformulation was New England historiography. Apess reserves his most abrasive language for his account of the landing of the Pilgrims. The much touted arrival at Plymouth Rock was, as Apess sees it, an invasion that would provoke Philip and the Wampanoags to try and enact the "American" Revolution a century before its time:

December (O.S.) 1620, the pilgrims landed at Plymouth, and without asking liberty from any one they possessed themselves of a portion of the country, and built themselves houses, and then made a treaty, and commanded them [the Wampanoags] to accede to it. This, if now done, would be called an insult, and every man would be called to go out and act the part of a patriot, to defend their country's rights; and if every intruder were butchered, it would be sung upon every hill-top in the Union, that victory and patriotism was the order of the day. (10–11)

Apess's use of the word "invasion" is perhaps the first extant example in Native American literature of Dee Brown's well-known demand that the history of white – Indian relations must be rewritten facing east rather than west.[65]

The Puritans' selling of Indian captives, especially Philip's son, into Caribbean slavery prompts Apess to turn the accusation of bestiality back upon the victors, turning the Puritan into the slave master. Apess's anger focuses in particular on the "sickening" language of Increase Mather, and the safe, smug judgments of his son, "the pious Dr. Mather," who never seems to have been aware that "God did not make His red children for him to curse."[66] Because Apess sees slavery as a multiracial practice extending from seventeenth-century New England to nineteenth-century Georgia, the sins of the New England clergy become original: "I do not hesitate to say, that through the prayers, preaching and examples of those pretended pious, has been the foundation of all the slavery and degradation in the American Colonies, towards colored people" (50). To thus hold Hubbard and the Mathers responsible for the legalization of slavery in the southern colonies and the Constitution is of course patently unfair, another example of ascribing more national influence to New England than New England can bear. But the primary intent of Apess's revisionism, despite his fleeting prejudice against Negroes, was to forge a bond between "colored people" as victims of slavery. The best way for all New Englanders – white, red, and black – to celebrate the arrival at Plymouth Rock would be to bury it (20). In words remarkably like those of Frederick Douglass's speech at Rochester on July 4, 1852, Apess insists that, for Indians as well as Negroes, the two celebrated dates of New England/American founding convey a special degradation: "We say, therefore, let every man of color wrap himself in mourning, for the 22nd of December and the 4th of July are days of mourning and not of joy" (20).

As the Whig candidate for Governor of Massachusetts in 1835, Edward Everett was afforded the perfect occasion, while commemorating the 1675 Nipmuc "Massacre" of "the flower of Essex County" at "Bloody Brook" near South Deerfield, for advancing himself by indulging in easy race-baiting together with heroicizing of ancestral martyrs. To his credit, Everett almost entirely resisted the temptation. Consistent with his bitter opposition to Jackson's Indian Removal Bill in Congress five years before, Everett refused to exonerate Euro-American land hunger, insisting that the Indian "fought for his native land" and that "no great reproach" should be leveled against the Nipmuc or Puritan in a war of such tragic inevitability.[67] Everett even invented a timeless Indian chief who questions, in words very like Tecumseh's in 1810, "How could my father sell that which the Great Spirit sent me into the world to live upon?"[68] After considerable preparatory research into historical sources, Everett had recognized that nearly everything asserted about Philip, by his romanticizers as well as his detractors, was legendary, nothing more than a sign of how "the terror of his name wrought powerfully on weaker minds" (604). Although the fertile cornfields around South Deerfield justified Indian dispossession within the stadialist perspective of civilization's progressive stages, Everett's controlling purpose for retelling the massacre of 1675 was fundamentally consolatory: to show why, by 1836, "that blood has sunk not forgotten but forgiven into the ground" (610).

Unfortunately, neither Everett's spirit of reconciliation nor active protest of the kind advanced by Child and Apess was to be the dominant response evoked by Philip's memory during the next half-century. The circulation of Mrs. Child's book and of the speeches by Apess and Everett were to be short-lived and very largely limited to Boston. Year after year until the late 1880s thousands of audiences in eastern, midwestern, and western cities went to see Edwin Forrest and his successors play King Philip in John Augustus Stone's melodrama *Metamora: Chief of the Wampanoags* (1829). Accounts of the play's effect need to be written in broad psychological strokes, as well as performance details.[69] *Metamora* proved to be the perfect vehicle for invoking the white American's guilt, and then releasing the white American's fear, without asking of its audience anything beyond a passive shudder.

Philip is introduced as "Metamora, the noble sachem of a valiant race – the white man's dread, the Wampanoag's hope."[70] Emphasizing both Puritan greed and the savagery of Indian retaliation, Stone's play centers on soliloquies in which Metamora becomes "dread" personified, calling down curses upon the white race. Very much as in captivity narratives, Metamora prophesies that "The war whoop shall start you from your dreams at night, and the red hatchet gleam in your burning dwellings" (23). The play ends as the dying Metamora calls down a curse upon the white race: "Murderers! The last of the Wampanoags curses be on you! May your graves and the graves of your children be in the path the red man shall trace! And may the wolf and panther howl o'er your fleshless bones, fit banquet for the destroyers" (40). While Indian nation after Indian nation was being dispossessed, killed and/or removed to a reservation, the audiences who kept coming to Stone's play surely knew that, in fact, exactly the reverse was occurring: the graves of red children continued to be in the white man's path, and the barren banqueting was still on Indian, not English bones. Whatever degree of thrilling guilt Metamora's denunciations may have momentarily induced, the audience could leave consoled by having seen the curtain drop on the suicidal death of a vengeful chieftain. Precisely because it lacked historical accuracy, the long cultural life of Stone's melodrama would end only after the Massacre at Wounded Knee and the official closing of the frontier.

In the year General Winfield Scott was assembling federal troops to remove the Cherokee, George Bancroft published the second volume of his *History* (1837), including his account of King Philip's War. At that time, Bancroft was a rising Massachusetts Democrat promoting workingmen's and educational issues. Understandably wary of offending Jackson and Van Buren over the bitterly contested policy of Indian Removal, Bancroft was also a friend and admirer of prominent New England Whigs, especially Edward Everett, whose recently published oration at Bloody Brook Bancroft read carefully. To evaluate King Philip's War under these circumstances was no easy task for a nationalist like Bancroft who was committed both to Anglo-American progress and to man's antecedent natural rights, individual and collective, as advanced during the Enlightenment.

Despite footnotes citing a commendably wide range of historical sources, Bancroft sweeps aside all arguments about the provoking incidents of the war, all the various allegations of Indian or white racial cruelty, all satanizing of Metacom, all accounts of the war's atrocities, all judgments that derive from the writer's religious creed.[71] Instead he sees the war in terms that approximate the long-term lens of an economic realist. By 1675 the insoluble problem for the Indian had become the prosperity of the English: "this prosperity itself portended danger; for the increase of the English alarmed the race of red men, who could not change their habits, and who saw themselves deprived of their usual means of subsistence."[72] The problem was not merely that the Indians misunderstood land sales, nor that the English broke treaties and land agreements. It was rather that, in 1675, the Wampanoags, Nipmucs, and Narragansetts rightly realized that they "were now shut in by the gathering plantations of the English and were thus the first to awaken to a sense of the danger of extermination" (98). As Hartford and New Haven plantations expanded from the southwest, as Boston expanded from the northeast, and as Providence expanded within their midst, New England's southern Indians realized "the ever urgent importunity of the English" for their territory (99). "As the English villages drew nearer and nearer to them, their hunting-grounds were put under culture . . . their natural parks were turned into pastures; their best fields for planting corn were gradually alienated" (99). Here is an argument for the primacy of economic and geographic enclosure that would have seemed secondary to Child or Apess, false to Hubbard or Cotton Mather, but essential to Francis

Jennings's insistence that King Philip's War was "the Second Puritan Conquest."[73]

However compelling Bancroft's argument may now seem, it left him in 1837 in a quandary over the issue of land ownership. Although Bancroft's phrasing continually admits Indian rights of land ownership ("their hunting grounds," "their natural parks," "their best fields"), to have explicitly argued for Indian ownership of land would have rekindled the controversy over Indian Removal at a time when Bancroft surely wished it resolved in the Democratic way. And so Bancroft wrote but one sentence addressing the general issue of land ownership as perceived by Indians being dispossessed: "But the unlettered savage who repented the alienation of vast tracts, by affixing a shapeless mark to a bond, might deem the English tenure defeasible" (98). Bancroft's usually clear and vigorous prose here falls into tellingly awkward syntax, abstract diction, and transparent hedging: Indians who "*repented* the *alienation* of vast tracts" "*might* deem the English tenure *defeasible*" indeed!

Bancroft's characterization of Philip aligns his *History* with the view of many a well-intentioned contemporary who believed that the sadly compromised dispossession of the Indian was nonetheless inevitable. Bancroft grants Philip honorable patriotism and strategic skill, but concentrates on rendering him a Man of Feeling, said to shed tears when the first white man was killed. Philip's weeping is then offered as a sign of his foresight into the inevitable:

For what prospect had he of success? Destiny had marked him and his tribe . . . The individual, growing giddy by danger, rushes, as it were, towards his fate; so did the Indians of New England. Frenzy prompted their rising. It was but the storm in which the ancient inhabitants of the land were to vanish away. They rose without hope, and, therefore, they fought without mercy. For them as a nation, there was no to-morrow. (101)

To Bancroft, Philip remains an admirable figure because the war he led was a past storm that, leaving no apparent Indian survivors, has presumably left no enduring Indian problem in New England.[74] The implication of Bancroft's storm metaphor for future Indian wars farther west (blue skies follow tribal extermination) is harshly dismissive. These sentences seem not to be penned by the same author who, in his preceding volume, had regarded the equally notorious Anne Hutchinson as a progenitor of democratic rights of conscience. To Bancroft, contemporary Indians remained a foreign people, or, at most, in John Marshall's memorable phrase, a "domestic dependent nation."

In comparison to Palfrey's rendering of King Philip's War, Bancroft's seems the essence of charity. Only with regard to Massachusetts's treatment of Indian captives does Palfrey acknowledge that there had been English injustice: "The selling of man, woman or child to be a slave, is a horrible act."[75] Beyond this one criticism, hardly daring in 1864, Palfrey grants white New Englanders everything and New England Indians nothing. Citing Josiah Winslow is sufficient evidence for Palfrey to deny that there had ever been forced land sales, misunderstood treaties, or fraudulent promises. Indians in their Natural State (i.e., precontact) are called "brutal savages" (140); King Philip's War is "a succession of ruthless ravages" committed by the Indians (214). In an implicit challenge to Bancroft, population figures are cited to demonstrate that in 1675 there was plenty of land left for both races to continue to live separately, hopefully forever. The troubling testimony of John Easton is to be disregarded because anyone whose spelling was so inaccurate must have been "grossly illiterate" (180). Behind Philip's phony title of "king," Palfrey claims, was only "the form of a squalid savage, whose palace was a sty; whose royal robe was a bearskin or a coarse blanket alive with vermin" (223).

So wholly racialist and racist an account of Metacom leaves the viewpoint of William Hubbard virtually intact. By the 1890s, Palfrey's attitudes were to become dominant; romantic writers were judged as racial sentimentalists, and the economic realism of George Bancroft was rarely mentioned. Even after passage of the Dawes Severalty Act in 1887, there were thought to be too many Indians still needing to be dispossessed. Robert Lowell's metaphor had become fully appropriate: Philip's head was grinning silently on its platter and anathema needed to be hurled across the racial divide. Those anathemas would not be fully voiced and widely heard, however, until the time of Vine Deloria Jr. and the Red Power Movement, twenty years after the publication of Lowell's prescient "At the Indian Killer's Grave."

CHAPTER 5

The axe at the root of the tree: Scarlet Governors and Gray Champions

UNANIMOUS RESOLUTION

To substantiate how universal progress was inexorably growing from new world Protestantism, nineteenth-century New Englanders needed to believe that England's "Glorious Revolution" of 1688 had at least prefigured, if not predetermined, the still more glorious revolution of 1775. As they saw it, the American Revolution had been courageously initiated by a sequence of popular *defensive* revolts in the Province of Massachusetts, beginning with the protest against the Stamp Act and closing with the fortifying of Bunker Hill. Because the Glorious Revolution of 1688 had resulted from the protestant need to wrest legislative power away from the absolutism of pro-Catholic Stuart monarchs, the creating of the American Republic by rebellion against England required that special attention be given to finding a New England precedent. Tracing Whig commitments to individual property, religious toleration, and representative legislatures back to John Locke, Algernon Sidney, or even John Milton was a useful public endeavor, well enough and good, but only so long as the pre-Revolutionary moment when the torch of Protestant Liberty had passed over to New England/America could still be clearly identified.

To antebellum New Englanders, the crisis moment of pre-Revolutionary revolution was not the Great Migration of 1630 (knowledgeable people recognized that the Massachusetts Bay Puritans had neither separated from England nor brooked toleration) but the 1689 revolt against Governor Edmund Andros. In 1820 Daniel Webster famously asserted that the revolt against Andros had been "the first scene of that great revolutionary drama, which was to take place nearly a century afterward."[1] The Websterian model was restorative: when third generation New Englanders rose against their first royally appointed governor and threw the minions of monarchy into jail for repeated violations of colonial rights, the beleaguered chosen people were thought to have defended British constitutional law, as well as

God's law, while engaging in a minimum of holy violence against England itself.

The second volume of George Bancroft's *History* (1837) ends with a climactic chapter on the crises of 1688–1689 that briefly summarizes the revolts in New York and Maryland, but which lavishes many pages on Massachusetts. Bancroft concentrates his readers' attention on the moment in front of the Boston town house when, after the British and New York appointees to Andros's council have been jailed, the last elected governor reappears before the people:

> Just then, the last governor of the colony, in office when the charter was abrogated, Simon Bradstreet, glorious with the dignity of four-score years and seven, one of the early emigrants, a magistrate in 1630, whose experience connected the oldest generation with the new, drew near the townhouse, and was received by a great shout from the freemen. The old magistrates were reinstated, as a council of safety; the whole town rose in arms, "with the most unanimous resolution that every inspired a people" and a Declaration, read from the balcony, defended the insurrection as a duty to God and the country.[2]

Except for the exalting phrase "glorious with . . . dignity," every detail of this passage may be traced back to a contemporary account, even the quotation about "unanimous resolution" which Bancroft took without attribution, and then slightly altered, from the *Magnalia*. (Cotton Mather had taken that same quotation, without attribution, and then slightly altered it, from "An Account of the Late Revolutions" written by "A.B." and dated June 16, 1689.[3])

To summon up the symbolic figure of Simon Bradstreet in this manner enabled Bancroft to imply the continuity of the Puritan will to independence without raising the specter of communal decline so prevalent in the sermons of the 1670s. Embodying the presumably unchanged spirit of New England "Freemen" (voters as well as church members) from 1630 to 1689 and beyond, Bradstreet emerges from the throng of angry citizens who acclaim his right to magistracy. Bradstreet's inspirational presence leads immediately to the reading of an unquoted "Declaration" that is said to defend insurrection as a duty, not only to God, but also to "the country." This climactic moment occurs at the end of a narrative that begins with Bancroft picturing "Sir Edmund Andros, glittering in scarlet and lace" disembarking at Boston to initiate a régime "the most vexatious and tyrannical to which men of English descent were ever exposed" (II, 425, 426). Among the tyrannies of empire, Bancroft emphasizes those that were to be imposed yet again during the decade after 1765: dismissing colonial legislatures, disbanding town meetings, censoring colonial publications, quartering redcoats in Boston, and especially, taxation without representation. From the pivotal year of 1689, Bancroft then projects the spirit of libertarian resistance backward and forward, portraying the region's clergy, magistracy, and people as united in one common effort. "The spirit which led forth the colonies of New England, kept their liberties alive," Bancroft insists: "in the general gloom, the ministers preached sedition, and planned resistance" (II, 431). Here is the Black Regiment emerging nearly a century ahead of its time.

To Bancroft, the sign of divine favor upon democracy had to lie in the spontaneity of popular uprisings on its behalf. The sanctity of the popular will demanded that New England's Freemen must have innately and immediately recognized the duty of libertarian resistance, not by authority of the biblical word, but as a principle of progressive protestantism. Accordingly, at the moment of crisis in 1689, there had to have been neither internal division nor advance planning. Response had been swift but leaderless; there had been no violence, no mobocracy. Bancroft acknowledged that Joseph Dudley, late born son of founding patriarch Thomas Dudley, had more than willingly done James II's bidding when he had agreed to serve as the president of New England's appointed, provisional government during the year before Sir Edmund's arrival. But after dismissing Joseph Dudley as "a degenerate son of the colony," Bancroft keeps Dudley off stage, preferring to emphasize how Andros and his "lean wolves of tyranny" enraged the local population (II, 425, 428). When the moment of uprising arrives, Bancroft's cast of historical characters has been handily narrowed into a stark contrast between a cabal of high-living British aristocrats and a rightly angered people grimly defending their land. Because there are no opposing interests within New England, nothing that suggests internal divisions of party, the revolt occurs with spontaneous integrity claimed in the sentence "Massachusetts rose in arms, and perfected its revolution without concert" (II, 448).

At the end of his narrative, Bancroft advances the sweeping claim that in 1689 the force of a "popular insurrection" whose "object was Protestant liberty" began to spread from the new world back to the old: "Boston was the centre of the revolution which now spread to the Chesapeake; in less than a century, it would commence a revolution for humanity, and rouse a spirit of power to emancipate the world" (II, 449). From this perspective, the "Glorious Revolution" had truly occurred, not in England in 1688, but in Massachusetts in 1689. Long before the Minutemen rose at Lexington and Concord, Boston had become the hub of the universe around which the revolutionary history of human liberty was to turn.

On this triumphant note, Bancroft's second volume ends, adding only a coda of tribute to Calvinism (astonishing for an historian so reputedly "Transcendental" or "Jacksonian") in which we learn, surely apropos of 1775, that "Calvinism rejected the herd of reprobates: Massachusetts inexorably disfranchised Churchmen, royalists, and all the world's privileged people" (II, 461). Instead of recalling that, once William and Mary had ascended the throne, the citizens of Massachusetts had professed the greatest loyalty to their protestant monarchs, Bancroft's second volume concludes with a claim better suited to John Endicott or Sam Adams. Both before and after 1689, Bancroft contends, "Massachusetts owned no king but the King of heaven; no aristocracy but of the redeemed" (II, 462).

The importance to Hawthorne of his tale about 1689, "The Gray Champion," cannot be understood apart from his desire to publicize himself as a New England author prepared to represent – not shyly withdraw from – the accepted historical attitudes of his time. First published in the *New England Magazine* in 1835, Hawthorne chose "The Gray Champion" to be the lead story in both the first and expanded editions of *Twice-Told Tales*. As much as any of his other fictions, "The Gray Champion" served Hawthorne as his signature piece, the story by which he might secure a regional and perhaps a national audience.

Hawthorne's opening and closing paragraphs are, if anything, even more ringingly patriotic than Bancroft's account, which was to be published two years later. Whereas Bancroft was to belittle James II through irony (James II "gave up three kingdoms for a mass," II, 444), Hawthorne appeals to long-standing anti-Stuart prejudice (James II is "the bigoted successor of Charles the Voluptuous").[4] Ignoring Andros's military service on New England's frontier as well as James II's Declaration of Indulgence, Hawthorne condemns Andros by introducing him as "a harsh and unprincipled soldier" sent "to take away *our* liberties and endanger *our* religion" (9, italics mine). In a deft summary with which Bancroft was fully to concur, Hawthorne's next sentence cites the specifics of imperial tyranny, thereby implying a direct continuity between the oppressive monarchies of 1689 and 1775:

The administration of Sir Edmund Andros lacked scarcely a single characteristic of tyranny: a Governor and Council, holding office from the King, and wholly independent of the country; laws made and taxes levied without concurrence of the people, immediate or by their representatives; the rights of private citizens violated, and the titles of all landed property declared void; the voice of complaint stifled by restrictions on the press; and, finally, disaffection overawed by the first band of mercenary troops that ever marched on our free soil. (9)

For once, Hawthorne approvingly quotes Cotton Mather, describing Edward Randolph as a "blasted wretch" and "our arch enemy" (13). Throughout the tale, Hawthorne's political values are so decisively regional that he even ascribes guilt to the unflappably ambitious Joseph Dudley. Hawthorne pictures Dudley riding beside Andros "with a downcast look, dreading, as well he might, to meet the indignant gaze of the people, who beheld him, their only countryman by birth, among the oppressors of his native land" (13).

After the Puritan Gray Champion has "emerged from among the people" (14) to face down Andros and the redcoats, Hawthorne's last paragraph pulls out all the rhetorical stops needed for a resounding New England Gloria. The Gray Champion, symbol of an aged yet timeless Puritan will to independence, will reappear during the crises of New England history: the Boston Massacre, Lexington and Concord, and Bunker Hill. The tale's last sentence, however, expresses a tellingly complex and divided response to the Grey Champion's reappearance in New England's un-Puritan future:

Long, long may it be, ere he comes again! his hour is one of darkness, and adversity, and peril. But should domestic tyranny oppress us, or the invader's step pollute our soil, still may the Gray Champion come, for he is the type of New England's hereditary spirit; and his shadowy march, on the eve of danger, must ever be the pledge, that New-England's sons will vindicate their ancestry. (18)

Pride here mingles with apprehension, regret with anticipation, resolution with worry. As a contemporary New Englander, Hawthorne acknowledges that he, perhaps like his readers, can no longer claim to welcome regional crises as a furnace of soul testing. "Providential Afflictions," to use a pre-1689 vocabulary, can no longer clearly demonstrate a communal will to "regeneracy." Nonetheless, Hawthorne affirms that an "hereditary spirit" originating in the Puritans is the means by which future New Englanders – at least those of Puritan ancestry – will (somehow) summon the courage to overcome new trials. A regional spirit of courageous self-definition has presumably survived its own outdated theology, but what henceforth is to be its spiritual foundation? Hawthorne imagines future crises arising from without the region ("domestic tyranny," "the invader's step") while disregarding the evidence, quickly accumulating in 1835, that regional complicity with slavery was to constitute New England's next and perhaps greatest trial. Clearly, Hawthorne's need at tale's end was to sustain confidence among

New England readers who still saw their region as origin and prototype for the nation.

First and last paragraphs do not an entire tale make. The sunset march of Andros and his redcoats on April 17, 1689, the appearance of the defiant Gray Champion, and the sullen withdrawal of the British have no historical validity except of the most general and symbolic kind. If, however, Hawthorne sought the freedom of fiction as a license for unalloyed vindication of New England ancestors, the narrative he devised raises formidable problems. Like Bancroft, Hawthorne pictures two groups of massed force (Andros with his wine-flushed redcoats confronting "the people") and thereby recognizes no party division within New Englanders. But Hawthorne does not, as Bancroft does, offer up Simon Bradstreet as the living embodiment of timeless Puritan courage. Instead, after the crowd shouts "Stand firm for the old charter Governor!" Hawthorne describes Bradstreet as "a patriarch of nearly ninety, who appeared on the elevated steps of a door, and with characteristic mildness, besought them to submit to the constituted authorities" (12).

Because Bradstreet the patriarch gives in with such surprising ease, the quasisupernatural appearance of the fictive Gray Champion becomes necessary. Hawthorne was caught in a quandary between historical accuracy and regional legend. His dispirited New Englanders have retained only the exterior strengths of Puritan forefathers ("sober garb . . . general severity of mien . . . scriptural forms of speech," 10). The popular will to resist must therefore come from without and not, as Bancroft would have it, from within. A literary symbol was needed to do the presumably heroic work of history. Surely, therefore, Hawthorne did not graft the Angel of Hadley legend from King Philip's War on to the events of 1689 merely because he found it dramatically useful to do so.[5] He recognized that the historical evidence for comforting assertions of unchanging regional courage was not there in the facts of the past. An affirmative conclusion had to be reached by other means. The revolution of 1689, Hawthorne knew, was soon to be followed by other crises: the Provincial Charter, the Salem witch trials, and a devastating sequence of French and Indian wars. And yet, in a story assuring us of the Gray Champion's ready reappearance, we are also told, "the men of that generation watched for his re-appearance, in sunshine and in twilight, but never saw him more" (17).

The historical prototype for the Gray Champion, Hawthorne suggests, was William Goffe, a British Puritan who, after signing the death warrant for Charles I, hid out in Hadley, Massachusetts after the Restoration, and then appeared unexpectedly to rally his townsmen against an attack by the Nipmucs. As a model of regional virtue, the figure of William Goffe would logically suggest that "the type of New England's hereditary spirit" actually originates in Old England rather than New, and that its innermost spirit is one of king-killing, rather than a defense of constitutional rights. These are, of course, implications that Hawthorne refuses to make explicit. Robin Molineux's nightmarish exposure to the eager violence of Boston's revolutionary patriots could, however, be cited in support of them.

Bancroft's version of Hawthorne's narrative remains a decidedly in-house disagreement about regional historiography. In Hawthorne's tale, as in Bancroft's history, the perception of the New England/American's hereditary spirit depends on emphasizing the three days in mid-April 1689 when Governor Andros's tyrannies were forcibly ended and he and his royalist councilors were imprisoned prior to extradition. By summarizing selected tyrannies of the royally appointed governor, by expanding on the unanimous uprising of "the people," and by predicting the restoration of regional liberties, the revolution of 1689 served both as the type of 1775 (Puritan teleological politics) and as the germ of progress within the common, property-owning people of America (Jacksonian teleological politics). Hawthorne's and Bancroft's strategy was to isolate the moment in which a determined people threw off the wine-flushed royalists. To have recalled the full historical context of the crisis of April 18, 1689 would have demanded an inquiry dangerous in kind and uncertain in outcome. Few of us willingly undertake the subversion of cherished cultural beliefs whose power to strengthen popular resolve has been repeatedly demonstrated. To those troubling facts we now turn.[6]

BRADSTREET: "HUMBLY BOLD TO SUPPLICATE"

Why did Edward Randolph, even more than William Blathwayt, Edmund Andros, or Joseph Dudley, acquire and long retain the mantle of New England's arch enemy? According to Michael Hall's amply substantiated account, Randolph was a doggedly diligent and law honest bureaucrat intent on carrying out the policies of the Lords of Trade – not a political subversive, not a Catholic absolutist, not a Puritan hater, not even an Anglophile wishing to be seen sneering at New England provinciality.[7] The underlying reason why New Englanders so detested Randolph should rather be sought in his four years of service as Collector of Customs for New England. Week after week, year after year, Randolph and his assistants walked the Boston waterfront trying with little success to enforce the Navigation and Plantation Acts. Of the thirty-six cases Randolph brought before the local courts, whose juries consisted entirely of Freemen, Randolph obtained exactly two convictions. Only in 1686, when Joseph Dudley became provisional president and appointed the Admiralty courts, did convictions under the various navigation laws become regularly obtainable.

Hostility to Randolph ultimately reflects a long-standing issue of jurisdiction. When the Stuarts were restored to the throne in 1660, New England officials of Puritan conviction assumed that the commonwealth status granted to Massachusetts in 1654 by Oliver Cromwell remained in force. As soon as the charter of 1629 was directly threatened by a writ of *quo warranto*, Deputy Samuel Nowell, ever the advocate of preparedness, was provoked to respond "By our Pattent we have full and absolute power to rule and governe, pardon and punish."[8] The General Court, however, did not fully support such independence of spirit. By the early 1680s many a Massachusetts deputy was willing to relent to British demands that the suffrage be widened to include freeholders and that the Anglican Church be tolerated. Moreover, it was difficult to argue convincingly that the Navigation and Plantation Acts were illegal. Nonetheless, from the time of Randolph's arrival until Andros's departure, inflammatory tinder was struck whenever British officials acting under British law tried to take cash from New England pockets. The members of the General Court knew that customs taxes eventually raised costs for all New Englanders, not just Boston merchants. Because enforcing of the "just price" had been abandoned, increased costs would eventually be passed along to country purchasers of imported goods. Despite increasing distinctions of religion and class, a common economic interest bound countryside to town.

After the old charter was revoked in 1684, the British government, with the encouragement of Randolph, Dudley, and Blathwayt, promptly reorganized select colonies as "The Dominion of New England." The ironies of this name remain almost inexhaustible. The four years of the Dominion's existence are the only time when the words "New England" have ever described a governing political entity, yet few New Englanders, however loyal to the King of England or cooperative with Andros, ever publicly acknowledged its legitimacy. Defenders of Massachusetts's old charter conveniently ignored parallel changes occurring in New York and Maryland, where old charters were being vacated by English courts, royally appointed governors were being challenged by the colonists, but new provincial charters with royal governors and partially elected legislatures were emerging as a compromise. Because these kinds of silence continued in Massachusetts for six years, they reflect more than an information lag or insularity fostered by the Commonwealth's now tarnished belief that God's chosen were preserved for special destiny. To deal extensively with the "Dominion of New England" was to legitimate the political reality of everything which most Massachusetts citizens, "puritan" or not, believed New England never had been and hopefully never would be.

By 1688 "The Dominion of New England in America," according to Governor-General Andros's newly revised commission, consisted of all lands from the mouth of the St. Croix River north to the St. Lawrence, south to the Delaware, and west from the Atlantic Ocean to the "South Sea."[9] That is to say, even if we set aside such an imaginary westward claim, the Dominion of New England comprised the land of eight present states and included peoples ranging from French Catholics in southern Quebec to Quakers in what is now Burlington, New Jersey. Dominion status not only nullified the old charter; its existence replaced the United Colonies of New England, whose commissioners and armies had done so much during King Philip's War to define what "New England" actually was (Massachusetts Bay, Plymouth, and Connecticut, with outposts in Maine and New Hampshire, and by 1680, though grudgingly, Rhode Island!). Disbanding the Massachusetts General Court led to the creation of a council appointed by an (appointed) governor-general. Although Massachusetts was to be allotted the greatest number of council members (ten), New York was allotted eight and Rhode Island seven, while Connecticut and Maine were each allotted two, and New Hampshire and the recently acquired "Narragansett Country" were allotted only one.[10]

The Dominion of New England was to be controlled by the council in Boston, but the lack of a quorum requirement enabled six or seven council members, including New Yorkers newly resident in Boston, to gather and to approve legislation. "With the advise and consent of our said Councill" Governor-General Andros was granted unilateral powers "to make, constitute and ordain lawes, statutes and ordinances," to "impose, assess and raise and levy rates and taxes," and to appoint all judicial officers without restriction of qualification.[11] Shortly after assuming office, Andros announced a penny per pound tax on imports. Because the old charter had been vacated, it was decided that not all colonial land titles would be confirmed; some would have to be repatented, for which a fee would of course be charged. Under the protection of King James II's Declaration of Indulgence, Anglican services were held in Boston's South Church while its Congregational members, some of whom had founded the church, waited outside for their turn to worship God in a now merely different manner. Old visual symbols came back to haunt in new forms. With council encouragement, maypoles were constructed in Boston and Charlestown.

The Dominion of New England even had its own ultra-royalist flag: a white background with a red cross and a gold crown embossed with the letters J. R. Even if the Gray Champion were still surviving in the hearts of the people, there seemed no longer to be a John Endicott to cut down Boston's Maypole or to cut the red cross from the flag of James Rex.

For the next century, French wars would prove to be as expensive a proposition for the British as for the Bourbons. Like the Stamp Act of 1765, a new import duty, the Penny Pound, was demanded of the colonists shortly after their costly victory over border Indians. The Lords of Trade believed that, by creating the Dominion of New England, a centralized system of taxation could extract needed funds from northern colonies whose treasuries had been suspiciously claimed to be empty since King Philip's War. By building eight forts along the New Hampshire–Maine frontier, Governor-General Andros believed he could fight France in the new world while simultaneously protecting militarily incompetent New Englanders from French and Indian attack. These were, however, the wider views of empire that it was not in New England's present interest to understand. Versailles and London were an ocean away. Although Virginians might have needed British troops to subdue Bacon's Rebellion, New Englanders had fought King Philip without British cash or British soldiers. Would God have permitted his chartered land to prosper, only now to favor Anglican newcomers who sought to nullify His political covenant with New England?

By such appeals Increase Mather in 1684 convinced the citizenry of Boston – or was it just the Freemen? – to vote unanimously at a town meeting not to submit to the *quo warranto* against the Charter.[12] The presumed unanimity of this moment became the prime source of the insistence on "unanimous resolution" that would resound in New England histories from Cotton Mather through George Bancroft. By slighting the likelihood that all voting Freemen had been church members sympathetic to Mather's appeal to chartered spirituality, Bancroft could write as if his contemporaries' notions of democratic vote and popular will had been fully operative in the 1680s.

In historical fact, by the time the revolt against Andros occurred, the balance of political and ecclesiastical power had shifted markedly. During the five years before 1689, merchants who were not church members had gained influence through quiet cooperation with the Andros government. Other merchants who had become church members, as well as the clergy who confirmed them (men as influential as William Phips, Bartholomew Gedney, Samuel Shrimpton, Reverend Samuel Willard, and Reverend Cotton Mather), had good reason to detest both the polity of the Dominion and the specifics of Andros's policies, but they also had a great deal to lose if they openly criticized the Council, urged disobedience to Andros's legislation, or led a revolt that failed.[13]

There is, consequently, a still unacknowledged discrepancy within the accounts written to justify the revolt against Andros. The unanimity of all New England in its presumably unplanned uprising against the Dominion is celebrated by dwelling on selected incidents: the simultaneous rising in Boston's north and south ends, the "coming in" to Charlestown of at least a thousand sympathetic citizens, the crowd's shout greeting Bradstreet's appearance, and the reading of the "Declaration" from the town house. In Bancroft's time, these incidents would be seen as prefiguring the uprising of the populace after Lexington and Concord, the "coming in" of the militia to besiege the British, and the eventual expelling of the redcoats from Boston in March 1776. Within the very same pamphlets, however, there are fleeting acknowledgments that there were conflicting interest groups within New England's citizenry. The official papers of Edward Randolph show why. Randolph had long been writing home about differences between what he called the Massachusetts "Faction" (tax dodgers, rebellious ex-magistrates and sanctimonious Puritan clergy) and the "moderates" (loyal patriots who understood the needs of governing an empire).

Clothing these inner divisions in binary rhetoric, the accounts of Nathaniel Byfield, Samuel Prince, Samuel Sewall, Edward Rawson, and Cotton Mather acknowledge only amicable differences between the "Gentlemen" or sometimes "Moderates" (the principal merchants and clergy of Boston) and "the Country" or "the Country party" (freeholders, farmers, ex-soldiers, rural clergy such as John Wise and Jeremiah Shepherd.) All extant accounts written by New Englanders were, however, penned by writers allied with and sympathetic to the Moderates and Gentlemen. In the absence of accounts by defiant leaders Randolph associated with the "Faction" (Thomas Danforth, Elisha Hutchinson, Elisha Cooke), we need to recognize the force of the long-standing need, from 1689 until at least Bancroft's day, to minimize if not to cover up complicating divisions. In 1840 as in 1690, the premise of unity did not allow the angriest voices an historical hearing, perhaps because their unwritten responses had been offensive in both senses of the term.

Whether written by Cotton Mather or not, the famous "Declaration" read on April 18 from the town house – the crucial document that made as well as recorded history – contains no claim for independence in the name of a whole people. Its very title, "The Declaration of the Gentlemen, Merchants and Inhabitants of Boston and the Country Adjacent" suggests separable constituencies. To be sure, the Declaration objects to many of the same policies that were to recur after 1765: abolishing colonial legislatures, raising taxes without an assembly, suspension of *habeas corpus*, "packt and pickt Juries," and forced quartering for imposed redcoats – all of which are specifically said to be violations, not of God's plan for New Israel, but of Magna Charta.[14] But the author(s) of the Declaration offer a collective justification revealingly mixed in the kinds of its claims. Although specific violations are enumerated in a way to suggest that reasonable colonial gentlemen are now addressing their British equals, "The Declaration" begins with a tirade against the "horrid Popish Plot" and "the great Scarlet Whore," alleging that "Sacred Concerns . . . in our Israel" have been "Discountenanced," and concluding "we do therefore seize upon the Persons of those few ill Men which have been (next to our Sins) the grand Authors of our Miseries."[15] The acknowledging of "our sins" has here been reduced to a parenthetical clause. "Our Israel" is to be restored by authority of Magna Charta rights rather than biblical word.

These muted appeals to Puritan heritage end in an insistence that New Englanders are colonials knowingly carrying out their part in the great protestant revolution begun when William of Orange arrived in England. But in the accompanying note which fifteen Boston "Gentlemen" sent to "Sir Edmund Andross Kt," the signers wish Sir Edmund to understand that they have all been "suprized with the Peoples sudden taking of Arms; in the first motion whereof we were wholly ignorant" (182). Quite possibly the unsigned Declaration and the signed note of disclaimer, taken together, reflect a deft double strategy suited to a divided society, rather than any mental confusion of the moment. The Declaration placates the Faction, while the Gentlemen offer a timely disclaimer to the Council. However, because there had been no provoking incident on April 18, 1689, as there would be on April 18, 1775, the revolt against Andros could have been neither an "Accident" nor a surprise. A 2,500-word declaration is not written early one morning, even by a pen as fluid as Cotton Mather's; nor do one thousand countryfolk, as well as residents and militia from both ends of a small city, arise simultaneously and unanimously, even on a lecture Thursday.

The two words that resound through the first of New England's self-justifications, written by Samuel Prince, Nathaniel Byfield, and "A.B.," are "gentlemen" and "country." Whether Boston's leaders genuinely feared the violence of a country mob, or wished not to appear as revolutionaries in the eyes of British readers, or perhaps both, is now impossible to determine. What is undeniable is the persistent importance of class distinctions and their political implications for a separation of a proto-Tory merchant interest from a proto-Whig farming and tradesman interest, with the Congregational clergy, both rural and urban, caught in between.

Cotton Mather's often quoted account of the Andros revolt reveals division without admitting it. Neither in 1689 nor 1702 could Mather abandon rhetoric about the solidarity of the New England community. He had to demonstrate that gentlemanly reason had controlled popular anger until unanimity had been attained.

Wherefore some of the Principal Gentlemen in Boston consulting what was to be done in this Extraordinary Juncture, They all agreed they would, if it were possible, extinguish all essays in the People towards an *Insurrection*, in daily Hopes of Orders from England for their Safety: But that if the Country People by any violent Motions push'd the Matter on so far, as to make a Revolution unavoidable, then to prevent the shedding of Blood by an ungoverned *Mobile*, some of the Gentlemen present should appear at the Head of the Action with a Declaration accordingly prepared. By the *Eighteenth* of April 1689, Things were pushed on so far by the People that certain Persons first Seized the Captain of the *Frigot*, and the Rumor thereof running like Lightning through *Boston*, the whole Town was immediately in Arms, with the most *Unanimous Resolution* perhaps that ever was known to have Inspir'd any People.[16]

The firm ending of this skillful paragraph obviates the reader's memory of its beginning. Accordingly, Mather's concluding phrases could become grist to Bancroft's democratic mill in one particularly inclusive way. To Bancroft as to Mather, progress derives from the timely restraining of an unruly but perceptive majority by educated gentlemen who guide the virtue of the common man. So, within Bancroft's history as a whole, the Great Migration needed its Winthrop, American Calvinism its Edwards, the Glorious Revolution its Mather, the Revolution its Jefferson and Adamses, the economy its Hamilton, and, ultimately, the nation its Lincoln.

By concentrating on ecopolitical issues of elective representation and the right to tax, post-Revolutionary Americans who needed to see 1689 as the precursor of 1775 ignored the force of anti-Catholic conspiracy fears in motivating the revolt against Andros. Similarly, anti-French and anti-Catholic fears provoked by the 1774 Quebec Act would long be underplayed in accounts of New England's revolutionary motivations. In 1689, however, conspiracy fears had been fueled by more than anti-Stuart resentment of James II's closet Catholicism and suspicion of the Declaration of Indulgence. Louis XIV's revocation of the Edict of Nantes in 1685 had led to the murder and extradition of many Protestants. By 1686, Louis XIV and James II had signed the so-called Treaty of Neutrality; the governors of

New York (Thomas Dongan), Maryland (Lord Baltimore), and Virginia (Edward Howard) were all Catholics. Andros's introduction of Anglican liturgy in Boston was thus plausibly regarded as the first step toward appointing a Catholic governor.

Moreover, the threat of Catholic incursion turned quickly into fear of territorial encirclement. The leaders of Massachusetts probably knew that in 1687 Louis XIV had instructed Comte Frontenac to march south from Montreal, capture Albany, descend the Hudson, and join a French fleet with which to capture New York. By the autumn of 1688, after settlements in the Connecticut River valley and Casco Bay had been razed, New Englanders had experienced the ravages of combined French and Indian attack. Samuel Sewall had nightmares of the French attacking Boston. New England's situation in late 1688 reminds us that the phrase "conspiracy fears" is commonly used only after a past possibility has become safely dead. Only in hindsight can we see that inadequacies of military technology made French and Indian conquest of Boston impossible. "Let the whole Nation judge," Sewall and Rawson were to recall in 1691, "whether these Men were not driving on a French design, and had not fairly erected a French Government."[17]

Dwelling on the conspiracy threat in the pamphlets of 1689–1691 can of course be regarded as New England rhetoric designed to appeal to their recent, protestant, Dutch king. But Cotton Mather's *Decennium Luctuosum* (1699) shows how historically powerful regional paranoia would continue to be. Mather's self-declared "History" defines the decade of sorrows (1688–1698) almost exclusively in terms of the quasi-epic but still unended war that the perfidious Gaul and the savage Tarratines have inflicted upon New England. In Mather's narrative, the triumphant revolt against Andros is regarded as the one redemptive incident within a ten-year waste of suffering and two-sided brutalities that culminate in Hannah Dustin's infamous revenge. The Virgilian epigraph ("Infandum iubes renovare dolorem") casts Mather the historian in the role of Aeneas, a tale-teller compelled to retell the horrible grief of a past in which we contemporary Trojans seem to be the losers. Only the implied link between the revolt against Andros and New England's intensely anti-French, anti-Catholic, and anti-Indian feelings can satisfactorily explain the strange composite Mather makes of his sorrowful decade. But Mather's link was to be one that post-Revolutionary Americans would prefer to ignore. The direct line to be drawn between 1689 and 1775 depended on obscuring the fact that France, recently the savior of the American Revolution, had served in 1689 as the provoking enemy for the very revolt through which New England had prefigured the national future.

Even if New England's resolution had been unanimous on April 18, the solidarity of the Saints soon faded. Bancroft and Hawthorne would lead their readers to assume that the nativist revolt against Andros restored the old charter government in a resurgence of the Puritan spirit of independence. In fact, sudden collective passivity turned a spirited revolt on behalf of self-determination into a paralyzing gesture of dependence upon England. Instead of declaring the continuance of the old charter government together with their loyalty to a new king, New England's leaders opted for the familiar face of aged governor-patriarch Simon Bradstreet, their last founding father, who told them that loyalty to the Crown was clearly a first priority, whatever form of government might follow from it.

Judged by the standard of a Puritan commonwealth, what followed the Commonwealth's gesture of revolt was a nearly complete unraveling. When the Corporation Bill relegitimizing the old Massachusetts charter became a dead letter in the House of Lords, Elisha Cooke withdrew into angry silence, leaving Increase Mather to make what terms he could. Faced with an empty treasury, the Bradstreet government repeatedly raised taxes and thereby incurred a tax revolt from its own country adherents. The year 1690, about which George Bancroft says practically nothing, offers a roll call of disasters that makes any other year in New England's history, including 1676 and 1692, seem benign. Andros, Dudley, and Randolph were all acquitted in London. The French and Indians attacked Berwick, Casco, Salmon Falls, and Haverhill, destroyed Wells and York, and razed Schenectady. Although New England's counterexpedition against Quebec began with the capture of Port Royal, it ended in Phips's disastrous defeat at Quebec City, costing the treasury 50,000 pounds of debt, which could only be paid by printing, for the first time in the colony's history, paper money that rapidly depreciated some 25 percent.

These setbacks were the preliminary. On February 12, 1690 the Massachusetts General Court unfastened the linchpin of the old charter government. The definition of "Freeman" was altered from church member to 40-shilling freeholder. If the purpose of the protestant commonwealth was to govern a Christian community by the laws of God, it was not likely to do so by extending the vote to all men of a certain property. Even though this change – surely the single most important outcome of the revolt against Andros – was heartily approved by the home government, it was not brought about by British pressure. New England merchant leaders, many of them church members, were benefiting from the triangular trade and eager to share political power within the British mercantile system.[18] The meaning of "New England" was shifting yet again. At the moment when the region's geographical definition was assuming its present shape, New England's founding identity as a commonwealth in which spiritual and political power derived from the franchise of the Saints was overturned from within. Ironically, this momentous change did not seem, given present stresses of an empty treasury and French/Indian warfare, even to be a crisis.

The Bradstreet government met these threats and changes with high-sounding public proclamations to New England and pleading private letters to Old England. A proclamation issued on March 13, 1690 "by the Governour and General Court" acknowledges that "this poor Land has laboured under a long Series of Afflictions and Calamities," so much so that "the *ax is laid to the Root of the Trees*" and the Commonwealth is in "imminent danger of perishing, if a speedy REFORMATION of our *Provoking Evils* prevent it not."[19] By 1690 Simon Bradstreet had to disclose the inadequacies of his government. To Increase Mather in London, Bradstreet wrote a long narrative about the Quebec disaster that borders on hysteria: "Shall our Father spit in our face and we be not ashamed!"[20] Seeking to explain why "the People in New England have not obtained all the Charter Priviledges which they have at several times Petitioned Their Majesties for," Increase Mather had to tacitly admit that, in the days immediately following April 18, there had been a failure of New England courage: "Had they at the time of the Revolution entred upon the full Exercise of their Old Charter-Government . . . wise Men are of Opinion that they might have gone on without disturbance."[21] Either God had not heard New England's righteous prayer (a possibility Increase Mather could never have seriously entertained), or deference followed by prayer were not responses adequate to show God that New Englanders were still worthy of His support.

As Hawthorne somehow knew, Simon Bradstreet's idea of his proper role as the "Moderate" had been to counsel New Englanders "to submit to the constituted authorities." Prominent members of "The Faction," however, had become equally submissive once the Deputies had made their decision on May 22 to wait upon the Lord and King William. No spirit of colonial independence, no criticism of the Bradstreet government, was to be forthcoming from Thomas Danforth or Elisha Cooke. In a Boston without newspapers, there could be no Sam Adams constantly reminding the citizens of their presumably violated rights. If 1689 is a portent of 1775, clerical leadership of an emerging Black Regiment would surely have been discernible in the words of Cotton Mather, especially considering his father's mission to recover the old charter in England.

On May 23, 1689, one day after the Deputies declined to reaffirm the old charter, Cotton Mather delivered the first Election Day sermon in four years. "The Way to Prosperity" denounces the Andros régime ("a company of abject strangers had made a mere booty of us") but says not a word about the old charter, or about any need to reestablish the former definition of a Freeman.[22] Mather implies that today's Way to Prosperity is to withdraw from political engagement. New Englanders are to return to the wisdom of the 1679 synod, to renew church covenants, to avoid contention amongst the Saints. Mather's controlling idea, "God will be with you, when you are with him," allows him to affirm the twin virtues of inner reform and outward peace: "so shall we be led and fed among the sheep of our God; He will restore us and His goodness and mercy shall follow us all our days" (138). Nor does Mather's Way to Prosperity link personal rebellion to money-making as Franklin's recollections of his Boston years so memorably would. Mather's sermon was in truth a curiously safe performance for a young cleric who may have helped plan the revolt against Andros, who may have penned the "Declaration of Gentlemen," and who was now speaking, he said, before "as much of New England in this great congregation, as can well be reach'd by the voice of one address" (127). By May 23 1689, to serve as a sheep of the Lord seems to have become, in Mather's eyes, a public virtue.

Almost two years later Cotton Mather delivered a Thursday lecture day address, "The Present State of New England," that was far more shrill in tone and worried in prophecy. New England has devolved into such "dismal Uncertainty and Ambiguity" that three outcomes seem possible: extinction through conquest, remigration to Europe, the beginning of a new world Millennium. To imagine three futures so different yet so equally overwhelming shows the extremity of the crisis Mather perceives. He persists in viewing the crisis, however, in predominately military terms. The blades now severing the root of New England's tree are specifically "a French ax, accompanied with Indian Hatchets."[23] Defining the present state of New England still requires no mention, however, of the profitless quiet recently fallen over Boston's commercial wharves. Having heard that an attack from New France upon Boston is imminent, Mather concludes, very much in the spirit of the Gray Champion, "He is no New Englander, (not worthy of the Name), who at such a time as this, will not venture his All, for this Afflicted people of God" (33). Venturing one's all demands individual reform of immoral behavior, public commitment to the war effort, and even "a reasonable *Tax*" to fund it (22). Venturing one's all does not, however, require New Englanders to stand up for the old charter, to restrict the vote to church members, to drive out religious error, or to elect their own governor. By 1691 Cotton Mather had silently made the accommodations that would justify the transformation of a Puritan commonwealth into a royal province. Bancroft's model of a gentlemanly leader controlling a people's rebellion is not applicable to such temporizing.[24]

Because the Bradstreet government did so little on behalf of the old charter, the ultimate consequence of the revolt against Andros would prove to be the new charter of 1691. *Habeas corpus* and trial by jury became the explicit constitutional rights of all British citizens. So too did Liberty of Conscience for all protestant Christians. The Congregational Way retained a crucial measure of its establishment by being permitted to continue to tax all of a town's citizens for the support of its Congregational church. In retaliation against Andros's tactics, all land and property contracts legal under the old charter were henceforth guaranteed. The House of Representatives, replacing the Deputies, continued to be an elected and representative body composed of two members per town. The House was to propose all candidates for the Governor's Council and to determine the Governor's salary. Most important, the power for proposing all laws regulating internal affairs was now clearly vested in the House of Representatives, not the Governor or the Council. The new charter thus retained many old charter "liberties" and conceded important new ones.

But the Charter of 1691 also retained crucial features of the Dominion of New England. The Governor, Deputy Governor, and Secretary of the Province were to be royal appointees. All customs officers, judicial officials, and militia officers were to be appointed by the Governor. The Governor was given a double veto power over the legislature; he could veto any law the House passed and any candidate the House proposed for the Council. The Provincial Charter legitimated the Massachusetts General Court's recent extension of voting rights to all 40-shilling freeholders, rather than to church members only. The new charter thus took away crucial old charter privileges and imposed new restrictions.

In sum, the charter for the Province was neither the triumph proclaimed by its first governor, William Phips, nor the defeat sullenly endured by Elisha Cooke. It was an inevitable compromise needed to bind a colony of growing commercial importance more tightly within the expanding net of British empire. Moreover, it was a compromise that a much weakened and therefore passive General Court, Congregational Church, militia, and merchant marine simply had to accept, even if many of the Country Party seethed beneath it. Moderates who cooperated with the new government, however, had much to gain, not only for themselves, but also for the new New England they saw emerging. The Provincial Charter's ambiguity concerning the two issues that would inflame Massachusetts for the next seventy-five years shows how important the force of commercial empire had now become. 1. The power to provide for the common defense was vested in both the Governor and the General Court without assigning how these powers were to be divided or who would pay. 2. The power to levy internal taxes on all "Estates and Persons" within the Province was explicitly vested in the House of Representatives, but whether the powers to tax inter- and intra-national commerce and to set customs duties were to reside in the Province's House of Representatives, in the appointed customs officers, in the Governor, in the Crown, in Parliament, or in some combination thereof, was not at all clear.[25]

What is clear is that the history of Massachusetts after the imprisoning of Andros and through the imposition of the new charter showed precious little popular independence. When post-Revolutionary New Englanders proudly claimed continuity between April 18, 1689, April 19, 1775, and July 4, 1776, they had to ignore the dependence mandated by submission to the Provincial Charter. Bancroft and Palfrey must have suspected that it was debatable, if not misleading, to end their volumes on seventeenth-century history with the parallel assertions that, after April 18, 1689, "Protestant liberty...would commence a revolution for humanity" (Bancroft) and that "again Englishmen were free and self-governed in the settlements of New England" (Palfrey).[26] By postponing analyses of the specific provisions of the Provincial Charter until the opening chapters of their next volume, Bancroft and Palfrey could acknowledge historical fact, yet separate their claim for the unanimous resolution of Liberty-minded New Englanders from the provincial status that had been immediately imposed upon them. In the writing of a comprehensive history that finds purpose and rational order in human affairs, careful subordination is everything.

Among the many tracts of the woeful, post-Andros decade, the only one that rises above dated polemics is Increase Mather's "A Brief Account . . . of the Agents of New England." Concise, factual, and fair, Mather's narrative shows the scant power of even the shrewdest Massachusetts provincial caught in the trammels of King James's and King William's courts. Behind all of Mather's shifting stratagems, first to restore the old charter, and then to obtain a favorable new one, lies the hard fact that no one in the English government, Puritan or Catholic, ever concedes that "the Agents of New-England were Plenipotentiaries from another Sovereign State."[27] Mather's determined defense of the new charter does not blind him to the crucial fact that an appointed governor's absolute veto "makes the Civil Government of New-England more Monarchical, and less Democratical, than in former Times" (291). (Does this statement contain the earliest commendation of Democracy by a person of authority in the New England record?)

The last sentence of Mather's "Brief Account" sums up his argument: in the new charter for the Province of Massachusetts, the Agents have obtained "a Magna Charta, whereby Religion and English Liberties, with some peculiar Priviledges, Liberties, and all Mens Properties, are confirmed and Secured" (296). The new charter is no longer to be cherished because it is a covenant with God that secures a Commonwealth for a select, chosen people. It is, rather, a state paper, worked out by men, through which "all English Liberties are restored" to British citizens in a transatlantic province (289). God's Providence figures hardly at all in Mather's recounting of the twists and turns of intra-empire diplomacy.

The young minister who in 1662 had made his reputation by opposing the leniency of the Half Way Covenant was now arguing for Liberty of Religious Conscience based upon the still evolving British Constitution. The same minister who, seven years before, had told the Freemen it was a "sin" not to stand up for the old charter, had now been, in his words, "forced to yield unto Necessity" and devote all his energies to secure a new one (287). The short, blunt words with which Increase Mather expresses this readjustment ("when they could not have what they would, [they] ought to submit to what they could get," 287) may reflect the plain style, but they also suggest the stagy pragmatism of Twain's Hank Morgan. Although Increase Mather may well be, in Michael Hall's title phrase, "the last Puritan," "An Account of the Agents" marks the moment in which the Massachusetts Puritan begins to sound like a Connecticut Yankee.

After 1692, Increase and Cotton Mather would continue to justify the Provincial Charter, to praise the Declaration of Indulgence, to seek support in the "protections" of British empire, and to claim political rights for New England deriving from Magna Charta and/or the Glorious Revolution. The Mathers would also assume, however, that New England could still remain a Bible commonwealth, salvaging its essence despite apostasies and signs of departing glory. To be sure, Cotton Mather refused to address the specifics of charter provisions while defining all "Good Things Propounded" before the General Court in June of 1692. And, after publishing "Ichabod" (1702), Increase Mather grew increasingly silent about New England's future.[28] But the Mathers' refusal to explicitly admit any fundamental inconsistency between the Bible Commonwealth and the British Province was to prove of immense importance. As New England's leading ministers, they advocated the continuity of God's spiritual Laws with English constitutional liberties. Even more important, by having served as the leading public accommodators of change for both church and state, the father and the son came to embody those very same continuities.

The eight years between the revocation of the old charter (1684) and the imposition of the new charter (1692) were also, ironically, the years when newly dependent New Englanders discovered that New England was indeed their "country." From Nathaniel Byfield's letter through Increase Mather's "An Account of the Agents," the word "country" resounds, carrying shifting meanings but always referring to a geographical land mass spreading out from Boston toward something like the six-state area we now know. The "Declaration" of April 18, 1689 opens with a paragraph identifying all the unnamed gentlemanly declarers as inhabitants of "a Countrey so remarkable for the true Profession and pure Exercise of the Protestant Religion as New-England is."[29] "The great Scarlet Whore," the document continues, is now determined "to crush and break a Countrey so entirely and signally made up of Reformed Churches" (174–175). All members of Andros's Council who have had the virtue to remain "true Lovers of their Country" are said to have consistently opposed the Council's tyrannical policies (180). The Declaration's concluding paragraph even claims that jailing the royal Governor has been nothing more than what "Duty to God and our Country calls for at our hands" (181).

What range of meanings did the word "country" signify in 1690? The second edition of *OED* lists five major meanings of the word, all of them current in the seventeenth century: 1. "a tract or expanse of land of undefined extent"; 2. "a tract or district having more or less definite limits in regard to human occupation"; 3. "the territory or land of a nation, usually an independent state"; 4. "the land of a person's birth, citizenship, residence"; and 5. "the part of a region distant from cities or courts." In 1635 only the first two of these meanings of "country" could have described the lands granted to the Massachusetts Bay Company, but by 1684–1685 all definitions except the third ("land of a nation") had become applicable to the Commonwealth of Massachusetts and to the Dominion of New England. When New Englanders put Governor Andros in jail out of "Duty to God and our Country," however, they were either conceiving of New England as "the territory or land of a nation, usually an independent state" (the third definition) or conceiving of their country in a more metaphysical sixth sense, namely that their "country" was embodied in the "rights" guaranteed to them by an unwritten British Constitution wherever the *terra firma* of empire might be located.

The problem of a New Englander's defining his "country" surfaces where least expected, in Increase Mather's "Brief Account of the Agents." Mather recalls his outrage against provisions inserted by the Lords of Trade into a draft of the new charter: "I expressed my Dissatisfaction, perhaps, with a greater Pathos than I should have done, earnestly protesting, that I would sooner part with my Life, than Consent to the Minutes, or any thing else that did infringe any Liberty or Priviledge of Right belonging to my Countrey" (283). Unless we regard this sentence as a sop designed to placate remaining members of "the faction," we must conclude that, to Increase Mather, "my countrey" still remained (or had recently become) New England, not England. New Englanders somehow still retained liberties and rights that both preceded and superseded the new charter that was attempting to codify them.[30]

In this regard, like father like son. Cotton Mather's biographical account of William Phips defines Phips's pervasive merit as "the old Heathen Virtue of PIETAS IN PATRIAM, or, LOVE TO ONE'S COUNTRY."[31] Clearly referring to New England, Cotton Mather then uses the words "the Country" or "of his country" four additional times in the same paragraph. It is in the life of Phips that Mather gives us his version of the revolt against Andros, with all its reassurances of how "the Gentlemen" controlled the threat of bloody revolution emanating from "the Country People" (294). The original "Patria" beloved by "Pious Aeneas," every eighteenth-century reader of the *Magnalia* would have recalled, had been Troy, the wondrous city recently ravaged by foreigners. And the "Patria" personally claimed by the poet Virgil, that "old heathen," had not been imperial Rome, but his beloved Mantua. To both Mathers, New England had now become their "country" in a similar sense – a semi-independent, culturally distinct region where love of local soil and rights of transatlantic empire hopefully would join.

The cross meanings of the word "country" in the aftermath of 1689 prompt a second glance at Samuel Sewall's hymn to Plum Island (1697). Sewall was, be it remembered, a Moderate whose lands Andros had recently tried to seize and who had retained conflicting feelings about the new Provincial Charter. By the late 1690s, Sewall's attachment to his New England's "patria" had become dependent on more than natural beauty, natural fecundity, and the passage of generations. It was a function of knowing how readily one's political patria once had been – and still could be – taken away. In the process of losing political independence, New Englanders were discovering how precious was "their country." After the passage of the new charter, a Massachusetts provincial might have seemed a rube in the eyes of a British Lord, but he was likely to be a voting freeholder jealously attached to his property and his Province.

If any New Englander initiated anything like a prophetic "revolution for humanity" during the revolt against Andros, the plausible revolutionary was neither passive Simon Bradstreet nor the cautious Mathers, but the Reverend John Wise, who publicly objected to taxation without representation.[32] When John Wise was subjected to abuse at a hearing before Andros's Council and then jailed without bail or a trial by peers, he became a symbol of country resistance to imperial tyranny. During the six months before April 18, 1689 different versions of the tyrannical threat Joseph Dudley or John West had voiced at the Council hearing ("Mr. Wise, you have no more priviledges left you than not to be Sould for Slaves"[33]) circulated throughout the Dominion. When in 1690 a committee of seven New Englanders, including Thomas Danforth and Elisha Cooke, drew up the bill of grievances against Andros and the Council for forthcoming trial in England, the first charge specified against Edmund Andros, Edward Randolph, and Joseph Dudley was the illegal imprisonment and disenfranchising of John Wise.

But to therefore accept the claim advanced in the Ipswich town seal, "The Birthplace of American Independence, 1687," would be to project a commitment to democracy and independence further backward into Wise's thought and conduct than the evidence warrants. Like many another New Englander, John Wise was conspicuously silent about old charter rights once Andros was overthrown. Not until twenty-five years later did Wise link political democracy with Congregational Church government, arguing that each covenanted church was a democracy of right-reasoning believers and that the Cambridge Platform protected a single church's autonomy. At the outset of *Vindication of the Government of New-England Churches* (1717), however, Wise makes it very plain that the advantages of democracy both in church and local government are enhanced and protected by the strengths of monarchy. Like Cotton and Increase Mather, John Wise had guided the spirit of revolt until the passage of the Provincial Charter had compromised the energies for rebellion.

HUTCHINSON: "THE AWFUL WEIGHT OF A PEOPLE'S CURSE"

Likening the glorious revolt of 1689 to revolutionary agitation of the 1770s proved to be a way of making history as well as reordering it. Two weeks after the Boston Massacre, for which many New Englanders were already holding Acting Governor Hutchinson responsible, the Reverend Samuel Cooke of Arlington delivered the Election Day sermon before the newly appointed Governor, "His Honor Thomas Hutchinson, Esq. Lieutenant-Governor and Commander in Chief."[34] Cooke took as his text a rather pointed verse from II Samuel in which God's everlasting covenant with the House of David is defined through David's "last words": "He that ruleth over men must be just, ruling in the fear of God" (327). Cooke then proceeded to implicitly chastise Massachusetts's newly appointed governor about God's Word concerning civil government, emphasizing a ruler's duties to make and execute laws only by "the general consent of the community" (328) and to exercise power only in a way to maintain "the rights of British citizens" (341).

To give these injunctions added force, Cooke elaborated, with his own kind of aphoristic staccato, upon a moral-political exemplum from the New England past:

Our Charter was dissolved and despotic power took place. Sir Edmund Andros – a name never to be forgotten – in imitation of his royal master, in wanton triumph, trampled upon all our laws and rights. Sir Edmund at first made high professions of regard to the public good. But it has been observed "that Nero concealed his tyrannical disposition more years than Sir Edmund and his creatures did months." But the triumphing of the wicked is often short. The Glorious Revolution under the Prince of Orange displayed a brighter scene to Great Britain and her colonies . . . I trust we are not insensible of the blessings we then received, nor unthankful for our deliverance from the depths of woe. (340)

The thrust of Cooke's warning against any future cloaking of tyranny depends on recognizing the irony of its source. The quotation linking Andros to Nero is from the newly appointed governor's own *History of the Colony of Massachusetts Bay* (1764). At this most public of moments, grandson was potentially pitted against grandson. As Thomas Hutchinson knew from writing his *History*, and as Samuel Cooke knew from reading it, both of their grandfathers (Elisha Cooke and Elisha Hutchinson) had in 1689 been prominent leaders of the Faction. If the newly appointed governor were not to prove true to the "blessings" of the "deliverance" of 1689, Cooke implied, let the New England House of David beware.

Thomas Hutchinson's *History*, as many in Cooke's audience surely remembered, had given qualified support to Massachusetts's glorious revolution. Borrowing a metaphor from Cotton Mather, Hutchinson had roundly condemned Andros's spoils-sharing Councilmen: "the harpies themselves quarrelled about their share of the prey."[35] Although the imprisoning of Andros and Randolph was judged to have been "a rash, precipitate proceeding," Hutchinson had acknowledged that the protest against tyranny in the April 18 Declaration "seems to have been necessary" (1, 322). As an historian who deeply admired Increase Mather's diplomacy on New England's behalf, Hutchinson understood the necessary connection between the rashness of the revolt against Andros, and the still workable compromise of the Provincial Charter. Accordingly, Hutchinson penned for his *History* an apprehensive variation upon Cotton Mather's praise for New England's "unanimous resolution." On the morning of April 18, 1689 Hutchinson had asserted, "The old magistrates and heads of the people silently wished, and secretly prayed, for success to the glorious undertaking [the accession of William of Orange], and determined quietly to wait the event. The body of the people were more impatient. The flame, which had long been smothered in their breast, burst forth with violence" (1, 317). As the Province's loyal historian, Hutchinson was clearly trying to allow for the potential benefit of popular violence; within the year after these words were published, the Boston mob was to sack Hutchinson's town house.

   By the time Hawthorne published "Edward Randolph's Portrait" (1838), the specific likening of Hutchinson to Andros had become as much a "Legend of the Province House" as the claim that 1775 had been a more glorious reenactment of 1689. The narrator of Hawthorne's short story, a bibulous "old tradition-monger" named Bela Tiffany, tells of how Hutchinson was compelled to realize, through seeing his own face in Randolph's portrait, that he himself was to replace Randolph as "the arch enemy of New-England."[36] In Bela Tiffany's legend, the importance of Cotton Mather's famous phrase is reaffirmed, especially because Hutchinson, priding himself on the historian's reason, dismisses the *Magnalia* as "old women's tales."[37] To be New England's "arch enemy" is redefined: the region's "Devil" is now native-born, a would-be aristocrat who, because he does British bidding, must henceforth bear "the awful weight of a People's curse" (262).

   The act that substantiates Hutchinson's identity as New England's anti-Revolutionary devil is his signing approval for the landing and quartering of three British regiments in Castle William and Boston. From his reading of Hutchinson's *History*, Hawthorne has combined two incidents that had occurred in October 1768 and July 1770.[38] Hutchinson had insisted that, on both occasions, British troops were ordered to Boston first by Governor Bernard and then by British military officers. As the Province's lieutenant governor, Hutchinson believed he was bound to enforce legal authority, especially because he suspected that troops would be needed. The immediate response of the House of Representatives, however, had been to resolve that imposing an internal tax and sending a standing army were violations of British constitutional rights and the Province's charter rights. These two resolutions, Hutchinson plausibly contended, contained "a greater tendency towards a revolution in government, than any preceding measures in any of the colonies" (III, 149). The presence and quartering of British troops in Boston were to be, of course, the necessary first steps toward the legendary event that would propel New England toward revolution – the Boston Massacre. A line had been drawn in the sand over an unresolved issue of the 1691 Provincial Charter.

If Bela Tiffany expresses his creator's opinions, Hawthorne's reading of Hutchinson had led him to believe that, during New England's two revolutions, popular feeling and not political fact was the force driving history. The similarly unhappy end of Randolph's and Hutchinson's lives confirms the tale's moral about "the awful weight of a People's curse" (262).

Our annals tell us . . . that the curse of the people followed this Randolph wherever he went . . . They say, too, that the inward misery of that curse worked itself outward, and was visible on the wretched man's countenance, making it too horrible to be looked upon (262) . . . And as for Hutchinson, when, far over the ocean, his dying hour drew on, he gasped for breath, and complained that he was choking with the blood of the Boston Massacre. (269)

The accusation of oppression, Hawthorne suggests, became an historical force through a dramatic, repeated gesture. Just as Samuel Cooke in 1770 had informed Governor Hutchinson of how Governor Andros had "trampled upon all our laws and rights," so Hawthorne's Alice Vane uses almost exactly the same phrase when she warns Hutchinson of how Edward Randolph had "trampled on a people's rights" (268). In Hawthorne's tale, the fictive Hutchinson remains a New Englander by birth only. We hear Hutchinson assuming a British identity and expressing pride in trampling upon provincials: "What to me is the outcry of a mob, in this remote province of the realm? The King is my master, and England is my country! Upheld by their armed strength, I set my foot upon the rabble, and defy them!" (266).

Despite Hawthorne's claim that Bela Tiffany's tale will offer "as correct a version of the fact as the reader would be likely to obtain from any other source" (258), "Edward Randolph's Portrait" distorts history in revealing ways. As Bernard Bailyn's biography has demonstrated, Thomas Hutchinson had no wish, even in his last years of virtual exile, to trample upon New Englanders. Neither Randolph nor Hutchinson was responsible for provoking a revolution by taking an aristocrat's delight in fleecing a provincial people. Nor does either of the two royal appointees appear to have been tormented by "hideous guilt" (267) during the years after New Englanders forcibly exiled him. Hawthorne's passing tribute to the presumably united and unchanging Puritan character (the Selectmen of Boston are said to be "plain, patriarchal fathers of the people, excellent representatives of the old puritanical founders, whose sombre strength had stamped so deep an impress upon the New England character," 264) dismisses all the inner divisions which, as Hawthorne well knew, had beset Massachusetts during the crises of 1770, 1689, and 1636.

Such observations, however, can be fairly advanced only from beyond and outside of the tale itself. With characteristically canny contrivance, Hawthorne has protected his fiction's politics by means of his narrative frame. "Edward Randolph's Portrait" is not, like "The Gray Champion," offered as a presumably accurate rendering of history to which a legend has been added to secure a triumphant ending. Because of its place in Bela Tiffany's four-story sequence, "Edward Randolph's Portrait" is presented from the outset as a "legend." We see Randolph and Hutchinson only as imagined figures in Bela Tiffany's thrice-told tale. As merely the tale's last teller, Nathaniel Hawthorne is not restoring the truth of historical events, but conveying the power of legend in the remaking of them. Within that legend, the past is symbolized for us as an indecipherably black painting that time has fully obscured. It is New England's will to tell tales of how Randolph had been its arch enemy, and Hutchinson the devil incarnate who had provoked the spirit of revolution. If past fact is but a blackened painting, and legends are the force truly moving history, then written history should at the very least take stock of such legends. As we read "Edward Randolph's Portrait," the linking of 1689 to 1776 becomes itself a "legend" of historical import, while Alice Vane's dramatic warning about the power of the people's curse acquires a witchery of its own.

The paucity of significant literature about the revolt against Andros written outside Massachusetts, and/or after Hawthorne's time, suggests that the Glorious Revolution of 1689 was far more important to nineteenth-century New Englanders than to twentieth-century Americans. As sectional nationalism waned in the aftermath of Civil War, the connections between the rebellious factions of 1689 and 1771 seemed less important than simultaneous connections across regions within either era. The Dominion of New England came to be wrongly remembered as a paper threat of no lasting consequence. Founding moments in Plymouth, Salem, and Boston were still thought to belong to the nation, but the revolt against Andros seemed, after Palfrey's time, to have mattered to Massachusetts antiquarians only.

CHAPTER 6

Race, war, and white magic: the neglected legacy of Salem

Since 1986 witchcraft ("Wicca") has been a constitutionally protected religion; witch/wizard covens are maintained across the country, though they are, perhaps understandably, concentrated in Massachusetts.[1] Nonetheless, the very mention of the seaboard city of "Salem," for all except those who live there, has never shed its association with the infamous "Salem witch trials," even though the trials arose in the neighboring inland community of Salem Village, now Danvers.[2] Three centuries of notoriety have made the bibliography of the Salem witch trials (hearings, transcripts, polemics, history, historical fiction, drama, scholarship) so voluminous that no one can hope to master its entirety. My emphasis here is on exploring one long-neglected cause of the Salem trials, and studying selected renderings of it. During the sessions of the 1692 Special Court of Oyer and Terminer, confusions of racial color symbolism (red, black, and white) were expressed in the testimony of the afflicted who swore they had seen specters. Before, during, and after these testimonies, Essex County was sending its militia to fight Indians and Frenchmen who had been threatening and overrunning the county's northern borders since King Philip's War. The interconnections between these two developments demand our continuing attention if we are to understand not only the trials of 1692 but also the historiographical tradition that follows them.[3]

It is particularly important that the racial and wartime dimensions of the Salem witch trials should have been so long obscured within the progressive New England historical tradition. Surely the most influential and revealing error George Bancroft ever made was his vehement misreading of the Salem witch trials as the linchpin of New England's change from credulous Puritanism to the Age of Reason. Historical literature dealing with the Salem trials would sometimes challenge the Bancroftian consensus, but not sufficiently so as to alter either today's historical textbooks or the audio tape still heard daily during the tourist season at the Salem Witch Museum. The roles in which George Bancroft cast the ministry, magistracy, and the people have long resonated at the deepest level of cultural belief. In our increasingly secular democracy, they may never be overturned, especially because they allow us the comfort of believing in Euro-American "progress" while avoiding its racial and military contexts.

INDIAN JOHN AND THE NORTHERN TAWNIES

Although economic displacement within Salem Village in the 1680s fueled if not caused the initial accusations, monetary and class grievances almost never surface directly in the trial transcripts.[4] Such motives, however real locally, can explain neither the intensity of popular fear nor the geographic range of the accusations. Throughout the Salem witchcraft hearings, exactly those fears that had been familiar from preceding New England crises reappear in altered ways and then coalesce. The Salem witch trials took place during King William's War, itself a northeasterly continuation of King Philip's War. Even though the Wampanoags and Nipmucs had been defeated by 1677, the Wabanaki peoples (Pennacooks, Nashaways, Sacos, Androscoggins, and Penobscots) soon prepared to continue the fight.[5] Issues of the Antinomian Crisis resurface in altered form. Anne Hutchinson, convicted of heresy, had been suspected of being a witch; two of her adherents were to be tried for witchcraft. When Martha Corey protested to Jonathan Corwin and John Hathorne "I am a gospel woman," she was insisting, in a telling reversal of Antinomian belief, that her years of sanctification as a Salem Village church member of good standing should be her soul's justification in the eyes of any earthly examiner.[6]

Without the context of the recent Indian wars and the turmoil over the new charter, Salem witchcraft cannot be convincingly explained. Cotton Mather's three narratives of the grievous decade of the 1690s all specify that Indian powwows, thought to be Devil's agents if not devils themselves, had been leading the assault of Satan's legions against New England, from the onset of the Pequots in 1636, to the intertribal conspiracy of King Philip's War and, most recently, all along the frontier line north of Salem Village. Because Massachusetts remained an uncharted colony for two years after the revolt against Andros ("between government and no government," in Robert Calef's words[7]), witchcraft accusations were allowed to multiply and jails to fill during the spring of 1692, a time when, in anticipation of the new charter, no colony-wide trials could be held. The authority to appoint judges, granted to the governor of the Province by the new charter, enabled William Phips not only to create the special Court of Oyer and

Terminer, and to appoint William Stoughton as its chief justice, but also to disband the special court five months later, and then to reconstitute it. Like Andros in March 1689, Phips let it be known that he momentarily left Massachusetts at a time of gathering turmoil (June 1692) in order to lead a New England army struggling to withstand the northern Indians and the French. While the two governor-generals were fighting their frontier battles, the not unrelated crises within coastal communities exploded behind and to the south of them.[8]

The importance of the northern war suggests that, at least during the Salem trials, the seventeenth-century New England witch wore a second, even more hidden face. As the careful statistics and biographical narratives of John Demos and Carol Karlsen have shown, the accused witch was likely to be a woman over forty years of age, without a secure social position or a male heir, but known to have a sharp tongue, skills at midwifery, familiarity with a tavern and/or a reputation for having practiced white or black magic.[9] By late summer 1692, both the afflicted and the accused reported seeing one particular kind of specter with suspicious frequency. This evasive specter-devil assumed the shape of the male Indian, who looked like the Black Man, the Red Man or a "Tawny," who had been "seen" either as a warrior or a powwow, and whose spectral presence in Salem Village, but more often to the north, was the surest sign of the Devil's impending war against New England. The qualities of the tawny man were very unlike the witch, but as a specter he was a source of intense fear to Essex County citizens who had known frontier warfare, particularly to afflicted young women who had experienced devastating Wabanaki attacks upon Falmouth Maine. To a populace threatened with invasion, the bonding of the Indian specter with their own white Christian minister could thus provide the unequivocal sign of New England's innermost corruption.[10]

The chronologies of the wars against witches and northern Indians must be put together in order to grasp the importance of frontier fears to the onset of legal accusation. In 1689, Saco Falls, Dover and Casco Bay had been attacked by Indians and/or the French; John Bishop and Nicholas Reed of Salem Village were killed in Indian warfare. In 1690, Schenectady, Salmon Falls, Casco, Berwick, Exeter, and Amesbury had been attacked; Godfrey Sheldon of Salem Village was killed. In 1691, Wells, York, Berwick (again), Rowley, and Haverhill had been attacked. At least thirty-five men from Essex County were then serving in the northern forces while at least twenty-one men were on militia-alert in Essex County. On January 25, 1692, a week after Tituba, Abigail Williams, Betty Parris, and Ann Putnam Jr. were playing with white magic in the Reverend Parris's household, the

French and Indians attacked York (again), burning the town, killing at least fifty people including the Reverend Shubael Dummer, and capturing about eighty more.

Northern service for select able-bodied Essex County men would continue throughout the summer. On June 11, the day after Bridget Bishop was hung and a month before Sarah Good, Rebecca Nurse, Suzannah Martin, Elizabeth How, and Sarah Wildes were sentenced to death, the French and the Indians attacked the town of Wells. The minister of Wells, a man of reputation most unlike that of the revered Dummer, was apparently not present. He had recently been "cried out" as a wizard in Salem Village by Ann Putnam Jr. and Abigail Hobbs; his name was George Burroughs, the former minister of both Salem Village and Falmouth Maine. The confessions of at least nine accused Andover witches would soon specify that they had been communicants in the black masses conducted by the Reverend Burroughs, some recently in the Reverend Parris's pasture in Salem Village, but many as long as three years before somewhere in Maine or in the forest.[11]

The conduct of the trials perpetuated differences between "Gentlemen" and the "Country Party." Although accusations and preliminary testimony came increasingly from the north, those called to judge the accused were sent from the heart of Provincial power in Boston. Of the seven new justices added to Jonathan Corwin and John Hathorne to make up the special court (William Stoughton, Bartholomew Gedney, John Richards, Nathaniel Saltonstall, Peter Sergeant, Samuel Sewall, and Wait Winthrop), only Bartholomew Gedney (himself very much a "gentleman") came from Salem or its environs. These men, who had been leaders of the seaport "Moderates" during the resistance against Andros, may have been especially prone to suspect the unreason of the Country Party, but they were equally likely to seek to maintain their dominance over rural communities.

Although the records of the trials are now lost, their presiding spirit was surely revealed in the beliefs of Chief Justice William Stoughton, who would continue to press for convictions after spectral evidence was disallowed, who resigned while the jails were emptying, and who refused ever to admit to any judicial error. Chief Justice William Stoughton, with his Oxford MA, his curacy in Sussex, and his years of service on Governor Andros's council, was not the kind of judge ultimately to care very much about poppets, village slander, or the preternatural death of an accuser's precious livestock. The title of the one published early sermon by which the man's spirit can be known suggests that, from 1668 onwards, William

Stoughton yearned for strenuous exertion on behalf of "New England's True Interest":

New England, thy God did expect better things from thee and thy Children; not Worldliness and an insatiable desire after perishing things; not Whoredomes and Fornications; not Revellings and Drunkenness; not Oaths & false swearings; Not Exactions and Oppressions; not Slanderings and Backbitings; not Rudeness and Incivility, a degeneracy from the good Manners of the Christian World; not Formality and Profaneness, to loath Manna, to despise holy things, to grow Sermon-proof and Ordinance proof; not Contentions and Disorders; not an itching after new things and wayes; not a rigid Pharisaical Spirit; not a contempt of Superiours, not Unthankfulness and disrespect to Instruments of choice Service; not a growing weary of Government, and a drawing loose in the Yoke of God: Not these things, but better things, *O New England*, hath thy God expected from thee.[12]

Until the early poetry of Robert Lowell, no passage in the jeremiad tradition would surpass Stoughton's in its relentlessly combative decrying of the darkness and decline of New England. The man who wrote these words could not be expected to believe that God would ever allow a black or red devil to appear in the shape of an innocent, especially at a time of political transition and northern warfare. Compared to William Stoughton, Cotton Mather was to prove a Moderate indeed.[13]

Whether the two household slaves the Reverend Parris had purchased in Barbados, Tituba and her husband John, were born among Indian peoples in the British West Indies, in South America, or in North America is not known, nor can we be certain that they were not of mixed Indian and African blood.[14] In seventeenth-century Massachusetts, such discriminations among unregenerate peoples of color were neither usual nor thought to be needed, especially for slaves. The warrant for Tituba's arrest refers to "titibe an Indian Woman servant."[15] Throughout the records of the preliminary hearings, Tituba's husband is referred to as "Indian John" or "John Indian." By 1692 (exactly two centuries after first contact), Columbus's misnaming had yielded a catch-all term that had been applied to the Guanahani, the Carribe, the Aztecs, and West Indies Africans, as well as to the Iroquois, the Penobscot, and the Wabanaki "Tarratines."

Although witchcraft seems to have been first practiced by Indian John (a rye cake soaked in children's urine), it was Tituba, not her husband, who was summoned to be examined at the first preliminary hearing. As soon as Tituba confessed to practicing witchcraft in order to protect the Reverend Parris's children, the associations of race and black magic became overpowering. Tituba the accuser quickly became Tituba the accused. With the advantage of the "cross and swift questions"[16] recommended for witchcraft hearings, examiners developed special interest in a suspected witch's misuse of Indian power or an afflicted person's confrontation of Indian deviltry. Although ailing, aged Sarah Osborne stoutly denied ever seeing the Devil, John Hathorne led her to confess that "shee was frighted one time in her sleep and either saw or dreamed that shee saw a thing like an indian all black which did pinch her in her neck and pulled her by the back part of her head to the dore of the house." Any reader of Mary Rowlandson's narrative, especially an honest, bed-ridden woman living near the frontier, might well have testified she "saw or dreemed that shee saw a thing like an Indian" who dragged her by the hair to the door of her house before the threat of scalping brought the Indian's spectral visitation, as in a dream, to its sudden close.[17]

Of the 141 suspected witches summoned to court, there was to be but one official resident of Boston. Captain John Alden, son of John and Priscilla, had provided transport shipping for the northern armies during the two years before he was "cried out" as a witch. During court recess "a Ring was made" around Alden in the public street. According to Alden's own account, "the same Accuser [probably Mercy Lewis] cried out, 'there stands Aldin, a bold fellow with his Hat on before the Judges, he sells Powder and Shot to the Indians and French, and lies with the Indian Squaes, and has Indian Papooses.'" Although Alden probably did sell powder and shot to French and Indian troops, no evidence of Indian consortship was forthcoming. His examination was a variant of a long past trial: the charges plausibly made against Thomas Morton were now ironically being leveled against the son of John and Priscilla Alden, admirers of Captain Miles Standish, who had apprehended Morton in 1628.[18]

Examiners Corwin and Hathorne did not obtain a voluntary, revealing confession from a white Christian until April 19, when the court heard the spectacular revelations of Abigail Hobbs from Topsfield, north of Salem Village. Abigail testified that she had seen the Devil only once, had signed his book only once, and it had all happened three or four years ago, "at the Eastward at Casko-bay," when she had lived in Maine. Once Abigail was examined in prison, however, she recalled more specific details. She had consented to afflict families living near the Casco Bay fort only because she had there known the Reverend George Burroughs. It had been Burroughs who had brought her a poppet in the likeness of Mary Lawrence (since dead) and who had urged her to stick thorns into it.[19]

Suzannah Martin, convicted June 30 and executed August 19, came from the frontier town of Amesbury, attacked by Indians in 1690 and then fleetingly again in July of 1692. No more specific evidence condemning Martin was found than the testimony of 27-year-old Joseph Ring of Salisbury. Returning from military service against the Indians under Captain Shadrach at Casco Bay, Ring had met the Devil in the forest near Hampton; there he had seen the specter of Suzannah Martin assisting the Devil in serving the red wine and red bread,[20] a devil's Eucharist that the young soldier was sufficiently strong to resist.

The centrality of George Burroughs's conviction in extending the prosecution of witchcraft is shown by the singular volume and length of the materials (thirty pages) devoted to Burroughs's case. Discovering a corrupted minister would reveal the source of the spiritual power needed to attract converts to a black mass and to proselytize on behalf of the Devil's New England congregation. What preternatural powers – or knowledge – had enabled the dark-complected Reverend Burroughs to twice escape injury during Indian attacks? Might not an unordained minister like Burroughs, who could not administer communion in church, subvert God's people by administering black communion in the forest?

The crux of the courtroom case against Burroughs was to be the inflammatory April 20 deposition of Ann Putnam Jr., testimony probably based on anecdotal gossip Mercy Lewis had obtained while living in Burroughs's household in Falmouth.[21] As soon as Ann had seen the apparition of a minister, she had instantly grasped its significance. In court she knew how to phrase her horror to best advantage: "oh dreadfull: dreadful here is a minister com; what are Ministers wicthes to: whence com you and What is your name for I will complaine of; you tho you be A minister." After revealing that it was George Burroughs's specter that had tortured her and had offered her the book to sign, Ann Putnam charged Burroughs with monstrous perversion of generational duty: "It was a dreadfull thing: that he which was a Minister that should teach children to feare God should com to perswad poor creatures to give their souls to the divill." She then listed three specific charges against Burroughs, all of them ostensibly told to her by Burroughs's specter: 1. he had bewitched his first two wives to death; 2. he "killed Mr. Lawsons child because he went to the eastward with Sir Edmon and preached soe"; and 3. "he had bewicthed a grate many souldiers to death at the eastword, when Sir Edmon was their."[22]

Historians of Salem witchcraft would have much to say about George Burroughs's wives, but they long neglected the significance of Ann Putnam's second and third charges. Ann Putnam was charging George Burroughs with bewitching the soldiers in Andros's army while they had been fighting Indians in Maine. For Burroughs to have "bewicthed a grate many souldiers to death" can only mean that he was a spiritual agent of the French and Indian army still killing New England's Protestant Christians. The very next day, Thomas Putnam wrote to Hathorne and Corwin to gloat that the unmasking of Burroughs was the finding of the "wheel within a wheel at which our ears do tingle."²³

The Indian wars made strange consorts among the witches. The recently widowed Mary Toothaker from Billerica (a town some fifty miles from Maine) was examined by Gedney, Hathorne, Corwin, and Captain Higginson on July 30. "The truth in this matter," Mary testified, was that, ever since last May, "she was under great Discontentedness & troubled w'h feare about the Indians, & used to dream of fighting with them." Now, however, "she is convinced she is a witch" because, at the time of her worst fears, "the Devil appeared to her in the shape of a Tawny man and promised to keep her from the Indians and she should have happy dayes with her sone." At that time, the Devil had repeatedly assured her that "she should be safe from the Indians," if only she would sign his book by rubbing off the "white scurff" on "a piece of burch bark." Not considering that the tawny man who had come to her was clearly able to use Indian powers, Mary had signed the birch bark. Wrong to have assumed that Red Indian and Tawny Devil were discrete, she is now frightened to have discovered that, in Salem Village, 305 witches convene at "the Beating of a drum" and "the sound of a trumpet" under the leadership of "a minister, a little man whose name is Burroughs" and who promises to set up "the Kingdom of satan." Mary Toothaker, who had made her covenant with the Devil in order to be saved from the Indian, had found that Satan, true to his nature, had tricked her after all. Through the Reverend Burroughs, Satan was setting up a heathen ministry throughout the country. Satan's promise to defend her from the Indians was his lure to persuade her to join them.²⁴

During the weeks preceding George Burroughs's execution, Satan appeared to be planning a maritime attack to the north. According to the careful account of the Reverend John Emerson, there were five occasions in July 1692 when citizens of Gloucester saw small groups of armed Indians and armed Frenchmen crossing swampland. The enemy was always wordless; the Gloucestermen's guns always misfired. There were, however, no specter sightings after the execution of George Burroughs. Nine months later, when attempting to account for the "wonderful and Surprising Things which happened in the Town of Glocester," Emerson would not for a minute consider that the sightings had been a delusion. "I hope the Substance of what is written, will be enough to Satisfy all Rational Persons, that Glocester was not Alarumed last Summer, for above a Fortnight together, by real French and Indians, but that the Devil and his Agents were the cause of all the Molestation, which at this time befel the Town."[25] Emerson's conclusion was exactly in accord with Cotton and Increase Mather's reservations about accepting spectral evidence, reservations that had influenced Governor Phips's decision to halt the trials the preceding October. Although the Reverend Emerson now knew that the Devil could have impersonated an innocent person, it was still true that no Frenchman and no Indian was to be presumed innocent. The fact that no attack had occurred did not prove that the diabolic specters had not been there; it should rather be understood that New England's resistance to the French and Indian threat had rendered those specters ineffectual.

The slave whom everyone called "Indian John" played a curious and important part in the apprehending and examining of suspected witches. Unlike his wife, Indian John was never formally accused and therefore never examined, even though, according to Parris's account, it was Indian John who had prepared the witch cake. Nonetheless, Indian John was to become a regular attendee and periodic witness at the hearings. As a waiter at Lieutenant Ingersoll's tavern, Indian John had ample opportunity to overhear the conversations of anyone residing beyond Salem Village who had been summoned to be examined. Indian John's testimony was, like the witnessing of the afflicted women, usually wordless; he too displayed convulsive symptoms of daemonic possession or hysteria when suspected witches were brought into court.

Indian John's testimony at the hearings of Sarah Cloyce, Mary Warren, Suzannah Martin, and Elizabeth Cary shows that he acquired a unique trial status. Never accused, he played a role of carefully limited authority very like the Praying Indians who had served as scouts for white troops during King Philip's War. Assumed to know the ways of wilderness witchery, John could give special insight into the place where the Devil's spirit might be found. For the court to trust too much to the spiritual scouting of Indian John would obviously be folly. To ignore him, however, would also be folly. Not only was he proving himself especially able in ferreting out instances of evil possession. Until October 1692 the court of Oyer and Terminer was to proceed under the assumption that the Devil's evidence could be used in discovering the Devil. Indian John's contributions to New England's latest war thus showed that Indian powers could be both used and triumphed over simultaneously.

Perhaps the most vivid of all George Bancroft's narratives is his compelling, error-ridden account of how Cotton Mather's supposed credulity, infatuation, and "boundless vanity" first promoted the Salem witch trials and then, with the help of other ministers and a few appointed justices, sustained guilty verdicts despite the growing opposition of New England's commonsensical people.[26] Many pages have been needed to successfully challenge, though still not to dispel, the seductive populism of Bancroft's thesis.[27] Its power to distort depends equally on omission and commission. One must ignore all evidence of the northern war, widespread popular hysteria and racial color-coding. And secondly, one must subscribe to the long-standing stereotype that New England ministers, for whom Cotton Mather serves as the prototype, had become marginalized, power-hungry intellectuals driven by biblical dementia.

Accusers of Mather and the ministry rarely consider that none of Mather's writings on Salem witchcraft, especially *The Wonders of the Invisible World*, was conceived as factual recollection, self-interest, or as self-defense. Instead, as was his wont, Mather intended his narratives to provide a representative voice for New England in order to explain New England's shifting viewpoint about Salem witchcraft to the world. Read in this spirit, so opposite to Bancroft's insistence on Mather's peculiarity, Mather's writings convey why local fears of Indian wars had led to so many widespread accusations, why the special court was supported by the people at least as long as by the ministers, and why, after nineteen trials and nineteen executions, the General Court approved Governor Phips's order to disband the special court by a vote as close as 33 to 29.

The Salem trials were not to be regarded, Cotton Mather believed, as a Salem or even an Essex County crisis; in compiling *The Wonders of the Invisible World*, he announced, "I have indeed set my self to Countermine the whole Plot of the Devil against New England."[28] The worth of New England's mission explains why Satan is now conducting, not just a battle, but his greatest and possibly his last war. Observing that no people have ever wished to be "more free from the debauching and the debasing Vices of Ungodliness" than New Englanders, Mather cites Richard Baxter to explain the extremity of the Devil's exertions: "Where will the Devil show most Malice, but where he is hated, and hateth most" (10, 11). And where in particular should the "Army of Devils" choose to attack but at Salem, the site of New England's origin, "the First-born of our English Settlements" (14). To convey the power of this "Army" of invading specters, Mather instructs his reader to picture an army of French and Indians still presumably hovering not far north of Salem Village. "Think on vast Regiments of cruel and bloody French Dragoons, with an intendant over them, overruning a pillaged Neighbourhood," Mather writes, "and you will think a little what the Constitution among the Devils is" (45).

To Mather, the alliance between Frenchman and savage is no present-day accident of international politics, but rather a coalescing of the Devil's identities. French Catholic and tawny pagan, though they flourish together in the fallen forest, are everything New England is not. Just as, in the time of our forefathers, "First the Indian Powawes, used all their Sorceries to molest the first planters here" so now "The Tawnies among whom we came, have watered our Soil with the Blood of many Hundreds of our inhabitants" (74, 75). No one should wonder that so many convicted or confessed witches have recently referred to the Devil as the black man. Witches know their own kind, and the afflicted have come to know them too.

At any time, at any gathering, but especially in New England's present extremity, one can perceive an agent of "the Black Man (as the Witches call the Devil; and they generally say he resembles an Indian)" (126). In these few words, Mather speaks on behalf of, not in opposition to, his people's racial attitudes. He assumes that all New Englanders accept as fact the undeniable bonds among the black man, female witch, male wizard, devil, and Indian, all gathering to form one concerted force that, with French aid, is breaking New England apart from within as well as from without. Seven years later, when Mather published *Decennium Luctuosum*, he was still convinced that "this inexplicable War might have some of its Original among the Indians, whose chief Sagamores are well known unto some of our Captives, to have been horrid Sorcerers, and hellish Conjurers, and such as Conversed with Daemons."[29] These were not, as Bancroft claimed, the idiosyncratic notions of a vain minister anxious about his loss of authority; they were – exactly as Mather presented them – beliefs woven into the inner web of New England's founding, but now reaching their most exclusionist expression. Believing as he did that "New England was a utopia," Cotton Mather hoped the founders' patterns of thought could still be applied to a time of rapid social and economic change.

When Cotton Mather finally saw a devil, he was in the same place where he was also to see an angel – Boston. But the devil he saw came from elsewhere. Throughout the winter of 1692/1693 Mather had helped to treat a neighbor's young servant woman, Mercy Short, for the trauma she had suffered during months of captivity following the burning of her home, the deaths of both her parents, and the deaths of three of her siblings during the Indian attack on Salmon Falls in 1690.[30] Among the "cursed Spectres" that afflicted Mercy Short (spirits whom Mather was too wary of spectral evidence to name) was the demon who had controlled them:

The Divel that visited her was just of the same Stature, Feature, and complexion with what the Histories of the Witchcrafts beyond-sea ascribe unto him; he was a wretch no taller than an ordinary Walking-Staff; hee was not of a Negro, but of a Tawney, or an Indian colour; hee wore an high-crowned Hat, with strait Hair; and had one Cloven-Foot.[31]

Cotton Mather found it "remarkable" that Mercy's Devil so closely resembled European descriptions he knew she could not have read. What seems much more remarkable, however, is that Mercy's Devil had qualities that no beyond-sea history would have enumerated. Mercy saw a particularly New England Devil "not of a Negro, but of a Tawny or an Indian colour." Her devil was small, lithe, straight-haired. Mercy spoke of how the Devil had spoken to her in foreign tongues, asked her to sign the book with red characters, threatened her with burning flames, and inflicted fasts upon her until she felt all "the Agonies of One roasting a Faggot at the Stake" (266). Mather's devil was, in sum, a figure originating in European folklore, made over by the experience of Mercy Short, and then given written identity with the help of new world folklore, well known to Mather, about the severe trials of Indian captivity.

WINKING THE TRUTH OUT OF SIGHT

Perry Miller's testy dismissal of the Salem witch trials from New England intellectual history is a tacit acknowledgment of their importance to New England historiography. To argue, as Miller did, that up to 1720 Salem witchcraft "had no effect on the ecclesiastical or political situation, it does not figure in the institutional or ideological development" may be perfectly true, but is very much beside the point – unless of course one has presentist motives for trying to consign post-1720 historiography of the witch trials to oblivion.[32] Thomas Brattle, who like John Hale had attacked the court's injustices while believing in the Devil, concluded his influential circular letter of October 8, 1692 with the prediction: "I am afraid that ages will not wear off that reproach and those stains which these things will leave behind them upon our land."[33] Perry Miller knew how prophetic Brattle's words had proven to be. Before Miller began his stunning argument about the misuse of federal covenant theology by Stoughton and his fellow judges, Miller fleetingly acknowledged that the witch trials had become "that blot on New England's fame which has been enlarged, as much by friends as by foes, into its greatest disgrace" (191). In the twenty-first century, the blot is still there, enlarged by the tourist dollar and recurrent productions of Arthur Miller's *The Crucible*.

Although Perry Miller does not say so, he surely selected 1720 because that year marked the London publication of the first regional history in which Salem witchcraft figured prominently, Daniel Neal's *The History of New England*. Neal assumes that responsibility for the spiritual plague of 1692 must be chargeable, not to agents of Satan, but to the collective follies of the young women, of the judges, and of a populace that has made "the Distemper spread like a pestilential Sickness thro' several Parts of the Province."[34] The afflicted girls are dismissively referred to as "these distemper'd Wretches that pretended to the Spectral Sight" (II, 527). Taking a cue from Robert Calef's *ad hominem* attacks on Cotton Mather, Neal elevates to historical respectability the easy game of quoting selected passages of *The Wonders of the Invisible World* against Mather himself. Ultimately, however, it was to New England's good fortune that "the whole Country were by Degrees made sensible of their Mistake" (II, 536). Neal's insistence that the witch trials were an isolated regional "mistake" laid the foundation for the smug belief, soon to flourish, that the credulous bigots of 1692, by denying themselves "our" advanced understanding of science and reason, had hastened the demise of benighted Puritanism. From the Enlightenment until at least the Civil War, dwelling on the Salem witch trials thus offered the ready assurance that an outbreak of so deadly a spiritual mania could never recur.

The familiar narrative of the Salem trials, beginning with the hiring of the Reverend Parris and proceeding through Stoughton's refusal to apologize, was first assembled, with typical care for detail, by Thomas Hutchinson. It was Hutchinson who first perceived that spectral evidence had been the central issue of the trials and gave it clear, forceful definition. Hutchinson acknowledged (as Bancroft would not) that the ministry had written letters warning that spectral evidence alone was insufficient for conviction. Having examined many of the transcripts, including some that have since been lost, Hutchinson was the first to perceive the essential irony of the court's proceedings: "The most effectual way to prevent an accusation was to become an accuser."[35]

The conclusion Hutchinson drew from his many perceptions, however, derived more from his own time than from 1692.

There are a great number of persons who are willing to suppose the accusers to have been under bodily disorders which affected their imaginations. This is kind and charitable, but seems to be winking the truth out of sight. A little attention must force conviction that the whole was a scene of fraud and imposture, began by young girls, who at first perhaps thought of nothing more than being pitied and indulged, and continued by adult persons, who were afraid of being accused themselves.(II, 47)

In Hutchinson's view, because the hysterical symptoms of all the afflicted could have been nothing but "fraud and imposture," all the executed become "innocents," and all judges and juries become credulous.

Such generalization winks a good deal of the truth from sight. Hutchinson ignores the convincing power of fits of hysteria. He does not consider that, even though the powers ascribed to a "witch" may be imaginary, witchcraft was a seventeenth-century New England reality, almost surely practiced by Bridget Bishop and Wilmot Redd. If the events of 1692 had been nothing more than an instance of "young girls" fraudulently manipulating fearful adults, why could the accusations not have multiplied anywhere, anytime, and often during the Bay Colony's Puritan era? The discomfiting truth is that Hutchinson's rationalist overview of the witch trials, like his later slightings of colonists's anger at the Stamp Act, the Townshend Duties, and the Boston Port Act, greatly underestimates the power of popular feeling at times when social dislocation becomes aggravated into crises. Hutchinson's view, however, was one which post-Revolutionary Americans, anxious both to place pre-Enlightenment credulity far behind them and to trust that the progress of their own era precluded further crises, would be especially prone to accept. Hutchinson's conclusions were to become the assumptions upon which Bancroft, Upham, Drake, and even Hawthorne would reconstruct Salem witchcraft narratives.

To Bancroft, the Salem witch trials were a cultural turning point of such magnitude that they needed a villain of greater intellectual stature than William Stoughton. Giving Cotton Mather the benefit of no doubt, Bancroft reclothed him as the very type of late medieval megalomania, "an example of how far selfishness, under the form of vanity and ambition, can blind the higher faculties, stupefy the judgment, and dupe consciousness itself."[36] Bancroft's way of damning the witch trials immersed him, however, in a problem of logical consistency Hutchinson had not had to face. The controlling idea of Bancroft's entire *History* was that the glorious progress of the western world, made possible by the spirit of rational protestantism, had been born during the Reformation but had migrated to the new world between 1607 and 1640. Although this spirit was most clearly embodied in New England Puritanism, protestant reason seemed to have received such a setback in 1692 that the skein of steady progress was no longer discernible.

If New England's God had been slowly evolving from punishing Jehovah into enlightened Liberty, Salem's intuitions into the nature of the deity had shown themselves to be embarrassingly retrograde during the very middle of the transition.

To argue away this problem, Bancroft amasses remarkable powers of historical ingenuity. Before beginning his narrative of the Salem trials, Bancroft advances an apparently unquestionable insight of his own: "it must be remarked that, in modern times, the cry of witchcraft had been raised by the priesthood rarely, I think never, except when free inquiry was advancing" (III, 84). Exactly when or how the ministers or accusers had cried out upon the spirit of an advancing "free inquiry" is left conveniently unspecified. In truth, Bancroft needed to assume the advance of free inquiry as his basis for a later, more crucial argument. At the end of his narrative of 1692, Bancroft claims that the disgrace of the witch trials enabled New England's enlightenment fully to emerge: "Employing a gentle skepticism, eliminating error, rejecting superstition as tending to cowardice and submission, cherishing religion as the source of courage and the fountain of freedom, the common mind in New England refused henceforward to separate belief and reason" (III, 98). The sudden and complete triumph of the New England common mind, in its turn, rests on nothing more than Bancroft's assumption that, throughout the gathering injustice of the trials, "the common mind of Massachusetts was more wise" than either its appointed judges or its credulous ministry. "It never wavered in its faith," Bancroft claims (III, 98). Stoughton and Mather had had their way, not because the common man believed them, but because the common man tacitly knew that Christianity was prophetic of a time of reason. In 1692 Bancroft's New Englanders suddenly emerge as ur-Unitarians, a people wary of the Word but "cherishing religion as the source of courage and the fountain of freedom."[37]

This remarkable piece of historical reconstruction is, however, only Bancroft's warm up to still more glorious things. The "reason" and "belief" that after 1692 have become inseparable in New England are of a particular kind:

The invisible world began to be less considered; men trusted more to observation and analysis; and this philosophy, derived from the senses, was analogous to their civil condition. The people in the charter governments could hope from England for no concession of larger liberties. Instead, therefore, of looking for the reign of absolute right, they were led to reverence the forms of their privileges as exempt from change. (III, 99)

Bacon, Locke, and Jefferson are here made one, so swiftly and so thoroughly are sense empiricism and notions of natural political right presumed to enter into post-Salem New England, and thereby into pre-Revolutionary American history! The fact that Cotton Mather, more than any judge on the special court, and certainly more than the common people, wished to examine the sensual data that would demonstrate witchcraft escaped Bancroft's notice. Liberation of spirit had to immediately follow the defeat of a theocratic judicial system. Without offering evidence, Bancroft could then conclude that, beginning in 1693, New Englanders looked to their stipulated political "privileges" as the tangible evidence of rational liberties.

A major historian is surely entitled to one major mistake. Specious though Bancroft's argument about the witch trials is, it put 250 years of Massachusetts history, Whig history, and western thought together in one seamless rainbow. Seen from the proper distance, each of its colors flows imperceptibly into the next. Even though the facts of 1692 do not confirm the progressive force of the popular will, the Salem witch trials had by the mid-nineteenth century become vital to the history of both New England and the nation. Although Bancroft distorted the record rather than subvert the cornerstone of his cultural belief, condescension toward him is not in order here. We still want to believe his version, because no small part of democratic faith must be abandoned if he was wrong. As long as religious conflicts seem important because they yield progressive politics, as long as the people's wisdom must prevail over benighted learning, the power of Bancroft's synthesis is not likely to disappear.

Palfrey's post-Civil War perspective enabled him, for once, to challenge Bancroft's dramatic generalities effectively. Palfrey could no longer have confidence in Bancroft's relentlessly progressive thinking. The clear connection between the Dred Scott case and the carnage at Antietam had shown Palfrey that the bloody consequence of assuming that judicial decisions reflect moral good had not been confined to America's pre-Revolutionary darkness. An "ingrained respect for law," Palfrey somewhat uneasily states, has been "at all times a characteristic of the people of New England."[38] If it was true that New Englanders in 1692 had worriedly agreed to mass jailings and select executions, thereby doing "violence to their sentiments of justice, humanity and honor" (exactly Bancroft's argument), then cowardly law-obedience has again surfaced in the many New Englanders who have recently acceded to the Compromise of 1850: "When they [New Englanders] echoed the maxims of Stoughton and his set, they were in much the same state of mind as were the loyal citizens of the same community who, a hundred and sixty years later, presented their thanks to the champion of the Fugitive-Slave Bill for refreshing their sense of obligation" (III, 131). The implied similarities between William Stoughton and Daniel Webster, between jailing a witch and returning a fugitive slave, were evidently much on Palfrey's mind. Not only was Palfrey a proud – and therefore ashamed – descendant of a founder of Salem; he had freed, at considerable personal cost, some thirty Louisiana slaves he had inherited upon the death of his brother.

In Palfrey's view, New England popular virtue was an assumption never fully realized. Bancroft's insistence that, after 1692, the common mind of New England "refused henceforward to separate belief and reason" had too often proved illusory. The most Palfrey will offer in its stead is his belief that Massachusetts was singular in the rapidity with which "reason, courage, and humanity have so soon resumed their sway" (III, 133). As Palfrey saw it – clearly anticipating much twentieth-century literature about the Salem trials – the only admirable participants in the tragedy of 1692 were the martyred few: "Nor can a thoughtful mind fail to consider of what stuff some men and women of that stock were made, when twenty of them went to the gallows rather than soil their consciences by the lie of a confession" (III, 133). Such a statement treads perilously close to acknowledging that, in the summer of 1692, to be an enemy of the New England people was the only way to be worthy of one's heritage. Only by adding the ethnically discriminating phrase "of that stock" can Palfrey claim that Anglo-Protestant New England had managed to retain a small fraction of its true Saints. To Palfrey, the Salem trials were still an entirely Euro-American, courtroom affair.

Even if the pertinence of the northern Indian wars had not been obscured by the historical authority of Hutchinson, Bancroft, and Palfrey, the post-Civil War imaginative literature of the Salem witch trials would have been likely to obscure it. By 1850 New England's Indians were no longer visible on the cultural horizon of the region's opinion leaders. Indian wars and Indian dispossession had become a trans-Mississippi western affair in which sympathy for distant victims was perfectly compatible with support for such destructive and divisive measures as the Dawes Severalty Act (1887). Indians and the northern wars do not figure in J. W. De Forest's novel *Witching Times* (1856–1857), nor in Longfellow's play *Giles Cory of the Salem Farms* (1868), nor in William Carlos Williams's pages on the Salem witch trials (*In the American Grain*, 1925), nor in Shirley Barker's novel *Peace My Daughter* (1949), nor in Ann Petry's *Tituba of Salem Village* (1964), nor, above all, in Arthur Miller's *The Crucible* (1953), a perfectly crafted melodrama in which adolescent lusts, community jealousies, and popular cowardice coalesce in an historical parable of the McCarthy trials. Within this long tradition, Tituba is the sole exotic, the executed are innocent victims of a superstitious witch-hunt, and titled community leaders (judges and ministers) are suspect from the outset. To varying degrees, Bancroftian assumptions are everywhere.

There have been exceptions. Esther Forbes, author of *A Mirror for Witches* (1928) and of *Johnny Tremaine* (1943), gathered evidence about the northern Indian wars for a novel on Salem in 1692, but she died before its publication. Two nonconsensus voices that would be widely heard – Nathaniel Hawthorne and Maryse Condé – differ widely. Hawthorne sometimes subscribes to Bancroftian progressivism, but more often resists it, because he can forget neither the legacy of Indian conflict nor the Puritan tendency to exorcise their inner evil as an Indian "other." Condé, denouncing the entire Matter of Salem from an outsider's perspective, would even distort facts in the understandable hope of questioning if not reversing received attitudes.

BLACK INDIANS AND RED WIZARDS: HAWTHORNE AND CONDÉ

Whenever Hawthorne considers the historical facts of the Salem witch trials, his condemnation of the deadly credulity of Puritan forefathers is at least as shrill as his two chief sources (Hutchinson's *History* and Upham's 1831 *Lectures on Witchcraft*). His hectoring of Cotton Mather exceeds Bancroft's even while anticipating it. The witchcraft hysteria had proven so malevolent that Hawthorne believed its full disclosure to be, for some audiences, unwise. Although the kindly patriarchal narrator of *Grandfather's Chair* (1841), a regional history for young readers, is prepared to divulge only those details "he thought it fit for them to know," Grandfather condemns the witch trials as a "frenzy which led to the death of many innocent persons" and which "originated in the wicked arts of a few children."[39] While the magistrates took delight in wielding deadly authority, "the ministers and wise men were more deluded than the *illiterate* people" (78, italics mine). The grandchildren are not to be told all the details, but they are to learn that, except for the innocent dead, none were guiltless, not even the children, and certainly not the people.

The full force of Hawthorne's contempt for the events of 1692 is to be found at the very end of "Alice Doane's Appeal" (1835), when the young male narrator, whose inchoate tale of witchcraft has failed to move his audience of young Salem women, decides to try "whether truth were more powerful than fiction."⁴⁰ Although his picturing of the executions of August 19 is explicitly intended to evoke "horror" and "woe," it is also assumed to convey the historical truth. We see no Bancroftian "common sense" in the restive crowd on Gallows Hill, only "the deep unutterable loathing and horror, the indignation, the affrighted wonder, that wrinkled on every brow and filled the universal heart" (278). Instead of a stifled popular protest that anticipates the Age of Reason, "the whole crowd turns pale and shrinks within itself, as the virtuous emerge from yonder street" (278). Cotton Mather does not need to quiet the crowd because, like the submissive populace in "The Gray Champion," they are too frightened to make any audible protest. All Hawthorne's Mather needs to do is to be there, "darkly conspicuous" on horseback, waiting to be made over by the narrator into "the representative of all the hateful features of his time," "the one blood-thirsty man, in whom were concentrated those vices of spirit and errors of opinion, that sufficed to madden the whole surrounding multitude" (279).

Although Hawthorne's narrator succeeds in evoking tears from his audience, their weeping seems as conventional as Hawthorne's adjectives. Hawthorne's historical tableau arouses no pity for the expectable "tragedy" of "delusion" so often claimed for the Salem trials. Nor is historical "progress" really at issue. For Hawthorne, the moment of climactic executions contains no seed of Republican virtue within it, no Bancroftian trust in the reason of the people. By the fall of 1692 there was nothing but disgrace for the afflicted, the accused, the judges, and for the silent citizen. In his closing sentences, Hawthorne sardonically proposes that, as a complement to the Bunker Hill Monument, New Englanders should raise "another monument" atop Gallows Hill if they would be true to their traditional belief in the "infirmity" of the human heart (280).

In Hawthorne's writings as a whole, the complexities of the past are more often to be found in his historical romance than in his romantic history. Although critics and readers understandably follow Melville in universalizing "Young Goodman Brown" ("Deep as Dante"⁴¹), reading through the Salem transcripts is the only way to appreciate how vivid and accurate a rendering of the psychology of the 1692 witch accusations "Young Goodman Brown" truly is. Nowhere more so than in Hawthorne's perception of the force of race psychology within the accusatory mind. The first reflection Goodman Brown has when he leaves Salem Village and enters the forest is, "There may be a devilish Indian behind every tree."⁴² The fatherly devil whom Goodman Brown immediately meets while passing a crook in the road resembles old Goodman Brown, and it was he, that gentlemanly devil, who "brought your father a pitch-pine knot, kindled at my own hearth, to set fire to an Indian village, in King Philip's war" (77). This is the kind of displacement of both desire and guilt that John Demos uncovers in the history of New England witchcraft, and Frederick Crews in the patterning of Hawthorne's psychological themes. But it is carefully historicized, suggesting the connection between the Salem witch trials and the prolonging of King Philip's War against the "devilish Indian" immediately to the north.

The specter of Deacon Gookin (surely an oblique, ironic reference to Daniel Gookin) soon tells Goodman Brown that, upon his arrival at the witches' communion, he will find "several of the Indian powwows who know as much deviltry as any of us" (81). After Goodman Brown has arrived at the black mass, he sees that the powwows are "scattered among their pale-faced enemies" (85) rather than separate from them, and immediately trembles with the need to have his faith restored to him. Such a linking of red Indian to white saint among the black devil's specters is an association Brown will not admit to exist within his own self. The irony of his refusal to accept it is made plain, not only in the churchly and moral signifiers of his name but also by his conduct in the forest. Whether the forest is real or psychological, it is the place in which Young Goodman Brown turns into the feared and disparaged Indian, running "at such a rate, that he seemed to fly along the forest-path," "giving vent to an inspiration of horrid blasphemy", and crying out "Come witch, come wizard, come Indian powwow, come devil himself!" (83). One of the tale's few editorial comments occurs in the next sentence, as the narrator informs us that "the fiend in his own shape is less hideous, than when he rages in the breast of man" (84). A compulsion to see the savage Devil has clearly empowered Brown momentarily to become one. Brown's refusal to admit to such an unwelcome self-discovery leads, not only to his relief in waking from a presumed nightmare, but to a lifelong projection of witchery of the sort whose results are legible in trial transcripts and visible on Gallows Hill.

The six short and simple words with which "Young Goodman Brown" closes ("for his dying hour was gloom" 90) linger in the mind no matter how often they are reread. Their effect depends on cumulative context, on the unwelcome supposition that some initiations into evil can be so overpowering that they cannot be transcended, even if the evils are a phantasy or a projection. But the effect of those six words also depends, more than is often recognized, on the tale's historical dimensions. Readers familiar with any variant of Bancroft's claim that the common New Englander "henceforth" refused to separate fact and reason will be brought up short by Hawthorne's ending. Half a century of living among the tangible decencies of Salem Village has done nothing to convince Young Goodman Brown that daily sense experiences have any reality, let alone that Reason is leading to Progress in New England. Participating in the nightmare of half-pleasurable accusation darkens the mind of the young good man literally unto death. If the line of mourners headed by Faith and by Brown's "children and grand-children, a goodly procession" stand for all those who continue to be happy believers in New England's spiritual mission, then it is Young Goodman Brown's bitterly transformative response to the Salem witchcraft delusion that ultimately counts, not theirs.

Maryse Condé has said that, while writing *I, Tituba, Black Witch of Salem* (1986), she would not reread Arthur Miller's *The Crucible* because "I knew that Miller as a white male writer would not pay attention to a black woman."[43] A harsh and true observation, even more widely applica-ble. From Deodat Lawson at least through Richard Weisman, white men and women who wrote narratives of Salem witchcraft, whether historians, novelists, or dramatists, saw Tituba as an exotic presence who set a cri-sis of spiritual accusation and legal trial into motion, but not as a person of significance in herself.[44] Condé's novel thus serves as an act of angry restitution, a revisionist slave narrative designed to recover the voice of an historically neglected black woman who always knew her parentage and identity.[45] As a loving "black witch" able to heal others through the use of herbal medicines and sportive specters (the so-called "white magic" that New Englanders forgot), Condé's Tituba signifies far more than tinder for the Puritan's self-disgrace. Her nurturing powers, derived from her African blood-mother, from her Barbados witch-mother Mama Yaya, and from the Caribbean earth in general, are explicitly and insistently feminine. They are the source of good that the white male Euro-American has chained up in slavery, thereby furthering his own self-destruction.

Condé's attack on white male authority in New England, unlike her attack on British plantation owners in Barbados, rests in great measure on environmental determinism. Boston is first seen as a place of "grayish mist" where "an icy wind blew" and slave master Parris appears "like a ghost in the dirty, foggy light" (43). The bitter winters, the impenetrability of the New England earth, force both wives and afflicted girls into sexual prurience, a fear of removing their clothes, a desire for the horror of sex so strong that Elizabeth Parris believes sex to be "Satan's heritage in us" (42). Although Tituba finds Salem town a livable seaport, the hardscrabble, property-driven farm life of Salem Village is so bleak that phantasizing about witches becomes the Puritan's entertainment. "They needed me," Tituba remarks, "to season the insipid gruel of their lives" (61). To recite

"In Adam's fall / We Sinned all" serves a purpose beyond an educational primer; it is New England's collective and perverse "revenge on their awful humdrum existence" (70).

The mark of the Puritan's inability to open himself to the earth is his sexual and financial hypocrisy. The taverns of Boston, Indian John remarks after working there, are gathering-places for "whores, sailors with rings in their ears, ship's captains with greasy hair under their cocked hats, and even Bible-reading gentlemen, with a wife and children at home. They all get drunk and swear and fornicate. Oh Tituba, you can't imagine the hypocrisy of the white man's world."[46] After a month of household slavery in Samuel Parris's drafty manse, Tituba is able to imagine Puritan hypocrisy to the full: "That was Salem! A community that stole, cheated, and burgled while wrapping itself in the cloak of God's name. And however much the burglars were branded with a *B*, were whipped or had their ears cut off or their tongues cut out, the crimes continued to increase!" (84) These particular criticisms, however valid, were not a new revelation obtainable only through the voice of a 1980s multicultural outsider. Condé's way of attacking Puritan sadism, hypocrisy, and sexual repression resembles H. L. Mencken's "Puritanism as a Literary Force," Randolph Bourne's "The Puritan Will to Power," and D. H. Lawrence's *Studies in Classic American Literature*, with the crucial proviso that women are now seen to bear the suffering. To include an avowedly feminist Hester Prynne in her novel shows Condé's awareness that Hawthorne had anticipated her in seeing woman's love as a redemptive force sacrificed to Puritan conquest.

Condé's contribution to representing injustice in Salem is to differentiate among kinds of witchcraft. The afflicting shapes of black magic as seen by the young women of Salem Village are described by Tituba in the manner and language of the trial transcripts. Throughout Tituba's Caribbean years and even in New England, however, the benign specters of Ebena, Yao, and Mama Yayo also appear to Tituba, giving her emotional strength, generosity of spirit, herbal remedies, and (disregarded) advice to keep her body out of male arms. Even in translation, these spectral appearances are rendered with a subtlety that prevents the reader from ever being certain whether Tituba is having a supernatural experience or an imagined conversation with the dead.

As in "Young Goodman Brown," however, the difference is ultimately unimportant ("Be it so if you will"), because the effect on Tituba remains the same. The contrast between the white magic of Tituba's specters, and the malefic power ascribed to spectral evidence in the Salem witch trials, becomes a persuasive way of separating Caribbean colonialism from its New England counterpart. After Tituba understands how the diabolic powers of envy, lust, and boredom have driven Samuel Parris, Abigail Williams, and Anne Putnam to accuse her, she expresses her bewilderment to her fellow prison inmate, Hester Prynne:

"Why in this society does one give the function of witch an evil connotation? The witch, if we must use this word, rights wrongs, helps, consoles, heals . . . "
    She [Hester] interrupted me with a burst of laughter. "Then you haven't read Cotton Mather."
    She puffed herself up and solemnly declared: "Witches do strange and evil things. They cannot perform true miracles; these can only be accomplished by the visible saints and emissaries of the Lord." (96)

Hester's mockery of Mather is based upon a defensible criticism of the position concerning black magic that Mather had advanced in *Memorable Providences* and *Wonders of the Invisible World*. For New Englanders to have denied the beneficent powers within the Invisible World, while dwelling on Satanic ones, was not only a self-destructive but a divisive act. The more Tituba thinks about Samuel Parris's tall stature, "greenish cold eyes," and love of accusation, the more Tituba becomes convinced that there is neither one new world, nor one western hemisphere (34). "We did not belong to the same universe," she says of herself and of the Parrises (63).

Separated by geography and spiritual belief, Barbados and Salem Village are linked by the oppressive male control exerted by Caribbean plantation owners and by Puritan ministers and magistrates. Affirming Hawthorne's comment that the whipping post was the Puritan's maypole, Condé portrays Calvinism as a means of enslavement just as powerful as the slave owner's whip. She thus subverts the long-standing hierarchy of postcolonial social control, in which the order of presumed worth was white male, white female, black male, black female. There are no admirable white males in Condé's Salem (John Procter, so central to *The Crucible*, makes but the briefest of appearances), and no unworthy women of color in Condé's Barbados. The wives of whites with authority (Jennifer Davis, Goodwife Parris, Ann Putnam Sr.) have become neurotic and sickly victims, while men of color tend to be unreliable seducers (John Indian) or youthful icons of revolt (Christopher, Iphigene).

Deploying characters in this revisionist way runs the risk of reverse racism and reverse sexism. After Tituba has twice watched minister Parris tolerate the fits and accusations of the afflicted girls, her uncertainty about the inner reality of the New England people resolves into a new understanding: "I confess that I am naïve. I was convinced that even a race of villains and criminals could produce some good, well-meaning individuals, just as a stunted tree can bear some healthy fruit" (76). Even if these words are to be read as an exaggeration prompted by momentary feeling, the sweep of Tituba's generalization ("a race of villains and criminals") replaces one system of symbolic absolutes with another. It is evidently "naïve" not to believe that the power of evil (no longer the power of blackness) is exclusively white.

Condé said that *I, Tituba* is "the opposite of a historical novel" because she had "really invented Tituba" and "was not interested at all in what her [Tituba's] real life could have been."[47] The headnote to the novel, signed by Condé, informs the reader: "Tituba and I lived for a year on the closest of terms. During our endless conversations she told me things she had confided to nobody else." Condé's writing of the novel is thus traceable to the same privileged conversations with dead spirits that Tituba experiences within the narrative. Such spectral muses provide a rich source for humor as well as authority for matters unknown.

But what of matters known? Once Condé's Tituba has been publicly accused, four ministers privately torture her in order to extort a confession: "One of the men sat squarely astride me and began to hammer my face with his fists, which were as hard as stones. Another lifted up my skirt and thrust a sharpened stick into the most sensitive part of my body, taunting me: 'Go on, take it, it's John Indian's prick'" (91). This atrocity, not the worst in Condé's narrative, raises a fundamental issue of any novelist's responsibility to the past. The two ministers present, who are named Edward Payson and Samuel Parris, were living human beings. Every reader familiar with the 1692 witch trials knows that the two unnamed ministers, said to be from Beverly and Salem, were John Hale and Nicholas Noyes. During the Salem trials, only three instances of torturing a prisoner were ever alleged; in each case, the suspected witch was bound neck and heels until the blood ran. There is no conclusive evidence, however, of any torturing of Tituba, nor is there reliable evidence for the charge that Samuel Parris beat her.

It may well be, of course, that the Salem judges, and perhaps even the New England ministry, were driven by the guilty, vicarious, and sadistic lust for black women that this torture scene describes. But does Condé's disclaimer "For me *Tituba* is not a historical novel" therefore entitle her to picture historical people committing brutalities for which there is no historical evidence? The scene suggests that there is in fact a second witch hunt occurring in Condé's novel, a crying out against white wizards by a woman of color. Such an urge is not unlike Arthur Miller's ascribing preternatural spiritual power to accusations made by both the afflicted girls and, by implication, of Senator Joseph McCarthy.

As the atrocities of accusation accumulate, the justifying of revenge becomes a vexing problem neither Tituba nor Condé can resolve. If a black woman's "witchery" lies in her nourishing spirit and healing hands, how then to explain away the fact that Tituba cried out upon others as evil witches? Tituba justifies her accusations as necessity, the perverse outgrowth of "the ravages that Samuel Parris's religion was causing" (10). "Even I was being poisoned in this putrifying atmosphere and I caught myself reciting incantations and performing ritual gestures at the slightest occasion" (65). Because she senses that her only defense lies in accusing others, she becomes "another woman," acceding to ministerial and judicial oppression and crying out upon Sarah Good (66). Given the forces assembled against her, her confession at her preliminary examination, quoted directly from the Salem court testimony, becomes a fully understandable, if not blameless act. Nonetheless, no moment in the novel is more effective and convincing than Tituba's response to Samuel Parris, when he condescendingly congratulates her for her confessional testimony: "I hate myself as much as I hate him" (106).

As woman and witch, Tituba rises above the cowardly complicity of her husband John Indian, whose belief that "the duty of a slave is to survive" leads him repeatedly to say "Yes Massa, Yes Missy," to snoop around the tavern for useful gossip, and to accuse anyone at any time it seems advantageous (22, 74). Tituba's eventual dismissal of the man who "had made a pact with my tormentors" (109) is wholly appropriate to the demeaning, self-serving role of the historical John Indian, but it leaves the fictive Tituba with no middle course once she returns to Barbados. For a while she attempts to live, somewhat in the manner of a Hester Prynne, as a womanly healer in a cottage on the margins of plantation society, carrying out the advice that black witch Mama Yaya had given her years before: "Don't let yourself be eaten up by revenge. Use your powers to serve your own people and heal them" (28). When the Maroon leaders solicit her aid in an armed slave revolt, however, Tituba agrees to support and to participate.[48]

Condé nowhere indicates that Tituba's joining in the Maroon uprising compromises Mama Yaya's advice. Tituba is hanged as an admirable martyr to racial oppression. In the novel's epilogue, Tituba lives on as the very shape of implacable racial vengeance, a woman who is "hardening men's hearts to fight," "nourishing them with dreams of liberty." "I have been behind every revolt. Every insurrection. Every act of disobedience" (175). America is "a vast, cruel land where the spirits only beget evil!," a spiritual desert where "they will lock up our children behind the heavy gates of the ghetto" and where, therefore, "blood will beget blood" (177, 178). Although the beginning of the novel establishes that the beneficent power of Caribbean witchery rests on its healing refusal of revenge, Condé also acknowledged, "I wanted to turn Tituba into a sort of female hero, an epic heroine, like the legendary Nanny of the maroons."[49] Ultimately, then, the virtue of becoming "I, Tituba, black witch of Salem" rests on knowing when to forswear revenge, when to exercise revenge, and when not to worry about the inconsistency between them. To discriminate justly and to choose wisely among these three responses remains a Gordian knot neither Maryse Condé nor any human society has yet found the way to untie.

Tituba's closing denunciation of America as a "vast cruel land" is based upon the premise that what she has experienced in Salem is not the nadir of past Puritanism, but rather the sign of a culture whose corrupt essence has not changed. Whether the witch trials of 1692 prepare the way for secular enlightenment or the progress of western republicanism is of no import in Condé's novel. Nor is Condé concerned, as writers from George Bancroft to Marion Starkey to Arthur Miller had been, to concentrate on the courage of the few who died for individualism of conscience. The deterministic forces of geography, gender roles, and race prejudice are collectively too overpowering to make such considerations tenable.

Like Hawthorne, Condé knows that spectral evidence remains the heart of the historical matter of the Salem trials. Tituba may not be concerned with the specific evidentiary question of whether Satan can assume the shape of an innocent person, but her assumptions about a person's motivation and conduct are based primarily upon the kinds of specter one envisions. The power of the diverse shapes seen by Barbados planters, Salem ministers and Caribbean women of color are all undeniable. Words such as "superstition," "credulity," or "delusion," so central to two centuries of historical accounts beginning with Hutchinson, do not appear in Condé's novel. In Tituba's specter-ridden worlds, such terms would only point up the blind futility of rationalists who try to snuff out the seeing of the Invisible. In their scorn for the blindness of Sadducees who would deny the spirit world, Maryse Condé and Cotton Mather become oddly and momentarily one.

PART THREE

Revolution

Headnote

It was in the stars, perhaps, for the American Revolution to have
flamed first in Boston. Wasn't the Jamaican rum drunk there spiced
with gunpowder to burn the tongue? Here debate was hottest, debate
changing to riot, then assuming the Army's anonymous uniform for
violence. Petitions, speeches, Sam Adams populism, all that fierceness
of the early pre-Revolution that somehow lost momentum and gained
the marmorial dignity of George Washington.

Robert Lowell, "New England and Further" (1977)

Jamaican rum notwithstanding, the crisis which in hindsight we call "the
American Revolution" cannot be imagined without the active resistance
of New England, particularly the Commonwealth of Massachusetts, from
1761 to 1775. Consider the sequence of forcing events in New England
during the two years between the passing of the Intolerable Acts
(May 1774) and the expulsion of the British from Boston (March 1776): the
increasing presence of the British army; the passing of the Suffolk Resolves;
the forming of the Provincial Congress; the defiance of the Mandamus
Councilors and Provincial courts; refusal to pay royal taxes or to import
British goods; the powder alarm, seizing Fort William and Mary in New
Hampshire; standing opposition to regular troops sent to Portsmouth and
Salem; the 115 deaths and 365 casualties on April 19, 1775 during the British
march to Lexington and Concord; the Green Mountain Boys' capture of
Ticonderoga; the raising of a 5,000-man army among the four New England
colonies; the Battle of Bunker Hill; the blockading of the British behind
Boston Neck; the fortification of Dorchester Heights; the British abandonment of Boston. Twenty months into which were compressed more
trials than most people endure in a lifetime, comprising a total overturn of
power. In other colonies during those twenty months there were protests,
meetings, boycotts, and sporadic violence, but nothing like the concerted,
sustained, and successful effort mounted by New Englanders to expel

British military rule – and with it British political authority – from their lands.

When the crisis of the Intolerable Acts erupted, New Englanders immediately drew upon the formidable weapon of their perceived past. Within less than three weeks, Josiah Quincy Jr. wrote his lengthy *Observations on the . . . Boston Port-Bill* (1774), laced with facts and footnotes to demonstrate the history of conspiracy within and against New England. "Providence from the beginning has exercised this country with singular trials," Quincy declared. "In the earliest periods of our history, New England is seen surrounded with adversaries and alternately vexed with foes foreign and domestick." For six pages, Quincy demonstrates how New England's chartered liberties were directly threatened in three particular crises: Thomas Morton's conspiring with Archbishop Laud; Mason's conspiring with Sir Ferdinando Gorges; Dudley's conspiring with Sir Edmund Andros. Readers' familiarity with recent recurrences of Tory conspiracy is assumed; one need only realize that "Our freedom has been the object of envy, and *to make void the charter of our liberties* is the work and labor of an undiminished race of villains." Just as New England has always been a godly land beset with "men who harboured the darkest machinations," so today "wolves will appear in sheep's clothing, knaves and parricides will assume the vesture of the man of virtue." Quincy's readership, however, was now fully intercolonial. References to *Cato's Letters*, to Plutarch, and to Shakespeare's *Julius Caesar* end in Quincy's urging the reader to resolve, like Cassius, to "march against the enemy." The double rhetoric succeeded in reaching both audiences. Rushed into print almost simultaneously in Boston and Philadelphia, Quincy's *Observations* helped rouse the Continental Congress first to protest the Boston Port Bill and then – even more importantly – to support the Suffolk Resolves.[1]

The specific provisions of the Suffolk Resolves (September 1774), approved by the Provincial Congress before planned military action began, show in embryo form the remarkable totality of the Massachusetts revolt. The Suffolk Resolves declared 1. that no obedience was due from any citizen of the Province to the Intolerable Acts, to the Mandamus Councilors, or to appointed judges; 2. that all taxes should be withheld from the Provincial Government until the "proposed Provincial Congress" should direct their expenditure; 3. that Boston Neck be fortified and the Commonwealth's militia resist by any necessary means the arrest of a Massachusetts citizen defending his chartered liberties; 4. that the Provincial Congress, elected by the several towns, shall henceforth pass all needed legislation; 5. that whenever "our enemies" threaten to abridge our rights, the Suffolk County

Committees of Correspondence shall communicate the danger to outlying towns; and lastly, 6. that we shall "abstain from the consumption of British merchandise and manufactures . . . until our rights are fully restored to us."[2]

Do not these provisions collectively comprise a *de facto* declaring of independence twenty months before July 4, 1776? In one regard, the Suffolk Resolves are considerably more daring than the Declaration of Independence; they explicitly construct an alternative government and provide for the economic and military means of defending it. Moderate patriot Joseph Galloway of Pennsylvania feared that "the inflammatory resolves of the County of Suffolk contained a complete declaration of war against Great Britain."[3] Is it any wonder that, when John Adams, Samuel Adams, and John Hancock arrived in Philadelphia to attend the Second Continental Congress, shortly after the Battle of Lexington and Concord, they were suspected to be volatile, dangerous incendiaries by many delegates from the middle and southern colonies? Or is it any wonder that the elder, tetchy John Adams would repeatedly insist that the American Revolution had been fully achieved before the Declaration of Independence was even drafted? In his 1820 Plymouth oration, Daniel Webster would not hesitate to assert: "In New England the War of the Revolution commenced. . . . No portion of the country did more than the States of New England to bring the Revolutionary struggle to a successful issue."[4] While praising the Pilgrims, Webster well knew that the origin of Forefathers Day (Old Colony Day) had been in Plymouth's celebration of the repeal of the Stamp Act. To him, honoring the forefathers and celebrating the Revolution had become one.

The difference between the Suffolk Resolves and the Declaration of Independence lies less in their immediate consequence than in crucial differences of wording. Joseph Warren, who drafted the Resolves, couched their preamble in the neo-Puritan rhetoric of defending the forefather's civil liberties; Jefferson, however, was to make a futurist appeal to the law of nature and the rights of man. Warren's argument required that he offer the Englishman's claim of strong loyalty to his king; Jefferson's universalist phrasing allowed him to treat George III as the very model of political tyranny. When, however, we compare the Suffolk Resolves to Jefferson's firm but quite unthreatening tract "A Summary of the Rights of British North America"(1774), written at the same time as the Suffolk Resolves, we see how and why it was to be the actions undertaken in eastern Massachusetts, as called for in the Suffolk Resolves, that would force the revolution of the colonies as a whole.

The problems for persuasive justification of the Suffolk Resolves for the nation, however, were daunting. The Commonwealth of Massachusetts had long defined its identity by its fidelity to its Calvinistic forefathers, to the charter of its origin, and to an ecclesiastical polity that emphasized local control at the expense of concerted power. Even if a backward-looking populace could be led to revolt, how were acts of "rebellion" to be ethically and logically defended? How could one convince contemporaries that seemingly offensive military actions were in truth defensive? Was it possible that Calvinistic patriarchs had actually believed in the Rights of Man? To maintain revolutionary leadership would demand solutions to these challenges of political presentation and literary representation. As "rebellion" became revolt, as revolt became revolution, as revolution became the founding of a new New England, and as New England then began to lose its authority within the Republic, these challenges only became more acute. After July 1776, the facile claim that Parliament and/or the King were the true rebels against Liberty promptly lost its cogency. My next two chapters, focusing on the crisis time of September 1774 to March 1775 as the centerpiece of New England's Revolutionary self-definition, will address only selected but crucial parts of that immense, troubled, and fascinating cultural narrative.

CHAPTER 7

Boston revolt and Puritan restoration: 1760–1775

Popular mythologizers often forget that the confrontations at Lexington, Concord, Ticonderoga, and Bunker Hill occurred as the culmination, not the onset, of revolt in Massachusetts. Historians' narratives of "America's" growing revolutionary agitation rightly start in 1761 with James Otis Jr.'s argument against government's use of Writs of Assistance to apprehend suspected smugglers in Boston ("An Act Against the Constitution is void"[1]). In accord with the Whig historical tradition described by Bernard Bailyn, Otis appealed to Liberty as a political virtue emanating from the proper balance of the powers of King, Lords, and Commons within the British Constitution.[2] However, as in the 1680s, citing such a right to self-governance while avoiding the issue of dockside taxation had a twofold appeal. For vivid imagery of a people's insurgency within (or against) Liberty's balance of powers, it has proven hard to surpass the sequence of incidents from the plundering of Andrew Oliver's and Thomas Hutchinson's houses, to the defense of Hancock's sloop *Liberty*, to the Boston Massacre in King Street, to the Boston Tea Party, and finally to the first meetings of the independent Massachusetts Congress and the gathering of the volunteer Army of New England.[3] As rebellious New Englanders aimed their rhetorical weapons first at Parliament (1765), then at the British magistracy (1768–1775), finally at the King (1775–1776), and constantly at the appointive Provincial government, they slowly became republicans, not from initial conviction, but almost *faute de mieux*, as if they had reluctantly discovered that Liberty must be invested, not in charter privileges, but in a new polity, albeit with a Roman precedent.

Sam Adams, agitator and propagandist extraordinaire, was the crucial figure behind the insurgency. Given their long-standing collaboration, we can be sure that Joseph Warren wrote nothing into the Suffolk Resolves of which Sam Adams disapproved. Adams's circular letters of the late 1760s built the network that enabled the colonies to respond in concert, an infrastructure soon formalized as Committees of Correspondence within and beyond

Massachusetts. The Suffolk Resolves put Massachusetts in the suspect position of leading any movement toward intercolonial independence – a radical advocacy leading Adams into committee politicking rather than public speaking as a member of the Massachusetts delegation to the Continental Congress. In after times, however, Jefferson called Sam Adams "truly the *Man of the Revolution*" and John Adams recalled that his cousin had been "a wedge of steel to split the *lignum vitae* that tied America to England."[4]

Even if we deny that Sam Adams's long-closeted drive for independence became a prevailing force in 1775, a formidable conceptual question, aggravated by etymology, remains about the motives of pre-Revolutionary resistance, especially in Massachusetts. Living in the aftermath of 1776, 1789, and 1917, we assume that the "Age of Revolution" must have involved a transformative overturn of the old (feudal monarchical) order and the formation of a new (national, republican, or socialist) order – a transformation exemplifying those nineteenth-century ideas of historical progress that have proven so difficult to abandon even while we discredit them. Since 1800 the gradual decline of Latin in schools has led us to ignore or to slight the fact that the word "Revolution" derives from *Revolvo/Revolvere* meaning "to turn backward" – not to turn forward. But the backward-looking force of the word would hardly have been lost upon James Otis, Josiah Quincy, Joseph Warren, or the two Adamses, whose Harvard education had implanted Latin etymologies in their bones. Even more important to all of them, the chief example of successful revolution had been the "Glorious Revolution" of 1688, which they understood to have been a glorious restoration of British constitutional rights from the tyrannical usurpation of the Stuarts. To conduct a successful "revolution" meant to form a government that would secure those rights vested in British constitutional tradition both in England and in New England. But how to do so? By restoring the 1629 Colonial Charter (impossible), by improving the 1692 Provincial Charter (not negotiable) or, *in extremis*, by forming a new government (almost surely treasonable)?

Noah Webster's 1828 *Dictionary* shows us what would happen to the word *revolution* in the combined aftermath of the Declaration of Independence, of America's written constitution, and of events in France that had presumably inaugurated a new era. Webster's first political definition of *revolution* is "a material or entire change in the constitution of government" – a nineteenth-century progressive definition if ever there was one. When Webster considers the example of 1688, however, he lists an alternative meaning, namely "the restoration of the constitution to its primitive state."

Finally, however, when thinking of "the revolutions in Poland, in the United States of America, and in France," he concludes that revolutions have "consisted in a change of constitution."[5] Obviously a "restoration of the constitution to its primitive state" is hardly the same as "an entire change in the constitution of government." Webster's way of minimizing the earlier restorative meaning of the word *revolution* may bring the word's connotations closer to us, but it leaves us farther from an understanding of Otis, Warren, and Sam Adams.

To the extent that New England's "revolution" was to be a restorative event, the prospect of revolution lent primacy to the achievements of Puritan forefathers in establishing an ideal status to which New Englanders might return. To justify revolution in this manner was to return to the essence of seventeenth-century Puritanism as Dwight Bozeman defines it – restoring the purity of first spiritual communities. But to do so inevitably recast the meaning of Puritan mission. Instead of establishing a Godly Commonwealth via the Congregational way, Puritans were now seen as sustainers of a free Commonwealth through steady resistance to British tyrannical incursions both ecclesiastical and political.[6] The key term defining the mission of the forefathers shifted from communal and individual "salvation" to the communal and individual "Liberty" that had made salvation possible. Combining the two meanings, Sam Adams argued in 1772 that Liberty always had been, and still was, the "salvation" of Massachusetts.[7] When Puritan "Liberty" was invoked in the 1770s, however, the word no longer had the same sense in which Nathaniel Ward used it to enumerate "the Liberties of the Massachusetts Colonie" in 1641 ("liberties, Immunities and priveledges as humanitie, Civilitie, and Christianitie call for as due to everie man in his place and proportion"[8]). By 1775 Liberty had become a civic right and divine spirit, deriving from God but guaranteed to every man through covenantal, usually chartered agreements both past and present. Less Nathaniel Ward's granted privilege than Sam Adams's demanded right.

Care not to overstate is needed here. A restorative model of revolution based on Puritan forefathers was but one cause of resistance and revolt in Massachusetts. Graeco-Roman models of republic building and universalist theories of natural right became of greater importance by the time of constitution formation in the 1780s. In the intercolonial context, Dickinson, Mason, Rush, Franklin, Jefferson, Hamilton, and John Adams – and sometimes Sam Adams – wrote of the rights of British citizens anywhere, irrespective of any particulars of the Massachusetts Puritan heritage. Nor do I presume to distinguish moments in which patriot Whigs acted in accord with Puritan virtues from other moments in which patriot writers and Sons of Liberty opportunistically appealed to the forefathers as a tactic for gaining power. The political leader who believes he can honestly and accurately separate propaganda from principle, even in his or her own words, has probably not been in public life for long. What I do propose is to describe how and why, after 1765, the idea of regressive popular "revolution" to the Liberty of the forefathers was first advanced, became an historical force in 1774–1775, and then gradually subsided. As the intermediary between the political caucus and the Black Regiment, Sam Adams is the key to both the fact and the memory of this process.[9] Without a consideration of Sam Adams's character, John Adams claimed, "the true history of the American revolution can never be written."[10] Moreover, Sam Adams's stature was not to be tarnished or greatly diminished until well after the age of Bancroft and Hawthorne. Around the figure of Sam Adams, even more than John, would be concentrated the retrospective meaning of revolution in defense of New England's heritage.

As Peter Shaw has shown, the violent underside of Puritan culture exerted direct influence on revolutionary agitation. The origin of organized resistance lies in the forming of the Boston Mob out of the North and South End gangs who, in the early 1760s, had gathered annually on November 5 to celebrate "Pope's Day" by a street fight whose purpose was to destroy the other gang's effigy of the Pontiff.[11] The Essex Street oak was selected to become the Liberty Tree because it was believed to have been planted immediately prior to the execution of Charles I. During his journey to join the Second Continental Congress, John Adams, who had little sympathy with the intimidation techniques of the Sons of Liberty, would nonetheless make a point, while in New Haven, of visiting the grave of regicide judge John Dixwell who, like John Bradshaw, was reputed to have said "Rebellion to Tyrants is Obedience to God." When Sam Adams followed Jonathan Mayhew in tarring Governor Bernard's administration with the threat of an American episcopacy, he roused fears of popery spreading to Massachusetts country towns, published them in the *Boston Gazette*, and signed them "A Puritan." When attacking the new practice of the king paying the governor's salary, Sam Adams signed his most inflammatory essay "Cotton Mather."[12]

In adopting the identity of the Puritan father, rather than "Vindex," "Candidus," or "Determinatus," Sam Adams may have been following his cousin's precedent. In the aftermath of the Stamp Act, supposed deist John Adams, observing that charter rights sometimes had to be fought for, observed that "The world, the flesh, and the devil have always maintained a confederacy against her [Liberty], from the fall of Adam to this hour, and will, probably, continue so till the fall of Antichrist."[13] John's way of lending authority to this biblical overview was to publish it in the *Boston Gazette* as part of a pseudonymous letter penned by "Governor Winthrop to Governor Bradford." Before July 1776, both Adamses evidently believed that a revolutionary argument for Liberty could acquire force in New England by advancing it in the terms and garb of Puritan forefathers.

James Otis and Peter Oliver, whose allegiances were totally opposed, both lent currency to the term "Black Regiment" because they recognized the importance of Boston's Congregational ministry (including Jonathan Mayhew, Samuel Cooper, John Lathrop, Andrew Eliot, and Charles Chauncy but probably not Samuel Mather) in promoting resistance to particular Provincial measures and in supporting independence once it had been declared.[14] Although the term "Black Regiment" separates clerical leaders from political leaders and the laity, the status of minister and political leader could on important occasions shade into one another. Surely the great size of Boston's Second Church was not the only reason why Massacre Day commemorations and meetings to resist the landing of East India Company tea were held there rather than in Faneuil Hall, "the cradle of liberty." What was it like for a Boston tradesman, long accustomed to observing Sam Adams at Town Meeting, to see him stand in the pulpit of Old South on the eve of the Boston Tea Party and declare "This meeting can do nothing more to save the country"?[15]

Perhaps even more to the point, what had it been like the year before to hear Joseph Warren, in the most remembered of Massacre Day Orations, declare from the same pulpit, then draped in black, the following creed:

None but they who set a just value upon the blessings of LIBERTY are worthy to enjoy her – Your illustrious fathers were her zealous votaries – when the blasting frowns of tyranny drove her from public view, they clasped her in their arms, they cherished her in their generous bosoms, they brought her safe over the rough ocean, and fixed her seat in this then dreary wilderness; . . . With one hand, they broke the stubborn glebe; with the other, they grasped their weapons, ever ready to protect her from danger. No sacrifice, not even their own blood, was esteemed too rich a libation for her altar. God prospered their valour, they preserved her brilliancy unsullied, they enjoyed her whilst they lived, and dying bequeathed the dear inheritance to your care. And as they left you this glorious legacy, they have undoubtedly transmitted to you some portion of their noble spirit, to inspire you with virtue to merit her, and with the courage to preserve her. You surely cannot, with such examples before your eyes, as every page of the history of this country affords, suffer your liberties to be ravished from you by lawless force, or cajoled away by flattery and fraud.[16]

To Warren, LIBERTY is a goddess only slightly subordinate to the Christian God. The forefathers brought LIBERTY with them in 1620, not just as a woman to be "enjoyed," but as a household god, similar to Aeneas's Lares and Penates, who would preside at the household "altar" while the hard land is broken into civilization. The citizen in Warren's audience is conceived as the legatee of the forefather's "noble spirit," half-farmer, half-soldier, ever ready like a militiaman to grasp his weapon and protect Liberty both against ravishment by "lawless force" (the redcoat standing army) or against an insidious form of inner seduction (the "flattery and fraud" of Governor Hutchinson and the Tory placemen). Nowhere in Warren's address does the Christian God, John Winthrop's "God almighty in his most holy and wise providence," receive the same adoration, or release the same energy of protection, as does fair LIBERTY.

Sam Adams not only introduced Joseph Warren on such semireligious occasions; he empowered the Black Regiment by two-way stratagems of correspondence. For example, the Election Day Sermon of 1773, delivered by the Reverend Charles Turner before Governor Hutchinson, informed the citizens of Massachusetts that "the Powers that be are ordained of God alone," that "avarice and ambition" lead magistrates into "worldly interests inconsistent with the publick welfare," that Massachusetts had resisted such governors during the "Revolution" of 1689, and that a prompt cleansing of New England's sins (the "extravagance and luxury" promoted by its present leadership) would now be in the Commonwealth's spiritual interest.[17] As soon as Turner's sermon was published, Adams sent a copy of it to his Virginia confidant Arthur Lee, surely for purposes of distribution as well as doctrine. Similarly, after Joseph Warren sent the Suffolk Resolves to Sam Adams in Philadelphia, the Massachusetts delegation brought them to the Continental Congress for approval. Immediately after approval, Sam Adams wrote to the Reverend Charles Chauncy in Boston praising the "spiritual and patriotic Resolves" of Suffolk County, enclosing the Continental Congress's endorsement, and noting that Josiah Quincy was about to set off for England to "do great service to our country there."[18] We may be confident that Charles Chauncy made Sunday use of Adams's communiqués and that Chauncy, like both Adams and Quincy, now conceived of "our country" as something other than Old England.

In an admirable instance of manuscript collecting, George Bancroft uncovered the reasons why the newly organized town Committees of Correspondence had embraced the Statement of Grievances which the Massachusetts House presented to Governor Hutchinson in July 1772. The local townships wanted it known that their defiance was motivated by a desire to connect the present to the past. Plymouth declared that, to redeem the sacrifices of their ancestors, "they were ninety to one to fight Great Britain." The people of Cambridge, in town meeting, resolved that they "were much concerned to maintain and secure their invaluable rights which were not the gift of Kings, but purchased with the precious blood and treasure of their ancestors." Roxbury wrote that "our pious Forefathers died with the pleasing hope, that we their children should live free; let none, as they will answer it another day, disturb the ashes of these heroes by selling their birthright." The small town of Pembroke resolved that "if the measures so contrary to our ancestor's traditions, and so justly complained of, were to be persisted in and enforced by fleets and armies, they must, they will, in a little time issue in the total dissolution of the union between the mother country and the colonies."[19]

Even if there was considerable arm-pulling by leaders of the local Committees of Correspondence, these community resolutions must have had the concurrence of the citizenry. Citizens in those towns that, like Cambridge, had formally voted support in town meeting, were exercising a political right that was a cornerstone of their Puritan legacy. The first extant American publication was not the Bay Psalm Book, as is often assumed, but the Freeman's Oath, published in Newtown (Cambridge) in 1639 per order of the General Court. A voter's sworn allegiance was to "the wholesome Lawes & Orders made and established" by the Commonwealth of Massachusetts with nary a mention of England, nor of colonial status.[20] The citizen's duty "to maintain and preserve all the liberties and priviledges" of the Commonwealth carried within it an ambiguity: whereas a "privilege" may have been a grant of the King's 1629 Charter, a "liberty" may be the inherent right/power of a "Free-Man." By taking the oath, an unincorporated man, "free" by what John Winthrop called "the Law of Nature," became incorporated into the "Freemen," one civic body whose common interest was explicitly defined as the common weal of Massachusetts. No recognition of any transatlantic authority was involved in swearing to "give my votes and suffrages as I shall judge in mine own conscience may best conduct and tend to the publick weale." Because the Freeman's Oath ended with the words "So help me God in the LORD JESUS CHRIST," it is likely that voters in turbulent town meetings in the 1770s remained aware of the ultimate legitimizing power of their vote.

Of all the public occasions in Massachusetts history, surely none was of more ceremonial importance than the inauguration of the Massachusetts Constitution, the formal reinstitution of the Commonwealth, on October 25 1780 – three years before the Peace of Paris, one year before the

Articles of Confederation, seven years before the United States Constitution. On that occasion, speaking before Governor John Hancock and Lieutenant Governor Sam Adams, the Reverend Samuel Cooper delivered a sermon on republican virtue that grew out of the Puritan Election Day sermon tradition. Cooper took the occasion to develop, in its most absolute form, the restorative model of revolution in Massachusetts. As Sam Adams's long-time closet associate and correspondent, the Reverend Cooper could now divulge the aggressively defensive politics he had shared with both the merchants of his Brattle Street church and with his Congregational brethren throughout the Commonwealth. He began with the traditional typological analogy between Puritan settlement and the New Israel, directing it toward a pointed conclusion exactly illustrative of Sacvan Bercovitch's model of American symbology: "Like that nation ["the ancient Israelites"] we were led into a wilderness, as a refuge from tyranny and a preparation for the enjoyment of our civil and religious rights."[21]

If Massachusetts Freemen will take the long view, Cooper insists, they will realize that nothing of fundamental value has changed. When the people of Massachusetts finally realized that, after 1691, their liberties as provincials were less than the liberties of British citizens in England, they redressed this "late dismal situation, from which Heaven then redeemed us by a signal and glorious revolution" (15). Discovering that their "written charter was but a thin barrier against all prevailing power," the citizenry first agitated, and then revolted, in order to recapture those rights. To Cooper, the recapturing of those rights was at least as important as national independence. The Declaration of Independence, he asserts, only stated, for British as well as American ears, "the principles upon which her own government and her revolution under William the Third were founded" (19).

By sermon's end, Cooper's assessment of the revolution has become fully reversionary. The blessed in heaven who look down upon today's inaugural are not Locke, Sidney, or Cato, nor those who have practiced Faith, Hope, and Charity, but the libertarian Saints of Massachusetts who, through town meetings and the Congregational way, have made the Commonwealth of 1780 possible.

What are those illustrious forms that seem, to hover over us on the present occasion, and to look down with pleasure on the memorable transactions of this day? . . . Are they not the venerable Fathers of the Massachusetts who, though not perfect while they dwelt in Flesh, were yet greatly distinguished by an ardent piety, by all the manly virtues, and by an unquenchable love of liberty? . . . With what pleasure do they seem to behold their children, like the antient seed of Abraham, this day restored to their original foundations of freedom, their Governor "as at the first and their Councillors as at the beginning." (54–55)

The Puritan saints bless the inauguration, not because any form of the *novus ordo saeclorum* has been created, but because their original "broad Charter of Liberty" has at last been renewed after decades of enduring the debilitating compromises of the Provincial Charter.

Thomas Paine's *Common Sense* had insisted that colonial children could become men only if they would have the courage to cast off the tyrannical British parent. Samuel Cooper celebrates a revolution of the opposite sort: the current generation has shown itself worthy to be true "children" of Puritan forefathers by the courageous way they have fought to have their polity "restored to their original foundations of freedom." Paine's appeal had had the broadest possible colonial readership; Cooper's speech, however self-congratulatory the occasion, foretells a diminishing of New England's influence into regional nostalgia, a smug hesitancy about a future in which little further apparently needs to be done. In Cooper's grotesquely over-written words, one finds a source of that decline in energizing purpose that would prevail among the next generation of New England's spokesmen, notably Fisher Ames.

The pre-1777 writings of rebellious New Englanders, however, had clearly been a major cause of revolution, even if the extent to which their writings provoked action remains impossible to gauge. Sam Adams's letters and editorials are especially impressive for the relentless consistency with which he asserted colonial rights against the Provincial government and/or the British ministry. Although any plausible argument seems to have been grist to Sam Adams's resistance mill, his appeal to the presumably libertarian legacy of the forefathers was never far from the surface. How, then, do we respond to the fact that Sam Adams's essays served, like *Common Sense*, as effective propaganda toward revolutionary action? Because New England's patriot shopkeepers, merchants, farmers, and clergy thought they were restoring the libertarian virtues of the forefathers, neo-Puritan filiopietism must have been a major cause of revolution, however intangible or mythic it began to seem as early as Samuel Cooper's inaugural address. Non-Separatist as well as Separatist Puritans were thought to have made, through covenanted exile, their *implicit* Declarations of Independence. And perhaps, after all, they had.

Set aside the friendly, innocuous Sam Adams who smiles at us from the label of today's beer bottle. The Sam Adams rightly remembered by contemporaries was the daunting anti-government strategist of the

Massachusetts House, a compelling voice in the Continental Congress, and the master of a seemingly sputtering but quite controlled (Puritan?) plain style that rouses to resistance. His forte was not protesting against ministerial taxation, which was potentially compromising, but denouncing British troops as a standing army. Here he was on sure historical ground that led back through Andros's downfall to Endicott's and Winthrop's defiance of a threatened British invasion in the 1630s:

Let any one imagine the distress of this people – a free city, I mean once free and still entitled to its freedom, reduc'd to the worst of tyranny – an aggravated tyranny! Was not an army of placemen and pensioners sufficient, who would eat us up as they eat bread, but an array of soldiers must be stationed in our very bowels – Where is the bill of rights, magna carta and the blood of our venerable forefathers! In this dilemma to what a dreadful alternative were we reduc'd! *To resist this tyranny, or, submit to chains.*[22]

Although the sense of crisis in Adam's phrasing would seem to date this passage to 1775 when Boston was under occupation by General Gage, Adams actually wrote it in 1769, a year after the first arrival of a redcoat regiment. Without delving into documentary detail, Adams here aligns the three sacred cultural-political traditions that would continue to support libertarian resistance: the Bill of Rights emerging from the Great Revolution, Magna Charta, and "the blood of our venerable forefathers." Such an appeal has little to do with democratic self-determination, but much to do with turning backward to a presumably collective tradition of Protestant protest.

The wonder of Sam Adams's writings (setting aside his managerial and strategic talent) is his skill in finding diverse ways of phrasing this appeal for different audiences. In addition to public rousers like the sentences above, Adams had, as early as 1765, fully thought through a quasi-legal argument to be heard in the British ministry, in Parliament, in the provincial government, in Boston town meeting, and in the Massachusetts House, of which he would soon become Clerk. In memoranda to the Province's London agents, in official statements of the House, and in pseudonymous articles in patriot newspapers and magazines, he repeated his political logic, with suitable variations, again and again and again.[23] To cite its 1765 formulation to the Earl of Dartmouth: Sam Adams and Thomas Cushing speak "for the People of New England," identifying themselves as "Descendants of Ancestors remarkeable for their Zeal for true Religion & Liberty." The theocratic ancestors of Massachusetts's citizens are said to have prospered both because of their spiritual integrity, which earned them the approval of "HIM, whose is the Earth & the Fulness thereof," and because of the "Charter granted them by King Charles the first," a charter that was a "Contract," "a *Compact*" that was "not a National Act" and that therefore left them "entitled to all the Libertys & Immunities of free & natural Subjects of Great Britain." In particular, "By this Charter, we have an *exclusive* Right to make Laws for our own internal Government & Taxation" (italics mine). Because "great Distance" renders it "impracticable" for any American colony to be represented in the British Parliament, New England legislative bodies have clearly been afforded the right to legislate for themselves, provided only that the laws of England (which in turn means the rights inherited from Magna Charta and the Rights of 1689) are not violated.[24]

As long as readers do not look too closely at the specifics of either the Charter of 1629 or of 1691, Adams has devised a perfect circular argument that allows him to proclaim New England's loyalty to Old England while simultaneously claiming New England's complete legislative independence. The unwritten constitution is assumed to be a gathering sequence of libertarian rights, not the continuing restrictions of the common law. The linchpin of Adams's argument is its appeal back beyond the Provincial Charter of 1691 to the moment of settlement in 1630, thereby assuming, without directly saying so, that a royally appointed governor with a veto, and "his Majesty's Council," also with a veto, are all Johnny-Come-Latelys who have no *foundational* authority. Through 1775 Adams's appeal to covenantal politics, by dint of its timely repetition and broad basis in religiocultural appeal, remained a devastatingly effective argument within the New England for which it was so clearly designed.

The stumbling block was the legal authority of the 1691 Charter under which Governor Hutchinson was acting. Adams's strategy of avoidance was to link the Glorious Revolution in England with the revolt against Andros in Massachusetts and to present both revolutions as restorative triumphs to be reenacted. The hectoring of Thomas Hutchinson thus thrived on comparisons tarring Hutchinson with the precedent of Andros. Adams rightly sensed that his contemporaries were preconditioned by their historical understanding of 1689 to regard royally appointed governors and London ministers as clever conspirers against civil liberties rather than as bunglers anxious to demonstrate their authority. But the analogy also served a tellingly reactionary purpose. If Hutchinson could only be expelled as Andros had been, Massachusetts could return to the charter provisions of 1629 rather than 1691. Any patriot who acted on this analogy was taking up arms to turn the clock very far back indeed.

Sam Adams was prepared to exploit differences between Andros and Hutchinson as well as similarities. When Adams learned that Hutchinson was willing to accept his salary from the King, Adams scornfully attacked him on the grounds that appointed Governor Hutchinson, unlike appointed Governor Andros, claimed to be a staunch New England Congregationalist.

It will be recorded by the faithful historian, for the information of posterity, that the first *American Pensioner* – the first *independent* Governor of this province, was, not a stranger, but one "*born and educated*" in it – Not an ANDROSS or a RANDOLPH; but that *cordial friend* to our civil constitution – that *main Pillar* of the Religion and the Learning of this country; the Man, upon whom she has (I will not say wantonly) heaped all the *Honors* she had to bestow – HUTCHINSON!![25]

The contempt here masterfully heaped upon Hutchinson, Andros, and Randolph urges good riddance to the imperial evils all three represent, rather than worrying about what might follow their demise. Posing as a New England historian (a revisionist Hutchinson!), Adams anticipates the strategy Hawthorne was to pursue in "The Gray Champion": to evoke New England heroism by focusing on sequential crises (1632, 1689, 1775) in which a momentary uprising frees Protestants from aristocratic privilege.

Sam Adams's ability to embody aspects of the Puritan tradition, in addition to invoking them, is conveyed by the famous Copley portrait, in which Adams's plain clothing, defiant glance, and hand pointing dramatically to the Massachusetts Charter all make him seem, unlike Copley's finely dressed loyalists at ease amidst symbols of wealth, to grow out of the tradition of Puritan limner portraits.[26] We should recognize, however, that Sam Adams could also, when desirable, set all charters aside in order to mount a strictly biblicist attack on British/loyalist policy, almost as if he were an eighteenth-century Roger Williams. Shortly after Hutchinson assumed the governorship, Sam Adams, writing as "Candidus," opened an article for the *Boston Gazette* with the sentence "We read that Jeroboam the Son of Nebat made Israel to sin," and then sustained the implied comparison to Hutchinson for six remarkably ingenious and forceful pages.[27] From first sentence to last, the reader is led to assume that Thomas Hutchinson and his placemen, not Adams and the Sons of Liberty, stand revealed as "a perjur'd Traitor and a Rebel against God and his Country." Civil war arises only from the continued sins of negligent kings (Solomon/Hanoverians) who enable self-seeking usurpers (Jeroboam/Hutchinson) to profit through patronage.

As if he were writing the application of a sermon, Sam Adams reveals the significance of Jereboam (Hutchinson) for present-day politics:

What has been commonly called rebellion in the people, has often been nothing else but a manly & glorious struggle in opposition to the lawless power of rebellious Kings and Princes; who being elevated above the rest of mankind, and paid by them only to be their protectors, have been taught by *enthusiasts* to believe they were authoriz'd by God to *enslave* and *butcher* them. (269)

The true rebel against civic virtue, Adams argues, is the unjust ruler who is most likely to appear in the form of a governor, supported by placemen, and by cowardly political idolaters. "Let us beware of the poison of flattery," Candidus (Adams) urges: "If the people are tainted with this folly, *they will never have* VIRTUE *enough to demand a restoration of their liberties in the very face of a* TYRANT" (273). When governors become tyrant rebels, the holy people must become the true loyalists, devoted to restoring their foundational liberties.

By 1775 Sam Adams had become less guarded in predicting that "revolution" in New England and/or the colonies as a whole would demand independence. But Adams's greater openness does not mean that his notion of "revolution" had somehow become synonymous with natural rights theory, with the first amendment, or with the kind of Bancroftian "democracy" that trusts the wisdom of today's popular will. For years he had been repeating his belief that "the Religion and public Liberty of People are intimately connected; their interests are interwoven, they cannot subsist separately."[28] When prodding country towns to set up Committees of Correspondence, he adapted Miltonic imagery to the service of Boston-led politics: "the Iron hand of oppression is dayly tearing the choicest Fruit from the fair Tree of Liberty, planted by our worthy Predecessors."[29] Now, in November 1775, even though the tyrannies of George III's ministry were producing "the grandest Revolutions the World has ever seen," the ultimate goal was the recovery of virtue: "the golden opportunity of recovering the Virtue & reforming the Manners of our Country should be industriously improvd." The goal must still be defined as restoration because "our Ancestors in the most early Times laid an excellent Foundation for the security of Liberty."[30]

The prospect of subsuming New England within an independent America tried Sam Adams's faith as well as his patience. By January 1776 the influence exerted by middle colony accommodationists such as Jonathan Dickinson and Joseph Galloway to delay declaring independence led Sam Adams to write in disgust to John Adams, "I would endeavor to unite the New England Colonies in confederating, if none of the rest would join in it."[31] As the British army pursued George Washington through New Jersey and Pennsylvania with little popular opposition, Adams became convinced that the middle colonies had no tradition of spiritual resistance that would enable them to rise up and fight for civil and religious liberty. "They seem determined to give it up," Adams wrote angrily to his wife, "but I trust that my dear New England will maintain it at the Expence of every thing dear to them in this Life – they know how to prize their Liberties."[32] Although Adams knew Washington's army was fighting for the newly united states, Adams's regional pride makes him sound like the first go-it-alone secessionist.

Forty years later, when John Adams declared "without the character of Samuel Adams, the true history of the American Revolution can never be written," he had in mind a particular idea, not then widely accepted, of what the American Revolution had truly been about: "What do we mean by the American Revolution? Do we mean the American war? The Revolution was effected before the war commenced. The Revolution was in the minds and hearts of the people; a change in their religious sentiments of their duties and obligations."[33] Combining these two statements reveals that the "character" of Sam Adams represents the essential "religious" force without which the Revolution cannot be explained. This statement, which so belies the presumed vanity of John Adams in his later years, involves much more than his recognition of Sam Adams's skills as a publicist, organizer, and tactician of resistance. As early as 1765, John Adams had written that Sam Adams "has the most thorough Understanding of Liberty, and her Resources, in the Temper and Character of the People, tho not in the Law and Constitution, as well as the most habitual radical Love of it." In sum, Sam Adams's career showed that Liberty had been the religion of the age, and John believed he knew whence Sam Adams's persuasive power had derived: "If he was a Calvinist, a Calvinist he had been educated, and so had been all his ancestors for two hundred years."[34] Love of civil liberty had been the essential Calvinist trait that Sam Adams had been able successfully to reaffirm, not just in Revolutionary New England but also in Revolutionary America. The victory of this New England/American "character," its transferring of the locus of the "religious sentiments" of the people from Monarch and Governor to the Continental Congress and to themselves, was the true American Revolution, complete by 1775, a revolution which battlegrounds could only confirm. Was not John Adams's retrospective pride, even if accurate, also a sign of New England's loss of centrality in the new nation? Doth not the old man protest too much?

In historical fact, as the Second Continental Congress moved toward declaring independence, Sam Adams's ability to foment resistance through resolute principles and adaptable tactics began to be supplanted in power by John Adams's skills at state building and diplomacy. John Adams's thinking about the grounds for revolution, student of Bolingbroke as he was, had always drawn upon wider sources. During earlier years, to be sure, John Adams had lent strongly worded, though contextually qualified support to Sam Adams's argument for a Puritan revolution. "A Dissertation on the Canon and Feudal Law" had praised the Puritan forefathers as models for today's defense of civil liberties. Such passages did not, however, represent the whole of John Adams's argument, even in 1765. The force behind the aspiration for liberty was the existence of universal natural rights that precede all charters and all great migrations: "I say RIGHTS, for such they ["the poor people"] have, undoubtedly, antecedent to all earthly government – Rights that cannot be repealed or restrained by human laws – Rights derived from the great Legislator of the universe."[35] John Adams's early commitment to a precedent universality of natural right demanded a more than Puritan consideration for "the histories of ancient ages" and for "the great examples of Greece and Rome" (18). Citizens suffering under tyranny who defend foundational rights of liberty do more than restore natural rights; they lay a basis for their continuing expansion in statutes. To John Adams, the settlement of America was to be revered because it was the "opening" of today's "grand scene of providential illumination," not its forever-defining moment (8).

LOYALISTS AND THE WEAK LINKS

There had been, from the beginning, discontinuities in the presumably seamless skein of New England history which could be cited to explain why today's violent revolutionary was not as saintly as John Adams's model Puritan forefather. Weak links would surface repeatedly to threaten the grand myth that a spirit of defensive revolution had descended from Puritan forefathers to republican sons. For commemorative patriot writers beginning in Mercy Otis Warren's generation, these discontinuities proved vexing because they seemed to admit but three equally problematic resolutions: to fully admit them (unacceptable), to omit them (surely detectable), or to rationalize them (quite possibly suspect). For loyalist writers, however, the discontinuities amounted to hypocrisies ripe for satisfying if futile exploitation.

The crux of the difficulty was the disparity between the grievances that had roused the 1630 Puritan, the 1689 colonial, and the 1770 patriot to revolt on behalf of civil liberty. Issues intractably different in kind and severity separated Laudian silencing of the Puritan ministry from the threat of episcopacy, the voiding of the old charter from violations of the Provincial Charter, appointing a governor from paying the governor's salary, and the financial consequences of the enclosure movement from a 3d tax on tea. The immediate provoking causes of the American Revolution in New England center again and again on issues of the right and agency of taxation, whether by Parliament, by a representative local legislature, by decree of the governor and the council, by judicial decision, or by imposition of the King's troops. The corollary issues of episcopacy and parliamentary governance were real enough, and the Boston Port Act was flagrant tyranny by any standard, but the inflammatory grievances of the 1770s were, even more than in 1689, mercantile and financial. After 1770, the provoking incidents involving Liberty had not centered on founding "Puritan" beliefs about the Christian spirit or ecclesiastical polity.[36]

The link to 1689 was not as unquestionable as writers for the *Boston Gazette* assumed. Although avoiding taxes under the Navigation laws had been a closet motive for expelling Andros, Cotton Mather had mobilized Bostonians to support a Country Party that had been plausibly fearful that an episcopacy in Boston might serve a closet alliance between Andros's government and French Catholic troops then on New England's northern border. By the late 1760s and 1770 the impetus for revolt had shifted. French Catholics no longer held political power in Quebec. Revolutionary feeling arose among New England's coastal merchants and tradesmen primarily because public controversies pertaining to the right of taxation, to the payment of Custom's Duties, and to measures for stopping smuggling were visibly affecting the daily life of the docks. The two infamous incidents reliable for lasting protest – the Boston Massacre and the Boston Tea Party – had little to do with religion. In 1689 the villain had been the closet Catholic King James, and the virtues of a restorative revolution had been gladly granted to Parliament. After 1772 the threat of the SPG and an American episcopacy was to subside until by 1775 it was no longer a major issue in New England's revolution, despite Sam Adams's and Josiah Hawley's passing attempts to revive it. For a short time after the Quebec Act, Bostonian patriots even continued to proclaim their loyalty to the King, while vehemently denouncing the king's ministry and/or Parliament for usurping the power to tax.

During the late 1760s the Boston mob repeatedly harassed and plundered Provincial officials, customs officers, and redcoats. The tarrings and featherings, forced recantations, and burning of houses remained deeply compromising to the new nation's need to believe in Revolutionary virtue. Not only did the mob's violence threaten the image of the Revolutionary as principled gentleman; it suggested there was an underlying motive of class resentment (seaport workingmen sacking the estates of wealthy Tories) that did not accord with the universality of the Revolution's libertarian cause. Here again, the supposed link back to the Glorious Revolution in Boston was problematic at best: from 1685 to 1689 there had been no recurring pattern of popular harassment of the Andros régime. When confrontation came to Boston's streets in 1689, it had been resolutely nonviolent and controlled, much like the celebrated but singular Boston Tea Party. Nor had there been, in the late 1620s or the early 1630s, any violent resistance to perceived British oppression. John Endicott's summoning of the trained bands and his cutting the red cross out of the British flag in anticipation of an invading British fleet were to be interpreted by Bancroft and Hawthorne as an important precedent of Revolutionary independence, but what remains so striking about the incident is the purely symbolic nature of Endicott's defiance. One may hypothesize that the Massachusetts Bay colony had been too safely distant to resist by force during the 1630s, and then too enfeebled to resist by force during the late 1680s, but the fact remains that these two moments established an admirable image of resolute nonviolent resistance that the mob hazings of the Revolutionary era belie.

Sam Adams repeatedly deplored instances of mob violence. Nor did he ever claim, as British Whigs had done, that under threat of tyranny a limited degree of popular violence was not mob anarchy but defense of Liberty.[37] However, there is no evidence that Adams tried to quell the Boston mob in advance. The Copleyesque image of Sam Adams as principled Puritan revolutionary, worthy of comparison to Winthrop or Bradford, remains tainted by Adams's written remark about the purpose of the Massacre Day orations: "it is a good Maxim in Politicks as well as War to Put & keep the Enemy in the wrong."[38] Even if we conclude that Adams truly believed his enemy was "in the wrong," his casual coupling of politics with war and his clear justifying of the means by the end cannot be dismissed. Some things, Sam Adams knew, had best remain forever hidden. In the very same paragraph in which John Adams credits Sam Adams with the "character" that reveals "the true history of the American Revolution," he provides us with a remarkable portrait of Sam Adams as shredder of the Revolutionary record: "I have seen him, at Mrs. Yard's in Philadelphia, when he was about to leave Congress, cut up with his scissors whole bundles of letters into atoms that could never be reunited, and throw them out of the window, to be scattered by the winds. This was in summer, when he had no fire; in winter, he threw whole handfuls into the fire."[39]

If we claim that, in the years preceding 1776, Civil Liberty became the Massachusetts Puritan's religion, thereby according priority to a political framework rather than the religion it served to protect, what then is to be concluded about Massachusetts's retaining an established Congregational Church in its Constitution? Or, to put the same question in the opposite way, if American Puritanism had been defined *ab ovo* by the Congregational Way, how could liberty of conscience in spiritual matters have later become a revolutionary credo that any true Puritan descendant was willing to advance? To abandon the establishment of the Congregational Church would be to forsake the tradition that had long defined you; not to abandon it would be to "turn back" from the religious tolerance increasingly associated with Revolutionary republicanism and which would be enshrined in the first amendment of the federal Constitution.

The problem came to dramatic visibility during the proceedings of the First Continental Congress. On an evening in October 1774 the Massachusetts delegation was summoned back to Carpenter's Hall to answer inquiries posed by the Pennsylvania delegation concerning "complaints from some Anabaptists and some Friends in Massachusetts against certain Laws of that Province, restrictive of the Liberty of Conscience."[40] Israel Pemberton informed Thomas Cushing and the two Adamses that "the Laws of New England and particularly of Massachusetts were inconsistent with Liberty of Conscience" and then demanded assurance that Massachusetts would promptly "repeal all those Laws, and place things as they were in Pennsylvania" (311). Although John Adams's personal opinion probably was no different from Pemberton's, he was caught in a contradiction between Commonwealth practice and Revolutionary ideology. His two rejoinders – "that the Laws of Massachusetts were the most mild and equitable Establishment of Religion that was known in the World" and that "the very Liberty of Conscience which Mr. Pemberton invoked, would demand indulgence for the tender Conscience of the People of Massachusetts, and allow them to preserve their Laws" (312) – amounted to nothing more than lame hedging, if not double-speak. In his diary, Adams was to interpret this summons as yet another attempt, fueled by Quaker envy of Massachusetts's power, to derail the independence movement. But the pertinence of the issue for Massachusetts's leadership of the Revolution remains. As early as 1774, New England's lead in advancing revolutionary values, threatened by its own past, showed signs of eroding. If Liberty of Conscience is a defining value of the Revolution, how can Puritan "restoration" logically have been its cause?

Shortly after their arrival in England, loyalists Thomas Hutchinson and Peter Oliver resumed work on their manuscript accounts of the recent Massachusetts revolt. Under such contentious circumstances, it is astonishing that the third and final volume of Hutchinson's *History* is as dispassionate, factual, even nonjudgmental as it is. The worst Hutchinson was publicly to write of Sam Adams was that he had "a talent of artfully and fallaciously insinuating into the minds of his readers a prejudice against the characters of all whom he attacked, beyond any other man I ever knew."[41] Hutchinson shows no awareness, anywhere in the third volume, of Adams's argument that revolt against today's tyranny was a glorious restoration of the civil liberties of New England forefathers. Hutchinson had heard the argument from pulpit and podium and probably read it *ad nauseam* in the pages of the *Boston Gazette*. But the "king killing" feeling that survived in American Puritanism, the conviction that the old charter still defined their rights to self-governance, and the measuring of self-worth through opposition to British authority – the popular power of these instinctive motives, reinforced by a select understanding of history, eluded Hutchinson as completely as had his fellow New Englanders' gut response to a standing army of redcoats.

Unlike Hutchinson, Peter Oliver wrote a full-throated polemic against what he termed "the Faction," using a wide range of satiric technique and a vivid rhetorical palette. Although Oliver had been Massachusetts's Chief Justice, he slighted Hutchinson's constitutional arguments in order to probe visceral issues Hutchinson chose to avoid: armed smuggling, street violence, tarring and feathering, outright demagoguery, ministerial hypocrisy, class envy, provable sedition, public lying – and government's folly in being too lenient until too late. Oliver's lively account is true to its title, "The Origin & Progress of the American Rebellion." Not only does Oliver consistently use the word "Rebellion" in contrast to "Revolution"; his interest in the "Origin" of rebellion drives him to demolish the model of heroic Puritan forefathers. To Oliver, the meaning of rebellion in Massachusetts is not the triumph of "Liberty", a term he derives from the British Constitution only, but rather the sordid victory of a cultural-political entity he derisively calls "Daemonocracy."[42]

Led by James Otis, Sam Adams, and Joseph Hawley (Oliver's evil trinity), "Daemonocracy" has emerged as a modern polity still thankfully restricted to New England. In its daily strategies, it foments anarchy to advance the self-interest of "the Faction," but its energizing "Daemon" is a demagoguery deriving from New England Puritan tradition. When Peter Oliver asserts that "Independence, it is true, was declared in Congress in 1776, but it was settled in Boston, in 1768, by [Sam] Adams & his Junto" (148), he advances the exact same claim John Adams would repeat a quarter-century later, but from an opposite political perspective. By claiming Independence for pre-Revolutionary Massachusetts, thereby sidestepping Virginia and the Declaration, Oliver undertakes to trace the origins of Daemonocracy back to the forefathers revered by fellow New Englanders.

Oliver's history is highly selective but lacks neither evidence nor compelling rhetoric. The claim that the Puritans sacrificed all for civil liberty is belied by the number of splinter sects that were driven out of the Bay colony, showing that "there is no surer Way of propagating a Cause, especially a Religious Cause, than with the Scourge of Persecution" (15). Oliver quotes sections of the 1629 Charter at length in order to prove that the King did not grant the Massachusetts Bay Company exclusive control over taxation. How could the settlement of New England logically have anything to do with Liberty, Oliver wonders, when the voting privileges of a "Freeman" were promptly restricted to Congregational Saints, thereby excluding all Church of England men "from this so natural Privilege."[43]

Oliver's ridicule of "red-hot zealotry" is broadcast among the Daemonocracy of all eras in New England's past (15). Roger Williams "seemed always to labor under the Hectick of Enthusiasm" (20). John Endicott "in his great Fervor of Zeal, cut the Cross out of the military Ensign, as he took it to be a Relick of Antichrist" (20). The zeal of the Puritans actually led them to be proud of harboring regicide *judges* appointed by their anointed monarch. By honorably negotiating the terms of the 1691 Charter, after the seriocomic rising of the "Mob" against Governor Andros, Increase Mather showed that he was "as shrewd & as sensible a Man as any of the Massachusetts" (24). As a reward for his acumen, Mather was to be relentlessly sniped at by New England's leaders so that they could first misconstrue and then violate the Provincial Charter.

Oliver's satiric skills are at their sharpest in portraying the Black Regiment dressing up Religion "into a Stalking horse, to be skulked behind, that Vice might perpetrate its most atrocious Crimes" (26). The dissenting ministers of Boston, "that Metropolis of Sedition," showed their special cowardice by "distinguishing theirselves in encouraging Seditions & Riots, untill those lesser Offences were absorbed in Rebellion" (41, 42). The aging Charles Chauncy was a man of "exorbitant Passions" that erupted into blasphemies scriptural and political (43). Jonathan Mayhew, slow of mind, awakened his congregation from his lumbering sermons only by becoming "a partizan in Politicks" (44). But Samuel Cooper, "the last of the sacerdotal Triumvirate" was the true representative of the Black Regimental type: "not deep in his Profession, but very deep in the black Art"; "His Tongue was Butter & Oil, but under it was the Poison of Asps"; "Proficient in Jesuitism, he could not only prevaricate with Man, but with God also" (44, 45).

One member of the Faction enraged Oliver to the very limit of satiric control. Oliver's opening salvo was to quote an (unnamed) "celebrated Painter in America" who had remarked "if he wished to draw the Picture of the Devil, that he would get Sam Adams to sit for him" (39). Sam Adams was "so thorough a Machiavilian, that he divested himself of every worthy Principle & would stick at no Crime to accomplish his Ends" (39). Metaphors of animal entrapment flood Oliver's mind. Because Adams needed cash to finance the rebellion, money-pockets merchant John Hancock, whose mind was "a meer Tabula Rasa," became "as closely attached to the hindermost Part of Mr. Adams as the Rattles are afixed to the tail of the Rattle Snake" (40). To corrupt the naïve enthusiasts of Massachusetts, Sam Adams "like the Cuddle-fish, would discharge his muddy Liquid & darken the Water to such an Hue that the other was lost to his Way, & . . . would again be seized & at last secured" (40). Unlike Otis or Hawley, Adams's mind "was all serpentine cunning" of the kind that cloaked rebellion in the dress of Puritan virtue: "The other [Sam Adams] had always a religious Mask ready for his occasions; he could transform his self into an Angel of Light with the weak Religionist; & with the abandoned he would disrobe his self & appear with his cloven Foot & in his native Blackness of Darkness" (41).

As Oliver finished recounting Adams's machinations as Clerk of the House, he dropped all animal and underworld metaphors in order to say it straight. Adams and others of the legislative Faction "were unwearied in their Arts of Calumny & assassination of Characters which stood in the Way of their Views of Independence. They used every low & dirty Art, from Mouth & press, to stigmatize those who would not coincide with their measures" (96). By manuscript's end Sam Adams has been fully vested as the King of Daemonocracy, successfully robing himself in the phony virtue of Puritan "independence" while avidly pursuing self-interest by any means that can be hidden.

In spite of all its literary skill, however, Oliver's satire revealed nothing more about Sam Adams than had Hutchinson's legalisms. Neither in his alliance with Whig merchants nor his steady opposition to appointed officials do Sam Adams's known conduct and published writings demonstrate class envy, a drive for money, or pursuit of power. Oliver's brilliant character portrait cannot help us understand the Sam Adams of the 1780s and 1790s, who suspected the central power of the Constitution, denounced the new mushroom gentry, futilely longed for a "Christian Sparta" in Boston, and wrote his last letter to Thomas Paine in order to grieve for Paine's leading the once pious American people toward a "defence of infidelity."[44]

In 1825 three historical romances were published in the hope of stimulating a fiftieth anniversary market for fiction commemorating Revolutionary events in New England. By that time, no informed patriot could accept at face value Sam Adams's view of Revolution as the heroic restoration of the liberty of the Puritan forefathers. Too many complicating and compromising details that looked more like a rebellion were now known. Even more important, "revolution" was rapidly acquiring its new meaning. The year 1775 seemed less a restoration of an older era than the opening of a new one whose originating principles were universal and timeless ("the rights of man") rather than regional and cultural (the protestant Commonwealth's Body of Liberties). Sam Adams's cherished view was venerable but a bit tired. Questions about its validity needed to be acknowledged, while the emerging model of secular progressive republicanism demanded its own voice. What emerged from these crosscurrents was, inevitably, historical literature with tellingly conflicted value systems and tellingly forced resolutions.

In Mercy Otis Warren's *History of the Rise, Progress and Termination of the American Revolution* (1807) these shifts are already apparent. The distinction between "revolution" and "rebellion" is of no discernible interest to Warren, but the change from aristocratic Province to democratic "Republic" is crucial. To be sure, Warren's pages center on high-minded New Englanders who act for Liberty and Independence. She even feels a need to justify her regional favoritism by remarking that her *History*'s "appearance of locality" is due only to the fact that "the town of Boston" was the place where "the sword of civil discord was first drawn."[45] However, Warren does not derive Liberty from John Calvin or John Winthrop, nor does she worry about the specifics of New England's charter rights. To be descended from a New England family that has avoided luxury is a much greater commendation than to be descended from a New England family that has maintained Puritan convictions. At times, Mercy Warren even presents Puritanism as an impediment to revolutionary advance. She accounts for "the unlimited confidence long placed in the specious accomplishments of Mr. Hutchinson" by emphasizing his stature in the Congregational Church. A Puritan people "prejudiced by the severities their fathers had experienced" trusted too much in Hutchinson's mere "profession of their own religious mode of worship," thereby allowing "a tincture of superstition" to become a "higher recommendation than brilliant talents"(1, 46).

Mercy Warren's perfunctory interest in Calvinism as a cause of Independence is apparent in her shifting characterization of Sam Adams. In *The Adulateur*, Warren's closet tragedy of 1773, Sam Adams is portrayed as Cassius, and James Otis as Brutus; together they contend for Liberty against the varied tyrannies of Rapatio (Hutchinson), Limpit (Andrew Oliver), Hazelrod (Peter Oliver), and Bagshot (Captain Preston of Boston Massacre infamy). Cassius/Adams's opening words, his declaration of faith, invokes the freedom of Puritan forefathers through secular reasoning that Sam Adams would have questioned:

> Oh, Brutus, our noble ancestors
> Who lived for freedom, and for freedom dy'd;
> Who scorned to roll in affluence, if that state
> Was sicken'd o'er with the dread name of slaves.[46]

By the time Warren published her *History* over thirty years later, summarizing Sam Adams's character required a full paragraph, but no mention of any Puritan heritage. Adams is wholly refashioned into a model of classical virtues: "Early nurtured in the principles of civil and religious liberty, he [Sam Adams] possessed a quick understanding, a cool head, stern manners, a smooth address, and a Roman-like firmness, united with that sagacity and penetration that would have made a figure in a conclave. He was at the same time liberal in opinion, and uniformly devout; *social with men of all denominations*, grave in deportment; placid, yet severe; sober and indefatigable" (1, 116, italics mine).

Allowing Sam Adams the reluctant Puritan to recede into Sam Adams the Roman affords Warren greater opportunity to see New England's Revolutionary virtue as the foundation of an expanding republican empire. The last paragraphs of her *History*, surely written in the immediate aftermath of the Louisiana Purchase, show her awareness of the need to recast lines of continuity. Plymouth, Boston, and Jamestown are not mentioned; it is the justice of the new Republican polity, together with the virtue of its people, which "render the United States of American an enviable example to all the world, of peace, liberty, righteousness and truth." Like Samuel Cooper's inauguration sermon, Mrs. Warren's *History* closes with an image of angels approving the new earthly order. Warren's angels, however, are not the spirits of the Puritan forefathers but angels of a deity called "the Divine Economist" who envisions how "the western wilds, which for ages have been little known, may arrive to that stage of improvement beyond which the limits of human genius can not reach" (II, 698).[47]

In early republican historical romances, Sam Adams's argument for a revolution-restoring Puritan liberty receives little more than a dutiful nod. Lydia Maria Child's *The Rebels; or, Boston Before the Revolution* (1825) voices a familiar claim when doctor-minister Samuel Willard insists "Our forefathers brought the spirit of liberty from their native land when it was in the greatest purity and perfection there; and it has not degenerated by change of climate." Because Willard's belief is not thereafter affirmed by other patriots, it becomes associated with the Black Regiment only.[48] Sam Adams is the only historical figure of importance in *The Rebels*, but Sam Adams's defining concern, as Mrs. Child characterizes him, is to distinguish popular liberty from popular license. Her historically preposterous way of elevating Sam Adams is to show him defying the mob in order to conduct Thomas Hutchinson to safety. The novel's hero, Henry Osborne, may be the son of a Congregational minister committed to independence, but his sturdy virtues are associated with no specified theological or historical principles. From novel's outset, Mrs. Child sees Liberty as an irresistible natural force, describable as a swelling ocean, an illuminating light, a torrential river or a consuming fire – a force freed from any and all origin in Puritan and Provincial charters. To be among "The Rebels" is to be a freedom-loving son or daughter of New England who never worries about how "Liberty" had been defined in the words of dead Puritans.

Catherine Sedgwick's *The Linwoods* (1835) views the Revolutionary Puritan in similarly worldy terms. Although Sedgwick's patriot hero, Eliot Lee of Westbrook, Massachusetts, is "a lineal descendant from one of the renowned pilgrim fathers," his admired father is neither a cleric nor a town representative, but "a laborious New-England farmer, of sterling sense and integrity."[49] Introduced as "a favourable specimen of the highest order of New-England character" (I, 43), Eliot Lee is equally at ease on the farm and among the gentlemen of King's College. When the war begins, Eliot is seen "pondering on the character of our New England people"; he concludes that the external façade of the Yankee ("industrious, frugal, provident and cautious") will always rise, when a worthy cause emerges, into "a fervid energy, an all subduing enthusiasm" (I, 101). New England "enthusiasm" (the very quality Peter Oliver had singled out for satire) leads neither to a search for grace nor to transgressing the restraints of gentlemanly honor. When Sedgwick describes Eliot Lee's "fine face, marked with nature's aristocracy" (I, 254), and pictures him serving as George Washington's favored *aide de camp*, it becomes clear that a New England Yankee gentleman is being refashioned as the model American of whom Virginia's natural aristocracy would approve. Like Mercy Warren's Sam Adams, Eliot Lee's revolutionary virtues turn out to have no fortifying link to his "renowned pilgrim fathers."

Any tenuous link Child and Sedgwick perceive between Puritanism and Revolutionary republicanism depends on granting regional character traits primacy over doctrine and politics. Fenimore Cooper's *Lionel Lincoln* (1825), by contrast, ascribes the Puritan heritage to a loyalist protagonist and then attacks it. The American branch of British major Lionel Lincoln's family had been founded, Cooper writes, by "an ascetick puritan" and "obstinant predestinarian" whose "mind became soured by the prevalent but discordant views of the Deity."[50] Despite numerous opportunities and good reasons to join the revolutionaries, Lionel does not abandon his loyalist political and military allegiances. The most outspoken patriots Lionel meets in Boston, the white-haired prophet named "Ralph" and the abused warehouse boy named "Job Pray," are revealed by novel's end to be not only Lionel's father and illegitimate half-brother, but also to have become, both of them, quite deranged. New England revolutionary fervor is thus associated, however momentarily and unintentionally, with insanity. Why Fenimore Cooper thought *Lionel Lincoln* might be a best-seller in 1825 has yet to be satisfactorily explained.

These three novels are models of clarity by comparison with the mishmash made of Revolutionary New England in novels by John Neal (*Brother Jonathan*, 1825) and John Lothrop Motley (*Morton's Hope*, 1839). All five novels, however, share common problems. Strong in separable scenes and incidental passages, these early Revolutionary War romances lack a consistent value system and the power of coherent conclusion. Insufficient historical distance is less their problem than irresolvable crosscurrents of ideology. In the first decades of the nineteenth century the restorative versus progressive models of revolution, the loyalist critique of patriot dishonesty, nascent feminism, and the need somehow to connect the Puritan past to a westward-looking future, together formed a strange mixture of cultural attitudes that seemed to be proving incapable of credible fictional rendering.

Hawthorne's usual way of dealing with these crosscurrents was to voice them separately in controlled, unified stories and sketches, rather than to assemble them for resolution in a novel. The darkly Toryish ambiguities of "My Kinsman, Major Molineux" have become so familiar that it is easy to forget how complex and varied Hawthorne's view of revolution in Boston truly was. Plausibly regarded as a writer of democratic sympathies, Hawthorne was nonetheless quite capable of praising John Adams because "no base subservience to the people, any more than to the government, could make him swerve from his own ideas of right."[51] Hawthorne could vividly render the mob's sacking of Hutchinson's house, but then, in "Edward Randolph's Portrait," consign Hutchinson to an afterlife of despair for signing a devil's contract.[52] The four "Legends of the Province House" begin with a vindictively triumphant exit procession of the Royal Governors out of Boston ("Howe's Masquerade"), but they end with a sympathetic portrayal of a Tory lady who has outlived her culture ("Old Esther Dudley"). The smallpox plague serves Hawthorne as a metaphor to condemn not only British pride in aristocracy but also the provincial's aping of British luxury in a Boston where scarcely one stern Puritan seems to be left ("Lady Eleanor's Mantle").

Readers of *Grandfather's Chair* are repeatedly told that the Revolution is a just popular uprising against tyrannical measures of the British ministry (the Stamp Act, the Townshend Duties, and the Boston Port Act all figure prominently), but "Legends of the Province House" minimizes politics, focusing instead on the Revolution as the gradual freeing of New England from envy of aristocratic lifestyles and class snobbery. Readers who insist on Hawthorne's underlying patriotic allegiance would do well to consider "The Old Tory," last of a triptych of sketches entitled "Old News." Identifying his viewpoint as that of "a modern Tory" who speaks as "a sturdy King-man," Hawthorne judges the tree of Revolution by its fruits: confiscation of private property, worthless currency, patriot deserters, privateers who in fact are pirates, and self-seeking agitators with mouths full of Liberty.[53]

Only once, in writing *Grandfather's Chair*, did Hawthorne express "a distinct and unbroken thread of authentic history" about Massachusetts from 1630 to 1783 that was in consistent accord with Sam Adams's overview.[54] Even here, however, in a history designed for children, the Revolutionary restoration of Puritan Liberty acquires a sinister aspect. The moment before the Stamp Act was passed, Grandfather explains, "New England appeared like a humble and loyal subject of the crown; the next instant, she showed the grim dark features of an old king-resisting Puritan" (151). The "grim dark features" of restored Puritanism are later ascribed to Sam Adams personally as if he and they were above criticism. The very qualities initially seen as "grim" and "dark" now brighten into democratic assertion:

His [Adams's] character was such, that it seemed as if one of the ancient Puritans had been sent to earth, to animate the people's hearts with the same abhorrence of tyranny, that had distinguished the earliest settlers. He was as religious as they, as stern and inflexible, and as deeply imbued with democratic principles. He, better than any one else, may be taken as a representative of the people of New England, and of the spirit with which they engaged in the revolutionary struggle. (173)

Hawthorne's reader is never allowed to associate Sam Adams with the divisive pressures of street gatherings, backroom politics, or agitprop demagoguery. The triumphant climax of *Grandfather's Chair* is the moment when Samuel Adams, not John Hancock, becomes Governor of Massachusetts. Even Hawthorne's narrative frame serves the same end. By saving the seventeenth-century chair in which Grandfather retells history, Sam Adams becomes for the children the very symbol of the continuance of New England's Puritan heritage.

There is no textual or extratextual evidence to suggest any duplicity in Hawthorne's characterizing Sam Adams in this manner. His portrayal of Adams serves, rather, to resolve problems in the evolution of New England Puritan into republican Revolutionary. Hawthorne can render, condemn, and/or rationalize scenes of Revolutionary violence while keeping Sam Adams, his symbol of Puritan resistance, conveniently above the fray. When Grandfather remarks, apropos of the destruction of Hutchinson's house and the hazing of Andrew Oliver under Liberty Tree, that "we must not decide against the justice of the people's cause, merely because an excited mob was guilty of outrageous violence" (159), Sam Adams's name has not yet been introduced. His organizing of the Massacre Day Orations and his chairing of the Old South meeting hours before the Boston Tea Party are not mentioned in Hawthorne's accounts of those events. Grandfather's careful alternation of prose history with fictive historical sketches, combined with his timely summary judgments, allow Hawthorne to have it both ways.

The young patriot heroes of Revolutionary romances published at the time Hawthorne was reaching maturity (Child's Henry Osborne, Neal's Walter Harwood, Sedgwick's Eliot Lee, even Motley's Uncas Morton) had all somehow understood the defining issues of the Revolution even before they experienced its violence. Although Hawthorne clearly conceived of Robin Molineux as a representative Puritan lad, the son of a country minister, armed with confidence and a cudgel, Robin in fact has no knowledge of the civil liberties of the forefathers, and not a clue about the nightmarish brutalities of revolt in Boston. More than the country innocent initiated into the evil of the city, Robin represents a type of Puritan descendant whom commemorators preferred not to notice. His mind is untroubled because he utterly lacks the New Englander's presumed awareness of history. Robin's only idea of the future is that his respected kinsman will secure him a place, perhaps regardless of merit, and certainly regardless of political circumstance. As a cultural type, Robin is Young Goodman Brown's foil and opposite: whereas Goodman Brown had been obsessed with the forefathers' sins, Robin is the young New England/American innocent of all history who relies on networking to get ahead while assuming that only the present moment of time's changeless continuum could possibly count.

During his one evening in Boston, Robin experiences everything the commemorative tradition of patriotic heroism wished to hide. The revolutionaries are not a momentary mob whose admitted excesses – a tarring and feathering for instance – precede a return to good order and popular concern for libertarian principle. The patriots are quite clearly a highly organized network (unlike the benign governmental network Robin anticipates) with connections that center upon the tavern and which reach into barbershops, homes of the merchant gentry, houses of prostitution, and perhaps even the seemingly empty churches. The tarring and feathering is a masquerade, procession, and public drama all in one. Robin's vision of Major Molineux, a tearing away of the veil of illusion, can be seen, however, in only one way, as "the foul disgrace of a head grown gray in honor."[55] Insofar as Robin and the reader ever know, Major Molineux has always been an honest, competent public servant, an "elderly man, of large and majestic person, and strong square features, betokening a steady soul" who happens to have been a "Tory" officeholder in the Province. To see his forehead contracted in agony, his eyes "red and wild" while "the foam hung white upon his quivering lip" is to witness a political torturing (228). Conversely, the leader of the patriot procession, half red and half black of face, resembles a professional revolutionary, not a little sadistic, who is finally said to represent "war personified" (227). The revolutionary procession he leads has nothing whatsoever to do with restoring the virtues of libertarian forefathers; it is power politics making fullest use of class envy. If Chief Justice Peter Oliver had had the opportunity to read "My Kinsman, Major Molineux," he would surely have relished every word except its closing speculation, "you may rise in the world, without the help of your kinsman, Major Molineux" (231).

How, as early as 1832, could a tale so thoroughly subversive of commemorative patriotism, and so superbly crafted, have even been written? Why, to begin with a neglected detail about an essential question, did Hawthorne give his disgraced Tory major the last name of one of the best known of the Sons of Liberty, Sam Adams's associate William Molineux?[56] What is to be inferred from the fact that the red-faced leader of the patriotic procession resembles the equally nameless and silent "tall gentleman in a red Cloak" who, according to a legend Sam Adams denied, was believed to have first organized, and then silently witnessed, the patriot violence that led to the Boston Massacre?[57] Why does Hawthorne's opening paragraph discuss the trying dilemma of royally appointed Provincial officials with no mention of

Sam Adams's model of restorative Puritan revolution – a model Hawthorne was later to validate? Was "My Kinsman, Major Molineux" designed as a debunking of commemorative history or a concise reply to the sprawl of recent historical romances by Lydia Maria Child, John Neal, and Fenimore Cooper?

What we do know is that Hawthorne placed "The Gray Champion," his tale most in accord with the restorative model of New England Revolutionary patriotism, at the head of *Twice-Told Tales*, but left "My Kinsmen, Major Molineux" in the obscure pages of *The Token* until he collected it, seemingly as an afterthought, in his last volume of stories, *The Snow-Image and Uncollected Tales* (1851). Clearly, Hawthorne knew how to highlight the version of the Puritan/Revolutionary (dis)continuum that would be appreciated among his New England readers. No consistent overview of New England's revolution would, however, be forthcoming from him. Hawthorne would not abandon either Sam Adams's "Puritan" virtue or the atrocities of the popular mob. The unwelcome connection between them remains as much our problem as it was his.

Bancroft, unlike Hawthorne, had to try to resolve the contradictions. By the time Bancroft wrote the five volumes of the *History* concerned with the Revolutionary era, he had grown somewhat at odds with his New England heritage. Living in New York and then Washington, with his politically difficult years as Collector for the Port of Boston behind him, he was now suspect, not only among both the Cotton and Conscience Whigs of Massachusetts but also among those New England democrats and Democrats who disapproved of Bancroft's seeming complicity with southern expansionist interests under Polk's presidency.[58] These circumstances render his adulatory treatment of New England's leadership in the Revolution all the more remarkable. Whatever memories Bancroft may have had about the uneasy mix of his farm country youth, his Harvard and Göttingen education, his unsuccessful guest preaching in Massachusetts pulpits, and his grinding experience of Boston politics, Bancroft as an historian was clearly determined upon a synthesis of the varying models of New England's patriot leadership, leaving out only (and it is a major omission) the loyalist point of view.

At the outset of his first volume on the Revolutionary era, Bancroft sets himself the task of demonstrating that the American Revolution was "most radical in its character" yet also a "civil war" through which, eventually, "a new plebeian democracy took its place by the side of the proudest empires."[59] Bancroft's use of the word "radical," like his use of the word "revolution," points both backward to new world roots and forward to

America's new democratic order. As Bancroft summarizes the conditions of the colonies in 1750, the Puritan heritage provides the most conspicuous force for colonial protest because it derives, originally from Augustinian tradition, but more importantly from Calvinism, "revolutionary wherever it came," "forming the seedplot of revolution" because Calvin established "a religion without a prelate, a government without a king" (IV, 152, 153). When Bancroft considers the institutions through which independent, democratic politics were to develop after 1750, he singles out the school systems, town meetings, and Congregational polity of Massachusetts and Connecticut, all working in concert "so that all New England was an aggregate of organized democracies" long before the word "democracy" became a term of commendation (IV, 149).

Those who continue to assume that Bancroft's "democracy" amounted to an unthinking trust in majority opinion and benign individualistic energy need to reflect upon his view of the next stage in the development of revolutionary democracy. For five pages Bancroft praises Jonathan Edwards as the exemplar of "the New England mind" (perhaps the first use of this phrase); the Edwards whom Bancroft presents for admiration, though subsuming the dire Great Awakening sermons, focuses on the Edwards who defined God as Love to Universal Being, a God who "is His own chief end in creation" (IV, 155, 157). Edwards's greatness lay in his ability to inspire "the common mind of New England" with "the great thought of the sole sovereignty of God," without losing "personality and human freedom in pantheistic fatalism" (IV, 157). If this admitted difficulty led Edwards into "a sublime inconsistency" with regard to the Freedom of the Will, Bancroft surmises, well then so be it. Embodying New England's crucial modification of Calvinism, Edwards recognized the necessity of action on behalf of the Right. In Edwards's great treatise we see how, in anticipation of the end of Edwards's century, "Action, therefore, as flowing from an energetic right, and lovely will, was the ideal of New England" (IV, 158).

The intellectual lineage Bancroft then seeks to unfold is not from Edwards to Emerson, but from Edwards to Sam Adams. When first introducing Adams, Bancroft draws him forth as if he were a statue emerging from New England granite.

In Boston, at the town meeting, in May, there stood up Samuel Adams, a native citizen of the place, trained at Harvard College, a provincial statesman of the most clear and logical mind . . . In his religious faith he had from childhood been instituted [sic] a Calvinist of the straitest sect . . . He was a member of the Church and in a rigid community was an example in severity of morals. The austere purity of his life witnessed the sincerity of his profession . . . His sublime and unfaltering hope had a cast of solemnity and was as firm as a sincere Calvinist's assurance of his election.[60]

While endowing Sam Adams with New England Puritan character, Bancroft defines his politics in a way to support the restorative model of revolution. "For his political creed," Bancroft writes, "Adams received and held fast the opinions of the Fathers of New-England, that the colonies and England had a common king, but separate and independent legislatures" (v, 195). Adams's origin, character, and politics together embody the power of regional continuity and thereby earn the accolade that lends continuity to history: "Such was his deep devotion, such his inflexibility and courage, he may be called the last of the Puritans, and seemed destined to win for his country 'the victory of endurance born'" (v, 197).

Bancroft implicitly accepts John Adams's late-life claim that the Revolution had been won before Independence was declared. Bancroft quotes at length Sam Adams's letter of 1771 declaring to Arthur Lee that "America must herself, under God, finally work out her own salvation."[61] He quotes as creditable and complementary both William Pitt's description of Adams as a "masterly statesmen" and Hutchinson's surmise, "I doubt whether there is a greater incendiary than he [Sam Adams] in the King's dominions" (vi, 430, 406). For Bancroft, the crucial moment of Adams's achievement is the creation of the Committees of Correspondence within and then beyond Massachusetts. The committees are first introduced as an outgrowth of New England culture ("There, in New England . . . Liberty, acquired by the sacrifices and sufferings of a revered ancestry, was guarded, under the blessing of God, as a sacred trust for posterity," vi, 425). The moment when Sam Adams rises in the Massachusetts House to move the creation of the Committees on Correspondence is described as "that motion which included the whole revolution" (iv, 429), presumably because insurgent self-government based on violated civil liberties affirms the restorative model of Puritan revolution. Bancroft praises the Provincial Congress's 1774 resolution to resume the old charter and highlights declaratory letters from Massachusetts town committees who were joining resistance measures in the name of Puritan forefathers. The frontispiece illustration for Bancroft's seventh volume (covering just the twenty months from May 1774 to January 1776) is Copley's portrait of Sam Adams pointing to the Massachusetts Charter. That Bancroft also intended, as John Adams probably had, to deflect patriotic memory away from southern slaveholders who had written and signed the Declaration of Independence is a less likely presentist reading of his purpose.

Bancroft's celebration of Massachusetts's moment of Revolutionary Puritan "democracy" has an historical authenticity we now slight. In addition to support for the Suffolk Resolves from the many towns, the Provincial Congress functioned as America's first independent state from July 1775 to July 1776. Before his death, the first president of the Provincial Congress, Joseph Warren, had been negotiating through Sam Adams for a polity more republican than a recreation of the 1691 Charter, which, Warren wrote, "contains in it the seeds of despotism." Even though the Continental Congress officially reinstated the Provincial Charter, Massachusetts's interim government was to function under James Warren with no governor, no lieutenant governor, an elective house, and an elective president. In essence it was government by unicameral republican legislature through a single executive and his advisors. Joseph Warren would no doubt have been pleased at a polity seemingly deriving, like the Puritan Church, from the will of the congregated towns. As the Suffolk Resolves were published, Warren had written to Sam Adams, "I never saw a more glorious prospect than the present. The generous Spirit of our ancestors seems to have revived beyond our most sanguine expectations." Defending the Massachusetts Provincial Congress against the likely disapproval of the Continental Congress, Samuel Cooper wrote, "if any should think we move too fast here, without waiting your Result, they must soon reflect, that we are the Frontier."[62]

Bancroft's recognition of New England's primacy led him, however, into misleading metaphors of limitless natural empowerment. At the end of a chapter describing how the Massachusetts House, led again by Sam Adams, called for the 1768 Convention to resist the Townshend Acts, Bancroft describes Boston's resolve to resist as if it were the birth and the rise of the power of the Republic: "While the earth was still wrapt in gloom, they [the citizens of Boston] welcomed the daybreak of popular freedom and like the young eagle in his upward soarings, looked undazzled into the beams of the morning"(vi, 243). Bancroft's account of the weeks prior to Lexington, Concord, and Ticonderoga unfolds as if John Winthrop's words on the *Arbella* ("the eyes of the world are upon us") had at last been fully realized: "All America, from Lake Champlain to the Altamaha; all Europe, Madrid, Paris, Amsterdam, Vienna, hardly less than London, were gazing with expectation towards the little villages that lay around Boston."[63] Surely Bancroft could risk the hyperbole of such passages because many of his readers (all volumes of the *History* were published by Little, Brown of Boston) would readily assume that only language so heightened could fit the extremity of these particular moments of crisis.

Regional pride notwithstanding, Bancroft opened his seventh volume with paragraphs written from a protonational perspective, insisting that, when "the hour of the American Revolution was come," "the people of the continent with irresistible energy obeyed one general impulse, as the earth in spring listens to the command of nature" (vii, 21). In language that anticipates Frederick Jackson Turner, Bancroft invokes the fecundity of an endless open land as the determining circumstance of Freedom's growth in America. Imagery of the heroic pioneer, in turn, leads Bancroft to racialist praise of Anglo-Saxon dominance, praise expressed in terms for which he can be, and has been, roundly criticized: "For the first time, it [the idea of freedom] found a region and a race where it could be professed with the earnestness of an indwelling conviction, and be defended with the enthusiasm that heretofore had marked no wars but those for religion" (vii, 22).

But if we seek to understand rather than to blame, we can find the informing difficulty in Bancroft's attempted synthesis. The very mention of seventeenth-century wars of religion immediately leads Bancroft back from the progressive to the restorative model of revolution.

When all Europe slumbered over questions of liberty, a band of exiles keeping watch by night, heard the glad tidings which promised the political regeneration of the world. A revolution unexpected in the moment of its coming, but prepared by glorious forerunners, grew naturally and necessarily out of the series of past events by the formative principle of a living belief. And why should man organize resistance to the grand design of Providence? Why should not the consent of the ancestral land, and the gratulations of every other, call the young nation to its place among the powers of the earth? (vii, 22–23)

Suddenly Bancroft's nineteenth-century perspective gives way to seventeenth-century Pilgrims and Puritans acting as St. Luke's shepherds heralding the birth of the Christ. Their courage in defying canon and feudal powers, rather than the American land or any universal spirit of Liberty, is to be regarded as the seed of Enlightenment. The full import of Bancroft's passage, however, goes far beyond Sam Adams's pointing his finger to chartered civil liberties. "The formative principle of a living belief," conveyed through Puritanism without a mention of Virginia's Declaration of Rights, leads to a "revolution" that promises nothing less than "the political regeneration of the world."

Bancroft's language aligns Puritanism and Enlightenment, coastal Massachusetts and westward expansion, in ways that will find support in diverse revolutionary acts described in the volume to follow. Whether these assimilations are coherent in logic and accurate in fact should always be a legitimate question. The point for understanding the power of Bancroft's *History*, however, is the way these generalities were invoked to make them seem to work together. We may criticize Bancroft's selectivity and rhetoric, but his Janus-like portrayal of the motivations for "revolution" in Massachusetts made a grand and overarching statement out of the uneasy confusions and loose ends of recent decades.

CHAPTER 8

Shots heard round the world

Because studies of the American Revolution understandably focus on politics, they are apt to slight the impact of military narratives in forming cultural values and national identity. In New England, the starting point for such narratives was self-evident. Sam Adams's and Joseph Warren's justification for the Revolution, whether regressive or progressive, had claimed the high ground of self-defense; the sons of Puritan forefathers were to defend chartered liberty at all costs. New Englanders were never to seem the aggressor. Whether their weapons were words or guns, they were to claim loyalty while acting for liberty, to respond to tyranny rather than to initiate change.

The Suffolk Resolves, while stopping short of declaring independence, had sanctioned defensive activities of the most aggressive sort. But before national independence would be declared in July 1776, New Englanders would push well over even those limits. Expanding on Artillery Company tradition, they would cultivate military preparedness, organize themselves into regiments, and march many miles to fire muskets at battle sites soon celebrated in regional, national, and even world history. Within the context of defending Puritan liberties, how would it be possible to justify the ambushing of British soldiers from behind a stone wall (Concord Fight), or the seizing of a British fort through a surprise attack at dawn (Ticonderoga), or assuming an advanced hilltop position, probably against orders, in order to shell the British army in Boston (Bunker Hill)? In these three confrontations, New Englanders were no longer pointing fingers at Provincial Charters; they were firing guns and killing the soldiers of Great Britain, the "country" that was still, nominally, their parent nation. Were such acts defensive? Could they be made to seem so? At the very least, detailed accounts of prior British offenses would need to be brought to the fore. Promptly published narratives must visualize moments (very like the "Boston Massacre") in which New England commoners had been the passive, standing victims of British military aggression. The killings at Lexington were the perfect starting point, but what of Concord Fight, Ticonderoga, and Bunker Hill? Clearly, the commemorating would require both bold assertion and great care.

LEXINGTON AND CONCORD: AGGRESSIVE DEFENSE

New England's most celebrated day, April 19, 1775, was, in military terms, to prove of little importance. The eight colonial militia killed on Lexington Green and the 235 casualties which 1,800 British troops suffered during the retreat from Concord had little lasting effect upon British General Gage's decision to withdraw from Boston. The skirmish at Lexington Green was a patriot defeat that the British troops cheered as they marched off toward Concord. The estimated total of American deaths on 19th April (about fifty) was not dramatically less than the total of British deaths (about seventy-five).[1] The Earl of Suffolk, the British Secretary of State, was both bemused and confounded by all the furor:

For the soul of me I cannot see why Opposition should be so elated at what has happened in the Massachusetts. That affair has turned out exactly as was expected. A detachment was sent on a particular service; the service was performed; and on their return the troops were shot at from every place where there was cover, after having routed the only body of men who attempted to oppose them . . . What have they to crow about now?[2]

The Earl of Suffolk did not understand, however, as Sam Adams, Joseph Warren and Benjamin Church all did, that the import of the day's events lay not in who would control the military stores at Concord, but who would control the narratives told and written about the journey to seize them.[3]

For commemorating the virtue of New England/America's revolution, the onset of battle at Lexington and Concord was to have no literary equal.[4] Even so seemingly distant an observer as Henry James was to write that Concord Fight had been the "hinge on which the large revolving future was to turn."[5] Justifiable defensive revolution became the underlying paradigm of narratives from the time of Benjamin Church's broadside (1775) through David Ramsay's *History* (1795) to Longfellow's "Paul Revere's Ride" (1860). The crux of the paradigm was that the opening shots of the American Revolution had been fired in New England, not by self-seeking rebels, but by invading British redcoats intent on killing farmer-militia quietly standing in defense of their Common and their inland village. The Minutemen who a few hours later had driven the British from Concord's North Bridge, and then harassed the British army on its retreat to Boston, could readily be perceived as a gloriously undisciplined people's army. Later writers contributing to this commemorative tradition would pay tribute to their predecessors either by recalling their especially pertinent phrases (Sam Adams's "Oh, what a glorious morning for America," Edward Everett's "the countryside rose as one man," Emerson's "the shot heard round the world," Longfellow's "a voice in the darkness, a knock at the door"). As Emerson would claim, both individuality and democracy came that day to the military field, "every one from that moment being his own commander."[6] Hesitant colonials were perceptually transformed, *en masse*, into vigilant Americans who would abide neither British raids upon their provisions nor the marching of British regulars through their lands. The long retreat of the grenadiers from Concord to Boston showed the world who the British truly were – a detested invading army who needed to be shut up in besieged coastal towns. As Sam Adams had known, the spectacle of the redcoat on New England soil could readily inflame the populace to virtue.

Before the declaring of political independence, this paradigm of the crisis of April 19th tacitly excised Great Britain from America, Old England from New. Gone were the vexing issues of whether Crown, Parliament, royal provincial officials, or the colonists themselves should have the powers to appoint judges, to summon and suspend legislatures, to provide payment for the common defense, to impose import duties, and, above all, to assess taxes. By January 1776, Thomas Paine was prepared to argue that it was common sense to recognize that "all plans, proposals &c. prior to the nineteenth of April, i.e. to the commencement of hostilities, are like the almanacks of the last year; which, though proper then, are superceded and useless now."[7] Since the glorious 19th of April in Lexington, America's Rubicon has been crossed, her War of Independence begun.

After the wartime calls to arms came the history. As the allegiances of her name suggest, Mercy Otis Warren was unlikely to believe that the Revolution had been won by the unaided resurgence of liberty in every farmer's heart. She knew full well what the voices, pens, and guns of her brother, her husband, and her martyred brother-in-law had done to evoke the spirit of libertarian resistance. Nonetheless, Mrs. Warren's rendering of New England's day of crisis remains true to what had by 1805 become accepted regional and national mythology. Raising the stakes of the atrocities alleged in Church's "Narrative," Mrs. Warren concludes that the British had acted throughout the day with such "perfidy and meanness," such "rancorous and ferocious rage," that their "barbarities" left an "indelible stain on a nation long famed for their courage, humanity and honor."[8] Emerson's famous phrase, "the embattled farmers," seems genteel indeed beside Mercy Warren's willingness to praise the Minutemen as "raw inexperienced peasantry, who had ran hastily together in defense of their lives and liberties" (1, 103). By 1805, Mrs. Warren's angry worry that true republican liberty might not survive the corruptions of Federalist aristocracy led her to echo the spirit of the 1775 broadsides and to present it as historical fact.

After first histories came the orators. By 1825, when Edward Everett gave the first of the important Concord orations, the so-called "Era of Good Feelings" was beginning to sour into worried claims for expansionism, internal improvements, and Indian Removal. Because New England's primacy in forming the nation's values could no longer be assumed, Everett took the high road and presented the revolutionary courage of April 19th as New England's gift to the nation. He gave his audience a vivid narrative of already legendary events from Revere's and Dawes's Ride, through "the rising of the people in their strength" to the despairing retreat of redcoated invaders from Concord's farmlands.[9] Concord Fight, he insisted, was no Middlesex County affair but a moment of American cultural definition in which "the national character . . . is formed, elevated and strengthened" (9). If the Lexington Militia had obediently dispersed, or if Concord's townsmen had given up their military stores, "then the Revolution had been at an end, or rather never had been begun" (5). A narrative framed in this way gave voice to sectional nationalism of an unalloyed kind.

In the seventh volume (1858) of his *History*, Bancroft put the matter of Lexington and Concord into a visionary form accepted as authoritative for almost a century. Bancroft, whose tutor at Harvard College had been Edward Everett, devoted five chapters and forty-two pages to describing the military, political, and teleological "Effects of the Day" of April 19. As plausible history claiming much from little, Bancroft's pages are hard to excel. In the rural Massachusetts dawn, even before the first shot at Lexington, a "mighty chorus of voices rose from the scattered farmhouses and, as it were, from the ashes of the dead."[10] This choral voice proclaims: "Come forth, champions of liberty; now free your country; protect your sons and daughters; rescue the houses of the God of your fathers, the franchises handed down from your ancestors. Now all is at stake; the battle is for all" (291). The unspecified "franchises handed down from your ancestors" derive from covenanted liberties that impose a duty in moments of crisis. The choral voice Bancroft invokes also resolves a problem of causation faced by earlier historians of the Revolution. As Lester Cohen has shown, Ramsay's and Warren's generation had been anxious about the part mere chance might play in a new world where the writing of Providential history was no longer tenable.[11] While endowing silent Minutemen with words,

Bancroft's "mighty chorus" deprives chance of any historical role in the events of April 19th. To fashion a variant of Cotton Mather's title, Bancroft is recording Providential signs of the *Magnalia Libertatis Americana* while still assuming, as Cotton Mather had assumed, that great American things were great New England things writ large.

By invoking this "mighty chorus of voices," Bancroft breaks down geographical and temporal boundaries separating the spheres of divine, political, and individual power. Summing up the import of the eight men who fell on Lexington Green elicits an ecstatic twenty-five line sentence beginning with a tribute to Lexington's dead, "village heroes" who, by offering their bodies in wordless testimony to the Rights of Man, continue to empower millions the world over (294–295). The light of liberty, tacitly synonymous with God, is traced forward from its first existence as pure essence, through the Hebrews, Greeks, and Romans, through Jesus Christ and Paul of Tarsus, through its glimmering survival in Anglo-Saxon forests, its rebirth in Luther and Calvin, its westward course to Massachusetts, and finally its remigration to inspire the *philosophes* with "analyzing inquisitiveness." Such an historical perspective has become too grand in scale for the terms of the Massachusetts Provincial Charter of 1691 to any longer be seen.

At sentence's end, all of history's spots of light coalesce and concentrate within the breasts of the martyrs on Lexington Green. From them the light of liberty reemerges in widening concentric circles as the guiding principle of the future.[12] For Bancroft, human history has replaced the Bible as evidence of divine law, but the central moment to and from which the religion of democracy moves is April 19, 1775 when mankind stood in silent witness to its own inner liberty. Only at this point does Bancroft, finishing his chapter, quote Sam Adams's legendary exclamation "Oh! what a glorious morning is this!," thereby linking the regressive view of New England's revolution to the dawning of American-led nineteenth-century progress. If there is one passage in the entire *History* that describes Bancroft's view of "the hinge of the future," his eulogy of those who stood at Lexington is the proper occasion and the only possible choice. In light of twentieth-century suffering, his confidence in peace, prosperity, and self-reliance seems naïve, but who can say, even in 2004, that his faith in a slowly emerging religion of democracy was wrong?

Emerson, when read attentively, habitually challenges our expectations, even in a ceremonial poem written for the dedication of a battle monument. It is now difficult even to think about the meaning of those ringing, overfamiliar words that end the first stanza of "Concord Hymn" ("Here once the embattled farmers stood / And fired the shot heard round the world"[13]). But these two lines, if we can still heed them, capture the essential paradox of the Revolutionary commemorative tradition. The defensive connotations of the phrase "embattled farmers stood" contrast perfectly with the aggression within the farmers' modest, world-changing response ("fired the shot heard round the world").

Considered as a whole, however, "Concord Hymn" is more than a summary tribute to New England's Revolutionary tradition; it ends in troubled meditation on probable regional decline. Reflecting upon the decay of the North Bridge, Emerson severs the sleeping present from the active past:

> The foe long since in silence slept;
> Alike the conqueror silent sleeps;
> And Time the ruined bridge has swept
> Down the dark stream which seaward creeps.

To describe Minutemen, grenadiers, and the North Bridge as all gone down time's dark stream could have been merely the prelude to a reassurance that past heroism was still recoverable. But in the closing stanzas the ceremonial votive stone is set in place with no purpose beyond redeeming the memory of a past event "When, like our sires, our sons are gone." The most the communal "Spirit" can be asked to do is to "gently spare the shaft" of remembrance. Whereas the Minutemen were "heroes," we contemporaries are only their "children." Unlike the exhortative end of many a contemporary New England oration, Emerson's poem leaves the children blessedly free but with no apparent way of proving that they are worthy of their ancestors.

Emerson's "Historical Discourse at Concord" (1836) expresses a similarly troubled affirmation. His Minutemen are "poor farmers who came up, that day, to defend their native soil."[14] Although Sam Adams's argument is acknowledged ("A deep religious sentiment sanctified the thirst for liberty"), Emerson does not trace the Minutemen's self-defense to Calvinism or to any Bancroftian light of Liberty descended from the Greeks. The freedom for which the farmers stood was simply a political expression of a now weakened religious heritage. "All the military movements in this town were solemnized by acts of public worship," Emerson insists. "They supposed they had a right to their corn and their cattle, without paying tribute to any but their own governors. And as they had no fear of man, they *yet* did have a fear of God" (75–76, italics mine).

Emerson's Concord is neither the crucial village in the world's history, nor a place to which one comes to give an oration, but rather a stagnant community with a noble past. At the end of his "Historical Discourse"

Emerson acknowledges, "Of late years, the growth of Concord has been slow. Without navigable waters, without mineral riches, without any considerable mill privileges, the natural increase of her population is drained by the constant emigration of the youth" (85). Here Emerson touches on a motive Robert Gross has shown to be crucial to Concord's resistance in 1775: an inner anger built up by economic frustration, an inchoate sense among landless sons of not-so-prosperous farmers that they have little to lose through revolt.[15] Although Emerson does not directly say so, the causes of Concord's slow decline were by 1837 becoming increasingly applicable to rural New England as a whole. No visible, present enemy was giving fresh purpose to the community's hard-won libertarian faith. Left behind in the midst of *laissez-faire* prosperity, Concord's sons have little to rebel against. Emerson regretfully closes his essay by acknowledging "every moment carries us farther from the two great epochs of public principle, the Planting, and the Revolution of the colony" (85). As in "Concord Hymn," the contemporary claim upon the legacy of the New England fathers is asserted with scant evidence for its continuance.

In barely avoiding mourning a victory, Emerson's Concord commemorations are atypical for his region and era. Most New England historians and orators uneasily combined regional loyalties with a universalist perspective that drew them toward congratulatory patriotism of an abstract kind. Their rites of commemoration, then thought to elicit words of higher persuasion, now seem especially suspect. Historical fiction, however, is still often granted a more objective niche among genres. To write convincing historical fiction forces responsible novelists – of whatever political persuasion – to immerse the reader in the confusions of particular days of the past. The recreations of the events of April 19th in Cooper's *Lionel Lincoln* (1825) and Hawthorne's *Septimius Felton* (1861, 1871) have an immediacy that, despite the authors' failure in fictional plotting, remain more compelling than – and may be as historically accurate as – the rhetorically freighted accounts of Everett, Bancroft, or even Emerson.

The divided loyalties of Cooper's Revolutionary heritage (paternal patriots, maternal loyalists) intersect in fruitful ways with his search for historical accuracy.[16] To be sure, the narrator of *Lionel Lincoln* often passes judgment from comfortably within the "Whig" tradition familiar in the histories of David Ramsay and Mercy Otis Warren. Cooper's overview of the causes of the Revolutionary War, for example, begins by stating that the American Revolution "established a new era in political liberty and founded a mighty empire" (57). The many readers who, like Herman Melville, saw Cooper as "our national novelist"[17] would have found in *Lionel Lincoln* more than enough historical instances of British ministerial and military oppression to justify the Revolution. But Cooper knew that conventional assurances obscured troubling facts. Accordingly he forces the reader to see the events of April 19, 1775 from the viewpoint of a self-divided loyalist. A major in the Royal 47th, Lionel Lincoln is Boston born but Oxford educated, heir to a British aristocratic family but the son of a convinced patriot. For the reader of 1825, Lionel's military experience is clearly expected to serve as a test case justifying conversion to the patriots' cause.

Cooper was well aware of the cultural need to validate Sam Adams's defensive justification for revolutionary violence. Applied to the events of April 19, 1775, this issue had already come down to the seemingly silly question of who had fired first. Twentieth-century historians Arthur Tourtellot and David Hackett Fischer both concluded that, on Lexington Green, the British and American forces found themselves facing each other with orders to stand firm, but to disperse rather than to fire.[18] At Concord's North Bridge, both sides had orders not to fire unless fired upon, but no mention was made of any dispersing.[19] On both occasions, one or two desultory shots, fired by no one knows who, caused the British to fire a volley. On Lexington Green, that volley would make patriotic martyrs of dead Minutemen; in Concord town, it would make martyrs of a few more but heroes of an entire populace. In neither episode does there seem to have been any deliberate decision on either side to begin battle. If the colonies' decision to declare independence can be plausibly ascribed to New England's immediate rise to arms after Lexington and Concord, logic would compel us to conclude that the reasoned deliberateness of Jefferson's words ("a decent respect to the opinions of mankind requires that they should declare the causes which impel them to the separation"[20]) is a deft verbal plank extended over an abyss of chaos and confusion.

After a dark and tiring inland march beside the grenadiers, Lionel Lincoln enters "a small hamlet of houses dimly seen through the morning haze" and sees "a small body of countrymen, drawn up in the affectation of military parade" (103). A British major of marines shouts "Disperse, ye rebels, disperse." There are "reports of pistols" from no identified source, then an order to fire. Not until six pages later does Cooper inform his reader that the hamlet was Lexington, the major Pitcairn. Similarly, while Lionel Lincoln is observing grenadiers searching for stored military goods in some town named Concord, "the report of fire-arms was heard suddenly to issue from the post held by the light-infantry, at the bridge" (112). Cooper then renders "the shot heard round the world" in this off-hand manner: "A few scattering shots were succeeded by a volley, which was answered by another, with the quickness of lightning, and then the air became filled with the incessant rattling of a sharp conflict" (112). These are the "realist" literary techniques we associate with the battle descriptions of Stephen Crane and Ernest Hemingway: war's senseless chaos, recorded as lived in the moment, not cleaned up into the orderly commemorative pattern that, in Cooper's day, made sense of "history."

If the word "enlightenment" connotes the perceiving of emerging light through retreating darkness, it is little wonder that commemorative rhetoric, like the Revolutionary War paintings of John Trumbull, offered its audience clearly defined tableaux flooded with light, centered in form, and apparent in meaning. Lionel Lincoln's scattered impressions of the retreat from Concord offer no panoramic view at all.

On either side of the highway, along the skirts of every wood or orchard, in the open fields, and from every house, barn or cover in sight, the flash of fire-arms was to be seen, while the shouts of the English grew, at each instant, feebler and less inspiriting. Heavy clouds of smoke rose above the valley, into which he looked, and mingled with the dust of the march, drawing an impenetrable veil before the view. (115)

Amidst such veiling of heroism in artillery smoke, who could ever prove that the fighting was defensive or offensive? To picture gritty clouds obscuring American triumph must have been disconcerting to patriotic readers, especially after they had been assured that the day would bring "an effect not unlike the sudden rising of the curtain at the opening of some interesting drama" (98).

Lionel's responses to armed revolt follow a revealingly consistent pattern. As the grenadiers fire on the Minutemen at Lexington Green, Lionel protests "Great God . . . what is it you do? ye fire at unoffending men! is there no law but force!" (104). His moral revulsion is immediately qualified, however, by his soldierly belief that "the power of Britain is too mighty for these scattered and unprepared colonies to cope with" (104). At each moment of crisis, Lionel Lincoln senses that his "countrymen" (75), the Americans, are in the right, yet he soon decides to rejoin his British "comrades." Nothing that Lionel witnesses at Lexington, Concord, or Bunker Hill ever leads him seriously to consider neutrality, let alone defection. And yet Cooper does not criticize Lionel's loyalty by labeling it a "Tory" failure of courage or political integrity – as Mercy Warren or Edward Everett would surely have done. Instead, Cooper immerses his reader in the experience of battle in order to show why, amid the murk of killing, a young man's "pride of arms," bred in him by institutional training, will determine his actions. As the controlling motive of human behavior, political principle proves decidedly secondary to training and to cultural upbringing.

The end of Lionel Lincoln's military service provides a suggestive link between Cooper's novel and Hawthorne's. In a memorable and revealing scene, to which we shall return, Cooper fuses historical climax with fictive anticlimax. At the moment when Bunker Hill is finally retaken by the British, Lionel Lincoln is suddenly and senselessly wounded by a patriot whose need to revenge Joseph Warren's death is all-consuming: "At this instant the trappings of his [Lionel's] attire caught the glaring eye-balls of a dying yeoman, who exerted his wasting strength to sacrifice one more worthy victim to the *manes* of his countrymen. The whole of the tumultuous scene vanished from the senses of Lionel at the flash of the musket of this man" (188). Challenging his reader's expectations, Cooper has transformed the patriotic ardor of the "dying yeoman" into a glare of insanity. The flash of the yeoman's musket recalls the sporadic musket fire by which Middlesex County yeomen had shot down British regulars retreating from Concord. In such moments, courage under crisis shades into madness; self-control seems a casualty of battlefield achievement.

To Hawthorne, unlike Cooper, such a glimpse of crazed violence would become the only lasting significance of Concord Fight. While living in the Old Manse, Hawthorne became increasingly troubled by an incident that Concord's patriots, including the town's historian Lemuel Shattuck, still preferred to ignore. After the fighting at Concord's North Bridge had ended, a local farm boy had come upon a British officer lying wounded beside the road. Whether driven by zeal, fear or both, the young man impulsively axed the British officer in the head. Hardly a defensive act. For Hawthorne, this one incident, so compromising to national faith in the embattled farmers' collective virtue, "has borne more fruit for me than all that history tells us of the fight."[21] To dwell on the import of this incident amounted to the exhumation of a suppressed but still living memory; David Hackett Fischer has noted that "For many years, the town of Concord threw a shroud of silence round this event."[22]

Although Hawthorne opens *Septimius Felton* in Concord on the morning of April 19th, the three people he assembles for our consideration sit together on a hillside enjoying the warmth of a spring day, oblivious to any historical context. Like the novelist, they have heard "stories of marching troops, coming like dreams through the midnight," "a steady march of soldiers' feet onward, onward into this land," but the stories mean little to them. Septimius Felton – old Concord farm stock, recent Harvard graduate, reluctantly preparing for the ministry – does not regret that he cannot engage in the history being enacted around him.[23] He retreats to his study when the British march into town. To block out the gunfire at the North Bridge, he tries half guiltily to read. After all but sporadic shooting is over, he snatches up his gun, runs outside with no clear purpose, climbs a hill to obtain an overview, and there discovers that Concord Fight is only "an unseen and inscrutable trouble" (23). Eagerness to defend New England's heritage of civil liberty is the last thing on his mind.

Septimius joins Concord Fight at its victorious turning point when the farmers, militia and Minutemen begin to harass the British retreating from the town. He sees the redcoats not as in "any way murderous, but, at most, only heavy, cloddish, good-natured, human" (21). It never occurs to him that the patriots' revenge against the retreating British is a rising of the people in collective self-defense. Instead, he gazes with horror as a straggling British regular is shot from ambush: "it was so like murder," Septimius thinks, "that he really could not tell the difference" (24). Although Septimius eventually contributes to the patriot cause by killing a British officer, he fires his gun only because he has been challenged to a duel by a man he has no wish to harm. He sought to be neither defender nor aggressor. The dying British officer admits that their duel has been "boy's play"; to Septimius "the whole thing scarcely seemed real" (27).

After completing the "lonely and terrible" (34) act of burying the British officer, Septimius returns in a guilty daze to his study. The only action he is able to take – replacing his musket over the mantelpiece – parodies the ceremonial gesture so integral to the legend of the Minuteman's triumphant return from Concord Fight.[24] In a parenthesis, Hawthorne pens his summary judgment of the day's events: "He longed, too, to know what was the news of the battle that had gone rolling onward, along that hitherto peaceful country-road, converting every where (this Demon of War, we mean) with one blast of its red sulphurous breath, the peaceful husbandman to a soldier thirsting for blood" (37). Hawthorne's words invert the assumptions of patriotic history. The arming of the people is in fact the moment of desecration, a communal decline caused by the "Demon of War" who has tempted peaceful farmers to give way to animal bloodlust.

When first hearing accusations against the British, Septimius had merely exclaimed, "And what matters a little tyranny in so short a life?" (16). Experiencing the British presence in Concord forces him to alter this wholly apolitical position, but only slightly: "It may be lawful for any man, even if he has devoted himself to God, or however peaceful his pursuits, to fight to the death when the enemy's step is on the soil of his home; but only for that perilous juncture, which passed, he should return to his own way of peace"

(38–39). On one level, these words can be seen as shrewd historical realism. Septimius is validating the principle of limited local self-defense which, at least in 1775, prompted many a patriot leader to believe that summer soldiers, sunshine patriots, and farmers with rifles might be enough to fend off the British. If New Englanders had followed Septimius's advice, however, the militiamen army would never have gathered from afar to shut up the British in Boston, and the glorious achievement of independence in revolutionary New England (which Hawthorne had often praised) could never have been consummated. As an older man, Hawthorne had come to believe that killing was justifiable only in momentary defense of one's home. As the Civil War began, he admitted that he so detested war that he could hardly bear to think about it, and that New England was as large a lump of earth as his spirit could embrace. Had not Hawthorne, too, conveniently forgotten that, even in 1775, military offense as well as defense had been needed?

Hawthorne conceived *Septimius Felton* before the fall of Fort Sumter, but did not begin writing it until shortly after President Lincoln called for 75,000 Union volunteers. Living physically and spiritually at the Wayside, Hawthorne found himself writing about Concord Fight at the same time he was watching the men of Concord volunteer for another and very different kind of war. Knowing that the grenadiers are marching toward him, Septimius responds to the drumbeat and mustering of the Concord Minutemen by muttering "Fools that men are" (16). Although Hawthorne surely sympathized with Septimius's cynicism, his sense of public responsibility was not so callous as to allow Septimius's dismissal to stand unchallenged.

Oh, high, heroic, tremulous juncture, when man felt himself almost an angel, on the verge of doing deeds that outwardly look so fiendish; oh strange rapture of the coming battle. We know something of that time now; we that have seen the muster of the village soldiery on meeting-house greens, and at railway stations; and heard the drum and fife, and seen the farewells, seen the familiar faces that we hardly knew, now that we felt them to be heroes, breathed higher breath for their sakes, felt our eyes moistened; thanked them in our souls for teaching us that nature is yet capable of heroic moments. (17)

Although the passage is suffused with prayerful gravity, Hawthorne's "devotion" is offered to the volunteer who has made life seem heroic and significant again, rather than to the political sanctity of the Union cause. Whether Lincoln's army was summoned to defend or to attack is not Hawthorne's concern. The mustering may well be the sign of a people's selfless faith, but one senses that it is a moment only. Try as he might, Hawthorne could not approve the ecstasy of warfare; his opening phrases seem almost parodic in their claim to feel ("Oh strange rapture of the coming battle").

The specter of civil war often informs the least expected of antebellum texts. Longfellow's "Paul Revere's Ride" is not, as is commonly assumed, the poem that created a national legend about "the eighteenth of April in Seventy-five."[25] Considered as a narrative, it is little more than a deft splicing together, a verse pastiche, made up of all those legendary details that had been the public currency of commemorative patriotism for eighty-five years. The important question raised by the poem is why Longfellow should have wished, late in 1860, to write about Paul Revere's ride at all? The poem was first published as a self-contained lyric in the January 1861 issue of the *Atlantic*, where it appears together with an apprehensive editorial on the outbreak of civil war entitled "The Question of the Hour." Longfellow closes his poem with the following lines:

> For, borne on the night-wind of the Past,
> Through all our history, to the last,
> In the hour of darkness and peril and need,
> The people will waken and listen to hear
> The hurrying hoof-beats of that steed,
> And the midnight message of Paul Revere. (29)

These lines suggest that Longfellow intended his poem, not as soothing antiquarianism in verse, but as an affirmation that the strength of the people was still sufficient for the nation's coming night. Unlike many previous versions of April 19th, which had stressed the victimized integrity of Minutemen standing still on Lexington Green, Longfellow's poem is full of a ceaseless motion implying that the Union retains the energy and flexibility to survive.

The vital commemorative literature of Lexington and Concord fittingly ends with Emerson, who in 1867 was asked to deliver the address for the dedication of Concord's Civil War Monument.[26] The memorial ceremony for Concord's recent dead was held on April 19th, the ninety-second anniversary of Concord Fight. It was an occasion, Emerson knew, for comparing monuments.

The old Monument, a short half mile from this house, stands to signalize the first Revolution, where the people resisted offensive usurpations, offensive taxes of the British Parliament, claiming that there should be no taxation without representation. Instructed by events, after the quarrel began, the Americans took higher ground, and stood for political independence. But, in the necessities of the hour, they overlooked the moral law, and winked at a practical exception to the Bill of Rights they had drawn up. They winked at the exception, believing it insignificant. But the moral law, the nature of things, did not wink at it, but kept its eye wide open. It turned out that this one violation was a subtle poison, which in eighty years corrupted the whole overgrown body politic, and brought the alternative of extirpation of the poison or ruin to the republic.

This new Monument is built to mark the arrival of the nation at the new principle – say, rather at its new acknowledgment, for the principle is as old as Heaven – that only that State can live, in which injury to the least member is recognized as damage to the whole. (31–32)

Emerson has anticipated late twentieth-century understanding of the Civil War as the bloody fulfillment of the American Revolutionary compact left incomplete in 1776 and in 1787. From the perspective of 1867, the underlying issue of Revolutionary times seems to have had regrettably little to do with the integrity of the "embattled farmers." The old monument memorialized a national, not a local rebellion ("taxation without representation"). What now seems most important about the founding fathers is the one thing they did not do. Even the Minuteman, the very symbol of vigilance and rectitude, had "overlooked" the overriding "moral law," a law that in 1775 as in 1861 had demanded an end to slavery as well as courageous defense of constitutional liberties.

Nineteenth-century Americans who commemorated Lexington and Concord were in search of that presumably pure moment of popular integrity that preceded General George Washington's need to subject an army to organized discipline. The purity of that moment may not have been illusory, but the prolonged search for it distracted antebellum Americans from considering how slavery's "subtle poison" would continue to infect the nation. Perhaps if post-Revolutionary generations had followed Cooper's and Hawthorne's mood of mourning a victory, rather than Sam Adams's proclaiming of a glorious morning, the national night might have been neither quite so long nor quite so brutal.

TICONDEROGA AND BUNKER HILL: DEFENSIVE AGGRESSION

It was one thing for sixty town militia to stand armed on their village green and then be shot at and killed by British regulars marching into town. It was quite another for 150 armed men, none of them members of any locally authorized militia, to attack a British fort in another province. The first was an act of defensive even passive resistance – a standing protest against the predawn incursion of redcoats who were known to be on a secret, destructive mission. The second was a secret predawn attack on His Majesty's troops and military property – legally an act of treason, punishable by death, because independence was still undeclared. Yet these two events – the British "Massacre" at Lexington and the Green Mountain Boys "Conquest" of Ticonderoga – occurred within only three weeks of each other (April 19 and May 10, 1775) at a time when the Rage Militaire in New England was at its peak, but there was no consensus (and therefore no control) over the proper means of colonial resistance.

The two famous statements by the commanding officers, both perhaps apocryphal, suggest the difference between the two kinds of armed defiance. Captain John Parker at Lexington: "Do not fire unless fired upon, but if they mean to begin a war, let it begin here." Colonel Ethan Allen at Ticonderoga: "I demand the surrender of this fort in the name of the great Jehovah and the Continental Congress." Both express determined assurance, but Parker's appeal to the simple rectitude of the invaded local ("let it begin here") contrasts sharply to Ethan Allen's bravado about the vexing problem of laying claim to larger authority ("in the name of the great Jehovah and the Continental Congress"). In three weeks the victims had turned into the aggressors, yet somehow, in the light of subsequent history, Lexington and Ticonderoga would have to be made into one consistent narrative of revolutionary popular virtue.

On the first anniversary of April 19, the Reverend Jonas Clarke, minister of Lexington Congregational Church and close associate of Sam Adams, insisted that the Lexington militia had had "no design of opposing so superior a force . . . much less of commencing hostilities."[27] He then recreated, in the past-present tense, the moment when the British regulars arrived on the green:

they approach with the morning's light, and more like murderers and cut throats, than the troops of a Christian King, without provocation, without warning, when no war was proclaimed, they draw the sword of violence, upon the inhabitants of this town; with a cruelty and barbarity which would have made the most hardened savage blush, they shed INNOCENT BLOOD. (27)

Although Clarke's words exactly fit the model of defensive resistance, how applicable were they to the conquest that followed hard on the killings at Lexington? Every detail of Clarke's picture except the reference to the shedding of "INNOCENT BLOOD" could rightly have been in the mind of a *British* soldier watching the Green Mountain Boys approach Ticonderoga at morning's light. Giving no warning and proclaiming no war, Ethan Allen and the Green Mountain Boys, who were surely clothed more like cutthroats than troops authorized by any Christian state, had drawn the sword of violence. How, in light of Jonas Clarke's and Sam Adams's model of defensive revolution, was so aggressive an act ever to be justified as standing for civil Liberty?[28]

This is the problem that Ethan Allen's *Narrative* manages, through literary skill, shrewdness, luck, and sheer chutzpah first to evade and finally to resolve. One of few books to be published in America during the Revolution, *A Narrative of Colonel Ethan Allen's Captivity* (1779) was reprinted in eight editions during the war years (five of them in New England), and nineteen editions before the Civil War.[29] Allen published his book, not in the Vermont hinterland, but in Philadelphia at a time when memory of Valley Forge privations was keen and personal testimony of patriotic triumph (Allen's release from the hell of British captivity) was greatly needed. The autobiographical self Allen fashioned to affront British captors and engage the American reader is an ever-shifting amalgam of the country commoner, honorable gentleman, would-be philosopher, cunning Yankee and ring-tailed roarer – a combination of inconsistent American selves that would prove readily adaptable to the expansive values of later eras.[30]

Before immersing his reader in horrific memories of British prisons, Allen needed to write an account of the taking of Ticonderoga that would justify the attack, as well as establish his own heroic credentials. He wrote knowing full well that, upon hearing the news of Ticonderoga's surrender, the embarrassed Continental Congress, still seeking an accommodation with England, not only had not issued him any official congratulation, but had even recommended that all captured supplies and munitions be held for the royal army. Nor had subsequent developments since the fort's capture vindicated his aggression. Although America's Northern Army, with the crucial aid of the Green Mountain Regiment, had forced Burgoyne's surrender, the war for independence was in 1779 far from over. To celebrate your own aggression in print was, therefore, to take a great risk. Moreover, informed readers of Allen's *Narrative* would have known that, during the two intervening years, Ticonderoga had been retaken by the British, New York had continued to block the Continental Congress's recognition of Vermont, and Ethan Allen had still not been appointed to active rank in the Continental Army.

Instead of complaint, accusation, or information about the early years, Allen began his *Narrative* with the effect of Lexington.

Ever since I arrived to a state of manhood, and acquainted myself with the general history of mankind, I have felt a sincere passion for liberty. The history of nations doomed to perpetual slavery, in consequence of yielding up to tyrants their natural born liberties, I read with a sort of philosophical horror; so that the first systematical and bloody attempt at Lexington, to enslave America, thoroughly electrified my mind, and fully determined me to take part with my country.[31]

Ignoring the Green Mountain Boys' controversial defense of their land titles against the titles of New Yorkers, Allen here creates a nameless, generic self that comes to manhood when the Lexington militia refuse to yield up their "natural born liberties." The origin of his claim to patriotic integrity is traced to defensive resistance at Lexington, but the New England liberties to which Allen lays claim are not those cited by Samuel Adams or Jonas Clarke. Although Ethan Allen's first American ancestor had migrated with Hooker to Hartford in 1635, the writer of this paragraph cares nothing for the legacy of Puritan forefathers. He reads "the general history of mankind," not the Mathers or Edwards, and he cites "natural born liberties" rather than the "civil and religious liberties" fought for by New England's protestant settlers.[32] Allen's telling use of the word "electrified" ascribes the force of liberty to natural powers rather than to Providence or divine grace; it aligns republican liberty with Franklinian science, not protestant theology.[33] Emanating from New England but not from Puritanism, Allen's kind of "revolution" turns forward and not backward, anticipating that Nature's liberties will increasingly burst through multinational forms of civil enslavement.

   Allen's universalist claim on Revolution and Liberty provides the context for understanding why his justification for the attack on Ticonderoga became so celebrated. The crux of the justification is its own bravado: when the British commandant had asked him "by what authority" Allen was demanding Ticonderoga's surrender, "I answered him, 'In the name of the great Jehovah, and the Continental Congress' (the authority of the Congress being very little known at that time)" (7). As Allen's most authoritative biographer points out, none of the Green Mountain Boys recalled any such exchange, though some of them remembered Allen's saying either "Come out of there, you damned old Rat" or "Come out of there, you sons of British whores."[34] When Allen wrote his account, he knew from the Continental Congress's embarrassed response to his conquest that he would not have received authorization from "the Continental Congress" even if he had asked for it. Twentieth-century Vermont historians would make merry over Allen's words, noting parenthetically that there has never been any evidence that either the great Jehovah or the Continental Congress had commissioned Ethan for the task.

The debunking is not only too late but also quite beside the point. A long line of prominent state and national historians – William Gordon, David Ramsay, Samuel Williams, Ira Allen, Mercy Otis Warren, George Bancroft, Zadock Thompson – were to quote Allen's words, accepting their authenticity, their power, and even perhaps their validity.[35] So did that sometime skeptic Nathaniel Hawthorne, and so too, in more recent years, has a writer for *American Heritage*, a cultural scholar of the New Hampshire Grants and a prominent biographer of Benedict Arnold.[36] What continues to render Allen's words so essential a moment in American Revolutionary hagiography is the seriocomic audacity of his claim. As an authorizing power, the "little known" Continental Congress is cited as the syntactic equal of the Great Jehovah. Any concern that an attack upon a British fort might not be a defense of liberty is made to seem petty beside the bravado of claiming the highest sources of divine and political approval. Here is a pre-Revolutionary appeal to independent authority made by a New Englander, but no longer advanced within the confiningly regional terms of New England tradition. "The great Jehovah" is, after all, a pre-Christian deity, certainly not the God to whom members of the Black Regiment, such as Samuel Cooper and Jonas Clarke, were then praying in the name of protestant forebears.

Allen's backcountry daring became an institutionalized legacy. The cannon captured at Ticonderoga proved essential to Washington's fortification of Dorchester Heights and the expelling of the British from Boston. When Vermont entered the Union, it provided new revolutionary qualities to New England identity that went far beyond its culture of small farming. Whereas the New York Constitution of 1777 allowed feudal land lease, slavery, and a property qualification for suffrage to continue, Vermont entered the Union as the first state whose constitution, also passed in 1777, explicitly outlawed slavery, adopted universal manhood suffrage, and redefined "Freeman" status as possession of the vote without property qualification. Together with Vermont's statute embracing absolute freedom of religion, all these provisions must be seen as deriving in no small degree from the beliefs of Ethan Allen, Ira Allen, and the Green Mountain Boys. Vermont represented a new New England and was so identified both by state historian Zadock Thompson and by George Bancroft. Within this more accepting climate of opinion, Ethan Allen's *Narrative* began to look like the book in which New England had finally broken fully free of its Old England identity. Not only had the outsized Ethan Allen loudly defied British snobbery, exposed British cruelty, and then shown what it meant to "come Yankee over" the Englishman; in the latter pages of the *Narrative*, as Burgoyne surrenders and the French alliance is formed, Allen had even written, as self-consciously as possible, "Vaunt no more Old England! As a nation I hate and despise you. My affections are frenchified" (68, 70).[37]

There is no evidence that Melville's knowledge of Ethan Allen extended beyond an amused but appreciative reading of *A Narrative of Colonel Ethan Allen's Captivity*. Nonetheless, into two short chapters of *Israel Potter* (1854), Melville managed to compress more of the contradictory strands of Allen's heroic image than any of his predecessors had done. To Melville, "Ethan Ticonderoga Allen" served as the vehicle for the most comprehensive statement Melville would ever make about the ideal national (*not* New England) character.

Allen seems to have been a curious combination of a Hercules, a Joe Miller, a Bayard, and a Tom Hyer; had a person like the Belgian giants; mountain music in him like a Swiss; a heart plump as Coeur de Lion's. Though born in New England, he exhibited no trace of her character. He was frank, bluff, companionable as a Pagan, convivial as a Roman, hearty as a harvest. His spirit was essentially Western; and herein is his peculiar Americanism; for the western spirit is, or will yet be (for no other is, or can be), the true American one.[38]

By denying Ethan Allen's New England credentials, Melville here challenges the stereotypical model of the Puritan/New England/American that had prevailed so long within and beyond New England. Traits of folk heroes from Europe and America blend into one colossal but essentially western hero. The gigantic laborer, jokester, chivalrous knight, and wrestler fuse into an ingenuous, wholly competent good fellow, whose skills in acting the Yankee Melville has momentarily and conveniently ignored. The gallantry of Bayard is redirected toward democratic ends; sheer physical strength blends into western conviviality. Though pagan in manner, the essential American spirit somehow remains Christian at heart. Surely Melville sought to turn the abrasively Deistic Ethan Allen into a Christian so that he might represent, for the last time in Melville's writing, that national spirit of "the unshackled democratic spirit of Christianity in all things" which Melville had passionately invoked when reviewing Hawthorne's short stories.[39] Only in a transformed Yankee like Ethan Allen can we see how America's finest potential is by mid-century passing beyond and outside of New England. Sectional nationalism, in Melville's view, is now a dead end.

In support of the cynical observation "Now that materialism has won, it is appropriate that Ethan Allen has largely vanished from the public imagination," Michael Bellesiles cites the fact that Ethan Allen was omitted from the 1975 *Encyclopedia of American Biography*.[40] Although the repeated linking of Noel Lord to Ethan Allen in Howard Frank Mosher's well-known novella *Where the Rivers Flow North* (1978) might suggest otherwise,[41] I would not contest Bellesiles's point, but would rather observe that a similar kind of effacement had occurred even before the publication of *Israel Potter*. Hawthorne's sketch entitled "Old Ticonderoga," published in *The Snow-Image* (1852) but written two decades before, remains a neglected anomaly among legendizing pre-Civil War accounts of the fort's history. Visiting Ticonderoga as a romantic tourist in search of New England historical associations, Hawthorne's nameless narrator finds himself "disappointed" by the fort's neglect and the site's surprising smallness of size.

I viewed Ticonderoga as a place of ancient strength, in ruins for half a century; where the flags of three nations had successively waved, and none waved now; where armies had struggled, so long ago that the bones of the slain were moldered; where Peace had found a heritage in the forsaken haunts of War.[42]

Hawthorne's self-conscious search for the "poetry" of historical association ultimately yields nothing. His narrator sits near the roofless barracks summoning up "pictures of the past" in their historical sequence from the French construction of the fort, through Ethan Allen's "shout" about "the great Jehovah and the Continental Congress," to Burgoyne's recapture of Ticonderoga. The sudden ringing of a bell, however, recalls the narrator to the realities of the fort's "gray and weed-grown ruins" (189–191). Whatever storied conquests Ticonderoga might once have witnessed, today's ruined fort is, fortunately, "as peaceful in the sun as a warrior's grave" (191). As the last imagined garrison marches out of the narrator's consciousness, all his scenes of warfare are revealed to have been nothing more than imaginary panoramas of equal insignificance. Every gory picture in the narrator's historical sequence is effaced by the reality of a sun-filled present in which militarism no longer seems to prevail. Wasn't it pretty to think so!

The shock caused by New England's arming after April 19 is vividly conveyed in a little-known letter sent from New York City on May 29th by Quebec postmaster Hugh Finlay. Finlay was traveling up the Champlain waterway near Albany on May 12th when the rebel capture of Ticonderoga blocked his way back to Quebec. The rebels of New England, Finlay wrote his brother-in-law, had now become uncontrollable: "There is nothing in my opinion that may not be done by the Massachusetts and Connecticut people after having taken possession of His Majesty's forts of Ticonderoga and Crown Point."[43] The only reason Finlay can imagine for such an "overt act of rebellion" is that "The Eathan Allan [*sic*] who commanded the party of that expedition is a man who defies every office of Government." Finlay has heard rumors that "General Allen intends to destroy Ticonderoga" and that "the New England folks talk of standing by themselves."

Returning to Quebec via Boston, Finlay discovered that the army of New England was very real indeed, but he could account for it only as systemic madness. "The misrepresentations of the Lexington skirmish have fired the people in New England to frenzy." Their alleging of violated "liberties" is a powerful fantasy, a "fever" promoted by the New England media: "their newspapers, their orators, their politicians and the ministers of the Holy Gospel have deluded the people who are now armed to defend their religion and their property." Such propaganda is becoming ever more fearsome, however, because New England Puritans are the credulous, exiled inheritors of Old England's "blessed Oliverean tyranny." Finlay trusts that no bond will form between crazed New Englanders and Virginians, who are "men of principles, of strict honour, men of fortune and liberal education." But if New England proves so "mad" as to try to stand alone, Finlay predicts that "the New England people will rule the southern provinces with a rod of iron." At letter's end, Finlay tries to descry the future, but can offer only four telling words: "I foresee horrid work."

Just two days after Finlay sent his letter, Samuel Langdon D. D., president of Harvard and chaplain to the newly gathered New England army surrounding Boston, delivered the Election Day sermon in Watertown. Since the passing of the Suffolk Resolves the preceding September, no one could have been sure whether Massachusetts was now a province governed by royal officials in Boston or an independent commonwealth governed by the "Provincial Congress" variously located in Salem, Concord, and, most recently, Watertown. Langdon denounces the Intolerable Acts, not only to indict the British government but also to inquire, in the traditional jeremiad mode, why God should have afflicted such oppressions upon His people. Like Urian Oakes, Increase Mather, and William Stoughton, Langdon has mastered the repeated accusatory question.

But alas have not the sins of America, and of New England in particular, had a hand in bringing down upon us the righteous judgments of heaven? Wherefore is all this evil come upon us? Is it not because we have forsaken the Lord? Can we say we are innocent of crimes against God? Have we not lost much of that genuine Christianity which so remarkably appeared in our ancestors?[44]

But by sermon's end such questioning is replaced by a newer vocabulary provoking his audience to armed resistance rather than accusatory self-examination. "By the law of nature," Langdon exclaims, "any body of people, destitute of order and government may form themselves into a civil society . . . may by common consent put an end to it [an oppressive government] and set up another"– exactly as the Provincial Congress has now done (369).

By such reasoning, the spiritual enemy within is replaced by the military enemy without; the defensive stand of individual militia units shifts toward the prospective duty of collective military action. "In the name of God," Langdon's last paragraph concludes, "we will set up our banners." As he was speaking, Langdon was probably able to see, among the Massachusetts, Connecticut, New Hampshire, and Rhode Island troops encamped in and near Harvard College, that there was not yet a New England banner, and certainly no national flag. Under such circumstances, God's support for New England's defense could best be earned by resolute aggression. Seventeen days after his Election Day sermon, in the early evening on Cambridge Common, Samuel Langdon was to pray, apparently at considerable length, with William Prescott's Massachusetts regiment moments before Prescott's troops marched out, under an order of the Committee of Safety, to fortify "Bunker's Hill."[45]

Textbooks have long noted that Prescott's troops fortified Breed's Hill, not Bunker's Hill, and that the Battle of Bunker Hill should therefore be renamed, which of course it never will be.[46] Insisting on the distinction between the two hills now seems to be nothing more than a pedantic historical footnote. On June 17, 1775, however, the distinction was anything but pedantic. To advance and fortify either hill was an act of defensive resistance, but to fortify Breed's Hill was also tactically an act of aggression. Bunker Hill was close to Charlestown Neck and a long artillery shot from or toward Boston; it was a good spot to defend against another British incursion into the countryside, but not a position threatening the British military in the city. To fortify the eastern slope of Breed's Hill, however, was to threaten the British at the elevation closest to Boston. When William Prescott's troops built the redoubt on Breed's Hill before dawn on June 17, it was, therefore, an act of consummate defiance, to which the four British generals (Gage, Howe, Clinton, and Burgoyne) would be obligated to respond.

For decades thereafter, in accord with the belief that New England patriots had been the most reluctant of revolutionaries, American accounts of the Battle of Bunker Hill were to insist that fortifying Breed's Hill had been a defensive response to Gage's preparations for fortifying Dorchester Heights. To the British military and to any onlooker atop Copp's Hill, however, Prescott's building of the redoubt must have seemed an act of aggression at least as daring, dangerous, and public as Ethan Allen's attack on Ticonderoga. For what purpose were those militiamen fortifying so advanced a position, if not to shell the British navy, the British army in Boston, or both? If William Prescott's men were not rebellious colonists planning to attack His Majesty's Forces, they certainly must, across those 500 yards of water, have looked exactly like that. Were the New England militiamen digging in on that hillside *defending* their civil and religious liberties, or were they provoking a battle to establish the independence of New England, if not of all the colonies? On the validity of the distinction would hang, not only Sam Adams's insistence on the Revolution as a defensive resistance on behalf of liberty, but the later Federalist/Whig belief that Americans were a republican people averse to violent change and rationally obedient to duly established legal authority.

Although by day's end Prescott's men showed that Americans could withstand the repeated attack of British regulars, the New Englanders were eventually driven from both Breed's Hill and Bunker's Hill. But the true import of the battle, the patriots soon and often said, lay not in the strategic importance of possessing either hill, but in the exhilarating display of the militia's deadly resistance against a professional British army that colonials had grown to abhor and fear. Almost every narrative, from the official accounts of William Howe and Peter Thatcher, through Revolutionary and state histories, was to echo Burgoyne's description of the battle as a sublime panorama of regulars moving slowly up through billowing smoke to attack a surprisingly impregnable rebel position while thousands of spectators watched the red-coated soldiers fall in the green grass.

There is, of course, much to be said in support of Burgoyne's kind of heroic military landscape. Only an absolutist who discredits all military heroism can fail to be impressed by the ability and courage of William Prescott and his men, as well as the bravery in the field of John Stark and Joseph Warren, William Howe and John Pitcairn. Patriotic iconography was to fasten, however, upon the supposedly defensive qualities of two particular battle moments: Colonel William Prescott in plain linen coat walking on the ramparts of the redoubt amidst British fire (William Wetmore Story's statue); and Major General Joseph Warren dying during the final retreat from the redoubt (John Trumbull's painting). Both moments create the impression that overwhelming numbers of British regulars had relentlessly attacked beleaguered American defenses. Both concentrate on the bravery of the volunteer civilian defender, thereby implying that Prescott's and Warren's conduct had been representative as well as inspirational.

Bunker Hill proved to be the costliest of victories for the British, but a reversible loss for the Americans. Revolutionary warfare in Massachusetts ended after George Washington successfully reenacted Prescott's strategy of a surprise overnight fortification on a height of land. By the time Washington fortified Dorchester Heights, however, he was commanding disparate regiments serving under one banner, the Union Flag. The Army of New England had been refashioned as the army of a still nonexistent nation, now fully able to attack thanks to the 55 cannon, 2,300 pounds of lead, and barrels of flint somehow dragged over the Berkshires from Fort Ticonderoga in mid-January.

The legendizing of Bunker Hill and Ticonderoga demonstrates that revolutionary New England was looking for a new kind of regional culture hero. More is at stake here than the obvious, necessary change from civilian to military leadership. Although William Prescott, Israel Putnam, Joseph Warren, and Ethan Allen were descendants of early planters, none of them came from Boston families prominent in the political or ministerial leadership of the Commonwealth. None was prominent or even active in the Congregational Church. All had grown up as the sons of small farmers in rural towns (Groton, Salem Village, Roxbury, and Cornwall, respectively). The heritage that would account for their bravery had not been the ministerial/lawyerly/diplomatic legacy of the Mathers, Dudleys, Winthrops, and Winslows, but the hard-scrabble life of the Yankee farm family, doing what needed to be done to achieve the appointed task. The military exigencies of 1775 were evolving a different kind of leadership, still traceable to New England roots, but now of the best, common kind. A new model of the New Englander to which the life of Paul Revere, city boy though he was, could be readily adapted.[47]

Although New England courage was to be embodied in Prescott, the death of Joseph Warren drew forth the immediate eulogies. Their importance resides in what they do not include. Warren is revered as America's Leonidas, or Sarpedon, or Brutus, or Cicero, or Cato; New England is viewed as America's Sparta or Lavinium, and Bunker Hill as America's Thermopylae. In none of these classicizing analogies is there room for the Joseph Warren who in 1772 had invoked the Puritans as haters of tyranny, and who, in front of British troops in 1775, had told the congregation gathered in Old South that "Your fathers ... sternly frown upon the human miscreant who, to secure the loaves and fishes to himself, would breed a serpent to destroy his children."[48] No elegist wished to emphasize that in the preamble to the Suffolk Resolves, Warren had insisted that "the blood and valour of our venerable progenitors" is the source of our "most sacred obligations" to act upon and to transmit the dearly bought inheritance of liberty.[49] An increasingly Federalist and secular New England preferred not

to recall language that seemed to incite to violence on neo-Puritan principles. Accordingly, the abrasive, angry voice within Joseph Warren, which
by shaming the sons in the name of the fathers had helped to provoke
aggression, was now to be muted in favor of the gentleman martyr, classical
hero, man of sentiment, and libertarian of Reason.

While completing historical research for *Lionel Lincoln*, Fenimore
Cooper realized that the fortifying of Breed's Hill could be perceived either as a defensive or an aggressive action, and refused to argue the issue.
Cooper was not willing, however, to accept the handy transformation of
Joseph Warren into a pacifistic Man of Reason and Sentiment. In a rare
historical anachronism, Cooper introduces Joseph Warren presiding over
the North End Caucus in Boston in June 1775, in order to show us that
Massachusetts's "open, fearless and engaging" gentleman-martyr had in fact
long been conspiring to promote "the boldest assertions of constitutional
principles" in long, narrow, and darkened Boston rooms.[50]

Cooper's narrative of Bunker Hill climaxes in a revisionist view of
Warren's martyrdom. Instead of picturing Warren expiring in central fore-
ground with all eyes upon him, as in John Trumbull's painting, Cooper
renders Warren's death from the vantage point of British Major Lionel
Lincoln hurriedly stepping over "many a lifeless body" as he passes through
the redoubt.

Notwithstanding the hurry, and vast disorder of the fray, his [Lincoln's] eye fell
on the form of the graceful stranger stretched lifeless on the parched grass, which
had greedily drank his blood. Amid the ferocious cries, and fiercer passions of
the moment, the young man paused, and glanced his eyes around him, with an
expression that said, he thought the work of death should cease. At this instant,
the trappings of his attire caught the glaring eye-balls of a dying yeoman, who
exerted his wasting strength to sacrifice one more worthy victim to the *manes* of
his countrymen. The whole of the tumultuous scene vanished from the senses of
Lionel at the flash of the musket of this man, and he sunk beneath the feet of the
combatants, insensible of further triumph. (188)

Challenging patriot tradition, Cooper renders Warren's death as a revelation
of the brutal insanity of war, a tearing away of the veil of genteel warfare.
The scene is one of senseless havoc; Joseph Warren is but an unnamed
corpse whose blood is "greedily" drunk by the parched earth. Warren's
death, as far as we know, provokes only the further senselessness of Lionel
Lincoln's wounding. The "glaring eyeballs" of the "dying yeoman" who,
enraged at Warren's death, lives only to kill another redcoat reveal a crazed
patriotism utterly unlike Prescott's valor. At day's end, the surviving British

can only "go and mourn for their victory" (188), but Major Lionel Lincoln, American-born though he is, will never convert to the patriot cause.

Cooper's historical vision is both informed and double-sided. Although he renders the Revolution in Boston from the point of view of an honorable British military officer, he also reaffirms, without a trace of satire, the cherished essence of the patriots' courage in holding Bunker Hill.

Ignorant of the glare of military show; in the simple and rude vestments of their calling; armed with such weapons as they had seized from the hooks above their own mantels; and without even a banner to wave its cheering folds above their heads, they stood, sustained only by the righteousness of their cause, and those deep moral principles which they had received from their fathers, and which they intended this day should show, were to be transmitted untarnished to their children. (177–178)

The parallel phrasing and rhythmic cadences of these words resemble but surpass Daniel Webster's eloquence. The sentence's exact center is the two single syllable words – subject and verb – "they stood." Whether the advanced position of Prescott's yeomen was offensive or defensive, the strong rhythmic accents on "they stood" affirm the virtue most essential to justifying New England resistance: the will to stand witness to one's inner faith in liberty. (Emerson's "Here once the embattled farmers stood" was to repeat the same trope with a similar rhythmic emphasis.[51]) Although Cooper was scornful of Puritan religious bigotry, his ascribing the cultural origin of patriot resistance to "those deep moral principles they had received from their fathers" shows his willingness to recognize great merit in New England's heritage. The heroism in the redoubt was only the greater, Cooper implies, because Prescott's men had no "banner" to sustain them. While affirming Sam Adams's regressive view of revolution, Cooper's novel minimizes Puritanism and leaves out the flag-waving.

In 1852 Bancroft wrote in tribute to Cooper, "Great as he was in the department of romantic fiction, he was not less deserving of praise in that of history. In *Lionel Lincoln* he has described the battle of Bunker Hill better than it is described in any other work."[52] High and deserved praise, surely, but Bancroft was soon to publish an account of Bunker Hill superior even to Cooper's. The three-chapter 32-page account of Bunker Hill concluding the seventh volume of the *History* illustrates the achievements of the American Romantic historians at their best. Bancroft's narrative pacing is perfect: a chapter on the decision to fortify Breed's Hill and preparations for battle; a chapter on the first two British advances, ending with the militiamen's foreboding upon realizing that their powder was almost spent; and a final chapter describing the British conquest, but ending with Franklin's insight into the lasting significance of Bunker Hill – "England has lost her colonies for ever."[53]

Bancroft includes the expected pictorial tableaux but continually returns to a narrative vantage point – very different from Trumbull's or Cooper's – looking outward from within Prescott's redoubt. On the third charge, the British attack the redoubt from three sides simultaneously.

> For some time longer they kept the enemy at bay, confronting them with the butt-end of their guns, and striking them with the barrels after the stocks were broken. The breastwork being abandoned, the ammunition all expended, the redoubt half filled with regulars and on the point of being surrounded, and no other reenforcements having arrived, a little before four, Prescott gave the word to retreat. He himself was among the last to leave the fort; escaping unhurt, though with coat and waistcoat rent and pierced by bayonets, which he parried with his sword. (429–430)

Four short visual phrases, summarizing the conditions of a gallant loss, precede Bancroft's terse wording of the inevitable, life-saving decision to retreat. True to historical fact, as recounted by Frothingham and Ketchum, these sentences recall Roland at Roncesvalles, Leonidas at Thermopylae, without mentioning either analogy. The essence of revolutionary heroism, for Bancroft, still lies in a patriot's last defense.

In Bancroft's chapters, William Prescott, not Joseph Warren, emerges as the representative man of military crisis. Bancroft accepts the accuracy of two statements about Prescott ("He will fight you to the last drop of his blood"; "Prescott will fight you to the gates of hell"), and two statements by Prescott himself ("Don't fire until you see the whites of their eyes"; "These are the works of our hands; to us be the honor of defending them," 404). By concluding "heedless of personal danger, he [Prescott] obeyed the orders as he understood them" (409), Bancroft deftly conceals the possibility that Prescott's decision to fortify Breed's Hill countermanded Artemus Ward's orders.

Bancroft seeks above all to convey the power of spirit in Prescott's unpublished letter to the Committee of Safety written the day after the Mandamus Councilors had been appointed.

> Be not dismayed nor disheartened in this day of great trials . . . We consider that we are all embarked in one bottom, and must sink or swim together . . . Our forefathers passed the vast Atlantic, spent their blood and treasure, that they might enjoy their liberties, both civil and religious, and transmit them to their posterity . . . Is a glorious death in defence of our liberties better than a short infamous life, and

our memories to be held in detestation to the latest posterity? Let us all be of one heart, and stand fast in the liberties wherewith Christ has made us free; and may he of his infinite mercy grant us deliverance out of all our troubles. (99)

Prescott's letter is proof that Sam Adams's ideal of revolution as defense of civil liberties inspired the climactic military act of the American Revolution in New England. In Prescott's words can be found echoes of John Winthrop in 1630 ("the liberties wherewith Christ has made us free"), of Joseph Warren in 1772 ("Our forefathers passed the vast Atlantic, spent their blood and treasure, that they might enjoy their liberties"), of Sam Adams in 1774 ("we consider we are all embarked in one bottom, and must sink or swim together") and of Thomas Paine in 1776 ("Is a glorious death in defence of our liberties better than a short infamous life?"). But all these principles emanate, without a wasted word, from a rural New Englander who sought no celebrity and held no ministerial or political position. Prescott had made New England's principles real, enabling the "defense" of civil liberty to lead to independence. The fact that Prescott's rediscovered letter provoked little response upon its publication, however, suggests that, amid the divisive concerns of the mid-nineteenth century, Bancroft's claim upon the Puritan forefathers' virtues seemed to belong to an increasingly irrelevant past.

While drafting his narrative of Bunker Hill in the aftermath of the Compromise of 1850, Bancroft, knew that the major moments of commemoration were past. The laying of the cornerstone of the Bunker Hill Monument in 1825 had drawn a crowd of 20,000, which gathered to see a mile-long procession of 200 Bunker Hill veterans, the chief elected officials of Massachusetts, the Masons, and General Lafayette. The completion of the monument in 1843 had drawn a crowd of 100,000, which gathered to see a two-mile procession including 108 Bunker Hill veterans, the elected officials of Massachusetts, the Masons, President of the United States John Tyler, Tyler's cabinet, and federal Congressmen from every state in the Union. In all probability, the ceremony of 1843 was the largest and most widely attended historical commemoration yet held during the Republic's sixty years of existence.[54] The speaker on both occasions had been none other than New England's revered leader Daniel Webster, Massachusetts's adopted son of New Hampshire farm origin, the orator who had consistently encouraged voters to believe that he voiced the spirit of New England, and who, as an ambitious Whig, had become one of George Bancroft's chief party opponents throughout the 1840s.

Although Webster's 1825 address began with the well-known line "We are among the sepulchres of our fathers," his speech as a whole subsumes

New England regional pride within national patriotism.[55] A short tribute to Prescott and a long tribute to Joseph Warren precede a pointed reminder that many of the militiamen who fought at Bunker Hill also fought at Trenton, Camden, and Yorktown. Webster may honor his region's primacy, noting that "the 17th of June saw the four New England colonies standing here, side by side, to triumph or to fall together" (21), but his final paragraph insists "Let our object be OUR COUNTRY, OUR WHOLE COUNTRY, AND NOTHING BUT OUR COUNTRY" (39–40).

The 1843 speech was to be even more aggressively national. Secretary of State Webster ignored the libertarian piety of Puritan forefathers entirely, and very nearly forgot New England. His only appeal to region is his compliment to ex-New Englanders who have, for the moment, come home from western *and southern* residences to appreciate the New England origin of "the shrine of liberty."[56] The shrine of liberty may have belonged to New England in America's infancy, but the maturing of the Republic has allowed us to replace regional with federal liberty. The national heritage of freedom derives from Bacon, Locke, Shakespeare, and Milton, a heritage first institutionalized, Webster claims, not in the General Court of Massachusetts, but in "the first popular representative assembly which ever convened on this continent, the Virginia House of Burgesses" (188). President Tyler, we may assume, was not displeased to hear the tribute.

This time, Webster did not even bother to retell the Battle of Bunker Hill, but summarized its essentials in one short paragraph, adding "the history of all these is familiar" (141). The meaning of the completed Bunker Hill Monument for today's American, however, remained very much his concern. The Monument, as Webster now understands it, really has nothing to do with New England heroism.

Woe betide the man who can stand here with the fires of local resentments burning, or the purpose of fomenting local jealousies and the strifes of local interests festering and rankling in his heart . . . Union, founded on the same love of liberty, cemented by blood shed in the same common cause – union has been the source of all our glory and greatness thus far, and is the ground of all our highest hopes. This column stands on Union. I know not that it might not keep its position, if the American Union, in the mad conflict of human passions, and in the strife of parties and factions, should be broken up and destroyed. (140)

Anyone in the audience aware of fractious national issues that had developed since Webster delivered his earlier Bunker Hill speech would have known what his words implied. If the slavery issue were now to cause the United States of America to divide, the significance of Bunker Hill would "be broken up and destroyed." If "This column stands on Union," then the monument symbolizes, not civil and religious liberty for the individual, but union for the nation as a whole. Webster would have his audience believe that, on June 17, 1775 the New England militiamen, who had in fact fought under no single banner, were fighting for the national "Union" of 1843. Chattel slavery is therefore, by implication, included among the values for which Massachusetts militiamen as well as Virginia Burgesses presumably had fought.

Webster's 1843 speech ends with four paragraphs describing the hero of today's memorial. Not William Prescott, who is scarcely mentioned, and not Joseph Warren, whose martyrdom is no longer of interest, but George Washington. Never mind that Washington had not been present at the Battle of Bunker Hill, nor that Washington had not yet assumed command of the army, nor that New Englanders had fought under state and local flags.

The structure now standing before us, by its uprightness, its solidity, its durability, is no unfit emblem of his [Washington's] character . . . Towering high above the column which our hands have builded; beheld, not by the inhabitants of a single city or a single State, but by all the families of man – ascends the colossal grandeur of the character and life of Washington. (150)

Webster was too politically savvy to state explicitly that George Washington had been a Virginia slaveholder, but Webster surely knew that the appropriate Unionist inference was there for his audience's taking. By 1843 Daniel Webster was well on his way to becoming the national politician who, by accepting the Fugitive Slave provision in the Compromise of 1850, would acknowledge that slavery was legal on New England soil. To omit mention of slavery while praising George Washington was a ruse for politely projecting the nationalization of slavery down New England's throat.

If Webster's 1843 speech was not hollow rhetoric, it certainly was false history. Even though Bancroft was as strong a national unionist, and as little an abolitionist, as Daniel Webster, Bancroft's regard for historical fact left him with no respect for Webster's second Bunker Hill speech. Brushing aside the monument and never mentioning its orator, Bancroft challenges Websterian political "spin" at every turn. He restores William Prescott to his rightful honors, leaving George Washington's arrival as commanding general to the opening of the next volume. Self-conscious nationalist though he was, Bancroft underscores the undeniable fact that the Battle of Breed's Hill had been New England's affair. "Here the character of New England shown out in its brightest lustre," declares Bancroft at the opening of his second chapter on the battle (416). In a lengthy paragraph of plain syntax, Bancroft enumerates the virtues of Joseph Warren, insisting that "as the moment for the appeal to arms approached, Warren watched with joy the revival of the generous spirit of New England's ancestors" (433).

Bancroft's most timely slap at Webster's view of the Bunker Hill battle was his insistence on the participation of free blacks among New England's forces: "Nor should history forget to record that, as in the army at Cambridge, so also in this gallant band, the free Negroes of the colony had their representatives. For the right of free negroes to bear arms in the public defence was, at that day, as little disputed in New England as their other rights."[57] To include this fact prevents the reader from believing that New England's militiamen had fought for a "Union" with slavery. The "free negroes" on Bunker Hill were fighting to end a complementary form of slavery that they, like Joseph Warren, associated with British rule.

Bancroft's seventh volume was published in 1858, shortly after the Dred Scott decision. The divisive consequences of Webster's Seventh of March Speech, in which he had accepted the Fugitive Slave law to secure the Compromise, were being lived out in the nation as a whole. Amid the gathering storm of civil dissent, Bancroft's chapters on the Battle of Bunker Hill were not likely to attract the attention they deserved, either as the art of history, or as regional/national commentary. This missed opportunity is not, however, entirely ascribable to boredom with yet another celebratory narrative of Bunker Hill. In brooding over the politics of slavery, Bancroft was so immobilized by slavery's legality that he could only mention, not emphasize, his own reminder about the presence of free blacks at Bunker Hill. Unlike Webster, Bancroft had not allowed his politics and pocketbook to be mortgaged to New England's banking and cotton mill interests, but by 1858 Bancroft could see nothing but bloodshed ahead for his beloved Republic if Separatist sectional feeling, south or north, continued to grow. Bancroft's self-imposed silence on the slavery issue is a compelling sign of the last crisis faced by antebellum New England/Americans as they tried to carry forward their Puritan and Revolutionary heritage in the midst of a deeply conflicted present.

CHAPTER 9

Abolition, "white slavery," and regional pride

Is liberty safe? Is man saved? They say, sir, I am a fanatic, and so I am.
But sir, none of us have yet risen high enough. Afar off, I see Carver
and Bradford, and I mean to get up to them.

Wendell Phillips, 1855

I regard you as providentially raised up to be the James Otis of the
new revolution.

William Lloyd Garrison to Wendell Phillips, 1857

Although Angelina Grimké's "Appeal to the Christian Women of the South"
(1836) arrayed the Bible and the Declaration of Independence against chattel
slavery with a moral force hard to excel, Grimké had precious little regional
tradition to sustain her demand for emancipation. There had been numerous antislavery Southerners and some Colonizationists, but there were
precious few southern Abolitionists, and virtually no Abolitionists of the
uncompensated, immediatist persuasion like those who, for the preceding five years, had been following the Garrisonian banner. Accordingly,
Grimké's appeal had to be profoundly ahistorical, based upon the presumably timeless divine commands imbedded in the two scriptural texts, one
religious and one political, that were most widely valued by Americans on
both sides of the line of the Missouri Compromise.

In Massachusetts the argumentative resources for abolition were at once
broader than Grimké's and oddly narrower, evolving almost as much from
a selective reading of regional history as from Jefferson and Jesus. In considering the argument for immediate abolition, we need to confront, more
directly than has yet been attempted, both the special power and the
special danger inherent in New England's calling upon its now regional
legacy of freedom crises. To appeal to Bradford or Otis as a model for the
Abolitionist's lonely pilgrimage toward God's truth surely marshaled some
New Englanders toward ending slavery, but such appeals were couched in a
language of regional pride that seems almost designed to alienate indecisive

moderates of the border states or the South. Accordingly, Garrison's and Phillips's linking of abolition to the revolts of New England forefathers became increasingly shrill as its national ineffectiveness became, during the 1850s, increasingly evident.

The eventual victory and vindication of the immediate Abolitionists' cause, as biographers have often and rightly emphasized, were to be the Emancipation Proclamation and the Thirteenth Amendment.[1] But the immediatists' often overlooked defeat – especially wrenching for a pacifist like Garrison – was the outbreak and prolonged killing of the Civil War itself. Pride in New England's legacy of protest for Liberty, I contend, lent special power to the immediatist movement, but also stoked the angers of militant southern secession. Treasured notions of regional identity led to self-blindfolding. Why did Garrison, Phillips, and Parker repeatedly denounce all Southerners as slave-drivers and man-stealers, even though only a minority of male Southerners owned slaves? Was it, in part, because immediatists were too proud to appeal to the goodwill of nonslaveholding Southerners? And why were immediatists so unwilling to consider that voluntary, bloodless emancipation would require confronting the economic as well as legal fact that, for slaveholders, their slaves were their essential capital? Was it only because immediatists detested the Constitution and scorned placing any monetary value on a human being? Or did their expressions of moral and spiritual outrage conveniently hide the fact that New England increasingly lacked the power to promote political change?

Women Abolitionists were troubled by the extreme rhetoric of their male counterparts. As early as 1833, Lydia Maria Child warned that immediate abolitionism could well founder upon "mutual recrimination," causing the crucial issue of slavery "to degenerate into a mere question of *sectional* pride and vanity."[2] Two years later, Catharine Beecher, a gradualist like most members of her family, protested that Garrison's accusatory tone was hindering national emancipation even as his rhetoric gained regional support. Beecher was so fearful of the likely result ("Must we rush on to disunion, and civil wars, and servile wars [slave insurrections] till all their train of horrors pass over us like a devouring fire?"[3]) that she did not try to ascertain why the Garrisonians wrote as they did. Their belief in an absolute good and an absolute evil, within and beyond all churches, is one undeniable explanation. Another is that immediatism attracted New Englanders who felt particularly disempowered and who found in abolition a forum for asserting the moral priority of their regional heritage, whether or not their words represented a practicable solution to slavery.

The legacy of New England forefathers, as formulated by Garrisonian Abolitionists, was to lead not only to celebrating the separatism of the neo-Puritan Abolitionist, but to trampling out the grapes of God's wrath with a millennial fervor that served the freedom of the slave at the expense of thousands upon thousands of national and New England dead. No one will ever be able to weigh the cost and achievement of the Civil War more fully and deeply than Abraham Lincoln, yet even he, moderate Whig Midwesterner though he was, would give primary credit for the Negro's emancipation to the Garrisonians. Here was a great progressive change initiated by a beleaguered minority but exacted at enormous earthly price. What could be more "Puritan"?

We are accustomed to thinking of the "cultural imperialism" and "nationalism" of antebellum New England, to use Lewis Simpson's telling terms,[4] as deriving from sectional self-confidence based upon the region's economic and political strengths. My account proceeds from the opposite assumption, namely that New Englanders were conscious, even when they did not admit it, of New England's continuing decline in the economic, political, and cultural leadership of the nation. In 1791, New England comprised five of the Republic's fourteen states, about 18 percent of its land area, and about 28 percent of the national population. By 1860, New England comprised only 6 of the nation's 28 states, about 8 percent of its land area, and about 13 percent of the nation's population, including Negroes. Massachusetts had been the second most populous state in 1790; in 1820 it ranked fifth, behind Ohio.

Worry about declining regional influence was apparent before immediate abolition became a national controversy. Prominent Federalists such as Josiah Quincy, who bitterly resented the virtual succession of two-term Virginia presidents, awarded Madison and Monroe the satiric accolade of being America's Stuarts, James the First and James the Second. Hating the Constitution's three-fifth rule for slave representation even more than they hated slavery, many New Englanders of the early Republic believed that the Constitution and the South's "Peculiar Institution" were working together to perpetuate southern dominance. Fisher Ames and Timothy Pickering, who were sure that any lasting republic must remain small in size, regarded new and future western states as the source, initially of democracy but ultimately of tyranny. Even if the Louisiana Purchase did not portend the swift decline of New England power, the admission of Louisiana to statehood in 1812 introduced French and Spanish influences to Anglo-America, while strengthening southern slavery. Although moderate Federalists managed to control the Hartford Convention in 1814, thereby thwarting any motion to secede, the final report, drafted by Harrison Gray Otis, assailed Virginia and the three-fifths rule, while proposing that a two-third vote of both House and Senate be required for the admission of any new states. Here was the onset of regional fear with a pointed legacy in the next generation. In a footnote to his study of the Hartford Convention, James Banner drew up an impressive list of prominent Federalists whose sons and daughters were to become ardent Abolitionists.[5]

The migration from New England to upper New York, across the Western Reserve, and into the upper Midwest was touted as the spread of New England democratic institutions, but also feared as an exodus from rapidly depleting and recently circumscribed farmlands. It was all very well for Wendell Phillips, Bostonian patrician as he was, to proclaim to a Boston Melodeon audience in 1852 that "the hundred gathered in a New England school-house may be the hundred who shall teach the rising men of the other half of the continent and stereotype Freedom on the banks of the Pacific," but Garrison himself had been worried about the exodus as early as *Thoughts on African Colonization* (1832): "The emigration from New England to the far West is constant and large. Almost every city, town or village suffers annually by the departure of some of its adventurous inhabitants."[6] To demonstrate the growing power of southern slavery, Theodore Parker would in the 1850s repeatedly remind his audiences that Texas alone had an area six times that of Massachusetts, and that only three of the first twelve presidents had come from the North. The three northern presidents, Parker was fond of noting, had all been single-termers, and the two Adamses had suffered strong disapproval because of their advocacy of moderate antislavery measures.

To many an antislavery spokesman, the changes within New England were as disturbing as its shrinkage. Although Shays Rebellion, the secessionist urge prior to the Hartford Convention, and the sacking of the Ursuline Convent could be slighted as aberrations of the past, continuing demographic patterns were too palpable to ignore. While the Yankee farm population remained relatively constant, Boston's population increased from 43,300 in 1820 to 178,000 in 1860. About 40 percent of that increase – a number larger than the city's population in 1820 – were Irish Catholic immigrants. Thoreau's and Parker's slurs against the Irish were directed less against their Catholicism than against their presumed intemperance and shiftlessness, competing as they were against free black labor, especially in Boston.

The national high point of the xenophobic Know Nothing Party occurred in the 1854 elections in the State of Massachusetts. Even Ralph

Waldo Emerson, who would surely have cut the personal acquaintance of any Know Nothing delegate, was not impervious to the appeal of Know Nothing rhetoric for the purpose of stirring an Abolitionist rally. Speaking at a July 4, 1846 Abolitionist gathering in Dedham, Emerson began by lamenting:

A despair has crept over Massachusetts, and over New England, in regard to those objects which our people naturally love and aim at. The active, intelligent, well-meaning, and substantial part of the people find themselves paralyzed and defeated everywhere, by the foreign and newly arrived portion of the citizens, by the youthful, by the uneducated, and by the unscrupulous voters, and by those reckless persons who have assumed to lead these masses.[7]

Such a passage lends substance to David Donald's much contested charge that the Abolitionists were a "displaced social élite" whose Federalist/Whig professional heritage and élite education left them voicing the "anguished protest of an aggrieved class against a world they never made."[8] Indeed, it sometimes seemed that the only sign of New England's leadership was the growth and prosperity of its manufacturers. By 1860, 217 mills in Massachusetts were turning southern cotton into saleable textiles. There were more than twice as many cotton mills in Massachusetts as there were in all the other states of the Confederacy; the median-sized Massachusetts mill employed twice the number of factory workers (so-called "northern free white labor") of its southern counterpart.[9]

The question faced by Abolitionists seeking to turn New England's past national leadership to present good was, therefore, "what to make of a diminished thing" without acknowledging that the shrinkage might be permanent. The creeping "despair" over regional decline voiced by Emerson, and felt by abolitionist reformers, transcendentalists, and Conscience Whigs, was to be expressed in a wide range of responses to slavery. One could avoid all mention of the Massachusetts cotton mills, insist on New England's historical primacy in the antislavery movement, assume a humanitarian purity of motive in today's New Englander, regard North and South as separate regions, and urge abolitionism as the crucial reform needed for progress toward New England's truly humanitarian, postmillennial or even perfectionist future. Or one could acknowledge New England's longstanding complicity with slavery, regard North and South as one increasingly corrupt national garment interwoven of slave, cotton, and mill, denounce the hidden corruption in the New England soul, and then urge that a cleansing division of the nation (Disunion or perhaps even civil war) must accompany a cleansing of the individual heart. Broadly speaking, the first line of argument would be pursued by Mrs. Child, by Samuel Sewall, by Whittier, by the younger James Russell Lowell, and by Emerson. The second, far more abrasive argument would be formed by Garrison, passingly embraced by Samuel May and Henry David Thoreau, but raised to revolutionary pitch in the addresses of Wendell Phillips and the sermons of Theodore Parker.

There were, of course, many shades and combinations between these binary arguments, which were not as easily divisible as my bipolar summary suggests. Depending on the political moment and the rhetorical occasion, the same New England Abolitionist could assert either or both of them, Wendell Phillips's orations providing the best example of such flexibility. Rather than classifying such arguments along a spectrum, it is more important to grasp what was at stake in their collective use. To follow the presumably seamless libertarian inheritance of William Bradford and Roger Williams, James Otis and Sam Adams, meant not only that slavery must be abolished in the nation, but also that the Abolitionist was worthy of the forefathers and that New England was not necessarily in decline. To acknowledge New England's complicity with slavery was to admit that contemporary New England had fallen indeed, but could become regenerate if the courage for measures of uncompromising resistance could be summoned. Either way, however, the past leaders of the Puritan forefather–revolutionary father – yankee farmer historical continuum had to be held up as a beacon of integrity and a model for Abolitionist action. Effective abolitionism allowed for a strident attack on New England's countenancing of slavery for the sake of money and power, but did not allow for sullying the spiritual purity and political rectitude of regional heroes whose memory could prove redemptive. Garrison and Emerson, Lowell and Parker, Thoreau and Phillips advocated abolition on different grounds and with different rhetorical strategies, but they all shared in the directive spirit of Boston's nineteenth-century seal: *Sicut Patribus, sit Deus Nobis*.

Those who sought evidence for the historical primacy of Massachusetts in advancing abolition found it in abundance. While the Merrimack River textile mills were humming, regional pride laid ringing claim upon a noble emancipatory past. The endpoint of the Abolitionist road might be unknown, but the many milestones passed by pilgrims' feet were clearly visible: the ninety-first provision of the Massachusetts Body of Liberties of 1641 stating that "there shall never be any bond slaverie, villinage or Captivitie amongst us unless it be lawfull Captives taken in just warres"; Samuel Sewall's "The Selling of Joseph" (1700) as America's first antislavery tract; Prince Hall's petitions to end slavery in Massachusetts; the antislavery

pronouncements of James Otis and John Adams; Crispus Attucks's martyrdom, presumably on behalf of Liberty, during the Boston Massacre; Phyllis
Wheatley's poetry in praise of American Independence; Samuel Hopkins's
tracts advocating immediate emancipation of slaves in Rhode Island and
the new Republic; Massachusetts Chief Justice William Cushing's ruling
against the continuation of slavery in 1783; the elimination of slavery in
Massachusetts according to the 1790 census; Joseph Story's vivid account
of the Middle Passage; the publication in Boston of David Walker's *Appeal*,
of the *Liberator*, and of the most important fugitive slave narratives; the
convening of Boston's first African Baptist Church; the first meeting of the
New England Anti-Slavery Society there in 1832; and, finally, the formation
of the American Anti-Slavery Society under Garrison's leadership in 1833.
An impressive legacy, even though forms of indenture for former slaves
lingered on New England soil.

The pressure of tracts and sermons reminding New Englanders of their
antislavery heritage was intended to bolster the courage of waverers, to
persuade them to join the emancipation movement, even to risk martyrdom at the hands of an anti-Abolitionist Boston Mob led by "gentlemen
of property and standing." Whenever reminders of the forefather's libertarian virtues began to sound like a litany, however, unintended effects
could result: doubt at being able to measure up to an heroic past; complacency amid all the antislavery movement had achieved; an empathy with
"our" self-declared virtue that encouraged passivity as soon as one left the
lyceum or stopped reading. Regionalist rhetoric often overreached itself,
as in Samuel May's recollection of the moment Garrison was let out of
a Baltimore prison and went back to Boston to found the *Liberator*: "the
spirit of freedom – the true American eagle – thus uncaged, flew back to his
native New England, and thence sent forth that cry which disturbed the
repose of every slaveholder in the land, and has since resounded throughout the world."[10] Those who saw the eagle of freedom as a New England
bird risked smug moralizing of the most provocative sort. Two well-known
antislavery poems of the 1840s, Whittier's "Massachusetts to Virginia" and
Lowell's "On the Capture of Fugitive Slaves Near Washington," conceive
of Massachusetts as a tyrant-hating land of freedom where slavery has never
existed, in order to describe Virginia as a state of chains and coffles whose
people have utterly betrayed the faith of their Revolutionary fathers.

Parading regional economic differences had the self-defeating effect of
making Abolitionist activity seem logically unnecessary. Whittier's "Justice
and Expediency," for example, expatiates upon the "beautiful system of
free labor as exhibited in New England," where, thanks to the heritage of

Puritan freehold and Revolutionary independence, "every young laborer may acquire... in a few years, a farm of his own."[11] This remarkably false model of New England agricultural prosperity is contrasted to the brutal, slothful system of slavery, which, in 1833, is said to have already produced a wasteland "of grass-grown streets, of crumbling mansions, of beggared planters and barren plantations" throughout the entire South (52). Whittier's ignorance of the current prosperity in recent southern states undermines his own argument. If slavery is rapidly collapsing through its own economic failing, why should anyone incur personal risk merely to hurry its end?

Rhetoric in praise of New England's antislavery heritage reached its self-destructive climax in the speeches of its greatest orator and bluest blood, Wendell Phillips. Descendant of Watertown's founding minister, inheritor of moneys that founded Phillips Andover and Phillips Exeter, and son of Boston's mayor, Phillips would as early as 1853 devote an entire speech to the "Philosophy of the Abolition Movement," in which he traced an always regional but variously "Abolitionist" tradition from Garrison, Lydia Maria Child, and William Ellery Channing through Mary Weston Chapman, the Come-Outers, John Quincy Adams and Charles Sumner, to the New England expatriate Theodore Weld, and finally to the New England repatriot Harriet Beecher Stowe. In the face of this tradition, how was the South to be described? "The South is one great brothel," Phillips declared, "where half a million of women are flogged to prostitution, or worse still, are degraded to believe it honorable."[12] Surely Phillips imagined no southern audience for this statement. High-minded New Englanders who believed Phillips's words, especially women, would be likely to turn their eyes entirely away from the "brothel"; low-minded New England males, or would-be Doughheads, might be enticed to go south to enjoy the fruits.

As the slavery crises of the 1850s mounted, Phillips's oratory became ever more Manichean in its regionalism. After Webster's acceptance of the Fugitive Slave Law, after the bloody fight for Kansas, after the election of a proslavery northerner (Buchanan) to the presidency, and after the horror of the Dred Scott decision, the model of libertarian New England forefathers needed to be burnished and held aloft all the more stridently. Consider a passage from the July 4, 1859 oration that Phillips delivered in Framingham.

Here, under the blue sky of New England, we teach the doctrine, that whenever you find a man downtrodden, he is your brother; whenever you find an unjust law, you are bound to be its enemy; that Massachusetts was planted as the furnace of perpetual insurrection against tyrants; that this is a bastard who has stolen the name of Winthrop; that the true blood of the Bradfords, the Carvers, the Endicotts, and the Winthrops creeps out in some fanatical abolitionist whom the church disowns, whom the State tramples under foot, but who will yet model both, by the potency of that truth which the elder Winthrop gave into our hands, and which we uphold today as an example for the nation. This is my speech for the Fourth of July.[13]

Because Phillips's true patria has become New England, Disunionist words are needed to defy the annual celebration of national union. The moral power of declaring independence now resides in New England's noble threat of regional secession, to which southern nullification is apparently irrelevant. The essence of Liberty in Massachusetts has become civil disobedience, practiced by abolitionists and directed against an unjust national law.

Separation on behalf of Liberty is exactly what Phillips had advocated, two years before, when he spoke of hoping to "get up" to the level of Carver and Bradford. His advocacy of disunion was leading him to a militancy well in advance of Garrison. Embracing the "fanatic" spirit of Cromwellian civil war, Phillips anticipated sectional warfare that would somehow restore the lost virtues of a Puritan Commonwealth. By acknowledging New England's complicity in slavery, Phillips was sacrificing the satisfying opportunity to contrast slavery's tyrants with freedom's Saints. In exchange, he tapped into long-standing yearnings to reestablish the purity of New England's origin.

As Joanne Melish has shown, few antebellum New Englanders were willing to call attention to the modified forms of apprentice slavery that continued in all New England states well into the nineteenth century.[14] Garrisonian Abolitionists, however, often called attention to the prevalence of slavery in pre-Republican New England despite the Body of Liberties of 1641. Garrisonians noted that Prince Hall's petitions for emancipation had failed to pass the Massachusetts House in the 1770s. They warned readers to remedy the blemish on those New England Revolutionary fathers, especially Sam Adams, who had failed to extend their protest against the "slavery" of George III into a protest against the American enslavement of the Negro.[15] Even though Samuel Hopkins had exposed the church's tolerance of the Newport slave trade, time-serving silence was still continuing in Congregational pulpits. Theodore Parker liked to remind his audiences that the first known American slaver had been the *Desire*, built and berthed in Marblehead in 1637; he was equally fond of noting that, in violation of Congress's 1808 prohibition of the slave trade, the brig *Lucy Anne*, built in Thomaston, Maine in 1839, registered in Boston, repaired in Boston, and captained by a man named Otis, had been captured off the coast of Africa in 1849 with 547 slaves on board.

The founding moment of Garrisonian Abolitionism – the first issue of the *Liberator* – is suffused with a recognition both of New England's complicity in slavery and of the regional tradition that could nonetheless combat it. Garrison's piercing, valid prophecy ("I am in earnest. I will not equivocate – I will not excuse – I will not retreat a single inch – AND I WILL BE HEARD") is frequently quoted, and rightly so, but the specific wording of his declaration of purpose is not.

I determined, at every hazard, to lift up the standard of emancipation in the eyes of the nation, *within sight of Bunker Hill, and in the birthplace of liberty*. That standard is now unfurled; and long may it float, unhurt by the spoliations of time or the missiles of a desperate foe; yea, till every chain be broken and ever bondman set free![16]

Garrison's metaphor already contains the seed of his later Disunionism. The anticipated struggle for emancipation requires, from the outset, the unfurling of a rival flag, the establishing of an alternative birthplace. Today's small band of abolitionists cannot claim to be fully one with the defenders of Bunker Hill. Because the Revolutionary tradition has been corrupted, today's Abolitionist has not (yet) risen to the virtue of yesterday's Minuteman. Nonetheless, it is crucial to Garrison that the abolitionist flag be unfurled "within sight of" Bunker Hill because Boston remains "*the birthplace of liberty*." It is proximity to New England's revolutionary and separatist tradition that Garrison seeks, a distance sufficient to avoid today's State Street corruption, but a nearness sufficient to draw upon New England's oppositional spirit.

The most formidable force sustaining New England's complicity with the South was the economic complex defined as "white slavery" by John Randolph of Roanoke during the early 1820s. Randolph's infamous taunt would stick in the craw of Northerners for decades.

We do not govern them [the people of the North] by our black slaves, but by their own white slaves . . . We know what we are doing. We have conquered you once, and we can and will conquer you again. Aye, Sir, we will drive you to the wall, and when we have you there once more, we will keep you there, and nail you down like base money.[17]

The white slave of the North, in Randolph's view, is any mill owner, ship owner, banker, or factory hand who profits, economically or politically, from the economic vitality of the South. The much touted growth of the "free" North thus depends directly upon the vitality of southern slavery, which Randolph regarded as morally indefensible but constitutionally protected and economically impossible to abolish. America's unlikely "Union" is being stitched together with threads of cotton so strong that they weave all men into one slave fabric, North and South, white and black. In the voice of John Randolph, eighteenth-century Agrarianism and Swiftian satire coalesce into a darkly triumphant exposure of the slavery emerging in nascent capitalism.

The regional implication of Randolph's sneer is that the free white protestant New Englander is proving to be nothing but "base money," just as purchasable as any slave or any Boston bank mortgage on a plantation. Because the South first conquered the North in the framing of the Constitution, New Englanders will continue to be bought and sold by the chattel slavery system until, despite their boasts of primacy in Freedom's cause, they will be "nailed down" permanently. Is it any wonder that, in excoriating Daniel Webster's Seventh of March speech, Emerson was to remark in 1851 that "the words of John Randolph, wiser than he knew, have been ringing ominously in all echoes for thirty years"?[18] Three years later, Thoreau devised a succinct essay title that summed up Randolph's concept but which gave it stunning local application: "Slavery in Massachusetts" (1854).

Although the admission of New England's complicity in the nation's sin begins with Samuel Hopkins in 1776 ("We have no way to exculpate ourselves from the guilt of the whole . . . but by freeing all our slaves"[19]), Hopkins was sure that New Englanders could still redeem themselves by supporting general emancipation and colonization of free blacks as a Christian mission in Africa.[20] Once Garrison abandoned colonization, however, he began advancing the morally logical argument that redemption for sinful New Englanders could come about only through immediate, uncompensated emancipation. In his July 4, 1829 address in the Park Street church, Garrison proclaimed "We are all alike guilty" because "New England money has been expended in buying human flesh; New England ships have been freighted with sable victims; New England men have assisted in forging the fetters of those who groan in bondage." Moreover, Garrison insisted, in a barb that must have enraged all antislavery moderates in his Boston audience, that if "by a miracle, the slaves should suddenly become white . . . the old Cradle of Liberty [Faneuil Hall] would rock to a deeper tone than ever echoed therein at British aggression."[21] These words mark the beginning of a rhetorical strategy that Garrison, Phillips and Parker would employ again and again for the next thirty years: force your New England audience to admit their own complicity with slavery, contrast their debasement with the integrity of Puritan and/or Revolutionary forefathers, and then challenge them to have the courage both to free the Negro, *and to redeem themselves,* through acts of separation, civil disobedience and/or, finally, violence.[22]

Even though Lydia Maria Child's perspective was declaredly national, she furthered the attack on New England's complicity, charging without naming names that "several fortunes in this city have been made by the sale of Negro blood" – words not to her advantage when the trustees of the Boston Athenaeum considered revoking her library privileges.[23] New England's conspiracy of silence, she argued, is in New England's worst long-term interest: "truly we have well earned Randolph's favorite appellation, 'the white slaves of the North,' by our tameness and servility with regard to a subject where good feeling and good principle alike demanded a firm and independent spirit" (202). Because "repressing" the issue of slavery prevails throughout New England, Mrs. Child believes it only logical that a Southerner should be the first to declare that New England's profit is New England's enslavement.

No Garrisonian Abolitionist, nor anyone else, was ever to expose the economic power of white slavery in New England with the relentless fury of Theodore Parker. Before considering the specifics of his accusations, it is crucial to remember how fully Parker was committed, by heritage and personal conviction, to the *patria* of New England and to its leadership in America's great democratic experiment. Thomas Parker had come to Lynn in 1635 and become a Freeman in 1637. Jonathan Parker had fought in King Philip's War. Theodore's grandfather Captain John Parker, a sergeant in the French and Indian wars, became captain of the Lexington Militia, fighting with the Army of New England through the Battle of Bunker Hill. It was Captain John Parker who, according to New England legend, had said on April 19, 1775 to the Minutemen on Lexington Green, "Don't fire unless fired upon, but if they mean to have a war, let it begin here."

Theodore Parker did not have the money to graduate from Harvard, but he eventually assembled the largest private library in New England, including many volumes written by Puritan divines whose theology he discredited. When he began his preaching career in the Watertown meetinghouse, he was humbled to learn that the Massachusetts Provincial Congress had met in that very building from April to November 1775. Of all his possessions, Theodore Parker most treasured the two muskets, which grandfather John Parker had carried home to Lexington after the retreat from Concord. The first item in Theodore Parker's will was to bequeath "the two firearms, formerly the property of my honored grandfather Captain John Parker . . . carried while fighting in the sacred cause of God and his country" to the Commonwealth of Massachusetts "to be placed in the Senate

Chamber of this Commonwealth and there sacredly kept *in perpetuam rei memoriam.*" The second item was to bequeath his eleven volumes on English state trials to "my much valued friend" Wendell Phillips.[24]

Parker thus saw New England's values from within a tradition of country militancy on behalf of farmers, village tradesmen, and Freemen with and without a capital F. Generations of Parkers had quite literally prepared him to fight. As a young man, he had served as lieutenant in the Lexington militia; he never abandoned his belief in the spiritual value of military preparedness. In his autobiography of 1859 Parker was to insist, anticipating civil war, "In New England, the most democratic country, we have too much neglected the military art I fear – a mistake we may bitterly regret in that strife between the Southern habit of despotism and the Northern principle of democracy."[25] As head of the Massachusetts Vigilance Committee, Parker made his witness against the Fugitive Slave Law through a letter to President Fillmore in which he stated his duty as a Christian minister to succor the fugitive slave and to "*reverence the laws of God, come of that what will come.*"[26] The President also needed to know that there were personal motives driving him to civil disobedience:

There hangs beside me in my library, as I write, the gun my grandfather fought with at the battle of Lexington – he was a captain on that occasion – and also the musket he captured from a British soldier on that day, the first taken in the war for Independence. If I would not peril my property, my liberty, nay, my life, to keep my own parishioners out of slavery, then I would throw away those trophies, and should think I was the son of some coward, and not a brave man's child. (II, 102)

Parker's Revolutionary "trophies" are more than a memorial to past family achievement; they are a standard for the courage of descendants who must interpret anew the meaning of fighting for freedom.

Impatient with Unitarian rationalism as well as Christian revelation, Theodore Parker nonetheless refused to leave the Congregational Church. His was a singular position. For a son of such forefathers to serve as the pastor of the uprooted "Twenty-Eighth Congregational Society," ministering to a so-called "congregation" of 2,500 people from the "pulpit" at the Melodeon, the Music Hall, or Faneuil Hall was to speak as New England's ultimate outside insider. Many an address Parker referred to as a "sermon" had no controlling biblical text, no explication, and an application often lasting two hours. He spoke as the voice of New England tradition ruthlessly criticizing contemporary New England in jeremiads that neither his fellow clergy nor Boston's civic leaders dared to share.[27] Moreover, he delivered those jeremiads in a secular forum outside the Congregational establishment to which he still technically belonged. There is truth in Parker's claim that by late 1850 he had become "one of the most odious men in this State. No man out of the political arena is so much hated in Massachusetts as myself" (the politician inside the arena could have been no one but Daniel Webster).[28] To his many followers, however, Parker, like Garrison or Phillips, was a prophet.

Parker's commitment to Garrisonian abolitionism as the essence of reform provoked a crisis over New England's response to the annexation of Texas and the Mexican War.[29] To Parker, the crux of the controversy was not the familiar charge of Conscience Whigs that the war was motivated by the desire of southern slaveholders and northern merchant/manufacturers to enlarge the slave territory. Parker's analysis cut far more deeply into the fabric of the national economic system. His "Sermon on Merchants" (1846) argues that the Mexican War signals a greed that is overcoming democracy everywhere in the nation, but New England in particular. Surely one of the great transitional texts in American intellectual history, the "Sermon on Merchants" argues that the ever-growing drive for money has come to dominate politicians and educators, scientists and artists, colleges and seminaries.

The mercantile class . . . enacts the laws of this state and the nation; . . . it buys up legislators when they are in the market; breeds them when the market is bare. It can manufacture governors, senators, judges to suit its purposes, as easily as it can make cotton cloth . . . Here trade takes the place of the army, navy and court in other lands. That is well, but it takes also the place in great measure of science, art and literature . . . The mercantile class is the controlling one in the churches . . . It buys up the clergymen . . . The merchants build the churches, endow theological schools; they furnish the material sinews of the church. Hence the metropolitan churches are, in general, as much commercial as the shops . . . Take Boston, for the last ten years, and I think there has been more clerical preaching against the abolitionists than against slavery.[30]

Here is a vision of a New England America in which the infections of Thomas Carlyle's "cash nexus" and John Randolph's "white slavery" have swollen into cultural control. Ironically, only one sentence from Parker's "Sermon on Merchants" ("The government of all, by all, and for all, is a democracy," v, 26) is now remembered – and remembered only because it is a possible source for Lincoln's words at Gettysburg. Surely Theodore Parker himself would understand why that one rhetorical detail has been remembered while the substance of his sermon continues to be ignored. The ease with which today's Big Money can buy the access needed to coopt the politicians of our "democratic republic" would have disgusted Parker, but not surprised him.

The link Parker saw between "the mercantile class" and New England's support for "All Mexico" is explored in his manifesto "A Sermon on War." After amassing pages of statistical evidence to prove, in a newly pacifist manner, that all war is destructive, costly, evil, and un-Christian, Parker turns to the causes of the particular war at hand.

The eyes of the North are full of cotton; they see nothing else, for a web is before them; their ears are full of cotton, and they hear nothing, but the buzz of their mills; their mouth is full of cotton, and they can speak audibly but two words – tariff, tariff, dividends, dividends. The talent of the North is blinded, deafened, gagged with its own cotton.[31]

To be stuffed with cotton money is to be literally impervious to spiritual change. The final measure of New England's complicity is its reversal of the founders' godly purpose: "Though we are descended from the Puritans, we have but one article in our creed we never flinch from following, and that is – to make money, honestly if we can; if not, as we can!" (IX, 319).

Once Parker had perceived the connection between white slavery and the primacy of money in republican culture, he would neither dismiss it, nor allow its logical end to be ignored. Six years later, in his 117-page "Discourse on Webster" delivered a week after the great apostate's death, Parker took the broadest possible measure of what it meant for the once revered antislavery leader from New Hampshire to have, at the last, accepted the Fugitive Slave Law and thereby legitimized slavery in New England. Fifty years of history were compressed into the narrative of one metaphor:

Slavery, the most hideous snake which southern regions breed, with fifteen unequal feet, came crawling north; fold on fold, and ring on ring, and coil on coil, the venomed monster came; then avarice, the foulest worm which northern cities gender in their heat, went crawling south; with many a wriggling curl, it wound along its way. At length they met, and twisting up in their obscene embrace, the twain became one monster hunkerism; theme unattempted yet in prose or song; there was no North, no South; they were one poison! The dragon wormed its way along – crawled into the church of commerce, wherein the minister baptized the beast, "Salvation." From the ten commandments, the dragon's breath effaced those which forbid to kill and covet, with the three inbetweeen; then with malignant tooth, gnawed out the chief commandments whereon the law and prophets hang. This Amphisbaena of the western world then swallowed down the loftiest words of Hebrew or of Christian speech, and in their place it left a hissing at the higher law of God.[32]

Parker here offers a sardonic "Argument" for an American *Paradise Lost* ("theme unattempted yet in prose or song") in which free will is retained, sectional blame is equally apportioned, and the end is apocalyptic rather than epic. Southern Slavery and northern Avarice (Milton's Sin and Death) have chosen to unite in an obscene copulation, but ever since their offspring "monster hunkerism" was born there has been no resisting the appeal of its poison. The fruit is no longer forbidden; eating it has become culturally sanctioned, legalized, approved by all voices save the "loftiest words" of those ancient texts that are still read from the pulpits but no longer felt in the heart.[33]

To name the conquering monster "hunkerism" is to turn a colloquialism for a northern political type into an inner quality (greed with all its respectable trappings) that is corrupting republicans both North and South.[34] Parker's language recalls Jacksonian rhetoric of the 1830s against the "monster Bank," but the corrupting evil, as Parker sees it, is far more than the oppression of a centralizing federal power. Parker's comparison of slavery to the mythological Amphisbaena (a serpent with a head at both ends) implies that the true monster is the hidden avarice in most every northern and southern heart, an avarice that spews its sinful poison in both directions, swallowing the truth of the spirit with each advance.

During the 1850s, Parker would prophesy the disappearance of sectional difference through the triumph of "St. Hunker" again and again. But for him it would be New England, and more particularly the Massachusetts heritage, that was vanishing. To define what Webster's Unionism truly meant, Parker declared, as Anthony Burns was being returned to Virginia, "There is no North," Boston has become "a North suburb to the city of Alexandria," "and you and I are fellow subjects of the State of Virginia.[35] In his post-1850 abolitionist sermons, Parker repeatedly treats the Fugitive Slave Law as a symbol of how the constricting coils of slavery's monetary power mark the disappearance of New England's distinct cultural identity as well as its national leadership. Parker's abolitionism, based as it is upon New England values, modeled in its visionary imagery on the great Puritan poet of the English language, often results in the paradoxical conclusion that the essential New England no longer exists.

The more stridently the Garrisonians preached the duty of immediate abolition in a Christian democracy, the more the New England churches avoided taking a public stand on slavery. The longer the churches' silence, the more their neutral ground became contested ground and the more the Garrisonians criticized them. The Congregational Church, the remaining institutional symbol of New England's Puritan tradition, declined to adopt any position, both because leaders such as Moses Stuart of the Andover Theological Seminary were openly opposed to a church statement on slavery and also, surely, because of "Hunker" influence within. The

Garrisonians soon recognized that no Black Regiment would emerge to support New Englanders during their second revolution on behalf of Liberty. The Unitarians were divided both over colonization and over the means of emancipation; William Ellery Channing's call for voluntary emancipation by slave owners had damaged his reputation among Unitarians as well as Congregationalists.[36] The futile fervor of the Come Outer movement, which did not emerge until the churches had remained silent for fifteen years, derived from its insistence that New Englanders still in search of spiritual purity now needed to resign their membership in the very institution that had once defined it.

Under such circumstances, the perspective of the abolitionist minister of Boston's "Twenty-Eighth Congregational Society" became particularly cogent. The opening section of Parker's "Spiritual Conditions" (1849) lists statistical evidence for a worldwide decline in the power of piety among protestant churches, and for "the same decline of piety... in America, in New England, in Boston."[37] Parker then settles into a 25-page narrative of quotations and paraphrases of the Reverends John Wilson, John Cotton, John Norton, Increase Mather, Cotton Mather, Samuel Willard, Benjamin Colman, and Charles Chauncy, who collectively demonstrate that the clergy, even in New England's supposedly purer times, made a tradition of complaining about the decline in piety – and reaping harvests of new souls because of it. Then, in another remarkable turn, Parker acknowledges that, this time, "the sins of Boston," and the reluctance of Congregational preachers to expose them, have indeed shown that "their ancient influence is already gone" (v, 325).

The immediate Abolitionists' terms of contempt for "Cotton Whigs" included "Hunkers," "Doughfaces," "Gentlemen of Property and Standing," "Molochs and Mammons," "kidnappers" (when enforcing the Fugitive Slave Law) and sometimes, descending to a lower level of invective, southward-gazing "lickspittles." In the context of regional history, Parker applied a different term, damning New England cotton interests as a "Toryism" that had again become "the prevailing influence" in Boston.[38] The "Tory" analogy could also strengthen the demand for civil disobedience. Speaking against the Mexican War in Faneuil Hall, Parker called the armed soldiers standing along the walls "the hireling soldiers of President Polk" and compared their weapons to "British bayonets" not seen in Massachusetts since "the Boston Massacre on the 5th of March 1770." After Parker declared "I blame not so much the volunteers as the famous men who deceived the nation" (perhaps George Bancroft, certainly President Polk and Robert Winthrop), cries of "kill him" burst from the audience.

Undaunted, Parker called upon all recent recruits to disband, whereupon many in the crowd rose in protest, leading Parker to declare he had just heard a "Tory groan" from New Englanders who were proving themselves even more cowardly than "the British Tories, when they had no bayonets to back them up." Instead of letting the Tory analogy drop, Parker pursued its implications, urging the potential recruit to recognize that, like all Tories, he would be taking up arms *against* his country: "Let it be infamous for a New England man to enlist . . . I call on the men of Boston, on the men of the old Bay State, to act worthy of their fathers, worthy of their country, worthy of themselves."[39] It remains a wonder that Phillips, Garrison, and Parker survived such confrontations without guns being fired at them.

Sicut Patribus sit Deus Nobis. If God shall *choose* still to be with us as he was with our fathers (the verb is the hortatory subjunctive "*sit*" not present tense "*est*"), then it would first be necessary for Bostonians to embrace the principles of the fathers before He would fill them with grace and courage. To Garrisonians, immediate, uncompensated abolition was thus inseparable both from regional religious reform and from New England history. Their speeches return again and again to historical conflations such as Parker's summons to Massachusetts's citizens after Webster's apostasy:

Will Massachusetts conquer her prejudices in favor of the "unalienable rights" of man? I think, Mr. President, she will first have to forget two hundred years of history. She must efface Lexington and Bunker Hill from her memory, and tear the old rock of Plymouth out from her bosom. These are prejudices which Massachusetts will not conquer till the ocean ceases to wash her shore and granite to harden her hills.[40]

Parker makes no attempt, in such statements, to discriminate between Pilgrims and Puritans, seventeenth-century Freemen and eighteenth-century Revolutionaries. All are subsumed under the "unalienable rights of man" that Massachusetts's sons are sure to defend as the innermost value of their ostensibly feminine yet granitic *patria*. Liberty of spiritual conscience is the value that links Puritan removal to Boston revolution to Yankee abolition, thereby comprising the essence of New England under crisis.

This kind of rhetorical summons, fusing Puritan history with New England geography and national abolitionism, occurs selectively in Garrison's writings, commonly in Parker's sermons, and regularly in Phillips's speeches. But it may also be found in less expectable genres intended for other audiences. Whittier's "The Prophecy of Samuel Sewall," a poem as memorable as "Ichabod" and far more complex, begins by picturing

Judge Sewall fasting and weeping for "the sin of his ignorance" in condemning innocent people to death at the Salem witch trials. Instead of waxing complacent about the cultural significance of Sewall's atonement, as historians had often done, Whittier connects Sewall's penitence to his later authorship of "The Selling of Joseph":

> And seeing the infinite worth of man,
> In the priceless gift the Father gave,
> In the infinite love that stooped to save
> Dared not brand his brother a slave.[41]

As Whittier sees it, Sewall's discovery that an executed witch had a divine soul led him to understand why the slaveholder's claim that a Negro's soul is chattel is equally false. But the poem posits no easy emancipation. Whittier imagines a meeting between Judge Sewall and today's Hunker Judge, "That brave old jurist of the past / And the cunning trickster and knave of courts." The Hunker, "scoffing aside at party's nod," remains unmoved by Sewall's inner transformation, preferring to "rot in the web of lies he spins."

The poem ends with the troubled poet overlooking the pastoral environs of Newbury. Changing Samuel Sewall's invocation of Plum Island from prose to couplets, Whittier celebrates the landscape as the fulfillment of the forefather's vision of rural plenty. The field corn Sewall had invoked in the 1690s serves as a eucharistic metaphor for New England's future:

> And let us hope, as well we can
> That the Silent Angel who garners man
> May find some grain as of old he found
> In the human cornfield ripe and sound,
> And the Lord of the Harvest deign to own
> The precious seed by the fathers sown.

Although the Angel of Death now looms over New England's fields, Whittier trusts that the "precious seed" sown by Judge Sewall may yet yield abolitionist grain "ripe and sound." Whittier's poem is so deftly written that it has been possible to quite overlook its subtle tribute to the most precious of Samuel Sewall's seed, his descendant and Whittier's fellow Abolitionist, Samuel C. Sewall.

Just as the contrast between Puritan and Abolitionist led to angry despair, so the connection between Puritan and Abolitionist promised regeneration in troubled times. In the same antislavery speech in which Emerson declared that "a despair has crept over Massachusetts, and over New England," he offered the Abolitionist cause as a source of redemption.

I value as a redeeming trait, the growth of the abolition party, the true successors of that austere Church, which made nature and history sacred to us all in our youth. I often ask myself, what is to take the place, to the young people, of those restraining influences which the old Calvinism, or Puritanism, under whatever form, exerted on the youth of such as are as old, or almost as old, as I am. The young men seem left to a frivolous, external, Parisian manner of living. What can better supply that outward church they want, than this fervent, self-denying school of love and action, which, too, the blood of the martyrs has already consecrated?[42]

This is a far cry from the Emerson who, ten years before, had criticized his retrospective age for building the sepulcher of the fathers, and who had dismissed concern about original sin as time wasted worrying about the soul's mumps and measles. Abolitionism has since become the "outward church" that is the true successor to the "old Calvinism" once "sacred to us all."

Few New Englanders advocated immediate, uncompensated emancipation, because they had taken a journey south to witness the cruelties of cotton-field and kitchen-house. The motive of conversion was often an immediate, visual experience of New England's complicity in "white slavery." Garrison's radical Abolitionism did not emerge until he saw the slave ship *Francis* in Baltimore, and discovered it was owned by Francis Todd of Newburyport, Garrison's home town.[43] Samuel May and Samuel C. Sewell, already sympathetic to Garrison's cause, became more outspoken after seeing the cotton mills along the Merrimack and discovering the connections between mill towns, Boston's merchant gentry, and the tonnage in Boston harbor. The famous image of Garrison being dragged by an anti-abolitionist mob with a rope around his neck across the site of the Boston Massacre became for antislavery men and women the defining moment of Abolitionist victimization and of New England's disgrace, a moment that would be recalled again and again in order to rally liberty-loving New Englanders for further confrontations. Even though Wendell Phillips was raised to cherish freedom of speech, he made no protest when Arthur Lovejoy, Abolitionist son of a Maine Congregational minister, was killed and his press destroyed by an anti-Abolitionist mob in Illinois. It was listening to the Attorney General of Massachusetts justify Lovejoy's murder in Faneuil Hall that first roused Phillips's sense of outrage. Similarly, James Russell Lowell had written strongly worded Abolitionist essays before the Mexican War, but *The Biglow Papers* would surely not have emerged had Lowell not watched the Massachusetts Regiment being recruited for the Mexican War in Court Square. In all these instances, the prompt that turns private citizens of antislavery sentiment into orators and writers demanding immediate abolition is inseparable from the perceived desecration of New England.[44]

Because John Winthrop had not advocated Liberty of Conscience, and Sam Adams had not advocated freeing slaves, the restoring of regional virtue required that New England's citizenry be invoked *en masse* as spiritual militants always ready to fight for freedom. Garrison's account of his near hanging transforms personal victimization into impersonal regional crisis.

The great question to be settled is not merely whether two million slaves in our land shall be immediately or gradually emancipated, but whether the liberty of speech and of the press, purchased with the toils and sufferings and precious blood of our fathers is still to be enjoyed ... whether the descendants of the Pilgrim fathers, the sons of those who fell upon Bunker Hill, and the plains of Lexington and Concord, are to fashion their thoughts and opinions ... or to obey Jehovah or worship Mammon at the bidding of Southern slave-drivers and oppressors.[45]

Which is more important here, the preservation of free speech as part of the New England heritage, or the freeing of the slave? The figure of the Negro is conspicuously absent from Garrison's formulation of "the great question." Evidently, new adherents to the *Liberator's* cause were more likely to be won through appeals to the freedom of speech collectively fought for at Lexington, Concord, and Bunker Hill than through half-fictive descriptions of the atrocities of the slave-fields or quotations of the words of past Puritan leaders.

The need to defend freedom of speech against attack by officials of the Commonwealth was the issue that made Wendell Phillips a convert to lifelong abolitionism. When, in the sacred ground of Faneuil Hall, Attorney General James Austin compared the antislavery mob that killed Lovejoy to the "orderly mob" that had thrown tea into Boston harbor, the disparity was too much for Wendell Phillips, hitherto silent about slavery issues, to endure.

When I heard the gentleman lay down principles which place the murderers of Alton side by side with Otis and Hancock, with Quincy and Adams, I thought those pictured lips [pointing to the portraits in the Hall] would have broken into voice to rebuke the recreant American – the slanderer of the dead.[46]

As Phillips warmed to his subject, he noted another desecration of almost equal moment. The Reverend Hubbard Winslow of Boston, sullying the honor of both his names, had recently opined that "no citizen has a right to publish opinions disagreeable to the community" (7). "Shades of Hugh Peters and John Cotton," Phillips exclaimed, "save us from such pulpits!" (8). Returning to his comparison to the Revolution, Phillips then insisted that Lovejoy was entitled to even "greater praise" than Joseph Warren, because "the disputed right which provoked the Revolution – taxation without representation – is far beneath that for which he [Lovejoy] died" (9). The "right" for which Lovejoy was killed was not the right of the Negro to be free, which was the occasion for Lovejoy's protest, but rather "the freedom of the press on American ground" (9). For Phillips, the inflammatory issue was not free soil in the Midwest, but rather the dishonoring of Massachusetts.

Phillips's twentieth anniversary speech on "The Boston Mob" shows how paltry New England's compromised sons seemed in the context of absolute abolitionist commitment. Delivered in 1855 when the textile mills were hugely profitable, Phillips voiced more than a few slurs against "cunning tradesmen who have wriggled their slimy way to wealth," "the bursting ledgers of Milk Street," and even "the cuckoo lips of Edward Everett." The mob's assault on Garrison and the Boston Female Antislavery Society twenty years before had first uncovered the spiritual rot of today's wealthy city. When Boston's mayor compelled a women's antislavery meeting to disband, "the ignorant were not aware, and the wise were too corrupt to confess, that the most precious of human rights, free thought, was at stake."[47] To Phillips, this moment arrayed the few Saints against the many sinners, but only the Abolitionist elect counted: "those howling wolves in the streets were not Boston. These brave men and women were Boston. We will remember no other." In Phillips's words, the 230-year process of exclusionary self-definition reaches its culmination. New England's corruption has become so extensive that only the principled white genteel reformers, mostly women, unpolluted by trade, separate from the mob of gentlemen and hired laborers outside, represent the integrity of the City on a Hill. All others are to be defined as outside of Boston's righteous remnant.

What the brave defiance of the Abolitionists achieved on that day, therefore, had to be a kind of historical reenactment: "When the Mayor forgot his duty, when the pulpit prostituted itself, and when the press became a pack of hounds, the women of Boston, and a score or two of men, remembered Hancock and Adams, and did their duty." But what of Wendell Phillips himself, who had watched the mob gather but who had passively turned aside? At that time, still two years before Lovejoy's murder, "my eyes were sealed, so that, although I knew the Adamses and Otises, the Mary Dyers and Ann Hutchinsons of older times, I could not recognize the Adamses and Otises, the Dyers and Hutchinsons, whom I met in the streets of 1835." Here Phillips's retrospective guilt makes a telling order of the protesting Saints of New England historical legend. The courage of the Abolitionist, women's defiance of the persecutions of Puritan forefathers, the free speech legacy of the Revolutionary fathers, and the empowerment of today's women are all said to coalesce against the power of money, the blackness of white slavery.

Just as one crisis begot another, so the literature of a previous crisis could be brought to the service of emancipation. In the aftermath of the French Revolution of 1848, James Russell Lowell predicted a second American Revolution. Its seed ground would be decidedly local.

The farmers at Concord Bridge, as Emerson has strikingly said, "Fired the shot heard round the world," but they were not conscious of the mighty effects to flow from that little touch of their fingers upon the trigger. If our people had understood their own Declaration of Independence, the roots of slavery would never have been allowed to strike into and split asunder the very foundations of our social institutions.[48]

Praise for the consequences of Concord Fight did not prevent Lowell from directly protesting the evils of New England's complicity ("At the time when the Texas plot was ripening... the heart of the old Bay State was so mummy-wrapped in cotton as to give no audible beat"[49]), but it did mean that Lowell was more willing than Parker to rest on the certainty that emancipation was an historical inevitability. Because farmers had fired the shot that must eventually end slavery, expressing a virtuous opinion might now suffice. By the end of the 1850s, Lowell's pacifist hope was to prove fatally naïve.

HOLDING ON TO IMMEDIATISM: CRISES WITHIN CRISIS, 1845–1860

Beyond great increase in adherents and their visibility, the abolitionist cause made precious little progress during its first fifteen years. The contraband Atlantic slave trade continued, as did the selling of Virginia's slave population from markets in Alexandria and Washington, DC to the newer states of the Old Southwest. Abolitionist mails continued to be suppressed in the South, fugitive slaves continued to be returned from the North, and the Gag Rule continued to be enforced in Congress. Among New England's immediatists, there was a growing sense of desperate determination. Each controversy, from George Latimer's removal from Boston to John Brown's raid on Harper's Ferry, seemed a crisis calling forth rhetorical extremities ranging from the pointed to the perfervid. There was to be no let-up in the pressure of defensive attack, because America's godly libertarian heritage, and New England's two-century leadership within it, were both at stake.

For Garrisonians in the 1840s, the immediate problem was to define the degree and kind of opposition now needed to achieve emancipation. Which form of protest would be both ethically defensible and tactically effective? Denouncing slavery, the Mexican War, and the Fugitive Slave Law as abominations against Christian democracy? Demanding the immediate disbanding of Massachusetts troops? Disrupting Sunday meeting in order to urge "coming out" of the church? Breaking into a Boston prison in order to free a fugitive slave? Joining the emigrants, or sending rifles, to Kansas? Or, as a last desperate measure, supporting a slave rebellion in the South? Wherever one drew the line along this spectrum, the challenge of aligning oneself with New England's cultural and political tradition was always present. Did not the high-minded New England women presently criticizing the Congregational ministry resemble Anne Hutchinson? Should not Garrison's new banner cry "No Union with Slaveholders" be seen as a reenactment of Pilgrim separatism rather than of Calhoun's Nullification? Was refusing to return a fugitive slave a nobler new way of carrying out Sam Adams's commitment to revolt as defense of civil liberty?

Although Parker knew that the shaming of New England had to continue, he concluded that, as slavery strengthened its hold, old claims must acquire new force. "A Letter on Slavery" (1847) implicitly advocates antislavery violence in accord with the revolutionary principles of 1775.

Do you speak of Lexington and Bunker Hill as spots most dear in the soil of the New World, the Zion of freedom, the Thermopylae of universal right? How then can you justify your oppression? How refuse to admit that the bondmen of the United States have the same right, and a far stronger inducement to draw the sword and smite at your very life? Surely you cannot do so, not in America; never till Lexington and Bunker Hill are wiped out of the earth; never till the history of your own Revolution is forgot.[50]

Militancy of word here shifts to a militancy of deed. Unless complacent New Englanders understand how white slavery supports chattel slavery and then resolve to combat it, a bloody slave revolution, justified by Massachusetts's libertarian heritage, is likely to "smite at your very life."

Subverting the didactic, genteel moralism of abolitionist poetic anthologies such as *The Liberty Bell*, James Russell Lowell's *The Biglow Papers* attacked slavery through Yankee dialect, calculated doggerel, and burlesque narrative designed to laugh the reader out of fear of losing social respectability. *Big* truths expressed by *low* characters whose rural origins are assumed to convey authenticity. The opening poem of Yankee farmer Hosea Biglow, his "Letter" on Mexican War recruitment, is a now forgotten masterpiece of protest literature. "Come down" for the day from his inland village to Boston, Hosea watches a sergeant enlist sullen, lifeless recruits with the aid of drum, fife, and flag. "Considerabal riled," Hosea pens his first poem.

> Ez for war, I call it murder –
>   There you hev it plain an' flat;
> I don't want to go no furder
>   Than my Testyment fer that;
> God hez sed so plump an' fairly.
>   It's ez long ez it is broad,
> An you've gut to git up airly
>   Ef you want to take in God.[51]

An entirely biblical if not particularly Puritan perspective, in which God's higher law counts for everything, is here made engaging by Biglow's running trochaic lines and unintentionally comic off-rhymes (murder/furder and broad/God). The persona of Hosea Biglow conveniently deflects problematic issues. To get up early to "take in God" is less Franklinian "industry" yielding a tradesman's profit than a farmer's fieldwork making him one with natural law. The more we learn about Hosea's daily round with farm and family, the more satirical and the less contentious he can afford to be. Integrity is clearly and always within him. Accordingly, the worlds of law, trade, and manufacturing, which Theodore Parker needs frontally to oppose, are experienced in *The Biglow Papers* as alien to truth from the outset.

Although Hosea Biglow has surely not read John Randolph's taunt about white slavery, he everywhere confirms that it is a reality. "Fact! it takes a sight o'cotton / To stuff out a soger's chest," Hosea observes; "Chaps that make black slaves o'niggers / Want to make wite slaves o' you" (50, 52). His climactic metaphor for complicitous New Englanders ("witewashed slaves an' peddlin' crew!") leads him to end his poem berating Massachusetts rather than the South. The standard by which Massachusetts kneels convicted is not, however, the biblical commandment but the same regional pride in the Commonwealth's Revolutionary Freemen that pervades Parker's sermons:

> *Wut'll* make ye act like freemen?
>   *Wut'll* get your dander riz?
> Come, I'll tell ye wut I'm thinking
>   Is our dooty in this fix
> They'd ha done't ez quick ez winkin'
>   In the days o' seventy-six. (54)

The exemplary act of '76, as Hosea sees it, was that New England Freemen summoned the courage for Separatism, a separatism that now in 1847 demands what Garrison, Parker, or Phillips were calling "Disunion." However, Lowell avoids the traitorous connotations of the word "Disunion" by having Hosea describe New England secession through a variation on St. Matthew's words describing marriage: "Man had ought to put asunder / Them that God has noways jined" (55). If disunion is only a needed divorce, there would be justice, if not joy, in dissolving an unnatural political union. Whether separation could be achieved without the "murder" of war is, fortunately, well beyond Hosea Biglow's present ken.

The highest pitch of Garrisonian accusatory rhetoric was reached in the excoriation of two slavery crises of the 1850s: Daniel Webster's Seventh of March Speech, to which New England's shrill, divided reactions are well known; and the removal of fugitive slave Thomas Sims from Boston, which has been unduly neglected. After the Compromise of 1850 asserted federal jurisdiction for enforcing the Fugitive Slave Law in Massachusetts, Thomas Sims was the first fugitive slave to be returned to slavery from the hitherto "free soil" of the Commonwealth. To the Garrisonians, the forced return of Sims marked the nadir of New England Abolitionism, and the total betrayal of Massachusetts's libertarian heritage. The major responses to Sims's removal – the four orations delivered by Phillips and Parker and Whittier's poem "Moloch in State Street" – testify to the almost unlimited symbolic importance that New Englanders could, in an extremity, invest in the fortunes of a single obscure individual. Unlike the Garrisonians' damning of Daniel Webster, however, the return of Sims was not an occasion in which the betrayal of New England could be blamed upon a single individual. Because the guilt was collective, the import of regional self-condemnation led to a more complex cultural understanding.

Fugitive stowaway Thomas Sims, 17 years old, had arrived in Boston harbor on, of all dates, March 5, 1851. Twice recaptured, he twice escaped, but was finally locked up one month later in Boston Courthouse. To prevent the Vigilance Committee from rescuing Sims, Boston Courthouse was surrounded by an iron chain and guarded by 65 police and 100 local militia, while 250 federal troops were held in reserve at Charlestown Navy Yard. During Sims's hearing, Massachusetts Chief Justice, Lemuel Shaw, who believed in enforcement of the Fugitive Slave Law, was seen bending his body beneath the iron chain in order to enter the courthouse. An attempt of the Vigilance Committee to rescue Sims from prison failed. On April 12, the day of Sims's removal, a large massed crowd, including laborers and tradesmen from cities outside Boston as well as backcountry farmers, gathered in Court Square. One hundred police and 300 soldiers formed an infamous "hollow square," with Sims in its center, and then marched Sims over the site of the Boston Massacre to Long Wharf. The Vigilance Committee carried a black-draped coffin with LIBERTY printed on its hood. On April 19 – again of all dates! – Thomas Sims was returned to prison in Savannah, where he was reclaimed by his owner and promptly beaten. Two weeks later, abolitionist Charles Sumner was elected Senator from Massachusetts; in all probability, the disgrace of Sims's quasi-legal extradition gained Sumner more votes than it lost.[52]

Both Phillips and Parker expected their speeches on Sims to begin an anniversary tradition like the Boston Massacre orations delivered annually from 1771 to 1783. Gauging the effect of Sims's removal on public opinion, Thoreau called it a "moral earthquake."[53] Parker declared Sims's removal to be the blackest day in New England's history, far more tragic than Benedict Arnold's treachery, which had been only one man's deed, and infinitely worse than the Boston Massacre itself, which Parker saw as a triumph of citizen resistance to foreign occupation. Wendell Phillips's perspective was still closer to home. The significance of Sims's removal is that "Thomas Sims is the first man that the city of Boston ever openly bound and fettered and sent back to bondage."[54] It was the betrayal of Puritan precedent that, for Phillips, most clearly marked his city's disgrace. "Either the flavor of our old religion, or some remnant of the spirit of 1649 and 1776, had made the city of the Puritans a house of refuge to the fugitive" (72). Phillips quoted the statute of 1641 guaranteeing Massachusetts's welcome to "any stranger who might fly to her from the tyranny or oppression of their persecutors" (97). Today's fugitive slave cannot be separated from yesterday's Puritan exile.

To Wendell Phillips, the betrayal of New England tradition in the forced return of Thomas Sims made civil war seem probable and immediatism futile. Because slavery now has legal standing in Massachusetts, the very basis from which New England's abolitionism must proceed has eroded to the point of no return. Every Massachusetts citizen has now become implicated in white slavery. Once the removal of a fugitive slave from free soil is accepted as legal, the consequence will be a violent uprising *in the North* by fugitive slaves and their benefactors – an uprising fully warranted in accord with the principles of 1776: "If our Revolutionary fathers were justified in wading through blood to freedom and independence," Phillips insists, "then every fugitive slave is justified in arming himself for protection and defence."[55]

Almost half of Theodore Parker's 69-page oration on Sims's extradition, "The Boston Kidnapping," is devoted to the Puritan ministry and the Revolution in Boston. To convey the evil of Massachusetts's betrayal of freedom, the supposedly "liberal" or "Unitarian" Theodore Parker uses the words "sin" sixteen times, "crime" twelve times, "guilt" eight times, and "affliction" four times. The old Puritan vocabulary is thoroughly reworked, applied everywhere until the complicity of all New England seems undeniable.

This is the first anniversary of a great crime, – a crime against the majesty of Massachusetts law, and the dignity of the Constitution of the United States; of a great wrong, – a wrong against you and me, and all of us, against the babe not born, against the nature of mankind; of a great sin, – a sin against the law of God wrote in human nature, a sin against the infinite God.[56]

Although Parker contrasts past heroes with present cowards (James Otis to Daniel Webster, John Adams to George Curtis, Jonathan Mayhew to Orville Dewey), his focus is on the popular spirit shown in communal deeds. His oration moves obsessively back and forth between instances of past courage and present complacency, past promise and present degeneracy, in order to indict New England's fall.

Parker defines New England's sin primarily by historical rather than biblical contexts. Before the arrival of the despicable George Curtis, the last appointed commissioner in Boston had been Sir Edmund Andros, whom the citizenry had had the courage to extradite. The undemocratic term "commissioner" should therefore have "lost none of its odious character when it became again incarnate in a kidnapper" (333). To see Chief Justice Lemuel Shaw crawling under the iron chain around Boston Courthouse provides a tangible sign of the triumph of white slavery, "a very appropriate spectacle, – the Southern chain on the neck of the Massachusetts court" (355). As the "Sims Brigade" was forming its hollow square, "a man by the name of Samuel Adams drilled the police in the street" (356). The lineage of cowardly Harrison Gray Otis, who approved Sims's removal, should never again be traced back to James Otis, a libertarian patriot who had died without a son. As Thomas Sims was "escorted" to the harbor, the Sims Brigade "took him over the spot where, eighty-one years before, the ground had drunk in the African blood of Crispus Attucks, shed by white men on the fifth of March, – brother's blood, which did not then cry in vain" (367–368). African American blood had been heroically shed at the Boston Massacre and at Bunker Hill, but after 1851 there could no longer be "free blacks" in Massachusetts.

Today's mercantile Boston, Parker derisively reminds his audience, was once God's holy city; "this is holy ground that we stand on: godly men laid here the foundation of a Christian church . . . Laid in blood . . . the foundation of a Christian state, with all the self-denial of New England men" (323). Now, however, Boston has rebecome "Tory town" in earnest. Thomas Sims's slow walk out of Boston, "weeping as he went, towards the waterside, passing under the eaves of the old State-house, which had rocked with the eloquence of James Otis, and shaken beneath the manly tread of both the Adamses," must therefore be understood as New England's tragic reenactment of Christ's sufferings along the Via Dolorosa. Libertarian revolution and imitation of Christ still are one, but now only in the person of the fugitive slave, no longer in the white, protestant New Englander.

As Parker describes Sims's forced return to Savannah on April 19th, his historical rhetoric reaches for a still more heightened climax. "Do you know what that day stands for in your calendar?" Parker challenges his audience (364). His summary narrative of the heroic resistance at Lexington, culminating in his grandfather's words ("Don't fire unless fired upon; but, if they want a war, let it begin here," 364), reveals that the Boston crowd watching Sims's removal, so lacking in courage and principle, quite literally stood for nothing. Parker's account of April 19, 1775, ending with Sam Adams's alleged exclamation "Oh what a glorious morning is this!" (365), thus serves as his ironic introduction to the gathering dark of Boston's present. "Boston is now a shop, with the aim of a shop, and the morals of a shop, and the politics of a shop" (369).

The new Boston clearly needed a Websterian monument to New England virtue, and Theodore Parker was prepared to provide it – an ironic inscription consisting of seven strophes on New England's "Salvation of the Union" with a concluding epigraph and a motto:

> Union saved by Daniel Webster's Speech at Washington, March 7, 1850
> Union saved by Daniel Webster's Speech at Boston, April 30, 1850
> Union saved by the Passage of the Fugitive Slave Bill, Sept. 18, 1850
> Union saved by the Arrival of Kidnapper Hughes at Boston, Oct. 19, 1850
> Union saved by the "Union Meeting" at Faneuil Hall, Nov. 26, 1851
> Union Saved by Kidnapping Thomas Sims at Boston, April 3, 1851
> Union saved by the Rendition of Thomas Sims at Savannah, April 19, 1851
>   *"Oh, what a glorious morning is this!"*
>   SICUT PATRIBUS SIT DEUS NOBIS (366)

Parker's mock memorial to New England's "Salvation" is, of course, New England's tombstone. The very act of commemoration, to which the New England historical tradition had been committed for two centuries, is here bitterly parodied by the most devoted of New England patriots. Sam Adams's exclamation and Boston's seal acquire reverse meaning. New England's glorious morning has given way to Chaos and Old Night and there seems no reason why God should now wish to be with us, as He was with the Fathers.

In the forced return of Thomas Sims and Anthony Burns to slavery, twenty years of immediate abolitionism seemed to have ended in the wearying recognition that cotton was indeed king and that even Massachusetts had become a complicitous slave state. How then, in the face of such exhaustion, to redeem New England from the nadir of its dishonor? There is the rather cynical possibility that the psychological basis for regeneration had in fact already been fashioned. In the villainizing of Daniel Webster for his Seventh of March Speech, one can see traces of a projective purgation (or is it merely scapegoating?) through which Webster – and only he – is declared to embody the sin of New England's complicity with white slavery. After Webster's spiritual death is proclaimed, all he now represents can be handily erased from the regional record merely by rhetorical flourish.[57]

Visible evidence for the cleansing began in New England's military and financial support of a free Kansas. When the New England Emigrant Aid Society founded towns in Kansas named Plymouth, Lexington, and Concord it became clear that immediate Abolitionists and gradualist-free soilers could forget their differences and join in effective, aggressive antislavery actions outside New England. When powerful Cotton Whig mill owners, Amos Lawrence and Samuel Cabot supported the sending of Sharps rifles along with Beecher Bibles to Kansas, it seemed that the grip of white slavery on New England was finally weakening. The cotton money of Lawrence and Cabot ironically enabled a Garrisonian of impeccable New England credentials, Thomas Wentworth Higginson, to lead a company of armed New Englanders into combat in Kansas, and to conclude "it is precisely like waking up some morning and stepping out on the Battle of Bunker Hill. The same persons whom you saw a year ago in Boston, indolent and timid, are here transformed to heroes."[58]

Because New England's support of a free Kansas was clandestine, it could not publicly augur Abolitionist redemption, especially after the Dred Scott decision. The revealing of Freedom's triumph had to await the emergence of John Brown out of Bleeding Kansas through Harper's Ferry to martyrdom. In many of the tributes to John Brown voiced by Abolitionists, the concentration on John Brown's New England (Connecticut) heritage is a telling constant. Garrison, who was troubled by Brown's avowal of violence, nonetheless praised Brown as an adherent of "the logic of Concord, Lexington and Bunker Hill," and imagined himself standing beside John Brown in Virginia "with our feet upon the old Pilgrim ground."[59] Wendell Phillips described John Brown as a Yankee "from the old Puritan stock," comparable both to the Minutemen ("Harper's Ferry is the Lexington of today") and to Joseph Warren, dead at Bunker Hill.[60] Emerson concluded that John Brown was "a fair specimen of the best stock of New England." Describing Brown as an Old Testament prophet, Emerson derived Brown's heroic devotion to the Higher Law from his Connecticut origins, insisting that "our farmers were orthodox Calvinists mighty in the scriptures; they had learned that life was a preparation, a 'probation,' to use their word, for a higher world, and was to be spent in loving and serving mankind."[61] James Redpath's 1860 biography relentlessly casts John Brown as an heroic martyr for Puritan principles.[62] In these tributes, the controversial issue of whether Brown's raid was a defense of civil liberty is submerged in the forwarding of his credentials as a born again New England Puritan.

Despite Thoreau's arch declarations that he preferred huckleberrying or contemplating the water lily to Abolitionist action, no one was to proclaim John Brown's New England sainthood more fully than he. "A Plea for Captain John Brown" begins its biographical summary by asserting that Brown was "by descent and birth a New England farmer." Although John Brown "was like the best of those who stood at Concord Bridge once, on Lexington Common, and on Bunker Hill," he was "firmer and higher principled than any that I have chanced to hear of as there." As a New England militant, John Brown can be compared only with "Ethan Allen and Stark" but they were "rangers in a lower and less important field."[63]

Thoreau successively ascribes five different identities to John Brown: the Puritan, the Transcendentalist, the New England American, the heroic liberator, and finally Jesus Christ. The process of characterization may be somewhat like Henry Adams describing the self as a manikin clothed by successive cultural forces, but Thoreau's purpose is entirely different. He seeks to explain why meteor-like John Brown has restored New England to its founding spirit of apostolic protest yet thereby inaugurated a new era:

The North, I mean the *living* North, was suddenly all transcendental. It went behind the human law, it went behind the apparent failure, and recognized eternal justice and glory. Commonly, men live according to a formula, and are satisfied if the order of law is observed, but in this instance they, to some extent, returned to original perceptions, and there was a slight revival of old religion. They saw that what was called order was confusion, what was called justice, injustice, and that the best was deemed the worst. This attitude suggested a more intelligent and generous spirit than that which actuated our forefathers, and the possibility, in the course of ages, of a revolution in behalf of another and an oppressed people.[64]

Thoreau's John Brown is the spirit of heroic Puritan resistance, reappearing during America's first Revolution and now restored at the onset of a second revolution in a Christlike/New England/American guise. What is such a charismatic regenerative figure but Hawthorne's Gray Champion in a new form, somehow creating new virtues even as he restores old ones? If I am correct in emphasizing mid-century worry about New England's decline, then it is all the more understandable why Thoreau and many a Garrisonian would want to see John Brown as a variant of the Gray Champion. But Hawthorne's own startling comment on John Brown, "Nobody was ever more justly hanged," should give us pause in granting plausibility to Thoreau's claim.[65] John Brown's family left New England when he was 5 years old; his family's claim to be descended from Peter Brown of the *Mayflower* is probably spurious; if he ever had a home, it was in New Alba, New York; it is hard not to call the Pottawatomie killings murder; the New Englanders who supported John Brown did not fight at Harper's Ferry; many New Englanders suspected or detested John Brown from his first notoriety until he was hung.[66] Thoreau's quest to redeem today's failings through John Brown's rectitude never allows him to pause to count up the likely cost of ending slavery by the gun. If John Brown's raid shed "clearest light" on the land, what light was shining during the five succeeding years, when at least 500,000 bodies lay dead on American fields in order that the second revolution be achieved?

If the Garrisonians, as they claimed, represent New England's exalted heritage of libertarian resistance in accord with higher law, what then are we to conclude about George Bancroft's troubled position on slavery? Bancroft's Massachusetts upbringing and his historical research had led him to believe, no less than Parker or Phillips, that resistance to tyrants was obedience to God, and that the Constitution had compromised man's inalienable right of freedom for the sake of national union. The first volume of his *History* (1833) and the article "Slavery in Rome" express strong antislavery convictions that he was never to retract. But Bancroft's conviction that slavery was an "unjust, wasteful and unhappy system" maintained by "covetousness and not a mistaken benevolence"[67] did not preclude his being aware, from the outset, of two interrelated facts. First, a contemporary economic reality of enormous political consequence: "Slaves are capital; the slave holder is a capitalist. Free labor will be the first to demand the abolition of slavery; capital will be the last to concede it." As defiant responses to uncompensated abolitionism written by Thomas Roderick Dew, William Harper, and James Henry Hammond would soon confirm, few southern planters were prepared to give up capital assets simply because of northern appeals to Liberty and the Higher Law, no matter how morally valid such claims might be.[68] Secondly – and in part as a consequence – Bancroft perceived that civil war was the likely outcome if the effect of Garrisonian immediatism was to strengthen southern intransigence. As early as 1834, Bancroft had become convinced that "The horrible inhumanity of civil war, and slave insurrection are the topics of the loudest appeal against the condition of slavery."[69] Immediate Abolitionists would provoke forms of southern repression leading to horrors worse than slave rebellion. Questioning the tactics of Abolitionists as well as nullifiers, Bancroft warns against the "reckless violence of men of desperate audacity who employ terror as a means to ride on the whirlwind of civil war."[70] Few of Bancroft's generation had the insight and the courage to voice this double-sided fear.

To Bancroft, who by the mid-1840s had become the nation's historian, the Garrisonians must have seemed dangerously and increasingly parochial. They were forming ethical absolutes out of a selective reading of regional history for purposes that seemed to have almost as much to do with the moral regeneration of New England as the abolition of slavery itself. Bancroft's biographers have shown his growing reluctance to speak out on slavery crises, to attend antislavery meetings, or to support the Free Soil Party even after he was no longer a Democratic appointee. In 1848 he wrote to his stepson, "I love the principle of popular power that lies at the bottom of our institutions and I love the Union . . . So I would decide questions relating to slavery by appeals to the collective judgment of the nation, and not to a local party organization."[71] His hope was that, within every state, the complementary forces of libertarian progress and popular sovereignty would, if followed with an honest respect for difference, bring about the gradual, voluntary abolition of slavery. Not surprisingly, Bancroft voted for Stephen Douglas in 1860, strongly supported the northern war effort as soon as the southern states seceded, urged Lincoln to emancipate shortly after battle began, and then voted for Lincoln in 1864.

Amid the extremist climate of the late 1850s, Bancroft's realistic stance toward slavery proved to be helplessly passive, but it is not to be confused with thoughtless optimism or the self-serving of a Democratic Party hack. Bancroft's unequaled knowledge of the country's history led him to conclude that slavery was a powder keg for which no solution that did not command a popular majority in all regions could ever succeed. He futilely wished that the entire nation could somehow imitate the Massachusetts constitutional convention of 1780 and quietly outlaw slavery without mentioning the word.[72] Unlike Webster, Bancroft was beholden to no cotton or banking interests for the success of his career. He accepted the annexation of Texas only in anticipation of the statehood of California, and he accepted the Fugitive Slave Law only in the hope of saving the nation. He found glory in neither measure. One of the consummate ironies in American intellectual history is that Bancroft's great, climactic eighth volume on the achieving of national independence in 1775–1776 was to be published in the very year the United States of America ceased to be united. To Bancroft, the onset of secession was a devastating and humbling fall causing a personal hurt inconceivable for long-declared Disunionists such as Garrison and Phillips.[73]

When it became evident that Secretary of the Navy Bancroft was not going to oppose Texas annexation or war with Mexico, Garrison described him as "an ambitious, unprincipled time-serving demagogue who would sell his country as Judas sold his Lord."[74] Six months later, James Russell Lowell sneered at Bancroft's belief that a slaveholding Texas within the nation was preferable to Texas as a slaveholding region within Mexico. Lowell distorted Bancroft's position into "Annex Texas, said the profound historian, and you strike a blow at the root of slavery."[75] Late in 1845, Theodore Parker wrote a purportedly friendly letter to Bancroft, alleging that Bancroft had forgotten that he had once denounced slavery and urging him to be true to his first beliefs, lest Boston's skies soon be darkened with a hundred bonfires fueled by the volumes of his *History*.[76] The failure of Garrisonian Abolitionists to discriminate among New England's Unionists surfaces in Parker's 1851 slur implying that Bancroft had long been serving as Webster's priest: "Till the Fugitive Slave law was passed, we did not know what a great saint Iscariot was. I think there ought to be a chapel for him, and a day set apart on the calendar. Let him have his chapel in the navy-yard at Washington. He has got a priest there already."[77]

Who had authority to speak for the Puritan heritage in assessing the crisis of Freedom posed by slavery? Was it Garrison and Phillips, determined to undo the corrupting effects of white slavery regardless of the price of advocating Disunion? Was it James Russell Lowell, whose comic perceptions might provoke peaceful withdrawal from further annexations, if not the desideratum of emancipation? Was it Theodore Parker trying to force Boston's purest heritage, not only upon the nation, but on Boston itself? Was it George Bancroft, the Massachusetts minister's son whose viewpoint had become so fully national that he believed the only prospect for a peaceful resolution of the slavery crisis lay in silent hope? Or was it a then powerful voice ignored in this chapter, the New England Cotton Whig with dirtied hands who was more averse to slavery than the Garrisonians would admit?

Even this selected range of options shows that speaking for New England now involved a compromise of regional autonomy and identity beyond anything imagined even by Cotton Mather in the midst of the *Decennium Luctuosum*. New England's rage against territorial expansion as a promotion of the slave interest was inseparable from worried awareness of New England's growing marginalization within the nation. Self-accusatory anger at white slavery was testimony to a fifty-year economic ligature that had made New England no longer New England. Or, to express the subversion in perceptual terms, the very fact of "white slavery" had made New England no longer the New England of collective historical imagination. The ringing, never-changed "Introduction" Bancroft wrote for his entire *History*, which ascribes the Republic's glory to its western lands, its changeable Constitution and technological future, without one mention of New England, of the South, or of slavery in any form, must be seen as the hopeful legacy of this regional loss.

Epilogue: "bodiless echoes"

The dignitary selected in 1866 to give the memorial address on the life of Abraham Lincoln before the joint Houses of Congress was the Honorable George Bancroft of New York. Speaking on Lincoln's birthday nearly a year after the assassination, Bancroft needed to assure congressmen that John Wilkes Booth's bullet had been no hideous, inexplicable accident: "nothing is done by chance, though men, in their ignorance of causes, may think so."[1] The Providential view of history, to which Bancroft remains fully committed, permeates his very first sentence, "That God rules in the affairs of men is as certain as any truth of physical science" (3). Although God's rule made slavery's end inevitable, regional jealousies had prolonged and deepened the crisis, so it was best not to mention them. The words "New England" do not occur in Bancroft's address; he resorts to "the North" and "the South" only when absolutely necessary. Abolitionist courage is traced back, not to Garrison and Phillips, but to those Virginians of the late eighteenth century who were opposed to slavery and presumably fought to eliminate it. Sectionalism, Bancroft believes, must henceforward be buried in Union: "the American people was the hero of the war; and therefore the result is a new era of republicanism" (50). Lincoln's genius was to lead slightly in advance of the popular will while being beholden to no regional economic or religious interest. Although Bancroft never directly says so, he no longer has faith in the value of sectional diversity. As a separable cultural entity, "New England" must go.

In late nineteenth-century America, the power of Anglo-Protestant New England continued to steadily erode. While the population in the middle west and new western states soared, the geographically enclosed New England region could claim few Congressional leaders and but one president. Epoch-making national events – the Philadelphia Exposition of 1876, the Chicago World's Fair, the completion of the Transcontinental Railroad and the Panama Canal, the development of the oil and steel industries, the rise of labor unions, the explorations of John Wesley Powell, the Homestead

and Pullman Strikes, the Indian Wars, the inventions of Thomas Edison –
occurred elsewhere. The immigration of Irish, Italian, and Slavic peoples
successively broke down Anglo-protestant hegemony until, as John Seelye
has remarked, both the Statue of Liberty and Ellis Island have thoroughly
trumped Plymouth Rock as the icon of Euro-American arrival in the new
world.[2] In the twentieth century, Protestants were to become the religious
minority in every New England state save New Hampshire. After the Civil
War, New England's treasured landscape of small city seaports and prosperous freehold farms quickly gave way to a patchwork of sprawling multieth-
nic cities, ungainly river towns whose mills employed rural and immigrant
labor, and depleted upland farms where aging Yankee losers remained.[3]
New England's railroads, built to bring people in, carried many a New
Englander out. Class, income, and ethnic stratification grew until not even
New England orators could ignore it. On a larger scale, the incorporation
of America, to use Alan Trachtenberg's apt term, threatened the survival
of regional distinctions, leading to a need to preserve those distinctions
in literature, statuary, and local historical societies before they disappeared
entirely.[4]

The range of post-war fiction, even in the age of regionalism, shows
New England's decline. By 1880 the novel had emerged as the chief form of
literary discourse, but none of the major novelists of the period – Howells,
James, Twain, Crane, Norris, Wharton, Dreiser – were of New England.
The five canonical novels written about New England during this period
all advance a bifurcated image of the region – a consistently split image
deserving greater critical attention than it has yet received. For 250 years
the very words "New England" had contained within them the premise of
a single culture; New England authors had long striven to represent the
region as one cultural entity, even when they knew otherwise. In Howells's
A Modern Instance, however, New England is suddenly divided between the
staid village of Equity, Maine and the insecurities of commercial Boston,
with Bartley Hubbard's unrelenting egoism and smarmy ambition as the
link between them. Silas Lapham's financial fall and moral rise take place
within the opposed environs of rural Vermont (moribund but honestly
ethical) and urban Boston (economically vibrant but increasingly amoral).
James's *The Bostonians* not only juxtaposes New England to the South, but
contrasts the tawdry sprawl of Cambridge manufactories seen from Olive
Chancellor's Back Bay window to the noble loss symbolized by Harvard's
Memorial Hall, and to the mellow dullness of Buzzards Bay. Sarah Orne
Jewett never allows us to forget that the pastoral charms of Dunnet Landing
are being recreated for us by an urban outsider, a summer visitor to the

Maine coast, who can never belong within Almira Todd's household or at the Bowden family reunion. The privations of Ethan Frome's Starkfield are also rendered for us by an urban outsider, a clear-eyed engineer who knows that Ethan's farm town has lost its future now that the newly built railroad has passed it by.

In all five novels the authors render the value of New England's communal remnants with engaging ambiguity; embarrassed nostalgia and hesitant satire cut quite literally in two directions, progressively forward toward a modern city with little regional character, and backward into a New England past that the author no longer quite wishes to join. None of these texts defines New England identity in the spatially fixed manner of *The House of the Seven Gables*, a novel in which the Puritan, Revolutionary and Federalist pasts are all conveyed through symbols deriving from one stationary house, and in which a disorienting trip on the railroad becomes an option only in one late chapter. Hawthorne's New England, as Henry James's 1879 biography implies, suddenly seemed an anachronism, however great the literary art derived from it might have been.

After the Civil War, regional self-assertion of the familiar kind recommenced bravely, but in a context that lessened the likelihood of its acquiring lasting power. The *North American Review*, now forty years old, was becoming venerably dull, and even the *Atlantic* was no longer the new news it had been in 1859. Compared to Bancroft's volumes, Palfrey's *History of New England* was parochial, pedantic, and stylistically dull, no matter how much information it contained. Parkman's narratives remained the great achievement of the era's romantic historians, but Parkman's concern with New England lay in the region's remote frontier past. Autobiographies of New England upbringing by Thomas Bailey Aldrich and Lucy Larcom cast a warm glow over regional origins, but the resonance of both *The Story of a Bad Boy* and *A New England Girlhood*, written as they were for near adolescents, remained decidedly childlike. To make matters worse, the reverence paid to Longfellow, Lowell, Emerson, Whittier, and Holmes was proving to be New England's literary undoing, especially as these presumed seers aged with minimal new creative accomplishment. Revolt had begun before Twain's infamous Whittier dinner speech. Acknowledging that "it used to be a matter of no little jealousy with us, I remember, that the manners, customs, thoughts, and feelings of New England country people filled so large a place in books," Edward Eggleston determined that he would challenge the presumption that the life of a Hoosier schoolmaster could have "no place in literature."[5] By the time Holmes wrote his biography of Emerson, with its assertions that Concord was "an ideal New England town" and that

Boston's seventeenth-century trimount had furnished the whole world with its three "beacons" ("civil liberty," "religious freedom," and "the lamp of the scholar"), the force of such claims could be directed only backward upon the New England past.[6]

Lowell's review essay, "New England Two Centuries Ago" (1865), shows the suddenly problematic nature, not only of particular claims advanced about New England, but of the very act of offering them. The honesty Lowell found through the voice of Hosea Biglow was not sustainable in the prose of Lowell the Harvard professor and editor of the *North American Review*. Lowell begins with the sweeping claim that "The history of New England is written imperishably on the face of a continent and in characters as beneficent as they are enduring."[7] He then acknowledges the population exodus from New England, but tries to claim that "the seed of the Mayflower" now spread across the land in churches, schools, and colleges, attests to the folly of those who would now "Leave New England out in the cold!" (4). Lowell's New England still does not, however, include its Irish newcomers, for he insists that the New England creed ("Faith in God, faith in man, faith in work") is consistent with the neo-Puritan refusal to have any "faith in the Divine institution of a system which gives Teague, because he can dig, as much influence as Ralph, because he can think" (4, 5). When Lowell concludes that "Puritanism, believing itself quick with the seed of religious liberty, laid, without knowing it, the egg of democracy" (16), old and tired cultural tropes have resulted in a mixed metaphor as repellent as it is absurd. Reading so complacent a speech, it is hard to remember that, at that particular juncture, James Russell Lowell was, with the possible exception of Emerson, America's most prominent and powerful man of letters.

In the short fictions of Rose Terry Cooke, Mary Wilkins Freeman, and Edith Wharton, New England's claims to Christian spirituality, republican leadership, and pastoral progress are indirectly but thoroughly upended. Again and again, we read of stagnant towns, depleted soil, abandoned farmhouses, hypocritical ministers, ineffectual selectmen, the poorhouse, unwanted pregnancies, shotgun marriages, domestic violence, child abuse, and the many forms of madness that near total isolation brings. Above all, we read of brutal Calvinist husbands, and of women who passively endure or desperately rebel against male oppression. The solitary rural farmhouse and declining village replace the thriving town community and the City on a Hill as the symbols of New England life. Unlike the novels of Child, Sedgwick, Hawthorne and Stowe, the short, pointed narratives of Cooke, Freeman, and Wharton take place outside of specific historical context and specific location. Whether these stories are set in Cranberry, Bassett or Wingfield (Rose Terry Cooke), Dover, Canton or Pembroke (Mary Wilkins Freeman), Starkfield or North Dormer (Edith Wharton), we are in a village where there are institutions but no community, aged people but no history, religion but no belief, hard labor but no interwoven economy.

In these fictions there is no need for the historicism of Sedgwick or Hawthorne because there is no possibility of a crisis by which the community could be regenerated. There is, apparently, only an eternity of decline, a noncrisis that is the worst crisis of all. Although the tone of these stories and sketches varies widely, many of them express a woman's revenge against patriarchy, whether in direct authorial voice or through identification with a sympathetic and defiant woman character. It is, therefore, not at all surprising that generations of prominent male critics who admired antebellum New England's male authors would have wished to prolong the minimizing of this fictional tradition by confining it under its 1864 designation as (women's) "local color."[8] The unstated stakes were high. Behind the dismissal of antebellum history in these sparse fictions lies a sweeping indifference to the outmoded national claims of a long dominant New England culture.

A complementary development to the rise of women's regional fiction was the fading reputation of George Bancroft among his historical peers. For decades after 1893, the many adherents of Frederick Jackson Turner's "The Significance of the Frontier in American History" were to remain convinced of the half-truth that American "Democracy" had not arrived with Puritans aboard the *Mayflower*, but that it had been wrought in the ethnic crucible of the West. The eroding of Bancroft's reputation can, however, be detected years before Turner and in the least expected of places – the pages of the *North American Review*. At first, Bancroft's *History* had been greeted with a reverence almost beyond limit. After the first volume was published in 1834, Edward Everett declared that it "does such justice to its noble subject as to supercede the necessity of any future work of the same kind."[9] After praising Bancroft's "patience of research," "impartiality and love of truth," and "vigor, sprightliness and beauty of diction," Everett had even suggested that the *History*, rising from divine beliefs, "presents no mean image of that superior power, whose duration is as boundless as its intensity" (122).

When Prescott reviewed the third volume of the *History* in 1841, he continued the praise of Bancroft's "brilliant and daring style," "picturesque sketches of character and incident," "acute reasoning," and "compass of erudition," but treated the *History* as if it were a masterly, ongoing professional project rather than a revelation of divine truth.[10] By the time Henry Adams reviewed the tenth volume in 1874, the worm was turning.

No doubt Mr. Bancroft entertains as ardent a faith now as forty years ago in the abstract virtues of democracy and "the gentle feelings of humanity," but time and experience have tempered this faith with a more searching spirit of criticism than was fashionable in the days of President Jackson. Not that Mr. Bancroft has or ever will have a strictly judicial mind, to whatever age he may live, but that his idiosyncracies are now less prominent in his pages; and an acquaintance with the details of his subject, far more extensive than that of any other individual, living or dead, now gives those pages a practical value which the critic must begin by acknowledging in the fullest and frankest terms. In order to criticize at all, one must use the materials which Mr. Bancroft himself has supplied.[11]

Henry Adams's suspicion of Bancroft's faith in "the abstract virtues of democracy" is as evident as Adams's dutiful defense of a monumental history he knows is beginning to be assailed. Who can be sure whether Adams intends a compliment or a criticism when he alleges that George Bancroft has never had, and never will have, "a strictly judicial mind"?

The fading of Bancroft's reputation and the achievement of women's regional fiction come together at a telling moment in Edith Wharton's novella *Summer* (1917). The awakening of Charity Royall's sexual desire occurs simultaneously with her overpowering "hate" for the deteriorating confines of North Dormer, Massachusetts. The power of Wharton's narrative, however, depends on the changing relationship between Charity and her middle-aged guardian Mr. Royall, the town's most prominent citizen and a widower, who has adopted Charity, given her his name, freed her from back-hills destitution, but then, in a dreadful moment of sexual need, tried to enter her bedroom. A few pages thereafter, Wharton pictures Mr. Royall in his "dusty office." It turns out that North Dormer's leading citizen, and probably the town's only lawyer, has almost nothing to do:

His hours there were not much longer or more regular than Charity's at the library; the rest of the time he spent either at the store or in driving about the country on business connected with the insurance companies that he represented; or in sitting at home reading Bancroft's *History of the United States* and the speeches of Daniel Webster.[12]

The drab reality of daily life in North Dormer gives the lie to Bancroft's and Webster's faith in protestant New England as the vanguard of the great Republic. Wharton's coupling of Bancroft with Webster, given their years of political enmity, and Webster's long-rumored sexual philandering, has its own characteristically sardonic edge. But the dominant effect of the passage is to reduce all Webster's and Bancroft's beliefs to mere words, a dreamed past that lends the illusion of significance to a dreary present.

As Joseph Conforti has shown, by mid-nineteenth century, Jonathan Edwards was widely thought to embody the spiritual aspirations of New England. Long after the time of his disciples Joseph Bellamy and Samuel Hopkins, Edwards's reputation had continued to grow in all save Unitarian circles, through the influence of Sereno Dwight's edition of Edwards's writings, the homage paid by Edwards Park at Andover, and the missionary activities of Mary Lyon and the American Tract Society.[13] However, those who continued after the Civil War to promote the apolitical Edwards as representative of all New England were at best touting a culturally narrowing anachronism. The attack then directed at the icon of Edwards was, I submit, of equal importance. Not the easy decrying of Edwards's stature by those who despaired of New England, knew nothing of Calvinism, resented any dominant male, or liked to debunk a monumental reputation, but rather the response of two major figures in New England intellectual life who would love their imagined region to the end: Harriet Beecher Stowe and Oliver Wendell Holmes.

Stowe's Christianity, not unlike Edwards's, was based on an affective and evangelical faith. In place of Edwards's reliance on theological doctrine and lifelong faith in church congregations of the Saints, Stowe substituted the heart's love of the missionary Jesus and the power of women's domesticity. The shift left her equally unwilling either to accept or to discard Edwardsean tradition. Insofar as later-day Edwardseans urged disinterested benevolence, acting in this world, as the essence of reformed faith, Stowe found New England Calvinism to be a regional tradition of indispensable purity and strength. Insofar as Edwardseans valued theological abstraction over Christian good works, or led individuals to despair of the grace God had forbidden them, they were becoming the errant male viceroys of a God whose cruel justice existed only in their imaginations.

Stowe would never be able fully to relinquish either possibility, but a shift in emphasis is detectable. *The Minister's Wooing* (1859) famously criticizes the entire Edwardsean tradition for holding out to eternity "a ladder to heaven" while knocking out every rung in the ladder except the highest "and then, pointing to its hopeless splendor, [saying] to the world 'Go up thither and be saved!'"[14] Nonetheless, Stowe praises Samuel Hopkins as a "good" man, and often, especially in his attack on slavery, praises him as a "great" one. *Oldtown Folks* (1869), however, sharpens the attack, emphasizing the harm Edwardsean tradition has done to New England culture. Although the first chapter begins with a tribute to the energy of New England Puritanism "burning like live coals" underneath the "obscurity" of theocratic dogma, Stowe soon ascribes to Puritanism those self-inflicted "needles of thought" peculiar to a religion that allows no intermediary between the individual soul and a very removed God.[15] Despite Edwards's abilities as prose-poet and metaphysician, Stowe attacks him, quite fairly, for his logic-chopping syllogisms, but also attacks him, quite unfairly, for "casting out of the Church the children of the very saints and martyrs who had come to this country for no other reason than to found a church" (358). When Stowe later alleges that Edwards's "Treatise on True Virtue" "was one of the strongest attempts to back up by reasoning the old monarchical and aristocratic ideas of the supreme right of the king and upper classes," we detect her desire, not only to cast Edwards as an opponent of American Revolutionary thought, but also to hold his theology somehow responsible for widening class divisions in New England (401).

Among the twelve essays Holmes collected into one volume of his complete works, "Jonathan Edwards" (1880) and "The Pulpit and the Pew" (1881) are conspicuous for their almost complete lack of his characteristic bonhomie and vacuous charm. Late in life, Holmes was no longer willing to try to laugh New England out of its Calvinistic theology, as he had been in "The Deacon's Masterpiece, or the Wonderful 'One-Hoss Shay'" (1858). Edwards's Trinity, Holmes now claims, was in fact a "Quaternity" with its fourth entity, God's brutal "Justice," controlling the other three.[16] Not only did the supposedly "brilliant" Jonathan Edwards believe that the Bible's palpable absurdities were God's Word, he also created a dominant theological system that was "barbaric, mechanical, materialistic, pessimistic" (395). The imputation of Adam's original sin to all mankind, Holmes unfairly alleges, led Edwards to emphasize infant damnation to such a degree that later generations would hate the Puritan God as much as they feared Him. Despite all Edwards's pseudo-logic about the freedom of the will, he never had an inkling of the fact that "physiological psychology" shows how man's will, his presumably "self-determined actions," are ascribable "more and more to reflex action, to mechanism" (378, 379). Holmes is ultimately bent on freeing New England entirely from the curse of Edwards: "The truth is, Edwards belonged in Scotland, to which he owed so much, and not to New England."[17]

Holmes's follow-up essay, "The Pulpit and the Pew," proceeds to empty out New England's protestant churches. Although it may have been logically true since Luther's time that "the priest is dead for the Protestant world," the New England pulpit has now in weekly fact become nothing but a rostrum and its minister a lost leader. The region's accomplished intellectuals

(Holmes provides a list from Everett and Emerson, through Bancroft and Motley, to Lowell and Parkman) are all, like Holmes himself, ministers' sons or grandsons who lack churchly allegiance. After pages hectoring Jonathan Edwards, Holmes seeks to define exactly what, in the absence of the Puritan tradition, New England now stands for. The Unitarian church hardly provides a vibrant or clearly definable faith. Holmes sees no community in New England's rapidly industrializing cities, no prosperity in the residual farm, and no self-control among Boston's recent immigrants. Science may be a worthy new religion, but it is by definition universal and not regional. There were, of course, the members of his own Harvard class and Brahmin caste, but Holmes was too wary of published snobbery to mention them. At essay's end there is nothing left but the prophetic image of an empty New England church in which "the preacher will by and by find himself speaking to a congregation of bodiless echoes" (433). In such phrasings, New England becomes its past.

I conclude with the assessments of New England, particularly of Massachusetts, in end-of-century texts written by three brothers descended in the fourth generation from John Adams. The special perspective of Charles, Henry, and Brooks Adams derives from more than the immense burden of filiopietism, a burden that provoked a perplexing mixture of pride, sarcasm, anger, melancholy, and ironic self-abasement in all three. The distinguished Adams heritage also demanded continued exposure to the polarities of New England life (urban mercantile Boston versus rural republican Quincy) and informed interest in regional history within national and international contexts. The fourth generation Adamses were positioned to detect the paradox that, while institutional and technological forces were integrating once distinguishable regions within a national culture, other forces had already disintegrated the New England heritage into which they were born. To their credit, all three brothers welcomed such confusions into their thinking, although only Henry was prepared to structure his writings, particularly his autobiography, around them.

The last part of Charles Adams's *Three Episodes in Massachusetts*, modestly entitled "A Study of Church and Town Government," is the worthy forerunner of the comprehensive New England town histories to be written by Charles Grant, Sumner Chilton Powell, Kenneth Lockridge, Phillip Greven, and others. For this last "episode," Adams provided well over four hundred pages of statistics and quotations drawn from the town records of Braintree and Quincy, linking economic, demographic, political, and technological developments with church and family history into a volume that is in one way admirably empirical, but in another full of undisguised "old family" Anglo-American prejudices. More interesting than Adams's distaste for stereotypical Irish immigrants and Democratic ward bosses, however, is the perspective he shares with contemporary observers of New England life, including, surprisingly, the women regionalist writers. Like them, Adams sees decades of agricultural decline in a community of widely separated farmhouses without books or newspapers. He too exposes the damages wrought by unchanging and ineffective agricultural methods, and by family bloodlines genetically weakened by "breeding-in."[18] Neither King Philip's War (which arose not far from Braintree) nor the revolt against Andros, nor even the American Revolution changed the blindly self-contained Braintree community. The only crisis in two hundred years came in the aftermath of the Great Awakening, when a forward-looking Arminian minister was ousted by a village congregation composed of "narrow-minded men of no great intellectual strength" who "could not grasp a new idea even when it was plainly set before them" (II, 639). Such descriptions could as readily apply to Rose Terry Cooke's characterization of Amasa Tucker or Mary Wilkins Freeman's characterization of Deacon Caleb Gale.

To Charles Adams, there would be little advantage in even referring to the Bancroftian sequence of crises, because Charles's view of New England's citizenry is that they have never been motivated by political, ethical, or religious values. When great grandfather John Adams bequeathed his library to the town, John's "ludicrously inappropriate" hope of benefiting popular education "wholly failed of accomplishment" because Quincy's townspeople, Charles claims, cared nothing for Shakespeare, Milton, or Locke (II, 941). If Charles perceived connections between his first two "episodes" ("The Era of Settlement"; "The Antinomian Controversy") and his study of the evolution of contemporary Quincy, he does not even try to specify them. In his view, the only truly important changes in the town's 250-year history are first, the construction of the railroad that in 1826 carried Quincy granite to build the Bunker Hill Monument, and second, the abandonment of the town meeting form of government when Quincy was incorporated as a city in 1889. The two developments are inextricably one. As the quarries and the railroad brought in Catholic Irishmen and others of "foreign blood" (II, 930), an urban center quickly developed; fifth generation farmers turned to profitable shopkeeping, and party bosses directed ignorant quarry and tannery laborers how to vote. Of the 1840s, Adams concludes: "The inrush of foreign elements had been too rapid. It tended to unsettle everything" (II, 949). As for "the new generation of Americans" (meaning "old family protestants"), "the more adventurous and enterprising went to the cities, or sought their fortunes in the West" (II, 949). What remains is a population so divided that Charles Adams, social Darwinist that he was, adopts the falsifying terminology of race conflict to describe it. "Quick of impulse, sympathetic, ignorant and credulous, the Irish race have as few elements in common with the native New Englanders as one race of men well can have with another" (II, 957). As Quincy's population quadruples, both "races" opt out of community responsibilities, government by town meeting becomes unmanageable, and Quincy must be reorganized as a managerial city if it is not to descend into anarchy.

The confusions of Quincy's future are further compounded by one of Charles Adams's most remarkable insights. He notes the beginnings in about 1875 of what he calls "suburban" life – surely one of the word's earliest uses. The completion of the Old Colony Railroad (Adams relishes the name's ironies) now links Quincy directly to Boston, making Quincy into "a species of sleeping apartment conveniently near to the great city counting-room" (II, 954). Adams is conspicuously unwilling, however, to consider that this bewildering amalgam of farm/factory/shop/suburb/city might be integral to defining a new New England. Instead, after having disparaged rural antebellum life for two hundred pages, he momentarily laments that "the last vestiges of village life now passed away, and the suburban town assumed shape" (II, 965). Guarding against sentimentality even as he gives way to it, Adams ends *Three Episodes* with a mock funeral for the democratic principle inherent in New England town government, acknowledging that the old system is now quite dead but remarking that it should perhaps be "laid away as a parent that was gone, – silently, tenderly, reverently" (II, 1009). An appropriate conclusion for a man who would shortly move his family's residence from urban Quincy to rural Lincoln, but then spend many a day returning to Quincy, as president of the Massachusetts Historical Society, to urge the city managers to set up memorials to the village's past.

The Henry Adams known to most readers – the author of the *Education* – is a protectively self-critical autobiographer contemptuously proud of his outmoded New England heritage of "resistance" and "moral law."[19] The *Education* portrays the "troglodytic" forces impinging upon Henry Adams's upbringing ("the First Church, the Boston State House, Beacon Hill, John Hancock and John Adams, Mount Vernon Street and Quincy") as the first "nest of associations" that was to shape his manikin self into both a worldly failure and a prophetic analyst of the emerging contradictions of twentieth-century life (3). His attitude toward his New England origins develops into a complex, conflicted blend of dismissive tribute and mock nostalgia. When writing professional history as a younger man, however,

Adams could not indulge in memories of sensual boyhood summers in Quincy, of President John Quincy Adams taking him in hand, or of Mt. Vernon Street's confidence in the material progress of Boston's educated citizenry. The suppression of strong personal reminiscences allows strong convictions about historiography to rise in their stead.

Adams's massive *History* of the presidencies of Jefferson and Madison begins with chapters surveying the separable regions of the country at the turn of the nineteenth century. In the spirit of Rose Terry Cooke or his brother Charles, Adams writes chapters entitled "Physical and Economical Conditions" and "Intellect of New England" in which he is clearly determined to concede "Old New England" almost nothing. He describes New England's wretched roads, dilapidated schoolhouses, rocky soil, and straggling orchards, noting with approval Alexander Wilson's observation that New England was "two hundred years behind the Pennsylvanians in agricultural improvements."[20] With its "crooked and narrow streets," its ill-lighted and unpoliced alleyways, "Boston resembled an English market-town, of a kind even then old-fashioned" (1, 20). Adams alleges that New England culture was everywhere dominated by an "oligarchy" of backward-looking Federalists who secured pulpit, bench and college against all innovation (1, 76). Fisher Ames is treated as if he represents all New England thought; changeless Harvard has become nothing more than "a priesthood which had lost the secret of its mysteries" (1, 77).

Adams is at special pains to disabuse his readers of the once cherished hope that the New Englander was to emerge as the representative American. "Even Boston, the most cosmopolitan part of New England, showed no tendency in its educated classes, to become American in thought and feeling" (1, 87). The Bancroftian notion that Puritanism was the seedbed of the Republic has become nothing more than a cliché to be upended by a sardonic twist. The reason Adams offers to explain why the Federalist oligarchy was so un-American is that they were infected with "the old spirit of Puritan obstinacy" (1, 86–87). Because the disgraceful prospect of New England secession during the Hartford Convention loomed around the historical corner, Adams would not relinquish his insistence that Federalist obstinacy derived from Puritan forbears.

The obstinacy of the race was never better shown than when, with the sunlight of the nineteenth century bursting upon them, these resolute sons of granite and ice turned their faces from the sight, and smiled in their sardonic way at the folly or wickedness of men who could pretend to believe the world improved because henceforth the ignorant and vicious were to rule the United States and govern the churches and schools of New England. (1, 87)

Even Henry's opinionated brother Charles would have great difficulty, given his regard for statistical record, in classifying such generalizations as the findings of "history." The cause of Henry's overt prejudice is his need to release anger, not only at the Federalist "Oligarchy" but also at decades of writing and oratory that had eulogized old New England as the source of national greatness. As Adams acknowledged in the *Education*, "the New Englander, whether boy or man, in his long struggle with a stingy or hostile universe, had learned also to love the pleasure of hating" (7).

The *Education* itself, however, transcends the regionalist formulation of such issues by making use of them for purposes at once personal and universal. The place titles for the first two chapters, "Quincy" and "Boston," begin as two New England communities, shift into opposed symbols of regional identity, but before chapter's end have become complementary opposites within the balanced personality. "Winter and summer, cold and heat, town and country, force and freedom, marked two modes of life and thought, balanced like lobes of the brain" (7). The ability to hold both Quincy and Boston within the self, without any irritable reaching after absolute certainty, would, in the manner of Keats's Negative Capability, allow for the fulfillment of a true education – if one could sustain such equanimity. Unfortunately, the bewildering variety of the self's experiences ("Washington," "Harvard College," "Berlin," "Rome," and so forth) never allows the lobes to be fully in balance, never allows Adams to see the unity of the present through its chaotic multiplicity. One might conclude that the chapter structure of the *Education* shows the ultimate submergence of regional origins within a self that becomes first national, then international, and finally concerned with such cosmic abstractions as the Dynamic Theory of History and the Law of Acceleration. But one might also conclude, with equal justification, that Quincy and Boston provide the manikin with worthy bases for assessing the multiple experiences and many chapters that will follow. To be the grandson of such dissimilar notables as John Quincy Adams and Peter Brooks, and to be the son of Charles Francis Adams ("the only perfectly balanced mind that ever existed in the name," 27) provide Henry with faculties much needed when he confronts the chaos of history that is Rome.

Brooks Adams's *The Emancipation of Massachusetts* (1887) accepts the long-standing premise that New England is to be understood through the ways it met the sequence of crises familiar to readers of Bancroft. Giving Sam Adams his due, Brooks contends that the successful defense of civil liberty must be regarded, in the main, as New England's special achievement for the nation. His purpose, however, is not to retread the most worn path of regional history but to challenge the received understanding of how the triumph of civil liberty came about. Instead of arguing that civil liberty came to the new world aboard the *Mayflower* and the *Arbella*, instead of searching out liberties in the Compact and the Charter, Brooks Adams attacks the seventeenth-century clergy, *en masse*, as autocratic tyrants. Not a speaking aristocracy in front of a silent democracy, but a repressive oligarchy in front of sullen semiliterates.

Brooks Adams's favorite noun for describing the Puritan clergy is "priest" and his favorite adjective is "sacerdotal." For a century, the Bay Colony was nothing but "a petty state, too feeble for independence, yet ruled by an autocratic priesthood whose power rested upon legislation antagonistic to English law."[21]

In the tempest of the Reformation a handful of the sternest rebels were cast upon the bleak New England coast, and the fervor of that devotion which led them into the wildernesses inspired them with the dream of reproducing the institutions of God's chosen people, a picture of which they believed was divinely preserved for their guidance in the Bible. What they did in reality was to surrender their new commonwealth to their priests. (213)

Such a slamming of the rhetorical door occurs again and again. A sentence lulling the reader into a familiar reassurance is undercut by the next sentence written in parallel syntax:

In the world's childhood, knowledge seems divine, and those who first acquire its rudiments claim, and are believed, to have received it by revelation from the gods. In an archaic age the priest is likewise the lawgiver and the physician, for all erudition is concentrated in one supremely favored class – the sacred caste. (212)

As exemplars of "the sacred caste," John Winthrop and John Cotton are granted no quarter, nor are Cotton Mather and Samuel Sewall. When reading Brooks Adams's glancing claims that Merry Mounters, Antinomians, Quakers, and witches were all freethinking victims of repressive church/state power, one might almost believe one is in the imagined world of William Carlos Williams's *In the American Grain* where "the Puritan" can be – and indeed is – held responsible for all the national ills.

Brooks Adams's view of the source of human conduct, however, is as distant from Williams as it is from Bancroft. Adams cannot believe that Puritan leaders could ever have acted on libertarian principle, religious or political, because human beings respond to "mechanical training" and "systems of education" with almost "mathematical precision" (407). Once the Puritan leaders were released from English law, they discovered that tyranny was necessary in constructing frontier theocracies; thereafter, "the human mechanism" took over, duplicating patterns of autocracy and obedience for generation after generation (533). By applying such absolute social determinism to the Puritan endeavor, Brooks Adams was denying the forefathers the capacity even for freedom of thought, let alone for free will.

The difficulty in Adams's argument lies in the need to provide an explanation of how "civil liberty" could ever have arisen in Revolutionary Massachusetts. He is forced into so vague a dodge as "An established priesthood is naturally the firmest support of despotism; but the course of events made that of Massachusetts revolutionary" (512). What "course of events" could possibly have brought about such a change if in fact priestly autocracy had ruled the human mechanisms in Massachusetts for the preceding 150 years? Echoing Bancroft's judgment that Sam Adams was "the last of the Puritans," Brooks Adams cites James K. Hosmer's biography to show that Sam Adams was in fact a "consummate agitator," but such recategorizing does not demonstrate why Adams should have written so continually of civil liberty in the Boston *Gazette*, nor why its readers should have followed him (514, 517). All Brooks Adams can offer as evidence of "civil liberty" is a series of impulsive gestures (Endicott mutilating the flag, Leverett insulting Randolph, Sam Adams challenging Hutchinson), gestures that are said to derive not from New Englanders' inner principle but from repressed memories of English statues and sermons that antedated the Great Migration. "For no church can preach liberality and not be liberalized," Adams asserts. "Of a truth the momentary spasm may pass which made these conservatives progressive, and they may once more manifest their reactionary nature, but nevertheless, the impulsion shall have been given to that automatic, yet resistless machinery which produces innovation" (533). New Englanders were, evidently, revolutionaries in spite of themselves.

An argument so vague, contradictory, and finally perverse only illustrates, in the end, how difficult it was to defend "the emancipation of Massachusetts" with the fashionable intellectual assumptions of the late nineteenth century. Brooks Adams could not have truly believed the determinism he so pointedly proclaimed. His book ends with a fulsome sentence that, in its highly oratorical rhythms, is an astonishing reversion to the era of Bancroft and Webster:

And so, through toil and suffering, through martyrdoms and war, the Puritans wrought out the ancient destiny, which led them to wander as outcasts to the desolate New England shore; there, amidst hardship and apparent failure, they slowly achieved their civil and religious liberty and conceived that constitutional system which is the root of our national life; and there in another century the liberal commonwealth they had builded led the battle against the spread of human oppression; and when the war of slavery burst forth her soldiers rightly were the first to fall; for it is her children's heritage that, wheresoever on this continent blood shall flow in defense of personal freedom, there must the sons of Massachusetts surely be. (534)

Here is Hawthorne's Gray Champion come yet again during the Civil as well as the Revolutionary War. The fact that Brooks Adams published a second and enlarged edition of his book in 1919 suggests that the Gray Champion may even have been put on alert to accompany the sons of Massachusetts into the Great European War.

No reader of the harsh post-Darwinian argument Brooks Adams unfolded in his preceding 500 pages could possibly find such a peroration to be logically convincing. If Puritan New England were to be defended for the benefit of twentieth-century Americans, a totally different, more flexible, and infinitely more scholarly method would need to be devised. The introduction to the 1962 reprinting of *The Emancipation of Massachusetts* was to be written by Perry Miller, who noted that in 1919 Brooks Adams was considered by his dwindling number of associates "to be unbalanced and dogmatic to the point of madness" (vii). Miller also noted that Brooks Adams "uttered many foolish statements, and he generalized irresponsibly without ever doing the requisite grubbing among factual records" (viii). In 1962, Perry Miller was in a position to offer both of these criticisms with well-deserved authority. Miller had persuaded historically minded Americans to understand Puritan origins according to the Puritans' own terms (Augustinian piety and covenantal theology) rather than, like George Bancroft, across the Revolutionary self-justifications of Sam Adams's generation.

Notes

INTRODUCTION

1. Among the many studies of American Puritanism, I am especially indebted to the following works, listed below in chronological order and in foreshortened footnote form, because of space limitations and their scholarly prominence: Perry Miller's *The New England Mind: The Seventeenth Century* (1939) and *From Colony to Province* (1953); Perry Miller's *Orthodoxy in Massachusetts* (1933), *Errand into the Wilderness* (1956), and *Nature's Nation* (1967); Edmund S. Morgan, *Visible Saints* (Cornell University Press, 1963); Alan Heimert, *Religion and the American Mind* (Harvard University Press, 1966); Robert Middlekauf, *The Mathers* (Oxford University Press, 1971); Larzer Ziff, *Puritanism in America* (Viking, 1973); Emory Elliott, *Power and the Pulpit in Puritan New England* (Princeton University Press, 1975); Sacvan Bercovitch *The American Jeremiad* (University of Wisconsin Press, 1978) and *The Rites of Assent* (Routledge, 1993); Philip F. Gura, *A Glimpse of Sion's Glory* (Wesleyan University Press, 1983); Harry S. Stout, *The New England Soul* (Oxford University Press, 1986); T. Dwight Bozeman, *To Live Ancient Lives* (University of North Carolina Press, 1988); Daniel Shea, *Spiritual Autobiography in Early America* (University of Wisconsin Press, 1988); Andrew Delbanco, *The Puritan Ordeal* (Harvard University Press, 1989); David Hall, *Worlds of Wonder, Days of Judgment* (Harvard University Press, 1989); Janice Knight, *Orthodoxies in Massachusetts* (Harvard University Press, 1995); Michael Colacurcio, *Doctrine and Difference* (Routledge, 1997); Darren Staloff, *The Making of an American Thinking Class* (Oxford University Press, 1998).

Among studies of Puritan and early Republican historiography, I have been especially influenced by the following: Peter Gay, *A Loss of Mastery* (University of California Press, 1966); Conrad Cherry, *God's New Israel* (Prentice Hall, 1971); Michael Kammen, *A Season of Youth* (Cornell University Press, 1978); Lester Cohen, *The Revolutionary Histories* (Cornell University Press, 1980); Donald Webber, "Historicizing the Errand," *American Literary History*, 2 (1990), 101–118; Stephen Arch, *Authorizing the Past* (Northern Illinois University Press, 1994); Nina Baym, *American Women Writers and the Work of History* (Rutgers University Press, 1995); Philip Gould, *Covenant and Republic, Historical Romance and the Politics of Puritanism* (Cambridge University Press, 1996); John Seelye,

Memory's Nation: The Place of Plymouth Rock (University of North Carolina Press, 1998).

2. George Bancroft, *History of the United States* (Boston: Little, Brown, & Co., 1869), v, 197. The fifth volume was first published in 1852.

3. Robert Lowell, "New England and Further," in *Robert Lowell: Collected Prose*, ed. Robert Giroux (New York: Farrar, Straus, & Giroux, 1987), p. 180.

4. In the introduction to *The Rites of Assent*, Bercovitch states that his own origins, upbringing and preacademic experiences led him to "an abiding suspicion of high rhetoric, especially as a blueprint of the future, and an abiding fascination with the redemptive promises of language, especially as a source of personal identity and social cohesion" (6). The value of such "suspicion" is its insight into the way language works as rhetoric; its danger is to detach words from life, thereby turning the past into concepts and concepts only.

5. Clifford Geertz, "Thick Description: Toward an Interpretive Theory of Culture," in Clifford Geertz, *The Interpretation of Cultures* (New York: Basic Books, 1973), pp. 15, 20.

6. See Bozeman, *To Live Ancient Lives*; Christopher Hill, *The Century of Revolution, 1603–1714* (New York: Norton, 1988); Stephen Foster, *The Long Argument, English Puritanism and the Shaping of New England Culture* (Chapel Hill: University of North Carolina Press, 1991).

7. See Lawrence Buell's *New England Literary Culture: From Revolution Through Renaissance* (Cambridge: Cambridge University Press, 1986), especially chapters 8 and 9, "The Concept of Puritan Ancestry" and "The Politics of Historiography."

8. In "New England and Further," Lowell observes that "The myth of the New Englander really comes into being in the nineteenth century. It was then that the great imaginative minds first clearly saw their heritage as something both to admire and to fear" (190). New England historical writing during the early Republic is a testament mostly to "admiration," as Lowell's own early poetry is mostly a testimony to "fear" (or perhaps contempt), but admiration and fear had certainly become inseparable by Hawthorne's time and were arguably inseparable once Cotton Mather had written the *Magnalia*.

9. Distinguished recent studies of New England's need to present its founding achievements as the germ of the Republic's virtue include David Waldstreicher, *In the Midst of Perpetual Fetes: The Making of American Nationalism 1776–1820* (Chapel Hill: University of North Carolina Press, 1996); Seelye, *Memory's Nation*; and Harlow L. Sheidley, *Sectional Nationalism: Massachusetts Conservative Leaders and the Transformation of America 1815–1836* (Boston: Northeastern University Press, 1998).

10. Bancroft has been fortunate in his biographers: Russell B. Nye, *George Bancroft, Brahmin Rebel* (New York: Knopf, 1944) and Lilian Handlin, *George Bancroft: The Intellectual as Democrat* (New York: Harper & Row, 1984). Whereas Nye saw Bancroft as a liberal Jacksonian democrat as well as a Democrat (much in the mold, one suspects, of Arthur Schlesinger's biography of Jackson), Lilian Handlin argues that Bancroft often praised the popular will because it worked

in cautiously conservative ways. This is an important distinction, similar to the differing ways in which nineteenth-century New England writers could derive the Puritan heritage either from John Winthrop or Roger Williams. With the notable exceptions of David Levin and Richard Vitzthum, Bancroft has not been as fortunate in his critics.

11. On early nineteenth-century historiography, and Bancroft in particular, see Joyce Appleby, Lynn Hunt, and Margaret Jacob, *Telling the Truth About History* (New York: Norton, 1994), chapters 2 and 3; also George Calcott, *History in the United States 1800–1860* (Baltimore: Johns Hopkins University Press, 1970).

12. Harlow L. Sheidley, *Sectional Nationalism: Massachusetts Conservative Leaders and the Transformation of America 1815–1836* (Boston: Northeastern University Press, 1998), p. 122.

13. Frank Kermode, *The Sense of an Ending: Studies in the Theory of Fiction* (Oxford: Oxford University Press, 1977), p. 4.

14. Stephen Nissenbaum has rightly observed that, as industrialization proceeded from the eighteenth to the twentieth century, the ideal New England was to be located ever further northward. "New England as Region and Nation," in *All over the Map: Rethinking American Regions* (Baltimore: Johns Hopkins University Press, 1996), pp. 38–61.

15. The traditional view of New England literature as the chronological development of literature written by Anglo-Americans living in New England is outlined in Perry Westbrook's *A Literary History of New England* (Bethlehem, Penn.: Lehigh University Press, 1988). Westbrook's major predecessor in studying New England regional literature in this manner is Van Wyck Brooks, *The Flowering of New England* (1936) and *New England: Indian Summer* (1940). Robert B. Slocum's two-volume bibliography *New England in Fiction: 1787–1990* (West Cornwall, Conn.: Locust Hill Press, 1994) is useful in tracking down fiction by authors left out of literary histories.

16. For other reflections on the contemporary meaning of "New England" see Nissenbaum's "New England as Region and Nation" and the introduction to Andrew Delbanco's *Writing New England: An Anthology from the Puritans to the Present* (Cambridge, Mass.: Harvard University Press, 2001), pp. xiv–xv. Dona Brown's *Inventing New England: Regional Tourism in the Nineteenth Century* (Washington, D.C.: Smithsonian Institution Press, 1995) shows how, after the Civil War, the decline of New England's rural and maritime economy was deliberately offset by the invention of "a mythic region called Old New England" (9) always ready to welcome full-pocketed urbanites to the seaboard and flatlanders to the up-country. From my perspective, "New England" was first invented by John Smith and reinvented many times before 1865.

17. Henry James, *The Bostonians* (Harmondsworth: Penguin, 1986), p. 189. The phrase "plain living and high thinking," already a cliché by the time James used it, occurs in a summary of Olive Chancellor's opinion of Miss Birdseye: "It struck Miss Chancellor (more especially) that this frumpy little missionary was the last link in a tradition, and that when she could be called away the heroic age of New England life – the age of plain living and high thinking,

of pure ideals and earnest effort, of moral passion and noble experiment – would be effectively closed" (189). Ironically, "plain living and high thinking" appears to have been first penned by Wordsworth; see David Shi, *The Simple Life: Plain Living and High Thinking in American Culture* (Oxford: Oxford University Press, 1985), p. 5.

18. Even a writer so interested in New England's separable identity as Hawthorne was to write a book on England entitled *Our Old Home*.

19. Robert Middlekauf, who dated "The Invention of New England" as late as the 1660s, coincident with the rise of the Jeremiads, argued that "the founders had no conception of New England apart from Old England." This view has been supported by Bozeman's insistence that, because the settlers of 1630 intended to restore the purity of the first Christian churches, rather than to construct a progressive theocracy, the first planters could have settled anywhere where there was no popish liturgical "invention." Both Middlekauf and Bozeman thus challenge the dominant view of New England Puritan "Errand" elaborated by Miller and Bercovitch. Given the absence of firm evidence, the debate upon the meaning of "New England" is unlikely to end. Although the Restoration of 1660 clearly created a need for the sons to publicly differentiate New England from Old, the settlers of 1630 must have had some concept of a future life that was decidedly different from Old England, and not merely a Catholic-free extension of it. Middlekauf, *Mathers*, p. 96.

20. In *Authorizing the Past*, Arch argues that the major Puritan narratives from Bradford through Cotton Mather "typify the way in which cultures use the past to generate and regenerate their sense of purpose about themselves and their futures" (viii). He demonstrates that it is not until Cotton Mather's *Magnalia* that a work even remotely similar to what we call "professional history" can be conceived (viii–ix and chapter 4).

21. Delbanco has argued persuasively that the new world experiences of the first generation were as much an immigrant "ordeal" as a messianic "errand." *Puritan Ordeal*, especially chapter 2 and pp. 116–117.

22. Oppositional self-definition is in some ways comparable to the model of seventeenth-century inter-Massachusetts hostilities advanced in Kai Erikson's *Wayward Puritans* (New York: John Wiley, 1966). Erikson, however, wrote about Puritan–non-Puritan confrontations in order to study "the sociology of deviance" – i.e., the societal causes that led to behavior predefined as deviance by the Puritan orthodoxy who presumably knew precisely who they were and what they intended. Quoting Durkheim on the "collective conscience," Erikson ascribed to the Puritans "that sense of firm ideological commitment, that willingness to participate fully in the rhythms of group life, that feeling of common heritage and common destiny which gives every society its underlying cohesion" (130). We now know, however, that there was not as much orthodoxy in Massachusetts as Erikson assumed. Collective surety emerged only rarely; defining others as "deviants" was a process more likely to lead to communal self-discovery than to its confirmation.

23. John Adams, "Governor Winthrop to Governor Bradford," *Boston Gazette*, January 1767, in *The Works of John Adams*, ed. Charles Francis Adams (Boston: Charles C. Little and James Brown, 1850), II, 485.

24. Consider the seven chapter titles within Mather's seventh, climactic book entitled *A Book of the Wars of the Lord*: "Mille Nocendi Artes," "Little Foxes: Separation and Familism," "Hydra Decapitato: First Synod, Antinomians," "Ignes Fatui: Quakers," "Wolves in Sheep's Clothing," "Arma Virosque Cano: Indian Salvages," and "Decennium Luctuosum: Indian Salvages 1688–1698."

25. William Hubbard, *A General History of New England from the Discovery to 1680* (Cambridge: Hilliard & Metcalf, 1815), p. 15.

26. Jedediah Morse and Elijah Parish, *A Compendious History of New England* (Charlestown: Samuel Etheridge, 1804), p. 351.

27. Alexis De Tocqueville, *Democracy in America*, ed. J. P. Mayer, trans. G. Lawrence (Garden City, N.Y.: Doubleday, 1969), p. 279.

28. Seelye's *Memory's Nation* provides a massive study of the way New Englanders insisted, with considerable success, that the Pilgrim legacy had long permeated the entire nation. Among academic historians, interest has recently emerged in the friction between regional and national loyalties in the early Republic. In the last chapter of *In the Midst of Perpetual Fetes: The Making of American Nationalism 1776–1820* (Chapel Hill: University of North Carolina Press, 1997), David Waldstreicher explores "the seeming contradiction of nationalist regionalism" (251). Harlow Sheidley's *Sectional Nationalism: Massachusetts Conservative Leaders and the Transformation of America, 1815–1836* (Boston: Northeastern University Press, 1998) shows how Massachusetts's Federalist/Whig establishment endeavored to speak for the nation. The very terms "sectional nationalism" and "nationalist regionalism" reflect the problem, not only of achieving *e pluribus unum*, but also of proudly insular regional cultures that advanced claims and made charges against little-known regions elsewhere.

29. Oliver Wendell Holmes, *The Autocrat at the Breakfast Table* (1858), in *The Complete Writings of Oliver Wendell Holmes* (Boston: Houghton Mifflin, 1892), I, 125.

30. Nina Baym has shown conclusively that, for the many women, mostly New Englanders, who wrote historical literature during the antebellum period, "historical memory placed them in the flow of world drama and gave their lives universal significance . . . The amalgam of Protestant Christianity, historicism, and national patriotism in women's historical writing is commonplace for the age, shared by men and women, visible in popular and scholarly texts alike" (*American Women Writers*, pp. 47–48). The phrase Baym uses to sum up these writers' sense of their place in history – "at the very vanguard of historical progress" (46) – could equally well describe one of Bancroft's basic premises about the American Republic.

31. Ralph Waldo Emerson, "Boston" (1861), in *The Complete Works of Ralph Waldo Emerson*, ed. Edward E. Emerson (Boston: Houghton Mifflin, 1906), XII, 188.

32. Cotton Mather, "A General Introduction" to *Magnalia Christi Americana* (1702), ed. Kenneth B. Murdock with the assistance of Elizabeth W. Miller (Cambridge, Mass.: Harvard University Press, 1977), p. 94.

33. Henry David Thoreau, *Walden*, ed. Sherman Paul (Boston: Houghton Mifflin, 1960), p. 227.

34. Norman Pettit has shown the high stakes involved in ascertaining where along the spectrum of assurance, certitude, and security the state of a saint's soul was thought to be. *The Heart Prepared: Grace and Conversion in Puritan Spiritual Life* (New Haven: Yale University Press, 1966).

1   OF CORN, NO CORN, AND CHRISTIAN COURAGE

1. Important studies of seventeenth-century New England's various trials, troubles, and controversies have continued the same tradition while redefining it in thoughtful and informative ways. See especially Andrew Delbanco, *The Puritan Ordeal* (Cambridge, Mass.: Harvard University Press, 1989); Philip F. Gura, *A Glimpse of Sion's Glory* (Middletown Ct.: Wesleyan University Press, 1984); and Janice Knight, *Orthodoxies in Massachusetts* (Cambridge, Mass.: Harvard University Press, 1995). Delbanco, for example, has effectively broken down the monolith of the "New England Puritan" by studying immigrants as varied kinds of British Protestants emerging from a world of oppressive enclosure.

2. The following historical studies of the first years of English settlement have proven especially helpful. On British and European backgrounds: David Hackett Fischer, *Albion's Seed* (1989); Stephen Greenblatt, *Marvelous Possessions* (1991). On British and Native American relations in New England: Francis Jennings, *The Invasion of America* (1975); Neal Salisbury, *Manitou and Providence* (1982); William Cronon, *Changes in the Land* (1983). On Virginia: Alden T. Vaughan, *American Genesis: Captain John Smith and the Founding of Virginia* (1975); Carl Bridenbaugh, *Jamestown 1544–1699* (1980); Leo Lemay, *The American Dream of Captain John Smith* (1991). On Plymouth: George D. Langdon, Jr., *Pilgrim Colony* (1966); John Demos, *A Little Commonwealth* (1970). On Massachusetts Bay: Edmund Morgan, *The Puritan Dilemma* (1958); Darrett B. Rutman, *Winthrop's Boston* (1965); T. H. Breen, *Puritans and Adventurers* (1980); Virginia DeJohn Anderson, *New England's Generation* (1991). George Percy, "Observations Gathered out of 'A Discourse of the Plantation of the Southern Colony in Virginia by the English, 1606,'" ed. David B. Quinn (Charlottesville: University Press of Virginia, 1967). First published in *Purchas his Pilgrims* (1625).

3. Edward Winslow, *Good Newes from New England* (1624), in Alexander Young, ed., *Chronicles of the Pilgrim Fathers*, 2nd edn (Boston: Charles C. Little and James Brown, 1844), p. 372. On the changing meaning of "profit" in the early seventeenth century, see William Cronon, *Changes in the Land: Indians, Colonists and the Ecology of New England* (New York: Hill & Wang, 1983), p. 76.

4. The first two New England settlements, Sagadahoc (1607) and Naumkeag (1628), suffered through a similar sequence. Half the settlers at Sagadahoc returned to England in *The Gift of God* in December 1607. Without knowing that the storehouse had burned, they informed Ferdinando Gorges that those remaining did not have enough food. Although vegetables had been planted in the fall, and a shallop sent to procure wild onions and grapes, "the winter proved soe extreme unseasonable and frosty" that the coastal Maine waters froze and "noe boat could stir upon any busines," leaving the remaining settlers virtually imprisoned in their fort for three months before Raleigh Gilbert decided to abandon the settlement. When the Winthrop fleet arrived in Naumkeag (Salem) in June 1630, they found that 80 of the 300 colonists sent over by the Massachusetts Bay Company were dead, that most of the living were sick, and that "all the corn among 'em [was] hardly sufficient to feed 'em a fortnight." On Sagadahoc, see Anon., "Relation of a Voyage to Sagadahoc" (1608), in *Early English and French Voyages*, ed. Henry S. Burrage (New York: Charles Scribner's Sons, 1932), p. 419. On the arrival in Naumkeag, see Thomas Prince, *A Chronological History of New England in the Form of Annals* (Boston: Kneeland & Green, 1730), p. 209 and *The Journal of John Winthrop, 1630–1649*, ed. R. S. Dunn and L. Yeandle (Cambridge, Mass.: Harvard University Press, 1996), p. 28, n. 58.
5. Percy, "Observations," p. 25. On the diseases that flourished in the swampy heat of Chesapeake Bay, see Fischer, *Albion's Seed*, pp. 247–252.
6. "The Proceedings of the English Colony," in John Smith, *A Map of Virginia: The Complete Works of Captain John Smith*, ed. Philip L. Barbour (Chapel Hill: University of North Carolina Press, 1986), 1, 275–276. Barbour glosses "to vild" as "too disgusting" and "occasion" as "cause."
7. William Bradford, *Of Plymouth Plantation, 1620–1647*, ed. Samuel Eliot Morison, introduction by Francis Murphy (New York: Random House, 1981), p. 75.
8. Thomas Dudley, letter to the Countess of Lincoln, March 28, 1631, in *Letters from New England: The Massachusetts Bay Colony, 1629–1638*, ed. Everett Emerson (Amherst: University of Massachusetts Press, 1976), p. 71. Hereafter cited as *Letters*. At the time Dudley's letter was written, Winthrop was beginning to suspect Dudley of hoarding corn for personal advantage.
9. Roger Clap, *Memoirs of Capt. Roger Clap* (Boston: Samuel Greene, 1731), pp. 14, 24, 25.
10. George Percy, "A Trewe Relacyon," *Tyler's Quarterly History and Genealogical Magazine*, 3 (1922), 267. I have normalized Percy's punctuation and spelling. The blasphemy and death of Hugh Price are not referred to in other early narratives of Virginia, nor is Price mentioned by Robert Beverley or William Stith. Some memory of Price's atheism must have survived in oral tradition, however, because John Fiske transformed the incident into a fireside anecdote about a madman and his Bible: "Such were the goings on in that awful time to which men long afterward alluded as the Starving Time. No wonder that one poor wretch, crazed with agony, cast his Bible into the fire, crying 'Alas! there

is no God.'" John Fiske, *Old Virginia and her Neighbours* (Boston: Houghton Mifflin, 1897), 1, 154. Since the publication of "A True Relation" in 1922, Percy's passage on Hugh Price has continued to be neglected, though Howard Mumford Jones in passing cited it as a curiosity, "a revelation of naïveté and religious faith." *Virginia Literature in the Seventeenth Century* (Charlottesville: University of Virginia Press, 1968), p. 18.

11. Among the reasons Virginia DeJohn Anderson cites to account for the comparative stability of early settlements in New England is the prevalence of families: "The ships carried mature couples, generally in their thirties, who had been married for about a decade." *New England's Generation* (Cambridge: Cambridge University Press, 1991), p. 22.

12. David Hall concluded that "seventeenth-century New Englanders were rarely able to articulate a real alternative to Christianity. Few were full-fledged atheists, and my cautionary 'few' should probably read 'none.'" *Worlds of Wonder, Days of Judgment* (Cambridge, Mass.: Harvard University Press, 1989), p. 162. T. H. Breen, contrasting the pre-revolutionary historiography of Massachusetts and Virginia, demonstrated the Virginians' comparative lack of interest in their history from the 1620s through Jefferson's *Notes on the State of Virginia*. *Puritans and Adventurers* (Oxford: Oxford University Press, 1980), pp. 164–196. Breen ascribes the difference between the two colonies to Virginia's concentration on future economic and political progress. The spiritual and civic disasters of early Jamestown, together with the consequences of single crop tobacco, surely suggest additional explanations.

13. letters of John Winthrop in *Letters*, pp. 45, 46, 47, 53, 54, 55. If Edward Winslow's July 26, 1830 letter to Bradford from Salem is accurate, the doubts John Winthrop felt about God's justice were expressed at the beginning of his Charlestown ordeal, rather than at its end. Winslow wrote that "Mr. [Isaac] Johnson received a letter from the Governor Mr. John Winthrop, manifesting the hand of God to be upon them and against them at Charlestown, in visiting them with sickness and taking divers from amongst them, not sparing the rightous but partaking with the wicked in these bodily judgments" (Bradford, *Of Plymouth Plantation*, p. 260). The subsequent sparseness of entries in Winthrop's journal during the Charlestown months may therefore indicate not only that Winthrop was harried by business, but also that he had resolved upon keeping silent about the possibility that God was "partaking with the wicked." Of such resolves is supportive endurance made.

14. *Letters*, p. 61. In fact, "our Indian corn" would not answer "for all" for at least three more years. As Winthrop was writing this letter, thirty-four hogsheads of wheat meal (English corn) were being sent from England to Massachusetts Bay, including one hogshead bought by John Cotton for delivery to future Antinomian William Coddington. See Sargent Bush, ed., *The Letters of John Cotton* (Chapel Hill: University of North Carolina Press, 2001), p. 151.

15. Perry Miller, ed., *The American Puritans* (New York: Doubleday, 1956), p. 213.

16. Samuel Sewall, *Phaenomena quaedam Apocalyptica, Ad Aspectum* NOVIS ORBIS *configurata; Or, some few Lines towards a description of the New* HEAVEN *As It*

makes to those who stand upon the NEW EARTH (Boston: Bartholomew Greene and John Allen, 1697), p. 5.

17. David S. Lovejoy argues persuasively that Sewall's hymn to Plum Island also has an unacknowledged personal motive. In his northern Massachusetts boyhood, Sewall had found a source of communal piety that might redeem him from his sinful participation in the Salem witch trials and release him from the many recent personal afflictions (the death of many family members) with which God had beset him. "Between Hell and Plum Island: Samuel Sewall and the Legacy of the Witches, 1692–1697," *New England Quarterly*, 70 (1997), 355–367.

18. Edward Taylor, "Preparatory Meditation," 1st series, 8, in *The Poems of Edward Taylor*, ed. Donald E. Stanford (New Haven: Yale University Press, 1960), pp. 18–19.

19. Nathaniel Morton, *New-England's Memorial* (Cambridge: S. Green, 1669), pp. 83, 84; Prince, *Chronological History*, p. 242; *Memoirs of Capt. Roger Clap*, pp. 4, 5.

20. Whereas Hutchinson never acknowledges the corn removal at all, Mather and Bancroft mention the discovery of the corn, but not the taking of it. There may be good reasons for the differing degrees of distortion. Although Hutchinson probably did not believe the event to be of any historical importance, Mather and Bancroft would surely have found the "taking" of the corn to be a collective embarrassment to the Saints and to the American people, respectively. Unlike Mather, Hutchinson and Bancroft, New England historians of lesser influence tried to justify the takings of the corn. William Hubbard contended that the pilgrims had "by accident stumbled upon some Indian beans, stored with baskets of their corn" which they removed "more to the apprehension of faith than of sense." William Hubbard, *A General History of New England from the Discovery to 1680*, (Cambridge: Hilliard & Metcalf, 1815), p. 55. Like Mather, Jedediah Morse avoided the word "take," preferring to insist, without claiming providential intervention, that "the corn which they [the pilgrims] *found* was the first fruit of the land to them, and incalculably important." Jedediah Morse and Elijah Parish, *A Compendious History of New England* (Charlestown: Samuel Etheridge, 1804), p. 41, italics mine.

21. The American Puritans' desire to restore the piety of the first-century Christian churches has been most fully explored by Dwight Bozeman. Bozeman's argument is the antithesis of Bancroft's long influential assumption that the Puritans are the seedbed of American liberty, democracy, and progress. Many quotations can be cited in support of either viewpoint. For my purposes, the crucial point is the greater cultural power of the progressive view. Bancroft's indifference to the possibility that the Puritans' essential purpose might have been restorative, even reactionary, was a major cause of his *History*'s resonance in its time.

22. Edward Johnson, *Wonder-Working Providence of Sion's Saviour in New England: 1628–1651*, ed. J. Franklin Jameson (New York: Charles Scribner's Sons, 1910), p. 66.

23. Cotton Mather, *Magnalia Christi Americana* (1702; Cambridge, Mass.: Harvard University Press, 1977), I, 72.

24. Hannah Adams, *A Summary History of New-England* (Dedham: H. Mann and J. H. Adams, 1799), p. 19.

25. George Bancroft, *History of the United States*, 9th edn (Boston: Little, Brown, & Co., 1841), I, 358. Volume I was first published in 1834.

26. "Discourse Delivered at Plymouth in Commemoration of the First Settlement of New England, Dec. 22 1820," in *Speeches and Forensic Arguments by Daniel Webster* (Boston: Perkins, Marvin, & Co., 1835), I, 26–27. John Seelye quotes the one extant response to Webster's famous speech: George Ticknor, not known for evangelical enthusiasm, remembered: "I was never so excited by public speaking before in my life. Three or four times I thought my temples would burst with the gush of blood . . . When I came out I was almost afraid to come near to him [Webster]. It seemed to me as if he was like the mount that might not be touched, and that burned with fire." John Seelye, *Memory's Nation: The Place of Plymouth Rock* (Chapel Hill: University of North Carolina Press, 1998), p. 66. On Webster's view of New England and American history, see Paul Erickson, "Daniel Webster's Myth of the Pilgrims," *New England Quarterly*, 57 (1984), 43–64 as well as *Memory's Nation* and Harlow Sheidley's *Sectional Nationalism* (Boston: Northeastern University Press, 1998).

27. Rufus Choate, "The Age of the Pilgrims the Heroic Period of our History," in *Addresses and Orations of Rufus Choate* (Boston: Little, Brown, & Co., 1905), pp. 76–77.

28. Delbanco, *Puritan Ordeal*, p. 191.

29. Prince, *Chronological History of New England*, pp. 242, 245, 246.

30. Bancroft, *History of the United States*, I, 467–468.

31. Bancroft regarded neither St. Augustine nor Santa Fe as settlements having a claim upon the nation's origin, and not for reasons of Anglo-Saxon prejudice only. To Bancroft, founding settlements were to be understood, not in their effect on native cultures, but rather as sites of origin for the central event in United States history, the American Revolution. Virginia was to produce Jefferson and Washington, and Massachusetts was to produce the two Adamses, whereas St. Augustine and New Mexico, being colonial outposts of the Spanish empire, could have provided nothing because they had been part of a separate economic, political and religious culture. The validity of the Black Legend was not, to Bancroft, the central problem of incorporating Spanish possessions north of Mexico into pre-1776 "America."

32. Bancroft, *History of this United States*, I, 313. This particular statement contradicts Bancroft's insistence elsewhere that liberty and independence had grown because of the impact of new world conditions *after* settlers in Jamestown and Plymouth had set foot on American land.

33. Robert Lowell, "Children of Light," *Lord Weary's Castle* (New York: Harcourt Brace, Jovanovich, 1946, 1974), p. 34.

34. Paul Mariani notes that in 1946 Lowell was reading Augustine's *Confessions. Lost Puritan: A Life of Robert Lowell* (New York: Norton, 1994), p. 141. What could be more suitable reading for so recent and decidedly Protestant a Catholic convert?

2 THOMAS MORTON: PHOENIX OF
NEW ENGLAND MEMORY

1. *The New English Canaan of Thomas Morton*, ed. Charles Francis Adams, Jr. (Boston: Prince Society), 1883, p. 278. Jack Dempsey has recently reedited the *New English Canaan* (Scituate, Mass.: Digital Scanning, 1999).
2. Among the scholarly studies of Morton and Merry Mount, the following have been particularly helpful. On Morton's life in England and New England: C. E. Banks, "Thomas Morton of Merry Mount," *Massachusetts Historical Society Proceedings*, 58 (1925), 147–193; D. F. Connors, *Thomas Morton* (New York: Twayne, 1969); Jack Dempsey, "Reading the Revels: The Riddle of May Day in New English Canaan," *Early American Literature*, 34 (1999), 283–312. On the *New English Canaan*: Robert D. Arner, "Mythology and the Maypole of Merrymount; Notes on Thomas Morton's 'Rise, Oedipus,'" *Early American Literature*, 6 (1971), 81–97; Daniel B. Shea, "'Our Old Professed Adversary': Thomas Morton and the Naming of New England," *Early American Literature*, 23 (1988), 53–69. On the historiography of the Morton–Puritan controversy: Karen Ordahl Kupperman, "Thomas Morton, Historian," *New England Quarterly*, 50 (1977), 660–664; Michael Zuckerman, "Pilgrims in the Wilderness: Community, Modernity and the Maypole of Merry Mount," *New England Quarterly*, 50 (1977), 255–277. On renderings of Morton and Merry Mount in fiction, poetry, drama, and opera: Richard Clark Sterne, "Puritans at Merry Mount: Variations on a Theme," *American Quarterly*, 22 (1970), 846–880; Connors, *Morton*, pp. 123–132. Karen Kupperman, Daniel Shea, and Jack Dempsey have provided new insight into the political and literary purposes of Morton's supposed obscurantism. This chapter represents a complete recasting of my article "Fictions of Merry Mount," *American Quarterly*, 29 (1977), 1–30.
3. *New English Canaan*, ed. Adams, pp. 312–313.
4. *The Journal of John Winthrop, 1630–1649*, ed. R. S. Dunn and L. Yeandle (Cambridge, Mass.: Harvard University Press, 1996), p. 259.
5. William Bradford, *Of Plymouth Plantation, 1620–1647*, ed. Samuel Eliot Morison (New York: Random House, 1981), p. 239.
6. Thomas Dudley, letter to the Countess of Lincoln, March 12, 1631, in *Letters from New England: The Massachusetts Bay Colony, 1629–1638*, ed. Everett Emerson (Amherst: University of Massachusetts Press, 1976), p. 74.
7. *Journal of Winthrop*, ed. Dunn and Yeandle, p. 39.
8. In all probability, the third section of the *New English Canaan* was written in 1634, just as the Charter revocation movement was gathering strength; the first and second sections of Morton's book were probably written later and perhaps shortly before publication in 1637. On the dating of Morton's text, see Connors, *Morton*, pp. 33–35. Shea, "Old Professed Adversary," pp. 62–65; Dempsey, "Reading the Revels," pp. 297–298.
9. Dempsey's ingenious and convincing unraveling of "Rise, Oedipus" has given Morton's poem the most coherent meaning it is ever likely to have ("Reading the Revels," pp. 287–296). It is important to remember, however, that Morton's poem was, in all probability, itself a late construct, composed in the late 1630s

as part of the historical artifice of the *New English Canaan*. If we are to believe that "Rise, Oedipus," which Morton claims to have "inserted" (277) into his text, had actually been affixed to the maypole in 1627, then we must account for Morton's removing the poem from the maypole and retaining it for ten years in spite of the razing of his plantation, three Atlantic crossings, and all the travails of his life.

10. In a letter to the Earl of Clarendon written in the 1660s, Samuel Maverick claimed that Morton had held a patent preceding those held by Endicott and Winthrop. No record of Morton's or Wollaston's patents for the land has been found ("The Clarendon Papers," *New York Historical Society Collections* [1869], 40).

11. On the dates of composition of *Of Plymouth Plantation*, see Jesper Rosenmeier, "'With my owne eyes': William Bradford's *Of Plymouth Plantation*," in *The American Puritan Imagination: Essays in Revaluation*, ed. Sacvan Bercovitch (Cambridge: Cambridge University Press, 1974), pp. 77–106.

12. Morton had been in great measure responsible for Winslow's being jailed in England for sixteen weeks during 1635.

13. Edward Johnson, *The History of New England: 1628–1651*, ed. J. Franklin Jameson (New York: Charles Scribner's Sons, 1910), pp. 154–155.

14. Quotations from four widely read histories before 1900 will serve to convey both the need to expunge and the pattern of perpetuation. Nathaniel Morton: "Wickedness was beginning, and would have further proceeded, had it not been prevented timely" (*New England's Memorial* [Cambridge: S. Green, 1669], p. 80). Cotton Mather: "a plantation of rude, lewd, mad English people, who did propose to themselves a gainful trade with the Indians, but quickly came to nothing" (*Magnalia Christi Americana* [1702], I, 59). Thomas Hutchinson: "One Morton . . . contrived to make himself chief, changed the name of Mount Wollaston to Merry Mount, set all the servants free, erected a maypole, and lived a life of dissipation, until all the stock, intended for trade, was consumed" (*History* [1764], I, 8–9). John Gorham Palfrey: "a witty and knowing but shiftless, reckless, graceless, shameless rake" (*History* [1859], I, 232). As Dempsey has remarked of Moses Coit Tyler's dismissal of the *New English Canaan* from the canon of American literature, "what other early American text has been treated this way?" ("Reading the Revels," p. 299).

15. C. F. Adams, Jr. "Thomas Morton of Merry Mount," *New English Canaan*, ed. Adams, p. 48.

16. For biographical details about the fourth generation of John Adams's family, see Paul C. Nagle, *Descent from Glory* (Oxford: Oxford University Press, 1983), especially chapter 15. Thomas Morton's book had resurfaced in New England intellectual life when John Quincy Adams found a copy of the *New English Canaan* in Berlin and brought it back to his father, who then wrote to Jefferson in October 1812 that, although Morton was "not worth much," "the Character of the Miscreant, however, is not wholly contemptible" because "Morton was not wholly destitute of learning."

17. Nagle, *Descent from Glory*, p. 303.

18. Charles Francis Adams, Jr., *Three Episodes of Massachusetts History* (Boston: Houghton Mifflin, 1892), 1, 170.

19. Earlier texts of self-consciously modernist and neo-Freudian Puritan-baiting include Van Wyck Brooks, *The Wine of the Puritans* (1909); H. L. Mencken, "The Last New Englander" (1926) and "Puritanism as a Literary Force" (1917); Randolph Bourne, "The Puritan Will to Power" (1917); and D. H. Lawrence's *Studies in Classic American Literature* (1925).

20. William Carlos Williams, *In the American Grain* (New York: Albert and Charles Boni, 1925), p. 63.

21. Williams's and Lawrence's attitudes would resurface in Richard Slotkin's influential *Regeneration through Violence* (1973). To exemplify the theory advanced in his title, Slotkin remakes Morton as a selfless prophet who offered earthy wisdom to white civilization. "Morton remains true to his major theme; that the Englishman must withhold nothing of himself from the wilderness and the Indian but merge thoroughly with them and refresh himself at the sources of human passions and affection." *Regeneration through Violence: The Mythology of the American Frontier, 1600–1860* (Middletown, Conn.: Wesleyan University Press, 1973), p. 62. To see Morton as a humorless prophet may tell us more about attitudes of the late 1960s than about the lawyerly royalist tactician who in 1637 had created "Mine Host."

22. See especially Dana D. Nelson, "Sympathy as Strategy in Sedgwick's *Hope Leslie*," in *The Culture of Sentiment*, ed. Shirley Samuels (Oxford: Oxford University Press, 1992), pp. 200ff.; Philip Gould, "Catharine Sedgwick's Recital of the Pequot War," chapter 2 of *Covenant and Republic: Historical Romance and the Politics of Puritanism* (Cambridge: Cambridge University Press, 1996), pp. 61–90; Judith Fetterly, "'My Sister! My Sister!': The Rhetoric of Catharine Sedgwick's *Hope Leslie*," *American Literature*, 70 (1998), 481–516; Karen Woods Weierman, "Reading and Writing *Hope Leslie*: Catharine Maria Sedgwick's Indian 'Connections,'" *New England Quarterly*, 75 (2002), 415–443.

23. Catharine Maria Sedgwick, *Hope Leslie; or, Early Times in the Massachusetts (1827)*, ed. Mary Kelley (New Brunswick: Rutgers University Press, 1987), p. 198. Although Gardiner and Morton had been in the service of Sir Ferdinando Gorges in England in the 1630s, and had almost surely known each other in 1629 during Morton's second sojourn at Merry Mount, Gardiner's return to Merry Mount in 1644 is entirely Sedgwick's fictional invention. Perhaps it is for this reason that Sedgwick decided to name him Sir Philip rather than Sir Christopher Gardiner.

24. As representative Puritan parents, William and Martha Sedgwick maintain an admirable devotion to family that derives from a religious faith conceived as oppressively narrow-minded. In his study of *Hope Leslie*, Philip Gould clarifies the contemporary thrust of Sedgwick's terminology by contending that, for her and her age, the term "Virtue" signified not only the tenets of classical republicanism, but also the benevolent piety so integral to Scottish common sense philosophy (*Covenant and Republic*, p. 62).

25. *The Correspondence of John Lothrop Motley*, ed. George William Curtis (New York: Harper & Bros, 1889), i, 8.

26. As Michael Bell showed many years ago, this particular variant of a happy marital ending was a recurrent paradigm in historical novels about the Puritans written during the antebellum period. *Hawthorne and the Historical Romance of New England* (Princeton: Princeton University Press, 1972).

27. John Lothrop Motley, *Merry Mount: A Romance of the Massachusetts Colony* (Boston: James Munroe, 1849), ii, 249. Page references are to the first volume unless otherwise noted.

28. John Lothrop Motley, "The Polity of the Puritans," *North American Review*, 69 (1849), 472.

29. "And next, among these Puritans and Roundheads, we observe the very model of a Cavalier, with the curling lovelock, the fantastically trimmed beard, the embroidery, the ornamented rapier, the gilded dagger, and all the other fop-pishnesses that distinguished the wild gallants who rode headlong to their overthrow in the cause of King Charles. This is Morton of Merry Mount." Nathaniel Hawthorne, "Main Street," in *The Snow-Image and Uncollected Tales*, ed. J. D. Crowley, Centenary Edition (Columbus: Ohio State University Press, 1974), xi, 62. The sentence offers only a limp stereotype, suggesting that, in his best historical tales, Hawthorne had known exactly whom not to write about.

30. Nathaniel Hawthorne, "The May-Pole of Merry Mount," in *Twice-Told Tales*, ed. J. D. Crowley, Centenary Edition (Columbus: Ohio State University Press, 1974) ix, 63.

31. Nathaniel Hawthorne, "Endicott and the Red Cross," in *Twice-Told Tales*, ed. Crowley, ix, 441.

32. In a late-life (1976) interview Lowell insisted that the apocalyptic pessimism of *The Old Glory* should not be lessened by confining the play's meaning to a topical protest against the Vietnam War. The trilogy aimed at a wider historical reach. "The plays were finished," Lowell said, "in 1962, before Vietnam was really in the air as an important disaster. I think they are prophetic in a way. I made changes to fit American history into an American catastrophe which was beginning to emerge." Lowell, interview with A. Alvarez, *Robert Lowell: Interviews and Memoirs*, ed. Jeffrey Meyers (Ann Arbor: University of Michigan Press, 1988), p. 126.

33. Robert Lowell, *The Old Glory*, rev. edn (New York: Farrar, Straus, Giroux, 1968), p. 9.

34. Lowell, interview with A. Alvarez, *Lowell: Interviews and Memoirs*, p. 126.

35. Peter Ackroyd, *Milton in America* (New York: Nan A. Talese/Doubleday, 1996), pp. 31, 30, 157.

3 TRYING ANNE

1. Michael Winship has plausibly argued that, because John Wheelwright's trial was the historical climax of the controversy, Anne Hutchinson was not the central figure of the "Antinomian Crisis," which should more accurately be

called the "Free Grace Controversy." Michael R. Winship, *Making Heretics: Militant Protestantism and Free Grace in Massachusetts, 1636–1641* (Princeton: Princeton University Press, 2002), p. 1. Because my interest is in the historiography of the trial, I accept the long-presumed centrality of Hutchinson and the customary use of the term "Antinomian."

2. David D. Hall, ed., *The Antinomian Controversy, 1636–1638* (Middletown, Conn.: Wesleyan University Press, 1968), p. 371. Hereafter cited in parenthesis in the main text.

3. Even among late twentieth-century scholars, the multidimensional nature of the Antinomian Conflict has led to startlingly different but quite plausible interpretations that often seem to pass one another along their several paths toward new understanding. To Emory Battis, following Bernard Bailyn, the conflict at base reflected an economic tension between new Boston merchants and established landowners, in which Anne Hutchinson's theology (given her presumed "psychological imbalance") was secondary. William K. B. Stoever's *A Faire and Easy Way to Heaven* counters Battis's economic interpretation by concentrating on Reformation theology, arguing for the determinative importance, not only of Perry Miller's model of covenant theology (minus preparationism), but also for the influence of an antinomian tradition in Old England at the time of John Cotton's and Anne Hutchinson's departures to New England. Janice Knight, however, sees two long-contending Puritan orthodoxies, derived from William Ames and Richard Sibbes, which led, in the constricted New England setting, to the effective quelling of Sibbesian notions of free grace. Daren Staloff subordinates theological and economic considerations to political ones, contending that the Antinomian Controversy shows the need for the ruling alliance of magistracy and clergy to find the measures and the theology needed to retain social control. Louise Breen has recently contended that Winthrop and most ministers were defending local authority against Hutchinson's form of transatlantic Protestantism.

Surely none of these viewpoints can be denied its importance, but if all remain plausible, no single one can be fully accepted. In the fullest study of the controversy to date, Michael Winship concludes: "As for what the free grace controversy was about, that cannot be reduced to a single issue" (*Making Heretics*, p. 228). See Emory Battis, *Saints and Sectaries: Anne Hutchinson and the Antinomian Controversy in the Massachusetts Bay Company* (Chapel Hill: University of North Carolina Press, 1962), p. 51; William K. B. Stoever, *A Faire and Easie Way to Heaven: Covenant Theology and Antinomianism in Early Massachusetts* (Middletown, Conn.: Wesleyan University Press, 1978); Janice Knight, *Orthodoxies in Massachusetts: Rereading American Puritanism* (Cambridge, Mass.: Harvard University Press, 1994), especially chapter 1; Darren Staloff, *The Making of an American Thinking Class: Intellectuals and Intelligentsia in Puritan Massachusetts* (Oxford: Oxford University Press, 1998), especially chapters 3 and 4; Louise A. Breen, *Transgressing the Bounds: Subversive Enterprises among the Puritan Elite in Massachusetts, 1630–1692* (Oxford: Oxford University Press, 2001), chapter 1.

4. *The Journal of John Winthrop, 1630–1649*, ed. R. S. Dunn and L. Yeandle (Cambridge, Mass.: Harvard University Press, 1996), p. 105.

5. Surely the elders' words were influenced by their memory of Paul's warning: "I appeal to you, brethren, to take note of those who create dissensions and difficulties, in opposition to the doctrine which you have been taught. Avoid them. For such persons do not serve our Lord Christ but their own appetites, and by fair and flattering words they deceive the hearts of the simple minded" (Romans 16:17–18).

6. George Bancroft, *History of the United States*, 9th edn (Boston: Little, Brown, & Co., 1841) I, 363. William Stoever noted Cotton's remarkable "capacity for verbal obscurity," and then wondered "whether Cotton, in a given instance, was obscure because he was in an unsettled interval between convictions, because his position was insufficiently thought through, or because he wished to conceal something is difficult to say" (*Faire and Easie Way to Heaven*, pp. 39–40).

7. John Calvin, *Institutes of the Christian Religion*, ed. John T. McNeill and Ford Lewis Battles (Philadelphia: Westminster Press, 1960), I, 745, 786. After extensive study of the meanings of biblical usages of the terms "Justification" and "Sanctification," the authors of *A Theological Word Book of the Bible* (New York: Macmillan Co., 1951) concluded: "it is tempting for the sake of logical neatness to make a clean division between the two; but the temptation must be resisted" because of "a certain inevitable looseness of definition" (218, 219).

8. *Journal of John Winthrop*, p. 115.

9. T. S. Eliot, "Burnt Norton," *Four Quartets*, in *The Complete Poems and Plays 1909–1950* (New York: Harcourt, Brace, & World, 1952), p. 121.

10. Alan Heimert, *Religion and the American Mind from the Great Awakening to the Revolution* (Cambridge, Mass.: Harvard University Press, 1966), p. 239. Staloff argues that the two trials, rather than posing a problem of church–state relations, coalesce to establish the control of "ministerial intellectuals and magisterial intelligentsia" within the Commonwealth (*Making of an American Thinking Class*, p. 72).

11. Charles Francis Adams, Jr., *Three Episodes of Massachusetts History* (Boston: Houghton Mifflin & Co., 1892), I, 514, 515.

12. John Cotton was to claim, in a letter to John Wheelwright in 1640, that he had been unaware of the "damnable opinions" of some followers of Wheelwright and Hutchinson until the convening of the synod in 1637, when he realized that "all these Bastard-opinions which were then delivered, would be fathered upon the members of our church." Sargent Bush, ed., *The Letters of John Cotton* (Chapel Hill: University of North Carolina Press, 2000), p. 303.

13. See Winship's account of the motives and circumstances of Thomas Shepard's "relentless heresy hunting" (*Making Heretics*, p. 227, chapter 1 *et passim*).

14. The scholarly work, which first effectively challenged Perry Miller's model of orthodoxy, is Philip Gura's *A Glimpse of Sion's Glory: Puritan Radicalism in New England, 1620–1660* (Middletown, Conn.: Wesleyan University Press, 1983). The related argument that Puritan orthodoxy struggled with the problems

of absorbing a sequence of sectarian splinter groups is developed in Stephen Foster's *The Long Argument: English Puritanism and the Shaping of New England Culture* (Chapel Hill: University of North Carolina Press, 1991).

15. Edward Johnson, *Wonder-Working Providence of Sion's Saviour in New England: 1628–1651*, ed. J. Franklin Jameson (New York: Charles Scribner's Sons, 1910), p. 203.

16. Thomas Shepard, "Memoir" of 1644, in *Chronicles of the First Planters of the Colony of Massachusetts Bay*, ed. A. Young (Boston: Charles C. Little and James Brown, 1846), pp. 550–551.

17. Samuel Eliot Morison, *The Founding of Harvard College* (Cambridge, Mass.: Harvard University Press, 1935), p. 179.

18. Hall, *Antinomian Controversy*, p. 325.

19. Nathaniel Ward, *The Simple Cobler of Aggawam in America* (1647), ed. P. M. Zall (Lincoln: University of Nebraska Press, 1969), pp. 6, 7.

20. On the resolution of the Antinomian Controversy as a victory of local autonomy over international Protestantism see Louise Breen, *Transgressing the Bounds: Subversive Enterprises among the Puritan Elite in Massachusetts, 1630–1692* (Oxford: Oxford University Press, 2001), chapter 1.

21. "A Coppie of the Liberties of the Massachusets Colonie in New England," in *Puritan Political Ideas 1558–1794*, ed. Edmund S. Morgan (Indianapolis: Bobbs-Merrill, 1965), p. 193.

22. Winthrop, "A Model of Christian Charity," in *Journal of Winthrop*, ed. Dunn and Yeandle, p. 8.

23. John Winthrop, speech to the General Court at Hingham, in *Puritan Political Ideas*, ed. Morgan, pp. 138, 139.

24. Michael Winship has surmised that George Bancroft was the first to use, or at least to popularize, the term "Antinomian Controversy" (*Making Heretics*, p. 247, n.1); Winthrop's and Weld's title and preface suggest that Bancroft was following long-established tradition.

25. On this point William Stoever concludes that "Weld had a point to make and was somewhat sweeping in his judgment . . . Weld's characterization of their [the Hutchinsonians'] manner of resolving these tensions was not, however inaccurate" (*Faire and Easie Way to Heaven*, p. 12).

26. See the fine discussion of these two patterns in Amy Schrager Lang's *Prophetic Woman: Anne Hutchinson and the Problem of Dissent in the Literature of New England* (Berkeley: University of California Press, 1987), especially chapters 3 and 4. I emphasize other important aspects of the historiography of the Antinomian Crisis (Bancroft, Palfrey, and Charles Adams) not in order to slight Lang's findings, but to avoid repeating them.

27. Edward Johnson, *Wonder-Working Providence of Sion's Saviour in New England*, ed. J. Franklin Jameson (New York: Charles Scribner's Sons, 1910), p. 124.

28. Cotton Mather, *Magnalia Christi Americana; Or, The Ecclesiastical History of New-England* (1702; Hartford, Conn.: Silas Andrus, 1820), II, 440. Robert Middlekauf has shown that, though Cotton Mather worried about compromising the Covenant of Grace with talk of Good Works, he also was fond of

proclaiming that "a workless faith was a worthless faith." *The Mathers* (Oxford: Oxford University Press, 1971), pp. 235, 243.

29. Charles Chauncy, *Seasonable Thoughts on the State of Religion in New England* (Boston: Rogers and Fowle, 1743), facsimile reprint edition, the Regina Press, 1975, n.p. On Chauncy and antinomianism, see Lang, *Prophetic Woman*, chapter 4.

30. Even if Chauncy had not intended to wield "Antinomian" as a smear word, the popularity of *Seasonable Thoughts*, together with the authority of Charles Chauncy's position, soon made it one. Eventually, even a leading New Light like Joseph Bellamy could express his worries about the excesses of the Awakening, and their possible connection to present heresies, by citing "Antinomianism" as the quality they possessed in common. Bellamy's *A Blow at the Root of the Refined Antinomianism of the Present Age* (1763) claims a distinction between the "Gross Antinomianism" of the past, in which the presumed Elect believed they were Justified *before* Faith, and the "Refined Antinomianism" of the present, in which the presumed Elect believe that, through Justification *by* Faith, they now have absolute Assurance. See Joseph Bellamy, *A Blow at the Root of the Refined Antinomianism of the Present Age* (Boston: S. Kneeland, 1763), p. 45. The distortion of "Antinomianism" here needed to keep Hutchinson's heresy applicable to a more latitudinarian and universalist age is nothing less than bizarre.

31. George Bancroft, *History of the United States of America*, 9th edn (Boston: Little, Brown, & Co., 1841), 1, 387. Parenthetical page references to Bancroft's *History* in this chapter are to volume 1.

32. Thomas Jefferson, letter to Benjamin Rush, September 23, 1800, in *The Life and Selected Writings of Thomas Jefferson*, ed. Adrienne Koch and William Peden (New York: Random House, 1944), p. 558.

33. John Gorham Palfrey, *The History of New England* (Boston: Little, Brown, & Co., 1859), 1, 509. Parenthetical page references to Palfrey's *History* in this chapter are to volume 1.

34. Charles Francis Adams, Jr., *Three Episodes of Massachusetts History* (Cambridge, Mass.: Houghton, Mifflin, 1892), 1, 396. Except as noted, parenthetical page references to Adams's *Three Episodes* are to volume 1.

35. Charles Adams is concerned to note, for example, that William Coddington owned Merry Mount's lands before the Adams family, and that John Wheelwright was the first minister in the vicinity. Whatever connection Adams intended to make between Merry Mounters and Antinomians remains, however, quite undeveloped.

36. *Three Episodes of Massachusetts History*, 1, 399. Behind Charles Adams's comment surely lies a reading of *The Scarlet Letter*, in particular of the passage in which Hawthorne connects Anne Hutchinson to the feminism of the 1840s. Houghton Mifflin began publishing its collected edition of Hawthorne's works during the decade prior to its publication of Adams's *Three Episodes of Massachusetts History*. The ways in which the characterization of Hester

Prynne reflects antinomian and/or 1840s feminist concerns has been the focus of much distinguished scholarship. See Michael Colacurcio, "The Footsteps of Anne Hutchinson," *ELH*, 39 (1972), 459–494; Sacvan Bercovitch, *The Office of the Scarlet Letter* (Baltimore: Johns Hopkins University Press, 1991); Lang, *Prophetic Woman*, chapter 7.

37. John Winthrop, *A Short Story of the Rise, Reign and Ruine of the Antinomians, Familists and Libertines* (1644), in Hall, *Antinomians Controversy*, p. 319; Jedediah Morse, *A Compendious History of New England* (Charlestown: Samuel Etheridge, 1804), p. 135; Nathaniel Hawthorne, "Mrs. Hutchinson" (1830), in *Selected Tales and Sketches*, ed. Michael Colacurcio (New York: Viking, 1987), p. 15.

38. Harriet Vaughan Cheney, *A Peep at the Pilgrims in Sixteeen Hundred Thirty-Six* (Boston: Phillips, Sampson, & Co., 1850), p. 330; Eliza Buckminster Lee, *Naomi: or, Boston, Two Hundred Years Ago* (Boston: W. M. Crosby and H. P. Nichols, 1848), p. 43. For interpretations of Mrs. Lee's paragraph that compare her view of Mrs. Hutchinson to her view of the Quakers, see Michael Bell, *Hawthorne and the Historical Romance of New England* (Princeton: Princeton University Press, 1971), pp. 96–97 and Lang, *Prophetic Woman*, pp. 155–160.

39. In *Saints and Sectaries* (Chapel Hill: University of North Carolina Press, 1962), Battis had described Hutchinson as a menopausal neurotic whose mysticism was traceable to the exaltations of repeated pregnancies, and whose "psychological imbalance" was expressed "in the concurrent and congruent roles of mystic, Antinomian, and religious agitator" (6, 51, 55).

40. The anachronisms of Heidish's novel pale in comparison to Selma Williams's 1981 biography of Hutchinson entitled, with minimal subtlety, *Divine Rebel* (New York: Holt, Rinehart, and Winston, 1981). Williams makes Hutchinson over into an advocate of "individualism," "progress," and "androgyny." In at least six passages, Williams contends that Hutchinson was a forthright disbeliever in the scriptural account of the fall of man and in the use made of it by Christian churches and theologians. To Williams, the Antinomian Controversy was about "individual responsibility versus tyrannic supervision" or "chaos versus stability" (94).

41. Andrew Delbanco, *The Puritan Ordeal* (Cambridge, Mass.: Harvard University Press, 1989), p. 138.

PART 2 HEADNOTE

1. Urian Oakes, *New England Pleaded With* (Cambridge: Samuel Greene, 1673), pp. 18, 19, 32, 25.

2. Ibid., pp. 19, 10, 21.

3. Increase Mather, "Preface" to Urian Oakes, *A Seasonable Discourse* (Cambridge: Samuel Greene, 1682), n.p.

4. Oakes, *A Seasonable Discourse*, pp. 19, 20.

4 A CLOUD OF BLOOD: KING PHILIP'S WAR

1. Robert Lowell, "The Park Street Cemetery," *Land of Unlikeness* (Cummington, Mass.: Cummington Press, 1944), n.p.
2. Robert Lowell, "At the Indian Killer's Grave," *Lord Weary's Castle* (New York: Harcourt Brace, Jovanovich, 1974), pp. 60–63.
3. Jill Lepore, *The Name of War: King Philip's War and the Origins of American Identity* (New York: Knopf, 1998), p. 219.
4. Benjamin Trumbull's *A Complete History of Connecticut* (New Haven: Maltby, Goldsmith & Co., 1818) made the first informed estimate of English deaths: "about one man in eleven was killed and every eleventh family was burnt out" (1, 351). The figures about Massachusetts's debt are from Michael Pugliosi's *Puritan Besieged: The Legacies of King Philip's War in the Massachusetts Bay Colony* (Lanham, Md.: University Press of America, 1991), p. 66. A recent and careful comparative estimate is that, by war's end, the "death rate was nearly twice that of the Civil War and more than seven times that of World War II." E. B. Schultz and M. J. Tougias, *King Philip's War* (Woodstock, Vt: Countryman Press, 1999), p. 4.
5. Richard Slotkin, "Introduction" to *So Dreadfull a Judgment: Puritan Responses to King Philip's War, 1676–1677*, ed. Richard Slotkin and James K. Folsom (Middletown, Conn.: Wesleyan University Press, 1978), p. 3.
6. Lepore, *Name of War*, pp. 5–8, 26 *et passim*.
7. James D. Drake has recently argued that King Philip's War was in fact a "civil war" because by the 1670s "the Indians and the English became one society by virtue of their shared social space and economy." *King Philip's War: Civil War in New England* (Amherst: University of Massachusetts Press, 1999), p. 14. Although Drake's argument helps to explain why Indians fought on both sides, insisting on the term "civil war" is a misleading overstatement. No group of Englishmen fought with the Indians. Except for isolated individuals, the Indians most amenable to English culture lived in the separate "Praying Towns." There seems no evidence that any New England Indian people accepted the *vacuum domicilum* argument for land-ownership. The Pequot War (1636) and the military readiness promoted by the forming of the United Colonies of New England (1643) demonstrate that "shared social space and economy" was not widespread.
8. On the ecopolitical system of the sachems, see William S. Simmons, *Spirit of the New England Tribes: Indian History and Folklore 1620–1984* (Hanover, N.H.: University Press of New England, 1986), chapter 2.
9. Francis Jennings, *The Invasion of America: Indians, Colonialism, and the Cant of Conquest* (New York: Norton, 1976), p. 298; Increase Mather, "An Earnest Exhortation to the Inhabitants of New England" (1676), in *So Dreadfull a Judgment*, ed. Slotkin and Folsom, p. 174. On Increase Mather's calculatedly Puritan self-identity during his youthful years, see Michael G. Hall, *The Last American Puritan: The Life of Increase Mather* (Middletown, Conn.: Wesleyan University Press, 1988), especially chapter 2.

10. Increase Mather, "Earnest Exhortation," p. 179.

11. Jennings, *Invasion of America*, p. 181.

12. Douglas Edward Leach, *Flintlock and Tomahawk: New England in King Philip's War* (New York: Macmillan, 1958), p. 250.

13. See Alden Vaughan, *New England Frontier: Puritans and Indians 1620–1675* (Boston: Little, Brown, & Co., 1965), pp. 55, 123.

14. Increase Mather, "A Brief History of the Warr with the Indians in New-England" (1676), in *So Dreadfull a Judgment*, ed. Slotkin and Folsom, p. 115.

15. Cotton Mather, *Magnalia Christi Americana* (1702; Hartford, Conn.: Silas Andrus, 1820), II, 480.

16. Increase Mather, "Brief History of the Warr," p. 141.

17. Cotton Mather, *Magnalia Christi Americana*, II, 501, 502.

18. John Foster's map of New England included in Hubbard's *Narrative* (1677) draws a regional borderline west of New Haven (very near the present New York border) and then projects it due north.

19. Samuel Nowell, "Abraham in Arms" (1678), in *So Dreadfull a Judgment*, ed. Slotkin and Folsom, p. 287.

20. Increase Mather, "An Earnest Exhortation to the Inhabitants of New England" (Boston: John Foster, 1676), p. 26.

21. Samuel Willard, "The Heart Garrisoned," sermon delivered before the Artillery Company of Boston, June 5, 1676 (Cambridge: Samuel Green, 1676), pp. 16, 17.

22. William Hubbard, "The Happiness of a People in the Wisdom of their Rulers" (Boston: John Foster, 1676), pp. 48, 49.

23. Urian Oakes, "The Sovereign Efficacy of Divine Providence" (Boston: printed for Samuel Sewall, 1682), p. 10. This sermon had been delivered before the Boston Artillery Company on September 10, 1677, five years prior to its publication, and at the moment when the war seemed to have ended in triumph.

24. Samuel Willard, "A Sermon Occasioned by the Death of the Much Honored John Leveret Esq." (Boston: John Foster, 1679).

25. John Easton, "A Relacion of the Indyan Warre" (1675), in Charles Lincoln, ed., *Narratives of the Indian Wars: 1675–1699* (New York: Charles Scribner's Sons, 1913), p. 17.

26. Wait Still Winthrop, "Some Meditations Councerning our Honourable Gentlemen and Fellow-Souldiers, in Pursuit of those Barbarous Natives in the Narragansit-Country" (1675), reprinted New London, Conn., April 4, 1721.

27. Nathaniel Saltonstall, "The Present State of New England" (1675), in Lincoln, *Narratives of the Indian Wars*, p. 46.

28. Benjamin Tompson, "Prologue" to "New England's Crisis" (1676) in *Benjamin Tompson, Colonial Bard: A Critical Edition*, ed. Peter White (University Park: Pennsylvania State University Press, 1980), p. 85.

29. Increase Mather, "The Day of Trouble is Near," sermon preached on December 11, 1673 (Cambridge, Mass.: Marmaduke Johnson, 1674), p. 26.

30. Jill Lepore's insight into Increase Mather's harshness and ambition eventually leads to her describing him as "the viciously unsympathetic Increase Mather"

(*Name of War*, p. 150). I do not share this judgment. Whatever Mather's personal motives, his refusal to temper his accusations made him one of the few eastern Massachusetts leaders able to conceive that New England might have wronged the Indian.

31. Increase Mather, "An Earnest Exhortation," in *So Dreadfull a Judgment*, p. 187.

32. Increase Mather, "Brief History of the Warr," p. 125.

33. Richard Hutchinson, "The Warr in New England Visibly Ended" (1677), in Lincoln, *Narratives of the Indian Wars*, p. 106.

34. William Hubbard, "Epistle Dedicatory" to *The Present State of New-England, Being a Narrative of the Troubles with the Indians* (1677), facsimile reproduction, ed. Cecelia Tichi (Bainbridge, N.Y.: Mail-Print, 1972), p. 11. On jealousies and differences between Increase Mather and William Hubbard, see Anne Nelson, "King Philip's War and the Hubbard–Mather Rivalry," *William and Mary Quarterly*, 27 (1970), 615–629, and Dennis R. Perry, "'Novelties and Stile which all out-do': William Hubbard's Historiography Reconsidered," *Early American Literature*, 29 (1994), 166–182.

35. Cotton Mather, *Magnalia Christi Americana*, II, 494.

36. The phrases in this paragraph are quoted *seriatim* from: Captain Thomas Wheeler, "A Thankefull Remembrance of Gods Mercy," in *So Dreadfull a Judgment*, p. 247; Hubbard, *Present State of New-England*, p. 33; Increase Mather, "Brief History of the Warr," p. 92; Saltonstall, "Present State of New-England," p. 36.

37. Hubbard, *Present State of New-England*, p. 32.

38. Bharati Mukerjee, *The Holder of the World* (New York: Knopf, 1993), p. 29.

39. Jill Lepore provides an effectively macabre summary of incidents of beheading (*Name of War*, pp. 178–180). On the Puritans' perceptions of wartime atrocities, see also James Drake, "Restraining Atrocity: The Conduct of King Philip's War," *New England Quarterly*, 70 (1997), 33–56.

40. Hubbard, *Present State of New-England*, p. 19.

41. Ibid., "Postscript," n.p.

42. Nathaniel Saltonstall, "A New and Further Narrative of the State of New-England," dated July 22, 1676, in Lincoln, *Narratives of the Indian Wars*, p. 91.

43. Benjamin Tompson, "New Englands Tears for her Present Miseries" (1676), in *Tompson: Colonial Bard*, ed. White, pp. 113–114.

44. Increase Mather, "Brief History of the Warr," p. 142.

45. Cotton Mather, *Magnalia Christi Americana*, II, 498–499.

46. Simmons, *Spirit of the New England Tribes*, pp. 141–142.

47. See Kenneth Silverman, *The Life and Times of Cotton Mather* (New York: Columbia University Press, 1985), pp. 19–20.

48. Jennings, *Invasion of America*, pp. 325–326.

49. Stephen Saunders Webb, *1676: The End of American Independence* (New York: Knopf, 1984), pp. 221–222.

50. Cotton Mather, *Decennium Luctuosum* (1699), in Lincoln, *Narratives of the Indian Wars*, p. 184.

51. Mary Rowlandson, *The Soveraignty and Goodness of* GOD, *Together with the Faithfulness of his Promises Displayed: Being a Narrative of the Captivity and Restauration of Mrs. Mary Rowlandson* (1682), in Lincoln, *Narratives of the Indian Wars*, p. 118.

52. Ibid., pp. 119, 120, 162, 163. The assumption that a frontier minister's wife in 1675 could not possibly have understood her geographical and historical circumstances has long since been shown to be fallacious. The Rowlandsons had begun housing Increase Mather on his trips to the Connecticut River valley as early as 1664. After her ransom, Mrs. Rowlandson lived for a time in Boston, where she became acquainted with William Hubbard and Thomas Shepard Jr. The histories of Hubbard and Increase Mather were available to her in Boston before she began writing her narrative. On Mary Rowlandson's life, and the circumstances of the narrative's publication, see Michelle Burnham, *Captivity and Sentiment: Cultural Exchange in American Literature, 1682–1861* (Hanover, N.H.: University Press of New England, 1997), especially chapter 1, and Kathryn Zabelle Derounian, "The Publication, Promotion and Distribution of Mary Rowlandson's Indian Captivity Narrative in the Seventeenth Century," *Early American Literature* 23 (1988), 239–261. Jill Lepore has explored the probable connections between Mrs. Rowlandson and James Printer, a "Praying Indian" who probably set type for both John Eliot's Indian Library and Mary Rowlandson's *Narrative* (Lepore, *Name of War*, pp. 137–159).

53. See Plutarch, "Life of Demosthenes," "Life of Phocion," translation by Ian Scott-Kilvert in *The Age of Alexander* (Harmondsworth: Penguin, 1973).

54. John Easton, "A Relacion of the Indian Warre," in Lincoln, *Narratives of the Indian Wars*, pp. 9, 11.

55. Benjamin Tompson, "New England's Crisis," in *Tompson: Colonial Bard*, ed. White, p. 84.

56. Hubbard, *Present State of New-England*, p. 103.

57. Nathan Fiske, "Remarkable Providences to be Gratefully Recollected, Religiously Improved, and Carefully Transmitted to Posterity," sermon preached at Brookfield, December 31, 1775 (Boston: Thomas and John Fleet, 1776). Imagining redcoats about to invade Brookfield, Fiske had intoned: "Are the deceased Indians risen out of their graves?" (28).

58. Hannah Adams, *A Summary History of New-England* (Dedham: H. Mann and J. H. Adams, 1799), p. 127.

59. Washington Irving, "Philip of Pokanoket," in *The Sketch Book of Geoffrey Crayon*, ed. Haskell Springer (Boston: Twayne, 1978), p. 235.

60. Lydia Maria Child, *The First Settlers of New England; or, Conquest of the Pequods, Narragansetts & Pokanokets* (Boston: Munroe & Francis, 1829), p. vi.

61. Biographical facts about Child's life are drawn from Deborah Pickman Clifford, *Crusader for Freedom: A Life of Lydia Maria Child* (Boston: Beacon Press, 1991), and Carolyn L. Karcher, *The First Woman of the Republic: A Cultural Biography of Lydia Maria Child* (Durham: Duke University Press, 1994).

62. For details of Apess's life, see his autobiography *A Son of the Forest* (1829) and Barry O'Connell's "Introduction" to *On our own Ground: The Complete*

Writings of William Apess, A Pequot (Amherst: University of Massachusetts Press, 1992).

63. Revd. William Apes, *Eulogy on King Philip as Pronounced at the Odeon* (Boston: published by the author, 1836), pp. 6, 5. O'Connell argues convincingly that, by the end of his life, the author wished his name to be spelled Apess. See O'Connell's "Introduction" to *On our own Ground*, p. xiv, n. 2.

64. Apess clearly believed that the legal status of Indian peoples should rise above John Marshall's conception of a "domestic dependent nation." Maureen Konkle's "Indian Literacy, US Colonialism, and Literary Criticism" places Apess's eulogy in the context of the 1830s state and Supreme Court disputes over Cherokee land rights. Konkle, "Indian Literacy, US Colonialism, and Literary Criticism," *American Literature*, 69 (1997), 457–486.

65. Dee Brown, "Introduction" to *Bury my Heart at Wounded Knee: An Indian History of the American West* (New York: Holt, Rinehart, & Winston, 1970), p. xvi.

66. Apess, *Eulogy on King Philip*, pp. 49, 30, 16.

67. Edward Everett, "Oration at Bloody Brook, September 30, 1835," in *Orations and Speeches on Various Occasions* (Boston: American Stationers Co., 1836), pp. 611, 595.

68. Confronting Governor William Henry Harrison, Tecumseh had denounced Shawnee land sales to the state of Indiana by protesting "Sell a country! Why not sell the air, the great sea, as well as the earth?" Frederick W. Turner III, ed., *The Portable North American Indian Reader* (New York: Viking, 1973), p. 246.

69. See Jill Lepore's informative account of the dramaturgy of *Metamora*, of Forrest's acting, and of the play's changing reception in different regions. Lepore believes it likely that William Apess attended a performance of *Metamora* in Boston in 1833 before writing his eulogy of Metacom. (Lepore, *Name of War*, chapter 8). My interest in *Metamora* is admittedly speculative: what was the lasting effect of the play on a nineteenth-century playgoer?

70. John Augustus Stone, *Metamora; or, The Last of the Wampanoags* (1829), in *Metamora and Other Plays*, ed. Eugene R. Page (Princeton: Princeton University Press, 1941), p. 11.

71. Bancroft's footnotes cite John Callender, Thomas Church, John Easton, Edward Everett, Daniel Gookin, William Hubbard, Washington Irving, Cotton Mather, Increase Mather, Mary Rowlandson, Nathaniel Saltonstall, and Thomas Wheeler; Bancroft does not cite Mrs. Child or William Apess. The easy conclusion to draw would be that Bancroft considers only the writings of white men to be important, even though he may oppose them. Against this assumption, however, must be set his respect for the courage and intelligence of Anne Hutchinson, of Quaker women, of Mary Rowlandson, of Gustavus Vasa, and of Mercy Otis Warren.

72. George Bancroft, *History of the United States*, 9th edn (Boston: Little, Brown, & Co., 1841), 11, 92; volume 11 was first published in 1837.

73. Jennings, *Invasion of America*, p. 298.

74. Bancroft refers to surviving Cape Cod Indians and he surely must have known that in the 1830s there were surviving communities of Abenakis, Penobscots, Narragansetts, Mohegans, Pequots, and probably smaller tribes as well. The frequency with which Cooper, Irving, Bancroft, and other northeastern writers could devise metaphors for tribal extinction, while knowing that the facts were otherwise, is telling.

75. John Gorham Palfrey, *The History of New England* (Boston: Little, Brown, & Co., 1859), III, 221.

5 THE AXE AT THE ROOT OF THE TREE: SCARLET GOVERNORS AND GRAY CHAMPIONS

1. "Discourse Delivered at Plymouth...December 22, 1820," in *Speeches and Forensic Arguments by Daniel Webster* (Boston: Perkins, Marvin, & Co., 1835), I, 28.

2. George Bancroft, *History of the United States*, 9th edn (Boston: Little, Brown, & Co., 1841), II, 446. The second volume was first published in 1837.

3. Cotton Mather's wording is "the whole Town was immediately in Arms, with the most *Unanimous Resolution* perhaps that ever was known to have Inspir'd any People." *Magnalia Christi Americana* (1702), ed. K. B. Murdock with the assistance of E. W. Miller (Cambridge, Mass.: Harvard University Press, 1977), p. 294. A. B.'s wording had been "all sorts of people were presently inspired with the most unanimous Resolution, I believe, that was ever seen." A. B., "An Account of the Late Revolutions," in *The Glorious Revolution in America: Documents on the Colonial Crisis of 1689*, ed. M. G. Hall, L. H. Leder, and M. G. Kammen (Chapel Hill: University of North Carolina Press, 1964), p. 50.

4. Nathaniel Hawthorne, *Twice-Told Tales*, Centenary Edition, ed. J. D. Crowley (Columbus: Ohio State University Press, 1974), IX, 9.

5. On Hawthorne's use of the Angel of Hadley legend, see G. Harrison Orians, "The Angel of Hadley in Fiction," *American Literature*, 4 (1932), 256–259, and Michael Davitt Bell, *Hawthorne and the Historical Romance of New England* (Princeton: Princeton University Press, 1971), pp. 27, 49–50.

6. The authoritative history of the rebellions in Massachusetts, New York, and Maryland in 1689 remains David S. Lovejoy's *The Glorious Revolution in America* (New York: Harper & Row, 1972). See also J. M. Sosin, *English America and the Revolution of 1688* (Lincoln: University of Nebraska Press, 1982).

7. Michael G. Hall, *Edward Randolph and the American Colonies 1676–1703* (Chapel Hill: University of North Carolina Press, 1960), pp. 219–222.

8. *Glorious Revolution*, ed. Hall *et al.*, pp. 22–23.

9. Ibid., pp. 25–26.

10. Viola Barnes, *The Dominion of New England* (New Haven: Yale University Press, 1923), p. 73.

11. *Glorious Revolution*, ed. M. G. Hall *et al.*, pp. 26–27.

12. For the conflicting accounts of exactly who voted at this meeting, see Lovejoy, *Glorious Revolution*, pp. 154–156. It is possible that only the Freemen present

voted on Increase Mather's resolution. By the 1670s it was common practice that resident citizens who were not church members could vote at town meetings on local measures, though not for elections to the General Court. See Thomas Breen, *Puritans and Adventurers* (Oxford: Oxford University Press, 1980), chapter 1.

13. See Bernard Bailyn, *The New England Merchants in the Seventeenth Century* (Cambridge, Mass.: Harvard University Press, 1959, 1979), chapter 7. Bailyn argues that once disenfranchised merchants sought political power first through Dudley's provisional government, then through Andros's Dominion, and finally, after the demise of Bradstreet's Council of Safety, through the Royal Province of 1692 (p. 191).

14. "The Declaration of the Gentlemen, Merchants and Inhabitants of Boston, and the Country Adjacent. April 18, 1689" appended to Nathaniel Byfield's "An Account of the Late Revolution in New-England" (1689), in *Narratives of the Insurrections*, ed. Charles M. Andrews (New York: Charles Scribner's Sons, 1915), p. 178.

15. Ibid., pp. 175, 176, 180, 181.

16. Cotton Mather, *Magnalia Christi Americana*, ed. K. B. Murdock with E. W. Miller (Cambridge, Mass.: Harvard University Press, 1977), p. 294.

17. Samuel Sewall and Edward Rawson, "The Revolution in New England Justified" (1691), in *The Andros Tracts*, ed. W. H. Whitmore (Boston: Prince Society, 1868), I, 87.

18. Bailyn revealed the coastal merchants' increasing resentment of the power of rural deputies elected by church members (*New England Merchants*, chapter 6).

19. "By the Governour and General Court of the Colony of the Massachusetts Bay in New-England," printed at the end of Cotton Mather's *The Present State of New England* (Boston: Samuel Green, 1690), pp. 47–52.

20. Simon Bradstreet, letter to the agents, *Andros Tracts*, III, 25.

21. Increase Mather, *A Brief Account concerning Several of the Agents of New-England* (1691), in *Narratives of the Insurrections*, ed. Andrews, p. 292.

22. Cotton Mather, *The Way to Prosperity* (1689), in *The Wall and the Garden: Selected Massachusetts Election Sermons 1670–1775*, ed. A. W. Plumstead (Minneapolis: University of Minnesota Press, 1968), pp. 130–131.

23. Cotton Mather, *The Present State of New England* (Boston: Samuel Green, 1690), facsimile reprint by Haskell House (New York, 1972), p. 34.

24. As the crisis deepened still further, Mather's worried caution would grow into counsels of near helpless passivity. *Optanda* (1692), *Fair Weather* (1692), and the "Political Fables" (1692?) are filled with metaphors of storm, earthquake, and fire, in which the ship of state is a "poor shattered, sinking bark," the people directionless and "discontent," and New England is left a sheepfold without a shepherd while the wolves approach.

25. Charter of the Province of Massachusetts, in *Glorious Revolution*, ed. Hall *et al.*, pp. 76–79. On the compromises of the new charter, see Richard L. Bushman, *King and People in Provincial Massachusetts*, (Chapel Hill: University of North

Carolina Press, 1992), especially chapter 1. The Provincial Chapter, approved in England in 1691, did not take effect in New England until 1692.

26. Bancroft, *History of the United States*, II, 449: John Gorham Palfrey, *The History of New England* (Boston: Little, Brown, & Co., 1859), III, 598. Without criticizing Bancroft directly, Palfrey challenged his account of New England's unanimity. The Moderates, in Palfrey's view, were a commercial class ready to profit from greater royal control: "The commercial activity had brought a large influx of wealth, and the instincts of wealth incline to the side of arbitrary power" (Palfrey, *History of New England*, IV, 359). Palfrey's argument anticipates Bailyn's, though perhaps to different end. Pre-Civil War controversies had caused Palfrey to fear and denounce the compromising effects of economic difference on party politics.

27. Increase Mather, *Several of the Agents of New-England*, p. 283.

28. On Increase Mather's disillusionment, see "History in Pieces," chapter 3 of Stephen Carl Arch's *Authorizing the Past: The Rhetoric of History in Seventeenth-Century New England* (DeKalb: Northern Illinois University Press, 1994).

29. "Declaration of the Gentlemen, Merchants and Inhabitants of Boston, and the Country Adjacent," p. 175.

30. Increase Mather's use of the phrase "my country" resembles Abraham Lincoln's repeated invoking of "the Union" in the midst of an even greater crisis. Effective leaders know that retaining group identity demands an insistence upon "country" or "union" as metaphysical realities at precisely the time when, as political entities, "country" or "union" has ceased to exist.

31. Cotton Mather, *Magnalia Christi Americana*, p. 288.

32. George Allan Cook, *John Wise: Early American Democrat* (New York: Columbia University Press, 1952), p. 48.

33. Samuell Sewall and Edward Rawson, "The Revolution in New England Justified" (1691), in *Andros Tracts*, I, 85.

34. Samuel Cooke, "A Sermon Preached at Cambridge in the Audience of His Honor Thomas Hutchinson" (1770), in *The Wall and the Garden*, ed. A. W. Plumstead (Minneapolis: University of Minnesota Press, 1968), p. 326.

35. Thomas Hutchinson, *The History of the Colony and Province of Massachusetts Bay*, ed. Lawrence Shaw Mayo (Cambridge, Mass.: Harvard University Press, 1936), I, 305.

36. Nathaniel Hawthorne, "Edward Randolph's Portrait," in *Twice-Told Tales*, ed. Crowley, IX, 257, 262.

37. Ibid., p. 262. Michael Colacurcio argues convincingly that, in Hawthorne's tale, Hutchinson's "historical failure is clearly a failure of imagination . . . In the end Hutchinson's study of history ought to have taught him that the Bostonians will respond to the troops of 1770 in much the same way they responded to those who followed the efforts of Randolph nearly a century earlier." *The Province of Piety* (Cambridge, Mass.: Harvard University Press, 1984), pp. 418, 409.

38. See Hutchinson, *History of the Province of Massachusetts Bay*, III, 146–162 and III, 221–225.

6 RACE, WAR, AND WHITE MAGIC: THE NEGLECTED LEGACY OF SALEM

1. Gustav Niebuhr, "Witches Cast as the Neo-Pagans Next Door," *New York Times*, October 31, 1999, pages 1, 28. Niebuhr estimates there are currently 100,000–300,000 members or attendees of Wicca meetings in the United States.

2. On the continuing association of Salem with witchery, see the concluding chapter, "Salem Story," of Bernard D. Rosenthal's *Salem Story: Reading the Witch Trials of 1692* (Cambridge: Cambridge University Press, 1993), pp. 204–28.

3. The first section of this chapter is a shortened revision of my essay "Indian John and the Northern Tawnies," *New England Quarterly* (1996), in light of Mary Beth Norton's authoritative study *In the Devil's Snare: The Salem Witchcraft Crisis of 1692* (New York: Knopf, 2002). Norton's book amply proves what I advanced only as a thesis. She concludes that "the term *Salem Witchcraft crisis* is a misnomer; *Essex County Witchcraft crisis* would be more accurate" (8).

4. In *Salem Possessed*, Paul Boyer and Stephen Nissenbaum advanced the influential argument that the Salem witch trials arose out of family and class tensions within Salem Village and between Salem Village and Salem Town. *Salem Possessed: The Social Origins of Witchcraft* (Cambridge, Mass.: Harvard University Press, 1974). Although this approach now seems restrictively local, I remain indebted to its findings.

5. On the northern aftermath of King Philip's War, see chapter 6 of Russell Bourne's *The Red King's Rebellion; Racial Politics in New England, 1675–1678* (Oxford; Oxford University Press, 1990). Salem's geographical position proved critical to this conflict. Although not on the frontier line in 1692, Salem was the largest English community north of Boston, the point of embarkation for northern wars against the French and the Wabanaki, and a major source of the Essex County militia, who would fight in those sporadic, seemingly endless wars from 1688 until 1763.

6. Paul Boyer and Stephen Nissenbaum, *The Salem Witchcraft Papers* (New York: Da Capo, 1977), 1, 248. Hereafter cited as *Salem Witchcraft Papers*. Whenever there are multiple quotations from these papers within one paragraph, they will be cited together in one note at the end of the paragraph.

7. Robert Calef, *More Wonders of the Invisible World* (1700), in *Narratives of the Witchcraft Cases 1648–1706*, ed. George Lincoln Burr (New York: Charles Scribner's Sons, 1914), p. 349.

8. Although William Phips led northern troops in late spring 1692, he was back in Boston and regularly attended Council meetings during the summer (see Norton, *In the Devil's Snare*, p. 237).

9. See John Putnam Demos, *Entertaining Satan* (Oxford: Oxford University Press, 1982), pp. 93–94 and Carol F. Karlsen *The Devil in the Shape of a Woman: Witchcraft in Colonial New England* (New York: Random House, 1987), pp. 39–40, 51, 65–66, 116–118. Women who shared more than one trait of this profile would include Anne Hutchinson, Mary Dyer, Ann Hibbens, Rachel Clinton, Elizabeth Garlick, Eunice Cole, and, at the Salem trials, Bridget Bishop, Sarah

Good, Susannah Martin, Elizabeth Procter, Dorcas Hoar, Martha Carrier, and Wilmot Redd.

10. Mary Beth Norton has assembled biographical evidence proving the crucial importance of the Maine wars to the patterns of accusatory testimony in 1692. While living in Falmouth (Casco, now Portland), Abigail Hobbes had known Mercy Lewis. The Burroughs, Hobbes, Lewis and Ingersoll families had known one another in Falmouth before reencountering each other in the houses, tavern and/or the meetinghouse of Salem Village. See *In the Devil's Snare, passim*, especially pp. 117–132.

11. My information about the war service and deaths of Salem area residents during the Indian wars of 1689–1693, is derived from Samuel G. Drake, *The Witchcraft Delusion in New England* (Roxbury, Mass.: W. Elliot Woodward, 1866) and Charles W. Upham, *Salem Witchcraft* (Boston: Wiggin & Lunt, 1867). See also James F. Kences, "Some Unexplored Relationships of Essex County Witchcraft to the Indian Wars of 1675 and 1689," *Essex Institute Historical Collections*, 120 (1984), 179–212. For the history of King William's War, see Cotton Mather's *Decennium Luctuosum* (1699), Jeremy Belknap's *The History of New-Hampshire* (1812), William D. Williamson's *History of the State of Maine* (1832), Francis Parkman's *Comte Frontenac and New France* (1877), and chapter 5 of Charles E. Clark's *The Eastern Frontier: The Settlement of Northern New England: 1610–1763* (1970).

12. William Stoughton, "New-Englands True Interest not to Lie," election day sermon preached April 29, 1668 (Cambridge, Mass.: Samuel Greene, 1670), p. 20.

13. Stoughton was New England's Talleyrand during its Time of Troubles. "New England's True Interest," as well as Stoughton's Harvard education, would seem to initially align him with Increase Mather, John Leverett, and Thomas Danforth as leading defenders of the old charter and the New England way. When Joseph Dudley was appointed by the Crown to head the provisional government of 1686, however, Stoughton served as Dudley's deputy president. Although Stoughton continued as one of Andros's Councilmen under the Dominion, when the revolt of April 18, 1689 arrived, it was Stoughton who was selected to issue the rebuke to Andros at Boston's town house. Never quite trusted by Bradstreet's Council of Safety, Stoughton nonetheless returned to office as lieutenant-governor under Phips, succeeding him as acting governor upon Phips's death. Despite – or perhaps because of – Stoughton's refusal to recant his record as presiding judge of the Salem witch trials, Stoughton would in later life be reelected to the General Court. His was a truly impressive lifelong performance of political trimming.

14. On the sequence of literary and historical renderings of Tituba's race, see Chadwick Hansen, "The Metamorphosis of Tituba, or Why American Intellectuals Can't Tell an Indian Witch from a Negro," *New England Quarterly*, 47 (March 1974), 3–12. Elaine G. Breslaw discovered that a slave whose name was spelled "Tattuba" was listed in a contract enabling Barbadian planter Samuel Thompson to lease his plantation in 1676. "The Salem Witch from Barbados:

In Search of Tituba's Roots," *Essex Institute Historical Collections,* 128 (1992), 217–238. In her book-length study of Tituba, Breslaw concludes that it is "possible, but in light of the very bitter heritage of the Puritan–Wampanoag hostility, somewhat improbable" that Tituba was a Massachusetts Indian sold into slavery in Barbados in 1676 after King Philip's War. *Tituba, Reluctant Witch of Salem* (New York: New York University Press, 1996), p. 9. William Hart has kindly informed me that Roger Williams lists three Alonginquin words phonetically close to "Tattuba:" "Tutteputch," "Tatuppuntuock," and "Ntatuppe." On the basis of Thomas Hutchinson's phrase "brought into the Country from New Spain," Mary Beth Norton speculates that Tituba may have been from Florida or the Georgia Sea Islands (*In the Devil's Snare,* p. 21).

15. *Salem Witchcraft Papers,* III, 745.
16. Cotton Mather, letter to John Richards, May 1692, in *Selected Letters of Cotton Mather,* ed. Kenneth Silverman (Baton Rouge: Louisiana State University Press, 1971), p. 38.
17. *Salem Witchcraft Papers,* II, 611, 610.
18. Ibid., I, 52. Carol F. Karlsen noted that the fathers of thirteen of the afflicted young women accusers had died before 1692, many of them in the northern Indian wars. Among them were two prominent accusers, Sarah Churchill and Mercy Lewis (Karlsen, *Devil in the Shape of a Woman,* pp. 226–228).
19. *Salem Witchcraft Papers,* II, 405; II, 410; II, 411; II, 423; II, 423; II, 423. Norton has provided convincing evidence that Abigail Hobbs had known Mercy Lewis as well as George Burroughs while living in Falmouth (*In the Devil's Snare,* pp. 118–119).
20. The curious and frequent mention of "red bread" in confessional testimony about witch communions still needs explanation. If ergot turned rye red, Linda B. Caporeal's now discredited explanation of the Salem trials (that ergot in rye caused hallucinations) might deserve a rehearing. However, Caporeal nowhere mentions that rye infected with ergot shows any such coloration. See "Ergotism: The Satan Loosed in Salem?," *Science,* 192 (April 1976), 21–26. The explanation for the red bread may lie in old world folklore, in new world fears of the Indian, or in both.
21. See Norton, *In the Devil's Snare,* pp. 122–123, 130.
22. *Salem Witchcraft Papers,* I, 164.
23. Ibid., I, 164; I, 165.
24. Ibid., III, 767; III, 767; III, 768; III, 768; III, 769.
25. John Emerson, "A Faithful Account of many Wonderful and Surprising Things which happened in the Town of Glocester, in the Year 1692" (1693), printed by Cotton Mather in *Decennium Luctuosum,* pp. 246–247.
26. George Bancroft, *History of the United States* (Boston: Little, Brown, & Co., 1861), III, 85. Volume III was first published in 1840.
27. Selma R. Williams, for example, remains convinced that Cotton Mather still deserves to be called "New England's intellectual witch hunter" and "intellectual inquisitor." *Riding the Nightmare: Women and Witchcraft from the Old World to Colonial Salem* (New York: HarperCollins, 1978), pp. 125, 200. David

Levin's two essays, "The Hazing of Cotton Mather" and "Historical Fact in Fiction and Drama: The Salem Witch Trials," neither of which is listed in Williams's bibliography, define the kinds of historiographical distortion she is repeating. See David Levin, *In Defense of Historical Literature* (New York: Hill & Wang, 1967).

28. Cotton Mather, *The Wonders of the Invisible World* (1693) (London: John Russell Smith, 1862), p. 4. Henceforth cited by parenthetical reference in the text.

29. Cotton Mather, *Decennium Luctuosum*, p. 242.

30. Richard Slotkin has made a vivid and compelling reconstruction of the historical circumstances and Puritan responses to the Salmon Falls raid. See chapter 5 of *Regeneration Through Violence: The Mythology of the American Frontier, 1600–1860* (Middletown, Conn.: Wesleyan University Press, 1973), pp. 117–128.

31. Cotton Mather, "A Brand Plucked out of the Burning," in *Narratives of the Witchcraft Cases*, ed. Burr, p. 261.

32. Perry Miller, *The New England Mind: From Colony to Province* (Boston: Beacon Press, 1961), p. 191.

33. Circular letter of Thomas Brattle dated October 8, 1692 in *Narratives of the Witchcraft Cases*, ed. Burr, p. 169.

34. Daniel Neal, *The History of New England* (London: J. Clark, 1720), II, 497.

35. Thomas Hutchinson, *The History of the Colony and Province of Massachusetts Bay* (1767), ed. Lawrence Shaw Mayo (Cambridge, Mass.: Harvard University Press, 1936), II, 23.

36. Bancroft, *History of the United States*, III, 97.

37. Bancroft's insistence on the post-Salem transformation of the New England/ American mind into enlightened reason continues to flourish. The end of the audiotape to be heard daily at the Salem Witch Museum perpetuates it. Stephen Krensky's *Witch Hunt: It Happened in Salem Village*, a title in the Random House Step Into Reading series, ends with the following sentence: "The Salem witch hunt was a time when fear and hate ruled over common sense" (New York: Random House, 1989) (48). Selma Williams reaffirms Bancroft's conclusion in its starkest form: "For all practical purposes the Great Witch Hunt petered out at Salem in 1692, laid to rest by the onset of the scientific revolution and the Age of Reason" (*Riding the Nightmare*, p. 202).

38. John Gorham Palfrey, *History of New England* (Boston: Little, Brown, & Co., 1877), III, 131.

39. Nathaniel Hawthorne, *The Whole History of Grandfather's Chair*, in *True Stories from History and Biography*, Centenary Edition, ed. William Charvat, Roy Harvey Pearce, and Claude L. Simpson (Columbus: Ohio State University Press, 1972), VI, 77.

40. Nathaniel Hawthorne, "Alice Doane's Appeal," in *The Snow-Image and Uncollected Tales*, ed. J. D. Crowley, Centenary Edition (Columbus: Ohio State University Press, 1974), XI, 278.

41. Herman Melville, "Hawthorne and his Mosses," *Herman Melville: Representative Selections*, ed. Willard Thorp (New York: American Book Co., 1938), p. 339.

42. Nathaniel Hawthorne, "Young Goodman Brown" in *Mosses from an Old Manse*, Centenary Edition, ed. W. Charvat, R. H. Pearce, C. M. Simpson, J. D. Crowley (Columbus: Ohio State University Press, 1974), x, 74.
43. Maryse Condé, from a 1991 interview with Ann Armstrong Scarboro, included in the afterword to *I, Tituba, Black Witch of Salem*, translated by Richard Philcox, foreword by Angela Y. Davis, afterword by Ann Armstrong Scarboro (New York: Ballantine Books, 1992), p. 202.
44. The historical narratives written by Hannah Adams and Marion Starkey are no exception to the exoticizing of Tituba. Nor is William Carlos Williams's inchoate libretto *Tituba's Children* (1950), which has precious little to do with Tituba or even with Tituba's metaphorical children. Restitution to Tituba began, however, in Ann Petry's *Tituba the Witch* (1964), published at least a decade before the upsurge of interest in writings by and about women of color.
45. Similar kinds of restitution to neglected black women occur, of course, in well-known fictions, contemporary to Condé, by Alice Walker, Toni Morison, Gloria Naylor, and others. To Condé, writing New England historical literature is in no way a regional endeavor.
46. *I, Tituba, Black Witch of Salem*, p. 71. Condé's observations find confirmation where least expected. Seventy years after the Salem trials young John Adams was so revolted by the diverse kinds of transactions he saw in Massachusetts taverns that he wrote editorial essays proposing their licensing and regulation.
47. Condé, 1991 interview with Ann Armstrong Scarboro, *I, Tituba, Black Witch of Salem*, pp. 200–201.
48. Although Condé's portrayal of Tituba's return to Barbados is quite possible, it cannot be confirmed. In April of 1693, Tituba was sold for the price of her jail upkeep to an unknown person. Thereafter she disappears from known historical record.
49. Condé, 1991 interview with Ann Armstrong Scarboro, p. 201.

PART 3   HEADNOTE

1. Josiah Quincy, Jr., *Observations on the Act of Parliament Commonly Called the Boston Port-Bill* (Philadelphia: John Sparhawk, 1774), pp. 52, 56, 58, 60.
2. *The Suffolk Resolves*, broadside, September 6, 1774.
3. Joseph Galloway, *Historical and Political Reflections on the Rise and Progress of the American Revolution* (London, 1780), p. 67.
4. Daniel Webster, "A Discourse Delivered at Plymouth, December 22, 1820" in *The Works of Daniel Webster* (Boston: Little, Brown, & Co., 1853), I, 33.

7   BOSTON REVOLT AND PURITAN RESTORATION: 1760–1775

1. From John Adams's summary of Otis's argument, *The Works of John Adams*, ed. Charles Francis Adams (Boston: Charles C. Little and James Brown, 1850), II, 522.

2. Bernard Bailyn, *The Ideological Origins of the American Revolution*, (Cambridge, Mass.: Harvard University Press, 1967), pp. 76–77.

3. Consider three well-known studies widely separate in time. John C. Miller's *Origins of the American Revolution* (1943 reprinted Stanford University Press, 1959) begins its chronology of conflict with Otis's speech on the Writs of Assistance; Miller states "One of the principal reasons why Massachusetts took a position of leadership in the struggle against Great Britain was that the Bay Colony had achieved a high degree of unity" (63). Edmund Morgan's *The Birth of the Republic* (1956; 3rd edn, University of Chicago Press, 1992) contains a number of variants on the sentence "But other Americans by now realized that Boston's cause was theirs" (49). Robert Middlekauff's *The Glorious Cause: The American Revolution, 1763–1789* (1982) contains a chapter entitled "Boston Takes the Lead."

4. Jefferson on Sam Adams, as quoted in John C. Miller, *Sam Adams: Pioneer in Propaganda* (Boston: Little, Brown, & Co., 1936), p. 343; Adams, *Works*, x, 263. Sam Adams's centrality has been called into question by Charles W. Akers (*The Divine Politician*, 1982) and Richard D. Brown (*Revolutionary Politics in Massachusetts*, 1970). Robert Ferguson's insightful, influential *The American Enlightenment* (1994) scarcely mentions Sam Adams. Pauline Maier's essay on him in *The Old Revolutionaries* (1980), contending for Adams's pervasive influence until the declaring of independence, establishes the viewpoint I find most convincing. See also Gregory H. Nobles, " 'Yet the Old Republicans Still Persevere'; Samuel Adams, John Hancock, and the Crisis of Popular Leadership in Revolutionary Massachusetts, 1775–1790," in *The Transforming Hand of Revolution*, eds. Ronald Hoffman and Peter J. Albert (Charlottesville: University of Virginia Press, 1996).

5. Noah Webster, *Dictionary* (1828), n.p.

6. Perhaps the clearest instance of this regressive use of the word *revolution* occurs at the end of Jonathan Mayhew's widely read sermon of 1766, "The Snare Broken," celebrating the repeal of the Stamp Act. The "late alarming CRISIS" has been averted, Mayhew claims, due to the resistance of a people who have only recently realized that "We only exercise that liberty, wherewith Christ hath made us free." Mayhew's words, so very like John Winthrop's 1645 definition of civil liberty ("the same kind of liberty wherewith Christ hath made us free"), lend a biblical authority for resistance that outweighs the admitted legal fact that "the colonies could not justly claim an exclusive right of taxing themselves." See *The Snare Broken* (Boston: R. and S. Draper, 1766), pp. 7, 19, 31.

7. *Boston Gazette*, October 5, 1772, in *The Writings of Samuel Adams*, ed. Harry Alonzo Cushing (New York: G. P. Putnam's Sons, 1906), ii, 336.

8. Nathaniel Ward, preamble to *A Coppie of the Liberties of the Massachusets Colonie in New England* (1641), in *Puritan Political Ideas*, ed. Edmund S. Morgan (Indianapolis: Bobbs-Merrill, 1965), p. 178.

9. Accounting for revolutionary resistance has long posed a problem of choosing among diverse kinds of evidence. Alan Heimert's *Religion and the American Mind* (1966) ascribed revolutionary fervor in Massachusetts to Edwardsean ministers

who, with scant help from the "liberal" clergy, created an evangelical spirit of liberty in the spring of 1775. Following Bernard Bailyn, Pauline Maier traced revolutionary fervor to the British Whig tradition that provided a vocabulary of resistance for colonial politicians and political writers (*From Resistance to Revolution*, 1972). Here are two major interpretations whose evidence moves on different paths. As the intermediary between Massachusetts's ministers and politicians, newspapers and the Congregational Church, Sam Adams caused events to happen. His accomplishments in enacting strategies of mediation comprise, I believe, the source of his power.

10. John Adams, letter to William Tudor, June 8 1817, *Works of John Adams*, ed. Adams, x, 263–264.

11. See Peter Shaw, *American Patriots and the Rituals of Revolution* (Cambridge, Mass.: Harvard University Press, 1981), pp. 15–18.

12. On the verbal war of Congregationalists and Presbyterians against the Archbishop of Canterbury's proposal to appoint an Anglican bishop, see Carl Bridenbaugh, *Mitre and Scepter* (Oxford: Oxford University Press, 1962). The three 1769 *Boston Gazette* essays that Samuel Adams wrote under the name "A Puritan" are collected in *Writings of Samuel Adams*, ed. Cushing, I, 201–212. The essay Adams signed under the name "Cotton Mather" is reprinted in II, 276–281.

13. John Adams, "Governor Winthrop to Governor Bradford," *Boston Gazette*, February 9, 1767, in *Works of John Adams*, ed. Adams, III, 489.

14. Important sermon passages that praise Puritan forefathers as models for courageous "revolutionary" defense of civil liberty include the following: Judah Champion, *A Brief View of the Distresses . . . Our Ancestors Encountered in Settling New England* (1770), pp. 10, 29–32; Charles Chauncy, *Trust in GOD* (1770), pp. 13, 25; Charles Turner, *A Sermon Preached Before His Excellency Governor Hutchinson* (1773), p. 42; Gad Hitchcock, *A Sermon Preached Before His Excellency Thomas Gage* (1774), pp. 48–51; Nathaniel Niles, *Two Discourses on Liberty* (1774), pp. 24, 59, 60; Judah Champion, *A Sermon Delivered Before the General Assembly of the Colony of Connecticut* (1776), pp. 16, 17, 28, 31; Samuel West, *A Sermon Preached Before the Honorable Council . . . of the Colony of Massachusetts-Bay* (1776), pp. 51, 56, 57, 67; Sylvanus Conant, *An Anniversary Sermon Preached at Plymouth, December 23, 1776* (1777), p. 22. See the summary description of Black Regiment sermons in Harry Stout, *The New England Soul* (Oxford: Oxford University Press, 1986), chapters 13–14. To risk an overgeneralization: before 1775 Black Regiment sermons usually urge liberty-loving congregations to wait upon the deliverance of the Lord, but by 1775 and 1776 they often urge congregations to act, not necessarily with a gun, in defense of their heritage.

15. See John C. Miller, *Sam Adams: Pioneer in Propaganda* (Boston: Little, Brown, & Co., 1936), p. 294.

16. Joseph Warren, *An Oration Delivered March 5, 1772 Commemorating the Bloody Tragedy of the Fifth of March 1770* (Boston: Edes & Gill, 1772), pp. 16–17. Warren's speech is a prime example of Sandra Gustafson's observation about revolutionary rhetoric invoking "the spectacle of besieged and suffering

Boston": "The body of the people became identified with the orator's body, their voice with his voice." *Eloquence is Power: Oratory and Performance in Early America* (Chapel Hill: University of North Carolina Press, 2000), pp. 199, 187.

17. Charles Turner, *A Sermon Preached Before His Excellency Governor Hutchinson* (Boston: Richard Draper, 1773), pp. 6, 16, 31.

18. *Writings of Samuel Adams*, ed. Cushing, III, 156.

19. George Bancroft, *History of the United States* (Boston: Little, Brown, & Co., 1867), VI, 431–441. The sixth volume was first published in 1856.

20. The Freeman's Oath (Newtown, per order of the General Court, 1639).

21. Samuel Cooper, "A Sermon Preached Before His Excellency John Hancock Esq., Governour, October 25, 1780, the Day of the Commencement of the Constitution" (Boston: J. Fleet and J. Gill, 1780), p. 2. On Samuel Cooper's life, see Charles W. Akers, *The Divine Politician: Samuel Cooper and the American Revolution in Boston* (Boston: Northeastern University Press, 1982).

22. Adams, *Boston Gazette*, October 2, 1769, in *Writings of Samuel Adams*, ed. Cushing, I, 392.

23. Bernard Bailyn's summary characterization of Sam Adams – "fierce, narrow, unbending, ungenerous, intolerant" – perfectly captures Adams's relentlessness, though Bailyn's choice of adjectives understandably reflects Hutchinson's wary, condemnatory perspective. *The Ordeal of Thomas Hutchinson* (Cambridge, Mass.: Harvard University Press, 1974), p. 292.

24. Adams, "To Reverend G– W– ," November 11, 1765, in *Writings of Samuel Adams*, ed. Cushing, I, 26–33.

25. *Boston Gazette*, October 7, 1771, in *Writings of Samuel Adams*, ed. Cushing, II, 248.

26. Paul Staits, "Accounting for Copley," in *John Singleton Copley in America* (New York: Harry N. Abrams for the Metropolitan Museum of Art, 1995), pp. 43–45, 275–278. Copley portrayed Adams pointing to the 1691 Charter during his confrontation with Hutchinson the day after the Boston Massacre.

27. "Candidus," *Boston Gazette*, November 11, 1771, in *Writings of Samuel Adams*, ed. Cushing, II, 268–274.

28. "Valerius Poplicola," *Boston Gazette*, October 5, 1772, in *Writings of Samuel Adams*, ed. Cushing, II, 336.

29. Letter of Correspondence to the Other Towns, November 20, 1772, in *Writings of Samuel Adams*, ed. Cushing, II, 372.

30. Letter to James Warren, November 4, 1775, in *Writings of Samuel Adams*, ed. Cushing, III, 234–235.

31. Letter to John Adams, January 15, 1776, in *Writings of Samuel Adams*, ed. Cushing, III, 260.

32. Letter to Mrs. Adams, December 9, 1776, in *Writings of Samuel Adams*, ed. Cushing, III, 325.

33. Letter to Hezekiah Niles, February 13, 1818, in *Works of John Adams*, ed. Adams, X, 282.

34. Letter to William Tudor, June 5 1817, in *Works of John Adams*, ed. Adams, X, 263.

35. John Adams, "A Dissertation on the Canon and Feudal Law"(1765), in *The Political Writings of John Adams*, ed. George A. Peek, Jr. (Indianapolis: Bobbs-Merrill, 1954), pp. 4–5.
36. On the political dimensions of the taxation issue during the decade preceding 1775, see Richard L. Bushman, *King and People in Provincial Massachusetts*, 2nd edn (Chapel Hill: University of North Carolina Press, 1985), pp. 176–210. Bushman observes: "Parliamentary taxation bypassed the Province's established line of defense and negated all the safeguards built up over the years . . . The decision to use taxes to pay for British regulars in America and to make governors and judges independent of the colonial legislatures realized all the old fears" (176).
37. See Maier, *From Resistance to Revolution*, pp. 22–26.
38. Samuel Adams, letter to Richard Henry Lee, March 21, 1775, in *Writings of Samuel Adams*, ed. Cushing, III, 206.
39. John Adams, letter to William Tudor, June 5 1817, in *Works of John Adams*, ed. Adams, X, 264.
40. John Adams, *Autobiography, Diary and Autobiography of John Adams*, eds L. H. Butterfield, W. D. Garrett, and M. Friedlaender (Cambridge, Mass.: Harvard University Press, 1966), III, 311.
41. Thomas Hutchinson, *The History of the Colony and Province of Massachusetts Bay* (1767), ed. Lawrence Shaw Mayo (Cambridge, Mass.: Harvard University Press, 1936), III, 212.
42. Peter Oliver *The Origin and Progress of the American Rebellion* (completed 1781 but unpublished in Oliver's lifetime), ed. Douglass Adair and John A. Schutz (Stanford: Stanford University Press, 1961), p. 84.
43. Ibid., p. 19. Oliver mentions loyalist printer John Mein, who had made similar use of similar evidence in his *Sagittarius Letters* (1775). It is probable that Peter Oliver wrote with a copy of Mein's text before him.
44. *Writings of Samuel Adams*, ed. Cushing, IV, 238, 412.
45. Mercy Otis Warren, *History of the Rise, Progress and Termination of the American Revolution*, ed. Lester H. Cohen (Indianapolis: Liberty Classics, 1988), I, 60, 59.
46. Mercy Otis Warren, *The Adulateur: A Tragedy* (Boston: New Printing Office, 1773), pp. 5–6.
47. Lester H. Cohen has shown how uneasy Mrs. Warren was about advancing Providential explanations of historical events. *The Revolutionary Histories* (Ithaca: Cornell University Press, 1980), pp. 63–65ff. It is important to recognize that, in the next generation, George Bancroft would be far more willing to write Providential history than Mercy Otis Warren had been.
48. Lydia Maria Child, *The Rebels; or, Boston Before the Revolution* (Boston: Cummings, Hilliard, & Co., 1825), p. 57.
49. Catharine Maria Sedgwick, *The Linwoods; or, Sixty Years Since in America* (New York: Harper & Bros., 1835), I, 42.
50. James Fenimore Cooper, *Lionel Lincoln; or, The Leaguer of Boston*, ed. A. Donald and Lucy B. Ringe (Albany: State University of New York Press, 1984), p. 53.

51. "John Adams," in *Hawthorne as Editor*, ed. Arlin Turner (1941; rpt. Port Washington, N.Y.: Kennikat Press, 1972), p. 43. Lewis Simpson argues persuasively that "My Kinsman, Major Molineux" affirms John Adams's suspicion that throughout the Age of Reason the logic of revolution had never been free of uncontrollable irrational desires. "The Fiction of the Real American Revolution," in Lewis Simpson, *The Brazen Face of History* (Baton Rouge: Louisiana State University Press, 1980), pp. 47–65.

52. Nathaniel Hawthorne, "Edward Randolph's Portrait," in *Twice-Told Tales*, ed. J. D. Crowley, Centenary Edition (Columbus: Ohio State University Press, 1974), IX, 265.

53. Nathaniel Hawthorne, "Old News," in *The Snow-Image and Uncollected Tales*, ed. J. D. Crowley (Columbus: Ohio State University Press, 1974), XI, 153.

54. Nathaniel Hawthorne, *Grandfather's Chair*, in *True Stories from History and Biography*, ed. R. H. Pearce, Centenary Edition (Columbus: Ohio State University Press, 1972), VI, 5.

55. Nathaniel Hawthorne, "My Kinsman, Major Molineux," in *Snow-Image*, XI, 229.

56. Peter Shaw, who sees the answer to this question as "expiation," describes Molineux's involvement in revolutionary rituals and speculates that the leader of the procession in Hawthorne's tale was modeled on crowd leader Joyce, Jr. (*American Patriots*, pp. 188–191).

57. See Samuel Adams, "Vindex," *Boston Gazette*, December 24, 1770, in *Writings of Samuel Adams*, ed. Cushing, II, 99. It may be more than coincidental that Copley painted Sam Adams in a red suit.

58. See Russell B. Nye, *George Bancroft: Brahmin Rebel* (New York: Knopf, 1944), chapter 5, and Lilian Handlin, *George Bancroft: The Intellectual as Democrat* (New York: Harper & Row, 1984), chapters 7 and 8.

59. George Bancroft, *History of the United States* (Boston: Little, Brown, & Co., 1868), IV, 12, 13. The fourth volume was first published in 1852.

60. George Bancroft, *History of the United States* (Boston: Little, Brown, & Co., 1869), V, 194. The fifth volume was first published in 1852.

61. Bancroft, *History of the United States*, VI, 408.

62. Letters of Joseph Warren to Samuel Adams, September 4, 1774 and May 14, 1775, in Richard Frothingham, *Life and Times of Joseph Warren* (Boston: Little, Brown, & Co., 1865), pp. 355, 483; letter of Samuel Cooper to Samuel Adams, September 5, 1774, in Akers, *Divine Politician*, pp. 185–186.

63. George Bancroft, *History of the United States* (Boston: Little, Brown, & Co., 1869), VII, 287. The seventh volume was first published in 1858.

8 SHOTS HEARD ROUND THE WORLD

1. David Hackett Fischer, *Paul Revere's Ride* (Oxford: Oxford University Press, 1994), p. 321.

2. Dispatch of the Earl of Suffolk, quoted in Ruth R. Wheeler, *Concord: Climate for Freedom* (Concord: Concord Antiquarian Society, 1967), p. 129.

346 Notes to pages 228–231

3. Fischer's detailed account of the war to control public opinion, which he calls "The Second Battle of Lexington and Concord," provides compelling details of the speed with which patriot riders conveyed the day's news and patriot writers wrote broadside press releases. *Paul Revere's Ride*, pp. 261–280.

4. A chronological listing of the writers who were to reflect at length upon the events of April 19 amounts to a sizeable roster of prominent historians, novelists, poets, and politician/orators during the antebellum period: William Gordon, David Ramsay, Mercy Otis Warren, Hannah Adams, Jedediah Morse, William Tudor, Edward Everett, James Fenimore Cooper, Daniel Webster, Sarah Josepha Hale, Elizabeth Peabody, George Bancroft, Ralph Waldo Emerson, Robert Rantoul, Henry David Thoreau, Henry Wadsworth Longfellow, Nathaniel Hawthorne, James Russell Lowell, John Greenleaf Whittier, Oliver Wendell Holmes. On the memorializing of Concord, see Robert Gross, "Commemorating Concord: The Story of How a New England Town Invented Itself," *Common-Place*, 4.1 (October 2003), http://www.common-place.org/

5. Henry James, *The American Scene*, ed. Leon Edel (Bloomington: Indiana University Press, 1968), p. 260.

6. Ralph Waldo Emerson, "Historical Discourse at Concord" (1835), in *The Complete Works of Ralph Waldo Emerson*, ed. E. E. Emerson (Boston: Houghton Mifflin, 1906), XI, 75. Fisher has shown that many of the men who stood on Lexington Green were not Minutemen but militia, and that, during the retreat from Concord, many patriots fought under order as members of militia units, rather than as the self-reliant New England individuals of regional and national legend. *Paul Revere's Ride*, pp. 153, 203.

7. Thomas Paine, *Common Sense* (1776), ed. Isaac Kramnick (New York: Viking Penguin, 1982), p. 82.

8. Mercy Otis Warren, *History of the Rise, Progress and Termination of the American Revolution* (1805), ed. Lester H. Cohen (Indianapolis: Liberty Classics, 1988), I, 103.

9. Edward Everett, *An Oration Delivered at Concord, April the 19th 1825* (Boston: Cummings, Hilliard, & Co., 1825), p. 35.

10. George Bancroft, *History of the United States*, 9th edn (Boston: Little, Brown, & Co., 1869), VII, 291. The seventh volume was first published in 1858.

11. Lester H. Cohen, *The Revolutionary Histories: Contemporary Narratives of the American Revolution* (Ithaca: Cornell University Press, 1980), p. 52. On the opportunities and difficulties posed to nineteenth-century historians by the Providential tradition, see Dorothy M. Ross, "Historical Consciousness in Nineteenth-Century America," *American Historical Review*, 89 (1984), 904–928, and Sacvan Bercovitch, *The Rites of Assent* (New York and London: Routledge, 1993), pp. 168–193.

12. Robert Ferguson has shown that American expressions of values associated with "The Enlightenment" are especially likely to be shaped by images of a future light glimpsed through the surrounding darkness. Robert A. Ferguson, "What is 'Enlightenment?': Some American Answers," *American Literary History*, 1 (1989), 246–272, and "The American Enlightenment, 1750–1820," in *The*

Cambridge History of American Literature, ed. Sacvan Bercovitch (Cambridge: Cambridge University Press, 1994), pp. 368–389.

13. Ralph Waldo Emerson, "Concord Hymn" (1837), in *Complete Works of Emerson*, ed. Emerson, IX, 158.

14. Ralph Waldo Emerson, "Historical Discourse at Concord" (1835), in *Complete Works of Emerson*, XI, 75.

15. Robert A. Gross, *The Minutemen and their World* (New York: Hill & Wang, 1976), p. 107.

16. As Donald and Lucy Ringe have discovered, Cooper not only examined the ground and consulted knowledgeable individuals; he read extant British accounts, including depositions of soldiers on both sides. "Preface" to *Lionel Lincoln; or, The Leaguer of Boston* (1825), ed. Donald A. and Lucy B. Ringe (Albany: State University of New York Press, 1984), p. 6.

17. George Dekker and John P. McWilliams, ed., *James Fenimore Cooper: The Critical Heritage* (London: Routledge & Kegan Paul, 1973), p. 244.

18. Arthur B. Tourtellot, *Lexington and Concord: The Beginning of the War of the American Revolution* (New York: Norton, 1959), p. 131; Fischer, *Paul Revere's Ride*, pp. 188–192. Fischer describes the recklessness of British lieutenant Jesse Adair, who led his advance column onto Lexington Green to confront, and perhaps provoke, the town's militia (*Paul Revere's Ride*, pp. 189–190). Of such impulsive, foolish actions is crisis history made.

19. Tourtellot, *Lexington and Concord*, p. 164; Fischer, *Paul Revere's Ride*, pp. 209, 212.

20. "The Declaration of Independence," in *The Portable Thomas Jefferson*, ed. Merrill D. Peterson (New York: Viking Penguin, 1977), p. 235.

21. Nathaniel Hawthorne, "The Old Manse," in *Mosses from an Old Manse*, ed. W. Charvat, R. H. Pearce, C. M. Simpson, and J. D. Crowley, Centenary Edition (Columbus: Ohio State University Press, 1974), X, 10.

22. Fischer, *Paul Revere's Ride*, p. 406, n. 49.

23. Nathaniel Hawthorne, *Septimius Felton*, in *The Elixir of Life Manuscripts*, ed. E. H. Davidson, C. M. Simpson, and L. N. Smith, Centenary Edition (Columbus: Ohio State University Press, 1977), XIII, 16.

24. Sarah Josepha Hale's "The Soldier of the Revolution," for example, had elevated the farmer-militiaman to the very pinnacle of human worth: "The name of citizen was the most gratifying title to the farmers who fought the battles of freedom, – and when the necessity for resistance ceased, they gladly relinquished their weapons, returning them above the firesides their valor had preserved from insult and spoilation. The generous devotedness of the American soldiery to the principles of liberty and equal rights, and their prompt obedience to civil government, have no parallel in human history." Sarah J. Hale, "The Soldier of the Revolution," in *Sketches of American Character* (Boston: Putnam & Hunt, 1829), p. 49.

25. Henry Wadsworth Longfellow, "Paul Revere's Ride," in *Tales of a Wayside Inn: The Poetical Works of Henry Wadsworth Longfellow* (Boston: Houghton Mifflin, 1886), IV, 25.

26. There were to be, of course, many other commemorative speeches and poems, including the ceremonial festivities in Concord of 1875, Robert C. Winthrop's centennial oration in 1876, James Russell Lowell's "Ode, Read at the One Hundredth Anniversary of the Fight at Concord Bridge" (1875), and Whittier's "Lexington" (1775). Compared to Emerson's 1867 address, these centennial writings convey little more than the author's strong sense of his civic duty to perpetuate the memory of venerable deeds.

27. Jonas Clarke, "Narrative of the Events of April 19" appended to *The Fate of Blood-Thirsty Oppressors* (Boston: Powars & Willis, 1776), p. 2. Fischer concludes that Captain Parker "did not wish to start a fight but was unwilling to run away from one" and that Parker wished to protect the retreat of John Hancock and Sam Adams, who had stayed the night of April 18 in Clarke's parsonage (*Paul Revere's Ride*, pp. 400–401). However, a fundamental question remains: what motives should we ascribe to the silent witness of the sixty militiamen standing in armed defense?

28. The earliest patriotic histories revealed their anxiety over this issue by protesting too much. William Gordon, for instance, justified "the necessity of securing Tyconderoga" by insisting that on April 19 "General Gage had commenced hostilities, so that retaliation appeared more than warrantable, even an act of self-defense." *The History of the Rise, Progress and Establishment of the Independence of the United States of America* (New York: Hodge, Allen, & Campbell, 1789), 1, 344.

29. See the list of editions of Allen's *Narrative* compiled by John Pell in *Ethan Allen* (Boston: Houghton Mifflin, 1929), pp. 276–277, and reprinted in Brooke Hindle's edition of the *Narrative* (New York: Corinth Books, 1961. With the exceptions of Paine's *Common Sense* and Allen's *Narrative*, the most celebrated books by patriots of the American Revolutionary era, such as Franklin's *Autobiography*, Jefferson's *Notes on the State of Virginia*, and Freneau's *Poems*, were to be published after the war was concluded.

30. On the adaptability of Allen's created persona, see Michael A. Bellesiles, *Revolutionary Outlaws: Ethan Allen and the Struggle for Independence on the Early American Frontier* (Charlottesville: University of Virginia Press, 1993), chapter 10, and John McWilliams, "The Faces of Ethan Allen," *New England Quarterly* 49 (1976), 257–282.

31. Ethan Allen, *A Narrative of Colonel Ethan Allen's Captivity*, ed. Stephen Carl Arch (Acton, Mass.: Copley Publishing, 2000), p. 5.

32. Michael Bellisles has discovered that, during Ethan Allen's Northampton years, but after his first exposure to the Deists, Allen had read a volume of Edwards's sermons and then "derided Edwards mercilessly" (*Revolutionary Outlaws*, pp. 22–23).

33. Thanks to Franklin, "lightening" became a divisive political metaphor. Fearing that future generations would neglect New Englanders who had defended civil liberty, John Adams sardonically commented to Benjamin Rush in 1790 that "the history of our Revolution will be that Dr. Franklin's electric rod smote the earth and out sprung General Washington." Quoted in Robert Ferguson,

"The American Enlightenment," in *Cambridge History of American Literature*, ed. S. Bercovitch, p. 348. Massachusetts historians were to seek legendary meaning in the death by lightning of their first Revolutionary patriot, James Otis. Mercy Otis Warren wrote of her brother's death: "After several years of mental derangement, as if in consequence of his own prayers, [Otis's] great soul was instantly set free by a flash of lightning, from the evils in which the love of his country had involved him" (*History*, ed. Cohen, 1, 51). Bancroft saw Otis's death as the freeing of the soul of liberty: "One flash and only one was seen in the sky; one bolt fell, and harming nothing else, struck James Otis, so that all that was mortal of him perished. – This is he who claimed the ocean as man's free highway; and persuaded to an American union." *History of the United States* (Boston: Little, Brown, & Co., 1867), VI, 432–433.

34. Charles Jellison, *Ethan Allen: Frontier Rebel* (Syracuse: Syracuse University Press, 1969), p. 118.
35. William Gordon, *The History of the Rise, Progress and Establishment of the Independence of the United States of America* (New York: Hodge, Allen, & Campbell, 1789), I, 346; David Ramsay, *The History of the American Revolution* (Dublin: William Jones, 1795; originally published 1789); I, 202; Samuel Williams, *The Natural and Civil History of Vermont* (Burlington: Samuel Mills, 1809; originally published 1794), II, 37–38; Ira Allen, *The Natural and Political History of the State of Vermont* (London: J. W. Myers, 1798) in *Ethan and Ira Allen: Collected Works*, ed. Kevin Graffagnino (Benson, Vt.: Chalidze Publications, 1992), III, 33; Mercy Otis Warren, *History*, ed. Cohen, 1, 114; Bancroft, *History of the United States*, VII, 340; Zadock Thompson, *History of Vermont* (Burlington: Chauncey Goodrich, 1842), p. 34.
36. Nathaniel Hawthorne, "Old Ticonderoga," in *The Snow-Image and Uncollected Tales*, ed. J. D. Crowley, Centenary Edition (Columbus: Ohio State University Press, 1974), XI, 190; Kenneth Davies, "In the Name of the Great Jehovah," *American Heritage*, 14 (1963), 74; Bellesisles, *Revolutionary Outlaws*, p. 118; Willard Sterne Randall, *Benedict Arnold: Patriot and Traitor* (New York: Morrow, 1990), p. 96. In the most recent life of Arnold, James Kirby Martin quotes Allen's words, but introduces them by stating that Allen had "putatively offered his famous reply." *Benedict Arnold: Revolutionary Warrior* (New York: New York University Press, 1997), p. 71.
37. The defaming of Ethan Allen, by Timothy Dwight, Ezra Stiles, and Lemuel Hopkins among others, waned quickly after the demise of the Federalist Party and of Dwight's generation. Until the end of the nineteenth century Allen would remain a favorite subject for historical romance, showing how the democratic pioneer gained strength from Revolutionary commitment. The important text here is Daniel Pierce's novel *The Green Mountain Boys* (1839), which would be reprinted in fifty editions by the outbreak of the Civil War. Later historical romances include Henry Hall, *Ethan Allen: The Robin Hood of Vermont* (New York: D. Appleton & Co, 1892); Eliza Pollard, *The Green Mountain Boys* (New York: Dodd, Mead, 1895); John De Morgan, *The Hero of Ticonderoga* (Philadelphia: D. McKay, 1896).

38. Herman Melville, *Israel Potter: His Fifty Years of Exile*, ed. Harrison Hayford, Hershel Parker, and G. Thomas Tanselle (Evanston: Northwestern University Press and the Newberry Library, 1982) p. 149.

39. Herman Melville, "Hawthorne and his Mosses," in *Herman Melville: Representative Selections*, ed. Willard Thorp (New York: American Book Co., 1938), p. 339.

40. Bellesiles, *Revolutionary Outlaws*, p. 370.

41. In Mosher's novella the town green of Kingdom Come contains "a life-size bronze statue of Ethan Allen, sword extended, capturing Fort Ticonderoga." The aged, belligerent logger Noel Lord lost his hand, and Ethan Allen's statue lost its sword, at one moment of collision in 1875. By the 1920s, as the electric company damns the river and drives out the loggers, the old men of Kingdom Come look out across the Green at the statue of Ethan Allen, with its now bladeless sword, and tell "the old stories of the men who had settled, cleared and defended the land." Howard Frank Mosher, *Where the Rivers Flow North* (Harmondsworth: Penguin, 1978), pp. 108, 140.

42. Nathaniel Hawthorne, "Old Ticonderoga," in *The Snow-Image and Uncollected Tales*, ed. Crowley, XI, 186, 187.

43. Hugh Finlay, letter of May 29th to his brother-in-law Ingram, *Documents of the American Revolution 1770–1783: Colonial Office Series*, ed. K. G. Davies (Dublin: Irish University Press, 1975), IX, 144–147.

44. Samuel Langdon, "Government Corrupted by Vice, and Recovered by Righteousness," a sermon preached May 31, 1775, in *The Wall and the Garden: Selected Massachusetts Election Sermons, 1670–1775*, ed. A. William Plumstead (Minneapolis: University of Minnesota Press, 1968), p. 367.

45. Resolution of the Massachusetts Committee of Safety, Cambridge, June 15, 1775, most readily available in *The Spirit of Seventy-Six*, ed. Henry Steele Commager and Richard B. Morris (New York: Harper & Row, 1976), p. 121.

46. Among the historical accounts of the Battle of Bunker Hill, Richard Frothingham's *History of the Siege of Boston* (1849), together with its collection of crucial documents, is not likely to ever be entirely superseded. See also Richard M. Kechum, *Decisive Day; The Battle for Bunker Hill* (New York: Doubleday, 1974), and Victor Brooks, *The Boston Campaign* (Conshohocken, Penn.: Combined Publishing, 1999).

47. The most influential rendition of the type during the Revolutionary era was David Humphreys' *An Essay on the Life of the Honourable Major-General Israel Putnam* (1788), reprinted four times before 1812. Humphreys, a graduate of Yale, presents Putnam as a New England farm boy whose deficiencies of education are redeemed by the unflagging energy, sturdy honesty, and Cincinnatus-like courage he shows in setting down his plow to serve the army at Bunker Hill. The example of Israel Putnam, Humphreys contends, shows how a self-sufficient agricultural life "converts the farmer into a species of rural philosopher by inspiring an honest pride in his rank as a freeman" (27).

48. Warren, "An Oration Delivered March 6, 1775 . . . to Commemorate the Bloody Tragedy of the Fifth of March 1770" (Boston: Edes & Gill, 1775), p. 21.

49. "Resolves of the County of Suffolk," September 6, 1774, broadside.
50. Cooper, *Lionel Lincoln*, p. 74. By June 1776 Joseph Warren was serving as President of the Provincial Congress, then convening in Watertown; the North End Caucus and the Sons of Liberty were no longer able to meet in Boston.
51. "Concord Hymn," in *Works of Emerson*, ed. Emerson, IX, 58.
52. George Bancroft, letter to the Cooper Memorial Committee, in *Memorial of James Fenimore Cooper* (New York: G. P. Putnam's, 1852), p. 16.
53. Bancroft, *History of the United States*, VII, 435.
54. Information on the Bunker Hill commemorations is drawn from Frothingham, "History of the Bunker Hill Monument," in *Siege of Boston*, pp. 337–359; Robert Remini, *Daniel Webster: The Man and his Time* (New York: Norton, 1997), pp. 347–52; E. P. Whipple, *The Great Speeches and Orations of Daniel Webster* (Boston: Little, Brown, & Co., 1880), pp. 136–137.
55. Daniel Webster, "An Address Delivered at the Laying of the Corner Stone of the Bunker Hill Monument" (Boston: Cummings, Hilliard, & Co., 1825), p. 4. The famous echoing words with which Emerson was to begin *Nature* ("Our age is retrospective. It builds the sepulchre of the fathers") chide contemporary New Englanders by suggesting that filiopietism encourages self-limitation, but they in no way discredit the achievements of the Puritan or Revolutionary fathers themselves.
56. Daniel Webster, "An Address Delivered on Bunker Hill, on the 17th of June, 1843 on Occasion of the Completion of the Bunker Hill Monument," *Great Speeches and Orations of Webster*, ed. Whipple, p. 140.
57. Bancroft, *History of the United States*, VII, 421. Bancroft is surely referring here to African American militiaman Salem Prince, who shot British Major John Pitcairn on Breed's Hill.

9 ABOLITION, "WHITE SLAVERY," AND REGIONAL PRIDE

1. Important biographies of the Abolitionists, to which I am indebted, include the following: Deborah Pickman Clifford, *Crusader for Freedom: A Life of Lydia Maria Child* (Boston: Beacon Press, 1992); Henry Steele Commager, *Theodore Parker, Yankee Crusader* (Boston: Little, Brown, & Co., 1936); Dean Grodzins, *American Heretic: Theodore Parker and Transcendentalism* (Chapel Hill: University of North Carolina Press, 2002); Carolyn L. Karcher, *First Woman of the Republic: A Biography of Lydia Maria Child* (Durham: Duke University Press, 1998); Henry Mayer, *All on Fire: William Lloyd Garrison and the Abolition of Slavery* (New York: St. Martin's Press, 1998); James Brewer Stewart, *Wendell Phillips: Liberty's Hero* (Baton Rouge: Louisiana State University Press, 1986). The most accessible recent collection of abolitionist writings is Mason Lowance's *Against Slavery: An Abolitionist Reader* (Harmondsworth: Penguin, 2000).

2. Lydia Maria Child, *An Appeal in Favor of that Class of Americans Called Africans* (1833), ed. Carolyn L. Karcher (Amherst: University of Massachusetts Press, 1996), p. 30.
3. Catharine Beecher, *An Essay on Slavery and Abolition with Reference to the Duty of American Females* (Philadelphia and Boston: Henry Perkins, 1837), p. 127. Beecher contended that the "measures of the Abolition Society" seem "calculated to generate party spirit, denunciation, recrimination and angry passions" (17). If Garrisonians continue to use "the vocabulary of Billingsgate" they will generate only "anger, fear, pride, hatred" outside their own following (46, 56). Catharine's criticisms were partly driven by family experience: Garrison had repeatedly attacked Lyman Beecher for clinging to Colonization.
4. Lewis P. Simpson, *Mind and the American Civil War: A Meditation on Lost Causes* (Baton Rouge: Louisiana State University Press, 1989), pp. 33, 35.
5. James H. Banner, *To the Hartford Convention* (New York: Knopf, 1970), p. 108.
6. Wendell Phillips, "Public Opinion" (1852), in *Speeches, Lectures and Letters by Wendell Phillips* (Boston: James Redpath, 1863), p. 51; William Lloyd Garrison, *Thoughts on African Colonization* (1832), facsimile reprint (New York: Arno Press, 1968), p. 16.
7. Ralph Waldo Emerson, "Antislavery Speech at Dedham, 4 July 1846," in *Emerson's Antislavery Writings*, ed. Len Gougeon and Joel Myerson (New Haven: Yale University Press, 1995), p. 41.
8. David Donald, "Toward a Reconsideration of Abolitionists," in *Lincoln Reconsidered* (New York: Knopf, 1959), pp. 35, 36.
9. Kenneth Stampp, *The Peculiar Institution* (New York: Random House, 1955), chapter 9 and p. 67.
10. Samuel J. May, *Some Recollections of our Antislavery Conflict* (Boston: Fields, Osgood, & Co., 1869), p. 17.
11. John Greenleaf Whittier, *Justice and Expediency; or, Slavery Considered with a View to its Rightful and Effectual Remedy, Abolition* (1833), in *The Abolitionists*, ed. Louis Ruchames (New York: Capricorn Books, 1964), p. 54.
12. Wendell Phillips, "Philosophy of the Abolition Movement" (1853) in *Speeches, Lectures and Letters*, p. 108.
13. Wendell Phillips, July 4, 1859 Address in Framingham, printed in *Liberator*, July 18, 1859, quoted in Stewart's *Wendell Phillips: Liberty's Hero*, pp. 191–192. Stewart reveals that in 1860 Phillips carried a gun and walked the Boston streets with a bodyguard (p. 214). In the Framingham speech, "the bastard who has stolen the name of Winthrop" refers to Robert Charles Winthrop (1809–1894), a direct descendant of John Winthrop. Robert Winthrop studied law with Daniel Webster, was a Member of the House of Representatives from 1842 to 1850, and Speaker of the House from 1847 to 1849. A politically powerful Cotton Whig who professed antislavery principles, Winthrop did little to oppose the Mexican War or impede the return of fugitive slaves. To Garrison, Parker and Phillips, Robert Winthrop became a chief example of New England's apostasy and decline from the integrity of the Puritan forefathers.

14. Joanne Pope Melish, *Disowning Slavery: Gradual Emancipation and "Race" in New England 1780–1860* (Ithaca: Cornell University Press, 1998), pp. 1–10, 163–165. Melish describes how the New England effort "to efface their history of enslavement" became so prevalent a strategy for opposing southern expansionism that "a virtual amnesia about local slavery and a kind of perpetual, indignant surprise at the continuing presence of people of color became common ingredients in the epic of preeminent New England as it was shaped in the years after 1815" (220). There is no better evidence of such "amnesia" than the tendency of certain Abolitionists – notably Whittier, Lowell, and Longfellow – sometimes to write as if there never had been a slave in New England. Melish's argument, however, slights the factual knowledge of New England's slave history that is evident in the writings of the Garrisonian Abolitionists – a knowledge that surely derived, in large part, from the Garrisonians' associations with Boston's free black community. On the importance of this association, see the essays in *Courage and Conscience: Black and White Abolitionists in Boston*, ed. Donald M. Jacobs (Bloomington: Indiana University Press, 1993).

15. On the reluctance of many Revolutionary leaders to regard slavery as a fact as well as a metaphor, see Patricia Bradley, *Slavery, Propaganda, and the American Revolution* (Jackson: University Press of Mississippi, 1998).

16. *Liberator*, 1.1, reprinted in *William Lloyd Garrison and the Fight against Slavery: Selections from The Liberator*, ed. William E. Cain (New York: St. Martin's Press, 1995), p. 71. From the windows of the *Liberator*'s shabby office in Manufacturers Hall, Garrison could see both Faneuil Hall and Bunker Hill (Mayer, *All on Fire*, p. 113).

17. John Randolph as quoted in Henry Adams, *John Randolph* (Boston: Houghton Mifflin, 1882) pp. 281, 282. A tidewater planter who inherited some two hundred slaves, Randolph believed that stable Republican government meant representing agrarian property and reelecting educated gentlemen. Although Randolph's unchanging belief that slavery was a "cancer" upon the body politic led him to free all his slaves in his will, his beliefs about national slavery policy, as the leader of the "Old Republicans" in Congress, became increasingly locked into defense of minimal government, voluntary emancipation, and states' rights. The acidity of Randolph's remarks on land speculators, manufacturing interests, political trimmers, and New Englanders (the Adams family is "the American House of Stuart") became legendary. See Russell Kirk, *John Randolph of Roanoke: A Study in American Politics*, 4th edn (Indianapolis: Liberty Fund, 1997), pp. 102, 156–189.

18. Ralph Waldo Emerson, "Address to the Citizens of Concord on the Fugitive Slave Law, 3 May 1851," in *Emerson's Antislavery Writings*, ed. Gougeon and Myerson, p. 64.

19. Samuel Hopkins, *A Dialogue Concerning the Slavery of the Africans* (Norwich: Judah P. Spooner, 1776), p. 6.

20. Samuel Hopkins, *A Discourse Upon the Slave Trade and the Slavery of Africans* (Providence: J. Carter, 1793), appendix, n.p.

21. William Lloyd Garrison, "Address to the American Colonization Society," July 4, 1829, printed in *William Lloyd Garrison: The Story of his Life Told by his Children* (Boston: Houghton Mifflin, 1894), I, 136, 134.

22. It could be argued that the most formidable force sustaining white slavery in New England was neither the Cotton Whig merchants, Doughface politicians, nor prejudice against the free Negro, but the large number of New England's intellectual and educational élite who, opposed to slavery though they might be, would neither speak nor act for emancipation or against slavery's expansion: George Bancroft, Rufus Choate, Caleb Cushing, Edward Everett, Cornelius Conway Felton, Oliver Wendell Holmes, Francis Parkman, William Hickling Prescott, Jared Sparks, Moses Stuart, George Ticknor. In general, the Garrisonians were reluctant to attack these much respected figures in public print, in part because they hoped to win them over by the power of positive persuasion. (Parker's attack on Prescott's *History of the Conquest of Mexico* is a notable exception.)

23. Child, *An Appeal,* ed. Karcher, p. 187.

24. Information on Parker's life is drawn from the following sources: Robert C. Albrecht, *Theodore Parker* (New York: Twayne, 1971); Henry Steele Commager, *Theodore Parker* (Boston: Little, Brown, & Co., 1936); John Weiss, *Life and Correspondence of Theodore Parker* (New York: D. Appleton & Co., 1864), 2 vols; Dean Grodzins, *American Heretic: Theodore Parker and Transcendentalism* (Chapel Hill: University of North Carolina Press, 2002). The quotation of Parker's will is from Weiss, *Life and Correspondence,* II, 443.

25. Theodore Parker, "Theodore Parker's Experience as a Minister" (1859), in Weiss, *Life and Correspondence,* II, 493.

26. Theodore Parker, letter to President Millard Fillmore, November 21, 1850, in Weiss, *Life and Correspondence,* II, 101.

27. In 1845 Parker noted in his journal: "I am excluded from nearly all the pulpits in the land" (Grodzins, *American Heretic,* p. 415). The Unitarians' Boston Association had made a public determination to bar Parker from guest preaching in all Association pulpits.

28. Theodore Parker, letter to President Millard Fillmore, Weiss, *Life and Correspondence,* II, 100.

29. In his diary for July 26, 1845, after the annexation of Texas had passed both houses of Congress, Parker dedicated himself to pursuing "the constant preaching of the truth" of antislavery: "I am resolved to spend what little strength I have in this way" (Weiss, *Life and Correspondence,* II, 76, 77).

30. Theodore Parker, "A Sermon on Merchants," delivered in the Melodeon, November 22, 1846, in *Collected Works of Theodore Parker* (Boston: American Unitarian Association, 1910), V, 10, 11, 22, 29.

31. Theodore Parker, "A Sermon on War," delivered in the Melodeon, June 7, 1846, in *Collected Works,* IX, 318.

32. Theodore Parker, "Discourse on Webster," delivered in the Melodeon, October 31, 1852, in *Collected Works,* VII, 337.

33. Thoreau was to pursue the Miltonic analogy for the narrower purpose of local accusation. The return of fugitive slave Anthony Burns shows that "the site of that political organization called Massachusetts is to me morally covered with volcanic scoriae and cinders such as Milton describes in the infernal regions." Whereas Parker applies Milton's imagery to the nation, Thoreau's concern is that complicity with the political demands of southern cotton interests is turning Massachusetts into Milton's hell. "Slavery in Massachusetts" (1854), in *Thoreau, The Major Essays*, ed. Jeffrey L. Duncan (New York: Dutton, 1972), p. 143.

34. Given Parker's repeated use of the words "hunker" or "hunkerism," it is curious that he should have chosen a term of condemnation so clearly associated, at least in its origin, with New York state politics. While locating the origin of the corrupting money powers outside New England, "Hunker" also implies that New York values, like those of the South, are now dominating New England. Through the power of New York banking interests, Hunkerism binds North and South together.

35. Theodore Parker, speech in Faneuil Hall, May 26, 1854, quoted in Weiss, *Life and Correspondence*, II, 130.

36. Many of Boston's textile manufacturers were Unitarians, including Amos and Abbot Lawrence. See Thomas H. O'Connor, *Lords of the Loom: The Cotton Whigs and the Coming of the Civil War* (New York: Charles Scribner's Sons, 1968), pp. 32–33.

37. Theodore Parker, "Spiritual Conditions," delivered in the Melodeon, February 18, 1849, in *Collected Works*, V, 299.

38. Theodore Parker, "The Slave Power," address to the New England Anti-Slavery Association, Boston, May 29, 1850, in *Collected Works*, XI, 281.

39. Theodore Parker, "The Mexican War," delivered in Faneuil Hall, February 4 1847, in *Collected Works*, XI, pp. 20, 26, 28, 29, 31.

40. Parker, "Slave Power," in *Collected Works*, XI, 268.

41. John Greenleaf Whittier, "The Prophecy of Samuel Sewall," in *The Complete Poetical Works of Whittier* (Boston: Houghton Mifflin, 1894), pp. 67–69.

42. Emerson, "Antislavery Speech at Dedham, 4 July 1846," in *Emerson's Antislavery Writings*, ed. Gougeon and Myerson, p. 44.

43. When Garrison returned to Newburyport after his trial in Baltimore for libel, he was blocked from public speaking in the town. Mayer, *All On Fire*, p. 102.

44. As a prior step toward these public moments, the influence of outspoken anti-slavery wives in prompting husbands toward public abolitionism was crucial. The influence of Ann Terry Greene on Wendell Phillips, of Maria White on James Russell Lowell, and of Lydia Jackson on Ralph Waldo Emerson confirm the historical reality of the powers of moral suasion that Mrs. Shelby and Mrs. Bird exert over their husbands in *Uncle Tom's Cabin*.

45. Garrison, "Triumph of Mobocracy in Boston," *Liberator*, November 7, 1835, in *Selections from The Liberator*, pp. 374, 380, 381.

46. Wendell Phillips, "The Murder of Lovejoy," in *Speeches, Lectures and Letters*, p. 3.

47. Even after the Civil War, Samuel J. May believed that the worst element in New England's complicity had been to deny first amendment rights to the Negro: "All in our country who were descendants from the Puritans, especially those of us who claimed descent from the fathers of New England, were imbued with the spirit of religious liberty, had much to say about the rights of conscience; but we gave no heed to the awful fact that there were millions in the land who were not allowed to express any of those rights." *Some Recollections of our Antislavery Conflict*, p. 26.

48. James Russell Lowell, "The French Revolution of 1848," essay of April 1848 published in the *National Anti-Slavery Standard*, *The Anti-Slavery Papers of James Russell Lowell* (Boston: Houghton Mifflin, 1902), I, 47–48.

49. James Russell Lowell, "Daniel Webster," July 1846, in *Anti-Slavery Papers of Lowell*, I, 43.

50. Theodore Parker, "A Letter on Slavery," December 22, 1847, in *Collected Works*, XI, 109.

51. James Russell Lowell, *The Biglow Papers [First Series] A Critical Edition*, ed. Thomas Wortham (DeKalb: Northern Illinois University Press, 1977), 51.

52. A vivid narrative of the capture and removal of Thomas Sims may be found in Lawrence Lader, *The Bold Brahmins: New England's War Against Slavery, 1831–1863* (New York: Dutton, 1961), pp. 173–180. On the connection between the Sims case and Sumner's election to the Senate, see David Donald, *Charles Sumner and the Coming of the Civil War* (New York: Knopf, 1960), pp. 197–202. Sumner's political prominence dates from an 1845 speech in which he had declared: "God forbid that the lash of the slave-dealer should descend by any sanction from New England! God forbid that the blood which spurts from the lacerated, quivering flesh of the slave should soil the hem of the white garments of Massachusetts" (Donald, *Sumner*, p. 140).

53. Thoreau, "Slavery in Massachusetts," p. 132.

54. Wendell Phillips, "Sims Anniversary," delivered in the Melodeon, April 12, 1852, in *Speeches, Lectures and Letters*, p. 73.

55. Wendell Phillips, "Surrender of Sims," delivered in Faneuil Hall, January 30, 1852, in *Speeches, Lectures and Letters*, p. 71. Compare Thoreau's famous declaration in "Civil Disobedience": "It is not a man's duty, as a matter of course, to devote himself to the eradication of any, even the most enormous, wrong; he may still properly have other concerns to engage him; but it is his duty, at least, to wash his hands of it." In *Thoreau, Major Essays*, ed. Duncan, p. 130. To Thoreau, washing one's hands by withdrawing from political corruption is a duty to the higher self. To Phillips, whose commitment to the mission of the Commonwealth was so much greater than Thoreau's, keeping one's own neck free from any mark of the slave collar is a very real but momentary temptation.

56. Theodore Parker, "The Boston Kidnapping," delivered in the Melodeon, April 12, 1852, in *Collected Works*, XI, 322.

57. Whittier's "Ichabod" (1850) is only the best-known example of the rhetorical mode of cleansing New England by denouncing and excising Webster. Consider the following ways of damning Webster's apostasy: Garrison, "His

(Webster's) strides from Plymouth Rock to Carolina lead as surely to perdition" ("The Great Apostate," *Liberator*, December 27, 1850); Phillips, "He is an enemy of the people . . . He knows well the Hancock and Adams of 1776, but he does not know the Hancocks and Adamses of today" ("Public Opinion," January 28, 1852, in *Speeches, Lectures and Letters*, p. 53); Parker, "The orator of Plymouth Rock was the advocate of slavery; the hero of Bunker Hill put chains around Boston court-house; . . . The Anglo-Saxon race never knew such a terrible and calamitous ruin. His downfall shook the continent" ("Discourse on Webster," October 31, 1852, in *Collected Works*, VII, 339, 345).

58. Thomas Wentworth Higginson, letter of 1857, quoted in Lader, *Bold Brahmins*, p. 200.
59. Garrison, "The Tragedy at Harper's Ferry," *Liberator*, October 28, 1859; Garrison, speech on John Brown delivered in Tremont Temple, December 2, 1859, in Cain, *Garrison and the Fight against Slavery*, pp. 154, 168.
60. Wendell Phillips, "Harper's Ferry," speech in Brooklyn, New York, November 1, 1859, in *Speeches, Lectures and Letters*, p. 291. Phillips sought to have John Brown buried in Boston within sight of Bunker Hill. In his eulogy, Phillips imagined John Brown's grandfather, a "hero saint" who had died in the Revolutionary War, bequeathing his sword to his grandson with the words "I give my sword to free the slave my fathers forgot" (*Speeches, Lectures and Letters*, p. 291).
61. Emerson, "John Brown," delivered January 6, 1860 in Salem, Massachusetts, in *Emerson's Antislavery Writings*, ed. Gougeon and Myerson, p. 122.
62. Redpath's preface begins with the claim that John Brown was "the last of the Puritans" and ends with the accusatory query: "How far as citizens have we wandered from the Hill where Warren fell?" James Redpath, *The Public Life of Captain John Brown* (1860) (Freeport, N.Y.: Books for Libraries Press, 1970), pp. 7, 10.
63. Thoreau, "A Plea for Captain John Brown," delivered in Concord Town Hall, October 30, 1859, in *Thoreau, Major Essays*, ed. Duncan, p. 148.
64. Thoreau, "The Last Days of John Brown" (1860), in *Thoreau, Major Essays*, ed. Duncan, p. 172.
65. Nathaniel Hawthorne, "Chiefly about War Matters," in *The Complete Works of Nathaniel Hawthorne*, ed. George P. Lathrop (Boston: Houghton Mifflin, 1883), XII, 327. After describing John Brown as a "blood stained fanatic," Hawthorne ends his reflections on Brown by appending a facetious footnote: "Can it be a son of old Massachusetts who utters this abominable sentiment? For shame" (XII, 328).
66. On John Brown's life see Stephen B. Oates, *To Purge this Land with Blood* (New York: Harper & Row, 1970).
67. George Bancroft, *History of the United States of America*, 9th edn (Boston: Little, Brown, & Co., 1841), I, 159, 171. Volume I was first published in 1833. "Unjust, wasteful and unhappy" are the first words describing slavery in the entire *History*. In the second volume, Bancroft argues that in Virginia "the institution of slavery renewed a landed aristocracy closely resembling the feudal nobility" (II, 194). In later volumes he blames the British for the

eighteenth-century slave trade and emphasizes the resolution of the Continental Congress to abolish slavery. The contemporary implications of "Slavery in Rome" are made clear in sentences such as "the large Roman plantations tilled by slave labor were the ruin of Italy" or "In a word, slavery subverted the Roman democracy." "Slavery in Rome," *North American Review*, 39 (1834), 433, 435.

68. See Drew Gilpin Faust, ed., *The Pro-Slavery Argument* (Baton Rouge: Louisiana University Press, 1981).

69. Bancroft, "Slavery in Rome," 424.

70. Bancroft, *Literary and Historical Miscellanies* (New York: Harper, 1855), pp. 437, 515.

71. Bancroft, letter of 1848 quoted in Russell B. Nye, *George Bancroft: Brahmin Rebel* (New York: Knopf, 1944), pp. 176–177.

72. One of the last acts of the Massachusetts Constitutional Convention had been to pass a resolution that any old extant laws inconsistent with the "rights and liberties" of a Massachusetts citizen would henceforth be dead letters. In the last volume of the *History*, Bancroft was to write: "So calm and effortless was the act by which slavery fell away from Massachusetts . . . The manner in which Massachusetts left slavery behind, as of the dead and irrevocable past, was the noblest that could have been devised. The inborn, inalienable right of man to freedom was written in the permanent constitution as the law of all coming legislation." *The History of the United States* (Boston: Little, Brown, & Co., 1874), x, 366.

73. Lilian Handlin describes Bancroft's mental state in the spring of 1861 as follows: "Secession came as a profound shock . . . The tension, uncertainty, and chaos of the new year seemed to belie everything for which Bancroft and his *History* stood . . . In a conversation with British journalist William H. Russell, Bancroft appeared confused, full of abstract philosophical speculations, but also sure that 'the republic, though in danger, was the most stable and beneficial government in the world.'" *George Bancroft: The Intellectual as Democrat* (New York: Harper & Row, 1984), p. 270.

74. Garrison, *Liberator*, June 14, 1844.

75. James Russell Lowell, "Texas" (1845), in *Anti-Slavery Papers of Lowell*, 1, 9.

76. See Nye, *Bancroft: Brahmin Rebel*, p. 153.

77. Theodore Parker, "The Chief Sins of the People," delivered in the Melodeon, April 10, 1851, in *Collected Works*, x, 28.

EPILOGUE: "BODILESS ECHOES"

1. George Bancroft, *Memorial Address on the Life and Character of Abraham Lincoln* (Washington, D.C.: Government Printing Office, 1866), p. 3.

2. John Seeley, *Memory's Nation: The Place of Plymouth Rock* (Chapel Hill: University of North Carolina Press, 1998), p. 2.

3. William H. Truettner's and Roger B. Stein's splendid collection of essays entitled *Picturing Old New England: Image and Memory* (Yale University Press, 1999) traces the evolution of imagined preindustrial rural and

marine landscapes from 1865 to the near present. The essays collectively suggest that images of the decayed underside of late nineteenth-century New England life were conspicuously absent until the Depression, and rare enough then.

4. Alan Trachtenberg, *The Incorporation of America* (New York: Hill & Wang, 1982). On the creation of regional associations devoted to preserving the presumed spiritual integrity of antebellum New England life, see chapter 6 of Joseph Conforti's *Jonathan Edwards, Religious Tradition and American Culture* (Chapel Hill: University of North Carolina Press, 1995). On the rise of the highly selective post Civil War New England tourist trade, see Dona Brown, *Inventing New England: Regional Tourism in the Nineteenth Century* (Washington, D.C.: Smithsonian Institution, 1995), especially chapters 2 and 3.

5. Edward Eggleston, preface to *The Hoosier School-Master* (1871), introduction by Vernon Loggins (New York: Hill & Wang, 1957), p. xiii.

6. Oliver Wendell Holmes, *Ralph Waldo Emerson* (1885) in *The Complete Works of Oliver Wendell Holmes*, Fireside Edition (Boston: Houghton Mifflin, 1909), VIII, 53, 20.

7. James Russell Lowell, "New England Two Centuries Ago" (1865), in *Among my Books* (Boston and New York: Houghton Mifflin, 1904), II, 3.

8. Among scholarly studies of New England regional fiction, I am especially indebted to Josephine Donovan's *New England Local Color Literature: A Woman's Tradition* (New York: Frederick Ungar, 1983) and *American Women Regionalists, 1850–1910*, ed. Judith Fetterley and Marjorie Pryse (New York: Norton, 1992). I differ from revisionist understanding of the "local color" movement in my belief that New England women regionalist writings should also be seen as a reaction against the long dominant male tradition of interpreting American identity through New England historical crises. Stephen Nissenbaum has rightly observed that "local color" was from the outset written for a national audience. "New England as Region and Nation," in *All Over the Map: Rethinking American Regions* (Baltimore: Johns Hopkins University Press, 1996), p. 59.

9. Edward Everett, review of volume I of Bancroft's *History of the United States*, *North American Review*, 40 (1835), 99.

10. William Hickling Prescott, review of volume III of Bancroft's *History*, *North American Review*, 52 (1841), 75–103.

11. Henry Adams, review of volume X of Bancroft's *History*, *North American Review*, 120 (1875), 434.

12. Edith Wharton, *Summer*, with introduction by Cynthia Griffin Wolff (New York: Harper & Row, 1980), p. 37.

13. Joseph A. Conforti, *Jonathan Edwards, Religious Tradition and American Culture* (Chapel Hill: University of North Carolina Press, 1995), chapters 1, 2, 4, 5.

14. Harriet Beecher Stowe, *The Minister's Wooing*, ed. Susan K. Harris (Harmondsworth: Penguin, 1999), p. 54.

15. Harriet Beecher Stowe, *Oldtown Folks*, ed. Henry F. May (Cambridge, Mass.: Harvard University Press, 1966), pp. 49, 71. Although the declared narrator of

Oldtown Folks is Horace Holyoke, who resembles Calvin Stowe, Mrs. Stowe's voice continually sounds through Horace's words. I have therefore assumed that Horace Holyoke's opinions are those of the author.

16. Oliver Wendell Holmes, "Jonathan Edwards," in *Pages from an Old Volume of Life: A Collection of Essays 1857–1881* (Boston: Houghton Mifflin, 1892), VII, 368.
17. Ibid., VIII, 394. Given the veneration of Edwards in 1880, we should recognize that Holmes's essay was not the anachronism it has been assumed to be. Holmes's attack on Edwardsean Calvinism is less an old fashioned defense of Unitarianism than a progressive defense of medical science with a Social Darwinist tinge. Holmes anticipates William James in believing that the combined study of mind and body must now replace treatises on God's determinism.
18. Charles Francis Adams, Jr., *Three Episodes of Massachusetts History* (Boston: Houghton Mifflin, 1892), I, 608.
19. Henry Adams, *The Education of Henry Adams* (1907, 1918), ed. Ernest Samuels (Boston: Houghton Mifflin, 1973), pp. 7, 33.
20. Henry Adams, *History of the United States of America During the Administrations of Jefferson and Madison* (New York: Charles Scribner's Sons, 1909), I, 19.
21. Brooks Adams, *The Emancipation of Massachusetts: The Dream and The Reality*, with introduction by Perry Miller (Boston: Houghton Mifflin, 1962), p. 348.

Index